WHAT
THE
BIBLE
TEACHES

Contributors

1 PETER

BOYD NICHOLSON

J.B. Nicholson was born in Blantyre, Scotland. He was saved as a teenager and moved to St. Catherines, Ontario, Canada, in 1946. Serving the Lord while engaged in secular employment, he was commended in 1960 to full-time ministry in Canada and the U.S.A. His extensive ministry has taken him to several countries in Central Africa, South Africa, India, the Far East, Central America, and the Caribbean. For many years he has been a contributor to assembly publications, and is currently editor of the magazine *Counsel*.

2 PETER

GEORGE WAUGH

G.P. Waugh was born in Newarthill, Scotland, and saved in Annbank, Scotland, in 1937. Throughout a very demanding secular career, he has preached the gospel and ministered the Word extensively in Great Britain. With retirement, his ministry has taken him further afield to Australasia. He maintains a deep interest in the spread of the gospel abroad, having been associated with the Home and Foreign Mission Fund for many years.

1, 2, & 3 JOHN

ARTHUR GOODING

Although a native of Ipswich, England, A.M.S. Gooding has spent most of his life in Scotland. For 33 years he was a director of John Ritchie Ltd, during which time he also engaged extensively in ministry throughout the British Isles. Since relinquishing his directorship, he has been fully engaged in the Lord's service at home and abroad. He is presently editor of Assembly Testimony, and has recently written a book on *The 13 Judges*.

JUDE

ALBERT McSHANE

Born in County Armagh, Northern Ireland, Albert McShane was commended to the work of the Lord in 1944. He has preached the gospel and ministered the Word widely throughout Ulster and also further afield, and has been closely associated with the Lurgan Bible Readings for many years. His recent writings include commentaries on 2 Corinthians and Philemon for this present series.

WHAT THE BIBLE TEACHES

with
Authorised Version
of
The Bible

IN ELEVEN VOLUMES
COVERING THE NEW TESTAMENT

VOLUME 5

JOHN RITCHIE LTD
KILMARNOCK, SCOTLAND

ISBN-13: 978 1 904064 42 8
ISBN-10: 1 904064 42 6

WHAT THE BIBLE TEACHES
Copyright © 2000 by John Ritchie Ltd.
40 Beansburn, Kilmarnock, Scotland

www.ritchiechristianmedia.co.uk

Re-typeset and printed 2007

Typeset at John Ritchie Ltd., 40 Beansburn, Kilmarnock.
Printed by Bell and Bain, Glasgow.

CONTENTS

ABBREVIATIONS

AV	Authorised Version of King James Version 1611
JND	New Translation by J.N. Darby 1939
LXX	Septuagint Version of Old Testament
Mft	New Translation by James Moffat 1922
NASB	New American Standard Bible 1960
NEB	New English Bible 1961
Nestle	Nestle (ed.) Novum Testamentum Graece
NIV	New International Version 1973
NT	New Testament
OT	Old Testament
Phps	New Testament in Modern English by J.B. Philips 1962
RSV	Revised Standard Version 1952
RV	Revised Version 1881
TR	Textus Receptus or Received Text
Wey	New Testament in Modern Speech by R.E. Weymouth 1929

PREFACE

They follow the noblest example who seek to open the Scriptures to others, for our Lord Himself did so for those two dejected disciples of Emmaus (Luke 24:32). Whether it is the evangelist "opening and alleging that Christ must needs have suffered and risen from the dead" (Acts 17:3) or the pastor-teacher "expounding ... in all the scriptures the things concerning himself" (Luke 24:27) or stimulating our hope "through the patience and comfort of the scriptures" (Rom 15:4), he serves well in thus giving attendance to the reading of the Scriptures (1 Tim 4:13).

It is of course of equal moment to recognise in the exercise of able men, the continued faithfulness of the risen Head in giving gifts to the Church, in spite of her unfaithfulness. How good to recognise that "the perfecting of the saints ... the work of the ministry...the edifying of the body of Christ" need not be neglected. Every provision has been made to ensure the well-being of the people of God. And every opportunity should be taken by the minister of Christ and those to whom he ministers to ensure that the saints "grow up into him in all things which is the head, even Christ" (Eph 4:15).

At various times in the post-apostolic period, certain teachers have come to prominence, sometimes because they succumbed to error, sometimes because in faithfulness they paid the ultimate price for the truth they had bought and would not sell. Some generations had Calvin and Luther, others Darby and Kelly, but in every generation God's voice is heard. It is important that we hear His voice today and recognise that He does speak through His servants. The contributors to this series of commentaries are all highly-respected expositors among the churches of God. They labour in the Word in the English-speaking world and have been of blessing to many throughout their years of service.

The doctrinal standpoint of the commentaries is based upon the acceptance of the verbal and plenary inspiration of the Scriptures so that their inerrant and infallible teachings are the only rule of conscience. The impeccability of Christ, His virgin birth, vicarious death and bodily resurrection are indeed precious truths worthy of the Christian's defence, and throughout the volumes of this series will be defended. Equally the Rapture will be presented as the hope of the Church. Before the great Tribulation she will be raptured and God's prophetic programme will continue with Jacob's trouble, the public manifestation of Christ and the Millennium of blessing to a restored Israel and the innumerable Gentile multitude in a creation released from the bondage of corruption.

May the sound teaching of these commentaries be used by our God to the blessing of His people. May the searching of the Scriptures characterise all who read them.

The diligence of Mr. J.W. Ferguson and the late Professor J. Heading in proof-reading is gratefully acknowledged. Without such co-operation, the production of this commentary would not have been expedited so readily.

T. WILSON

K. STAPLEY

1 PETER

J. B. Nicholson

1 PETER
Introduction

1. **General Observations**
2. **The Writings**
3. **The Writer**
4. **The Outline**
5. **Peter's Theology**
6. **A Word List**
7. **Bibliography**

1. General Observations

It is most helpful to view the epistle in the light of the writer and his calling and the recipients and their character.

Peter was given charge of the keys of God's kingdom (Matt 16:19) and the sheep of God's pasture (John 21:15-17). As in the writings of James and John and in the epistle to the Hebrews, the rapture is not in view, but rather the Appearing (1 Pet 1:7).

Prophetically 1 Peter will have a special significance and will provide a deep solace for the suffering scattered remnant passing through tribulation, "the great one", after the rapture of the Church.

Practically it has a present message for all believers who recognise their pilgrim character and suffer for it. Not only suffering by the pains of experience, but also by patient endurance.

Personally to Peter was committed "the gospel of the circumcision" and he held the "apostleship of the circumcision" (Gal 2:7-8). It should not be surprising then to see Israel's history shining through this epistle. John in his writings unfolds Christ for the deliverance of God's people from the world, its sins and its pleasures, as once Israel was delivered from Egypt by blood and water. Paul bears witness of the Church and the heavenlies, as eventually Israel entered the inheritance to fight the foe and eat the fruit.

Particularly it is left to Peter however, in this first epistle to shepherd the pilgrims through the wilderness of the alien world with its trials and tears, by the consolation of a living hope and a call to the consecration of loving obedience.

John and Aaron would seem to have something in common. Both were singular men of unique privilege. Aaron entered the innermost sanctuary of the tabernacle in the wilderness and beheld the glory of God in the midst of the cherubim. John leaned on the breast of the Son of God as He tabernacled here and he heard the innermost heartbeat of God manifest in flesh. Later he beheld the glory of God in the midst of the churches.

Paul and Joshua also seem to have something in common. They each were told to rise and enter into their ministry: Joshua to being the people into the enjoyment of their earthly inheritance (Josh 1:2), Paul to bring God's people into the enjoyment of heavenly places, the realm of their spiritual inheritance (Acts 26:16-18) where they are "no more strangers and foreigners" (Eph 2:19).

Peter and Moses also had something in common. Both were commissioned as shepherds of God's people to care for them as sheep in their pilgrimage through the wilderness as "strangers" (1 Pet 1:1). This is the character of Peter's first epistle, not to meet some theological heresy, but to console and strengthen the suffering saints and to call them to fragrant lives of sanctity in an alien scene, in hope of future glory and reward.

This epistle is both timely and relevant to the present day believer. We need this letter in a day when many seem to have lost sight of the unfading inheritance and are diverted by the glitter of gold and tinsel. Others are suffering deeply and can find no immediate answer to their sorrow. These need a glimpse of the glory and of the consummation of their faith to lift up their hearts and spur them on. It is a day of peculiar and sustained attack on the minds of the saints and the enemy seeks to defile and distract.

We need to hear Peter's clarion call to holiness. Values are tumbling and morals decay. The institutions of social propriety are mocked and dismantled with godless glee. It is good for the believer to be reminded by Peter of the abiding value on which his redemption rests and the enduring word upon which his hope is based.

These are days of profound need in the Church. The great doctrine of the priesthood of believers is being eroded by a flood of carnal alternatives. The holy and royal privileges of this sacred office are being lightly discarded. Peter's reminder regarding this ministry is most relevant. For many, honest toil and happy homes are but a distant memory of "good old days". Submissive wives and loving husbands are considered in the west a humourous violation of the present libertinism. Spiritual leaders amongst God's people need again solemnly to consider the obligations of their ministry and the inspired exhortations of the apostle that they might be true examples to the flock.

Perhaps above all we urgently need a fresh vision of the One we love though unseen to the eye. Then our joy will be restored, unspeakable and full of glory. This love for the Lord Jesus Christ will then distil that fragrant unity of the brethren. It will dispense blessed harmony in our homes. It will dedicate us to sacrificial service to the flock of God. It will inspire true piety in the world and in the workplace. Then when our brief day as strangers and pilgrims here is done the doxology of Peter may well become our epitaph: "To whom be praise and dominion forever and ever. Amen".

2. The Writings

The epistle opens with the signature of Peter, marking it at once as his own writing. He appends a confirmation of this at the conclusion of the letter, "I have written" (5:12). Whether by this he signified that he actually penned the epistle, or used the services of an amanuensis, perhaps Silvanus, is not clear.

The authenticity of the epistle has been accepted from the earliest times. "Citations from the epistle are abundant, in Greek writers from the time of Polycarp onwards; in Latin writers from that of Tertullian" (Hasting's *Dictionary*, Vol. 3, p. 779). It is an epistle of whose authority was never any doubt in the Church. " Among all the writers of christian antiquity, there is not one who doubted the genuineness of the Epistle, or had even heard of any doubts concerning it" (Olshausen).

Critics, of course, have challenged the Petrine claim and assigned the epistle to Silvanus or to some unknown disciple who used Peter's name as a pseudonym for greater credibility. Others have suggested that because of its "affinity in doctrine, thought and language with the Pauline epistles" and that it "breathes the Pauline spirit", Paul himself was the writer and-strangely enough-used Peter's name.

The main objections of the critics seem to be on the basis of linguistics. "Such a letter", wrote one, "could not have been written by [Peter], the illiterate fisherman, if he had lived to be over a hundred" (F.W. Beare, *1st Epistle of Peter*, p.29). Another suggested that the "formally good, rhythmic, polished and elegant style" (*Tyndale NT Commentary*, p. 23) of the Greek used, seems to some to be inconsistent with the education and background of a Galilean fisherman.

Some commentators seem to equate Peter's noticeable north country dialect (Matt 26:73) with an intellectual dullness or mental constriction. They point to Acts 4:13 where he and his companions are called "unlearned and ignorant men". Thus they assume that these were illiterate fishermen. But were they?

The word *agrammatos* ("unlearned") can mean without formal training. Robertson defines the word as being used to describe "Unlettered men without technical training in the professional rabbinical schools ... Jesus Himself was so regarded" (John 7:15). Similarly, *idiōtēs* "does not mean 'ignorant', but a layman, a man not in office" (Robertson, *Word Pictures in the NT*, Vol. 3, p.52).

Galilee was bilingual and no doubt Peter had used that language from his boyhood. Being the apostle of the circumcision (Gal 2:8) it would not be difficult to assume that he would hone his use of the language to reach the Hellenistic Jews in Jerusalem and to write to Greek-speaking believers.

Consider Peter's sermons in the Acts. In ch.2, he delivers a masterful exposition of OT Scriptures. In ch.3, he "taught the people" by reference to the patriarchs and the prophets (4:2). In ch.4, Peter confounds the high priest and his theological peers with his deep spiritual insight and knowledge of Scripture.

How was this possible for an "unlearned" Galilean fisherman? The answer surely is in 4:8, "Peter, filled with the Holy Ghost".

Why should it be thought a thing incredible that the risen Lord should keep His promises as recorded in John 14:26; 16:13-15? Why is it a problem to some that the same Holy Spirit who controlled Peter's mind at Pentecost and enabled him to speak a foreign language (*glōssa*) he had not learned, then controlled his tongue so that he spoke it in a local dialect (*dialektos*) he could not mimic, should also inspire him to write by the vehicle of a vocabulary "rich in contrast, spontaneous in style, replete with epithets and synonyms and sparkling with imagery drawn almost entirely from the Old Testament".

In John 7:15 the Jews wondered that the Lord Jesus knew "letters" (*grammata*) having never "learned". His teaching was "of God" (vv.16-17). Peter was filled with the Holy Spirit of God, we read. It should be no difficulty to the believing soul to accept that whatever erudition is conveyed in the language of this epistle was the result of the breathing of God through His instrument, as he was "moved by the Holy Ghost" (2 Tim 3:16; 2 Pet 1:21).

3. The Writer

It would be difficult to grasp the feeling of this epistle without considering, even in a limited way, the man who was inspired to write it. As we read about him, his words, his emotion, his strengths and weaknesses, and the Lord's dealings with him, we cannot help but be deeply moved to recognise ourselves in his failures and yearn to share the exuberance of his victories.

Brought up in Bethsaida ("the House of Fish") on the shores of Galilee, he and his brother Andrew were members of a fishing family. Simon must have been good at his trade for he eventually had his own boat and was able to buy a house when he settled in Capernaum (Matt 8: 14). His declaration "we have left all and followed thee" was no empty boast. It had cost him substantially in the context of life as he knew it then.

Names being more significant then than they are now, "Simon" or "Simeon" may well indicate that he was born in answer to the prayers of his parents. The Simeon of the OT (from *shama* "to hear") was so named by his mother Leah because she believed the Lord had heard her cry for a son.

Little did Andrew the fisherman of Bethsaida realise just how great was his catch that day when he brought his brother Simon to the Master, saying "We have found the Messiah" (John 1:40-42). "Such a *Eureka*! never before was uttered by a man. He was found for whom the world had waited forty centuries" (Bengel).

It was then that the Lord Jesus gave Simon the name *Kephas*. This is a Syro-Chaldaic word which interpreted into Greek is Petros, meaning "a piece of rock". It conveys something larger than *lithos*, a stone, and is diminutive of *petra*, a mass of rock, the latter ascription being used of Christ Himself (1 Cor 10:4).

The giving of a new name by God is always noteworthy in Scripture. As with Abram, Sarai and Jacob, the new name incorporated something from the divine name and signified a new relationship with God, a new responsibility to God and a new reflection of God.

His Call

John Baptist was thrown into prison and, in fulfilment of the prophecy of Isa 9:1-2, the Lord Jesus left Nazareth and dwelt in Capernaum (Matt 4:12-16). Peter also moved there from Bethsaida. Married and with his wife's mother living with them, he continued to ply his trade from there. Those who teach a doctrine of compulsory celibacy for their ministerial class should keep in mind that Peter had a wife and they should at least forbear to boast themselves of Peter's name.

It was nearby on the shores of Galilee, on what seemed an ordinary working day as the fishermen cleaned their nets, that Peter was called to the greater work of fishing for men. He had heard the Master preach. He would shortly see His power demonstrated at home when his wife's mother would be delivered from a "great fever".

Now it was time for Peter to learn some lessons vital to his new calling as a fisher of men. These lessons would teach him about the sovereignty of Christ, his Lord and Master, and the necessity for absolute and unquestioned obedience.

The first important lesson was that his Master's sovereign purpose transcends human reason. Having taught the people from the boat secured in the shallows near the shore, the Lord Jesus told Simon to launch out into the deep water and to let down the nets for a draught of fishes. Simon's first response was that the Lord's command seemed inconsistent with human reason. If these skilled fishermen had not been able to catch anything when the fish were near the surface at night, reason might well question how anything could be caught when the sun was climbing in the sky and the fish had gone down to the darker and cooler waters of the deep.

Simon may also have thought that the Master's command was inconsiderate of human limitations. They were already weary, having toiled all the night. "Toiled" (*kopos*) is laborious toil that results in weariness. Muscle-tired and bone-weary, those fishermen were no doubt anticipating with relief good rest and food. Then came the word, "Launch out into the deep and let down your nets for a draught" (Luke 5:4). Not exactly what Peter had planned.

This word may also have been seen by Simon as inconvenient to their human schedule. The nets had just been mended, washed and folded into the boat in readiness for the next night's fishing. Now the whole job would have to be done over again. What vital instruction there is in all this for those who would be fishers of men! The Lord's work is work indeed. Many aspire to it, thinking it is a glamorous life of travel and leisure. Some indeed may seek to make it so, but it is still the labourers that are few! "Nevertheless. . .", in spite of his own reasoning, Simon concedes to let down one net.

The second important lesson for the fisherman to learn in his new calling was that his Master's sovereign power transcends human resources (Luke 5:1-10). A long night of laborious toil using all the knowledge, skill and experience of their trade had not brought to the surface one small struggling fish they could keep. Now the Lord speaks of a "draught" of fishes. Simon would thus learn for future reference that the Lord knows all the secrets of the deep, whether of sea, circumstance, souls or sorrows. The deep and silent realms beyond the sight of men are all known to Him. "In his hand are the deep places. (Ps 95:4). What a lesson for fishers of men.

The third great lesson of the call of Simon was that his Master's sovereign resource transcends human requirements. So many were the fish caught that day that the net broke. Far beyond their immediate needs the Master provided abundantly above all that they could ask or think.

Why then was their valuable net damaged and broken under the strain of the catch? Because Simon's "nevertheless" did not include full and perfect obedience. The Master had said, "Let down the nets (*diktua*)". Simon replied, "At thy word I will let down the net (*dikton*)". But that was not the Master's word. Simon Peter modified it ever so slightly to fit his faith and let down one net only. Of course it broke. Implicit obedience is a basic requirement for all acceptable service. Those who would fish for men are not at liberty to adapt the Lord's commands nor to modify His word to suit either their faith or their convenience. The fish will still be caught, but the servant will suffer loss.

Those were most timely and needful lessons for Simon and his companions. This graphic instruction from experience would stand them in good stead in the tests and toils of their most noble and arduous calling. Those lessons would minister stamina to their spirits and strong confidence to their faith. They would produce quietness of heart and rest of mind when reason would object. By these lessons those fishers of men would be inspired and enlivened when weary and discouraged in the work. They would remember that obedience matters more than convenience. They would be delivered from the snare of appealing to men for supply when their resources were diminished and when their efforts seemed fruitless.

These are salutary lessons for those who would fish for men today. What distresses and what excesses would have been avoided, what humbling of self and what honour to Christ would have resulted, what blasphemy and what mockery against the precious name of the Lord would have been prevented, if only the divine instruction had been followed explicitly by all who claim the distinction, evangelist or missionary.

Simon at once recognised this miracle as a manifestation of the sovereign might and supernal majesty of the Son of God. The effect was to fill him with a deep sense of personal unworthiness. Much like Isaiah, at his calling, Peter cried "depart from me, for I am a sinful man". The reply of the Lord Jesus confirmed the purpose behind it all. It was to remove fear at the demonstration of divine power and to reassure faith by confirmation of the divine purpose, "Fear not, from henceforth thou shalt catch men".

There, at the feet of the Master in the boat, Simon learned in a way he would never forget, that this Jesus for whom he and the others would forsake all was indeed the Lord from heaven. From this school of divine instruction Peter came forth to catch men for God.

> "Fisher of men, the Blest,
> Out of the world's unrest,
> Out of sin's troubled sea
> Taking us Lord, to Thee."
> (Clement of Alexandria)

The time came for the appointment of the twelve and after a night alone upon the mountain in prayer, the Lord Jesus "ordained twelve, that they should be with him, and that he might send them forth to preach, and to have power to heal sicknesses and to cast out demons".

Those ordained men are listed differently.

Matthew	Mark	Luke	John
Simon Peter	*Simon Peter*	*Simon Peter*	*Simon Peter*
Andrew	James	Andrew	James
James	John	James	John
John	Andrew	John	Andrew
Philip	*Philip*	*Philip*	*Philip*
Bartholomew	Bartholomew	Bartholomew	Thomas
Thomas	Matthew	Matthew	Bartholomew
Matthew/Publican	Thomas	Thomas	Matthew
James/Alphaeus	*James/Alphaeus*	*James/Alphaeus*	*James/Alphaeus*
Lebbaus Thaddeus	Thaddeus	Simon Zelotes	Simon Zelotes
Simon/Canaanite	Simon/Canaanite	Judas of James	Judas of James
Judas Iscariot	Judas Iscariot	Judas Iscariot	-

It will be noticed that they are in groups of four. Each group is headed by the same name. The sons of Jonas and of Zebedee always constitute the first four and Peter always heads the list. Matthew expressly calls him "the first". Order of precedence however does not imply supremacy as some would claim, else why, just before the cross, was there dispute "which of them should be the greatest"?

Nevertheless Peter was the spokesman for the twelve on at least three occasions.

1. In the matter of watchfulness (Luke 12:41).

2. In the matter of forgiveness (Matt 18:21).

3. In the matter of renunciation (Mark 10:28).

It was Peter who was perceived as the leader of the disciples when the tax collectors came with their question (Matt 17:24).

On three occasions it was Peter, James and John who were selected to go with the Master. In each, death is in view. In the house of Jairus there was a cancelling of death and mourning. On the mount of transfiguration there was a conversation about death and glory. In Gethsemane there was a contemplation of death and sorrow. These three men had a signal honour in respect to death. Peter was to be the first preacher of the Church to publicly declare victory over death by the resurrection of Christ. James was to be the first of the twelve to experience death as a martyr. John was to be the rearward of the twelve to pass through the portals of death. By those three special convocations with death, Peter was prepared for a special ministry, James for an early grave and John for a long life.

His Confession

The Lord Jesus withdrew with His disciples to the quiet precincts of Caesarea Philippi which nestled at the foot of mighty Hermon. Far from the crowds and the confrontations of His detractors, His disciples were introduced to the significant events soon to take place in Jerusalem. He had been instructing them in the mysteries of the kingdom and establishing their faith by glimpses of His glory. Now the Saviour would lead them into the deeper mysteries of His sufferings, His betrayal and violent death.

Before this, the Lord sought to elicit from His own, a confession of their faith as to His own person. He had rebuked and warned them about the hatefulness of unsound doctrine with its insidious and corrupting influence which, like leaven, works silently within (Matt 16:1-12).

The bedrock and foundation of all true doctrine is Christ Himself. If the superstructure is built upon Him the edifice will stand and glorify God. If it is built on any other foundation, be it ever so grand, ever so glorious, ever so ancient, it will fall at the last.

Having asked "Whom do men say that I the Son of man am?" (16:13b), and hearing their response, the Lord Jesus then called for their own personal confession. It was Peter who answered for them all, "Thou art the Christ, the Son of the living God". The blessing of God rested upon this plain fisherman from Bethsaida, Simon Bar-jona. He had been the recipient of a special revelation from the Father. Now he is doubly blessed with a revelation from "the Son of the living God". Jesus said, "And I say also unto thee, that thou art Peter [*Petros*], and upon this rock [*petra*] I will build my church; and the gates of hell shall not prevail against it" (Matt 16:18). The Lord Jesus moves from addressing His servant by his old identity with all its restrictive and local connotations, Simon Bar-jona. He confirms him as Peter, his new name with its far-reaching implications and eternal consequences.

Peter is not the foundation of the Church. While the distinctions between

Petros and *Petra* are noteworthy, argument on this alone can hardly be used as a final evidence to identify the foundation of the Church. "The feminine, *Petra*, is predominantly used in secular Greek for a large and solid rock. The masculine, *Petros*, is used more for isolated rocks or small stones ... the emphasis should be noted, though in practice one cannot differentiate too strictly between *Petra* and *Petros*; they are often used interchangeably ... Rightly understood [however] Christ alone is *Petra* " (Friedrich). Other Scriptures make it crystal clear however that there is only one true foundation for that which is built for God, personal, local or universal, "which is Jesus Christ" (1 Cor 3:11).

The person of Christ, the work of Christ and the doctrine of Christ can be distinguished, but they cannot be separated any more than can length, breadth and height in space. They are distinct, yet indivisibly one of the other. This glorious person, His word and His work are together the impregnable Rock upon which the church is built.

In this declaration "I will build my church" are invested five indispensable principles.

"*I*"-the Church is to be *erected* by the power of Christ and not the programmes and energy of the flesh.

"*Will*"-the Church is to be *subject* to the will of Christ and not the will and desires of the flesh.

"*Build*"-the Church is the *project* of the design of Christ and not the religious ingenuity of the flesh.

"*My*"-the church is the *object* of the love and possession of Christ and not the perverted loyalties of the flesh.

"*Church*"-the Church is the called-out-company, to go forth unto Him, outside the camp, and to *reject* the systems of the flesh.

Great privilege brings heavy responsibility and Peter was given "the keys of the kingdom of heaven" (Matt 16:19)-not the keys of heaven, but the responsibility to unlock the treasures of truth to Jew and Gentile that they might enter by the obedience of faith that realm of heavenly rule where Christ is sovereign Lord.

This he did for the Jews at Pentecost, "This is that. . ." (Acts 2:16) and ''Therefore let all the house of Israel know assuredly that God hath made that same Jesus, whom ye have crucified, both Lord and Christ" (Acts 2:36). He performed this ministry also for the Gentiles in Acts 10 when he preached Christ to Cornelius and his companions, "to him give all the prophets witness, that through his name whosoever believeth in him shall receive remission of sins" (Acts 10:43).

Once Peter had used the key and opened the door to Jew and Gentile there was no further need for it. Therefore any claims to apostolic succession are spurious, misleading and arrogant. The counterfeit nature of all such profession is exposed by the evident lack of apostolic power and the departure from apostolic doctrine and practice.

His Crises

On the Water (Matt 14:22-27)

The Lord Jesus had called His own aside to Himself for a brief time of rest and refreshing. He knew their need and being the kind Master He is, saw it was time to "come apart".

They had suffered deep emotional strain, having just gone to Herod's prison and claimed the headless body of John. They would not forget that it was from this great servant's lips they first heard Christ preached. They had claimed that corpse and by their own hands carried it to the burial. We can only imagine their deep sorrow.

They had experienced a daily spiritual drain as they went about doing the works and teaching the words of the Master. We can understand a little of their dissipated strength.

They had experienced a distinct physical weariness having had no moment for relaxation, even briefly, to break away for a meal. They were learning about disrupted schedules. After a few brief hours of refreshing and having ministered to the multitude which had discovered them, they were constrained by the Master to get into their boat and return to Bethany.

It was not yet dark. It was evening (v.23) and they were "in the midst of the sea". Between vv.23 and 24 some very difficult hours intervened. We are told nothing about them save that a contrary wind had risen up and they were tossed with waves. Mark adds that "they toiled in rowing". No voice from heaven was heard. No intervention of the Lord relieved their toil. They just keep rowing hour after hour. "As this was 'about the fourth watch of the night' (Matt 14:25), or from 3-6 am, the disciples must have been struggling against the wind and waves some eight or ten hours" (Andrews).

The Master's eye is nevertheless upon them. His ear is open to their cry and He comes "unto them". It is not the conquering of the elements that is before Him, but the consolation of His own beloved disciples. He comes "walking upon the sea" thus showing that He is the Master over all life's changing circumstance.

They are terrified, supposing "it" was a spirit. Men always fear the "its" of life. We fear what we do not understand. The answer comes back across the waves from the One who knew their hearts, "Be of good cheer; it is I; be not afraid". The "it" they feared was really the Lord Jesus coming into their circumstances as Master of wind and wave.

It was Peter who responded, "Lord, if it be thou. . ." He still was not sure if this was an "it", a disembodied spirit, or "thou". One word of command was sufficient, "Come", and Peter stepped out of the boat on to the heaving waters of the sea. If this was an "it" he was going down. If it was the Lord he would remain on the surface and emulate his Master's walk upon the water.

So it was, he found the water firm beneath him and he set out towards the Master. "Faith was his only hold upon the power that could support him there, and when that failed, the miracle ceased for him" (Green).

He turned his eye away from the Lord Jesus and saw the strength of the wind. Then beginning to sink, he cried out "Lord, save me". Jesus already having stretched out the hand took hold of him. There, out on the water, beyond earshot of the others, the Master of the elements speaks a word of gentle rebuke "0 thou of little faith, wherefore didst thou doubt" (v.31). Let us not be too hasty to present Peter here as an example of failing faith. Who among us has walked on water recently?

It would seem to the reader of this narrative that here was an action embodying very great faith, yet the Lord called it "little faith". On another occasion He called a simple expression of the Syrophenician woman the evidence of great faith. We may learn from this that, for us, faith is not always easy to measure nor actions easy to evaluate by observation. Only the Lord can properly weigh actions (1 Sam 2:3), accurately measure faith and carefully discern motives in the light of eternal values.

In this experience on the water, Peter discovered the power of Christ as Saviour from the forces of nature, but more significantly, from the limitations of his own faith.

On the Mount (Matt 17)

Little wonder that it is recorded of Peter on the mount that he "wist not what to say" (Mark 9:6). It is always a safe rule that when we do not know what to say it is better not to say. Peter again is diverted by another "it" as, with James and John, he beheld the blazing Christ. Confused by fear, he said, "It is good for us to be here".

Diversion from Christ is the great ploy of Satan. The enemy does not mind what it is that turns God's people aside. It may be the ways of this world, the weakness of the flesh or the wiles of the devil. As in Peter's case it may even be a good and holy thing, a subjective experience that becomes the preoccupation of the soul, exciting the cry "it is good for us. . ." While not all translations have "for us" and read "It is good [beautiful, fortunate, excellent] we should be here", the context would seem to support that Peter was indeed taken up with "it", the experience.

The Father will permit nothing, not even a holy thing, to divert the mind's attention and the heart's affection away from His beloved Son without intervening. Holy things are still not Him! While Peter was speaking there was a divine interruption in his conversation (Matt 17:5). A bright cloud overshadowed them and the Father spoke. He directed Peter and the others to centre their attention on His beloved Son and be occupied only with Him and what He had to say.

"Moses represents the law and Elijah the prophets; both together comprising the whole extent of bygone divine revelations. The law and the prophets point to Christ: the ministry of the gospel was to point to Christ. The past and the present meet upon that mountain, to show that Jesus is the central figure of all time" (Green).

The Lord Jesus fulfilled the law and, as the effulgence of God, He is in Himself the full expression of the mind of God and the consummation of the prophetic Scriptures.

There on the mount, Peter, James and John saw a foregleam of millennial glory and a preview of the kingdom. As representing a separated remnant, their eyes beheld "the king in his beauty". He alone must be the focus of the soul, the filling of the vision and the first-love of the heart.

Many, in our day, seem to be diverted from Christ as the great preoccupation of the soul. Altogether apart from being distracted by what is evidently wrong, there are those who pursue a subjective experience as the main thing in their christian lives. Indeed they often make this the measure of their spirituality and the test of others. Service is performed, duties are discharged with earnest zeal and the exulting shout is heard " It is good for us. . ." and it is good, but it is not the best. It may be high endeavour, but not the highest. The familiar adage is right, that "The good is the enemy of the best".

Peter's experience on the mount can be most instructive to all who seek to know God's order of things, enabling the believer to distinguish what is of the soul and what is of the spirit. The soul with its emotion is not wrong; God made it, and there must be feeling in all our service or else it is cold, calculating and without compassion. But the spirit is the highest part of us and it is the spiritual that is eternal. The danger comes when we confuse the soulish and the spiritual and think that because our emotions are moved we have had a spiritual experience. This is not necessarily so. It is the word of God, "living and operative, and sharper than any two-edged sword, and penetrating to the division of soul and spirit. . ." (Heb 4:12 JND) that can enable the exercised believer to distinguish that which differs.

The great religious systems of the day place much emphasis on the emotion of the soul and not enough emphasis on the exposition of the Word. These systems divert the soul by a preoccupation with subjective experience at the expense of the spirit's occupation with the Lord Jesus Christ and the personal enjoyment of Himself.

It is of vital importance that we properly assess true values and establish the correct priority between right and holy aspiration, such as the psalmist's, "I shall be satisfied . . ." (Ps 17:15) and holy admiration, such as of the prophet, "He ... shall be satisfied" (Isa 53:11). We must be able to distinguish between

"it" and "Him" and to settle the priority of ministry between that which goes
out to the house of God (Ezek 44:11) and that which goes in to the heart of
God (v.15).

> "What do I really desire in this life?
>   Is it something for me, and a little for Thee?
> To what do I grandly aspire in the strife?
>   Is it Thee, my God, is it Thee?
>
> What drives me onward to serve day by day?
>   Is it something for me, or glory for Thee?
> What motive enlivens each nerve in the fray?
>   Is it Thee, my God, is it Thee?
>
> What is it draws my first love to impart?
>   Is it something for me, or Thee only Thee?
> What is it, below or above fills my heart?
>   Is it Thee, my God, is it Thee?
>
> Help me to more understand by Thy grace,
>   That the best thing for me, is enjoyment of Thee;
> That blessings and service, though grand in their place,
>   Are not Thee, blessed God, are not Thee."

In the Room (John 13:6-11)

On the water, Peter had seen the power of Christ as the Saviour. On the holy
mount he saw the glory of Christ as the Sovereign. He had more lessons yet to
learn as the cross drew near. He was going to see the grace of Christ as the
perfect Servant.

Gathered with the Lord Jesus and the others in the upper room Peter
discovered the danger of limiting the ministry of the Lord in his life by self-will.
We must be careful in considering this to remember that the Lord Jesus was
never limited in His attributes at any time. He never laid aside His deity to become
a man. He did however voluntarily limit the expression of those attributes as
occasion demanded.

The brief dialogue that surrounds the washing of Peter's feet is formed by
three exchanges. The first is a query and an explanation. Peter's query, as the
Lord approached him with the basin and towel was, " Lord, dost thou wash my
feet?"

Peter was not questioning the act itself. Feet washing was a hospitable custom
of the day. He was not questioning the need, for his feet, soiled by the dust of the
roads, needed to be washed. What Peter questioned was the propriety of the act,

the Lord washing his feet. The pronouns are emphatic and we could read "*Thou* Lord ... *my* feet?"

Why was the Lord, into whose hands the Father had given all things, interested in taking into those hands Peter's lowest members? First, because they were defiled, and no defilement, be it ever so slight, is unimportant to the Master. Secondly defilement is a hindrance to fellowship, and fellowship was important to both the Lord Jesus and to Peter. Thirdly because cleansing from that defilement was possible and that is important for the joy and peace of the disciple.

The explanation of the Master was given to Peter in three parts. He begins, "What I do. .." If the Lord had merely been removing the grime from his feet there would be no need for explanation. It would be self-evident what the Lord was doing. By those words He conveyed there was a deeper meaning behind the circumstance.

The Lord Jesus goes on ". . . thou knowest not now. .." That is, Peter could not know merely by observation what the Lord was doing. This word "know" (*oida*) is from the same root as *eidon*, "to see" (W.E. Vine). There was a spiritual lesson to be learned by this circumstance. More than this, "Thou shalt know hereafter". The word "know" is different here; it is "*ginōskō*" to get to know by instruction or experience, to get insight, to understand. This would tell Peter that there is an ultimate answer to the present experience. Many of God's beloved people passing through an experience they could not understand have found comfort in these words of the Master, "What I do thou knowest not now; but thou shalt know hereafter".

The second exchange of the dialogue is a refusal and a warning. Peter responds, "Thou shalt never wash my feet". It is not "Lord" now simply "Thou", for when we raise our own will we challenge the Lordship of Christ over us. There is great force in these words. Literally they may be read, "In no wise mayest thou wash my feet forever". By this refusal he raised three barriers against the ministry of the Lord towards him. The first was the exercise of the power of his own will: he said to the Lord "never"; it was self-will before the Lord's will. The next was the reservation of rights to the members of his body: he said "my feet". Then he extended the control of his own life to "forever".

By this refusal, he implied two things. He saw no pressing need for cleansing "now". He saw no profit to instruction "hereafter".

The Lord's solemn reply was a warning to Peter. "Unless I wash thee, thou hast not part with me" (John 13:8 JND). By these words the Lord reveals the consequences of Peter's refusal. It would be to remain untouched by the ministry of the Lord, to remain unwashed from the defilement of the way and to remain unblessed by the allotted portion (*meros*) of the Lord. The unsubmissive spirit must forego all these benefits.

The third exchange of the dialogue is a reaction and a principle. Upon hearing the warning of the Lord Jesus, Peter's reaction is one of enthusiastic submission, "Lord, not my feet only, but also my hands and my head". Peter moves back again to the literal and the physical, still seemingly unaware of the spiritual lesson, but that would shortly come. Peter wanted to make sure now that he was not going to miss the blessing. He wanted to have his share and not be excluded from the Lord's portion.

While we can hardly blame Peter for his enthusiasm, enthusiasm is not enough; it must be controlled by the rein of truth. To go beyond the will of the Lord is an error as serious as lagging behind. So the psalmist admonishes, "Be ye not as the horse, or as the mule. .." (Ps 32:9).

The Lord now gives an assuring principle. "He that is washed all over needs not to wash save his feet, but is wholly clean" (v.10 JND). This principle expresses three important truths. Once the disciple has been bathed at salvation, this need never be repeated. If the disciple becomes defiled in the way, he needs to be cleansed. Once this defilement by contact with the world has been dealt with, the disciple need never doubt the blessed portion of the Lord's fellowship is his to enjoy.

At the Fire (Luke 22:54-62)

Those few sacred hours spent in the upper room with the Lord Jesus were full of instruction for Peter and the disciples as the Lord led them gently to the realisation of His betrayal, His imminent death and future glory. Not only was He to suffer, but He told those beloved men that they too would come under the direct attack of Satan, the great adversary. This diabolical enemy desired to have the disciples to sift them as wheat. Thorns, and briars are burned; wheat is sifted. Actually the word "desired" is "asked, demanded, petitioned", from *aiteō*. The verb is in the middle voice, indicating the strong personal interest of Satan that these men be given up into his own hand.

Having warned the disciples that, as a special company, they were under Satanic surveillance, "Satan has demanded to have *you*" (*humeis*), the Lord now assures Peter personally of His prayers, "But I have besought for *thee* [*sou*] that thy faith fail not". Here we see the activities of the adversary and the intervention of the great Advocate, speaking on behalf of Peter, personally.

Note

It is of significant note in a day when, in English speaking lands at least, some have fallen into the use of the common "You" when addressing the God of heaven in public prayer. These state that it is acceptable to them to do so because, they would point out, there is no special word used in the Greek of the NT when addressing deity.

However they fail to follow the Lord Jesus in His careful use of pronouns. When speaking to the disciples as above, He used the second person plural but when addressing Peter, He used the second person singular. In speaking to His Father, the Lord Jesus always used the second person singular. This is carefully distinguished in the AV as "thou" or "thee". This is not an archaism to be lightly discarded but an accuracy to be carefully noted.

This lovely accuracy has been sacrificed by most modern translations, so that the careful reader is often at a loss to know, without further reference to the AV or the Greek text, whether one person or more is being addressed. This is a significant loss to the reader and greatly impoverishes any translation so modified. It is especially incongruous when "higher accuracy" is given as a reason for the existence of such a translation.

We never address God in plurality, but speak to the Father, or to the Son through the Spirit. It is only spiritually intelligent then to make the effort to learn and use that form of language available to us, which accurately and properly expresses the persons addressed. Indeed in our day, such a form of language can be reserved, in prayer, alone for God in singular reverence.

Other reasons for using the common form are given of course. One is that the NT believer has a place of intimacy with God as a Father and therefore may feel at liberty to be more familiar. The question must be asked, Do we know the Father more intimately than the Son who never used the wrong pronoun when speaking to His Father? Are we closer to God than the apostle Paul whose address of God was always correct and with carefulness?

Others say it is too difficult and awkward to use "thee" and "thou" and their attendant forms. Those who have worked with children in the past, quickly discount this excuse, because they have awarded many a prize to boys and girls for the word-perfect learning of even whole chapters from the AV.

The lisping prayers of a young child, the hesitant expressions of a newborn soul or the stumblings of the untaught, are quite another thing. For those who claim superior knowledge in things theological however, it may be well, before they meet the Lord at the Bema, to review their address of God and ask if peer pressure or religious fashion are more important than the Lord's lovely example.

Those plain men who had left all and followed this beloved One had been pointed away from the realm of mortal suffering and death to things eternal, to a kingdom to which they had been appointed, to heavenly fellowship and to thrones. The intense emotion and ardent feelings of that moment would be hard for us to imagine. It was then in that atmosphere of the impending clash of kingdoms, of fierce spiritual conflict and of the highest and holiest endeavour that Peter stepped forward with his oath of loyalty, "Lord, with Thee I am ready to go both to prison and to death" (JND). This was not the proud and arrogant boast of a thrill-seeking mercenary. It was the passionate allegiance of a loving heart courageously expressed in the face of seemingly overwhelming and merciless opposition.

The Lord knew His Peter better than Peter knew himself. He was well aware that this sturdy fisherman, skilled with the nets would prove clumsy with the sword, getting an ear instead of a head. He understood that Peter knew neither the full implications of his brave oath nor the frailty of his own heart.

In the conflict of the ages where battle is engaged with the cohorts of hell, where the legions are thunder-blasted demons and the issues are eternal, moral courage, be it ever so variolous and resolute, is a frail and brittle weapon indeed. "The christian's safety is in the knowledge of his weakness which sends him to the Lord for strength" (H. Martin). When that courage would fail, and tears and night would envelop a sorrowing Peter, would not those words of the Master penetrate his gloom, "Simon, Simon, ... I have prayed for thee . . .".?

Gethsemane, the disciple's sleep of sorrow, the Saviour's anguished praying, the ruffian mob with swords and staves, the traitor kiss, the futile flailing sword and the night walk into the valley of the Kedron and up the other side through the east gate of the old city to the palace of the high priest, and Peter followed ". . . afar off". But he did follow; let us say that much for him. Coming to the place he stood outside the door. At the request of John already inside, Peter was admitted to the courtyard.

A fire was kindled there by the servants and Peter drew near for a little warmth. There he sat down "together" with them "to see the end". What end? The end of that lovely life? The end of the prophetic purpose? The end of all his hopes? No battle lines were drawn, no phalanx of armoured soldiers stood to fight or else he might have drawn the sword again and slashed away. But the weapons were lies, slander, insult, mockery, unbelief, hatred and false witness. Against these, raw courage was futile and the sword had no target.

Bereft of weaponry, unskilled in advocacy, surrounded by the enemy, Peter's heart failed. Then came the threefold challenge as to his association with the Lord Jesus and the other disciples. Those three sad denials with cursing and swearing are almost too painful to recount in any detail. These were punctuated first and last by a cock crowing as the Lord had said. Flushed and frightened Peter takes a last look at his Master standing in solitary, suffering dignity, being treated as a common criminal before the scribes, the chief priests, the elders of Israel and Caiaphas, the high priest. The Lord turned and looked on Peter. Surely that was a look of unutterable sadness, tender and full of pity for His failing disciple, and "Peter remembered. .." Oh what memories as he went out into a dark night of remorse and inconsolable grief. He would never forget that look.

> "The cock crows coldly, - Go, and manifest
>   A late contrition, but no bootless fear!
> For when thy deathly need is bitterest,
>   Thou shalt not be denied, as I am here: -
> My voice, to God and angels, shall attest, -
>   'Because I *know* this man, let him be clear'."
>   Mrs Barrett Browning

Another Fire (John 21)

Remorse is a bitter grief indeed. How many of us have touched with this at the death of a loved one. How we wish then that we had done more, loved more, served more, given more, spoken more kindly, and then realise it is forever too late to change the past. Can we imagine Peter's remorse? Did he remember the words of his beloved Master, "Whosoever shall deny me before men, him will I also deny before my Father which is in heaven"?

Yet as he would recall the words of the Master concerning his denial, those very words would inspire hope again, "When thou art converted, strengthen thy brethren". It was "when" not "if". His recovery was certain. The other disciples would still be his "brethren". He was not lost after all. His soul was secure. "Strengthen" showed he still had a ministry to fulfil, he was not dismissed. His service was preserved. He had learned with bitter tears however that it would no longer be in his own fragile strength. He would strengthen his brethren in the Lord.

Ever after, as he wakened, morning by morning at the crowing of the cock, it would be for him a daily warning never again to trust in his own strength. Thus he would teach his brethren out of his own sad and unforgettable experience to draw upon the strength of the Lord.

Then came those three breathless women, having run from the sepulchre into the city (Matt 28:8). The message they brought was so amazing it seemed like "idle tales" (Luke 24:11). They had a special word for Peter from the risen Lord, and while the others "believed them not", Peter rose immediately and with John, ran to the sepulchre. Peter stepped in and saw the linen clothes "lying there alone" and full of wonder returned to their own home in the city.

We do not know exactly how or where it happened, but Paul reports in 1 Cor 15:5 that the Lord was seen of Cephas then of the twelve. What transpired between Peter and his Lord that glorious day we are not told. That must remain a secret between Peter and his Lord. The Lord never violated His own principles. He had taught His disciples, "If thy brother shall trespass against thee, go and tell him his fault between thee and him alone". We do know however that hope was begotten again in him by that mighty resurrection. The consolations of the risen Saviour healed his broken spirit so that he could stand up at Pentecost with his brethren and preach in the power of the Holy Ghost with a heavenly courage that confounded the crucifiers so that they cried out "Men and brethren, what shall we do?"

In the midst of all these astonishing circumstances life must go on, the men must provide food to eat and obtain money for the normal living expenses. So we see those fishermen again on the water honestly plying their trade.

It was a poor night for fishing, "that night they caught nothing" (John 21:3). The call from the early-morning Stranger to try the other side of the ship, resulted in a great multitude of fish being enmeshed in that single net (which did not break!). Whether it was the memory of the last great catch and the broken net that dawned upon John, or the growing light of the morning sun that dawned upon the Stranger on the shore we do not know, but John, ever the seer, recognised it was the Lord.

Characteristically, Peter throws himself into the situation, in this case, the cold water as yet unwarmed by the sun, not now, "If it be thou, bid me come to thee on the water". It certainly was the Lord, and his powerful stroke was faster in the water than the windless sails could move the boat, dragging its weight of fishes.

Reaching the shore they saw that the Lord had already set and lit a charcoal fire (*anthrakia*), hotter and longer lasting than a wood fire, for the ensuing conversation must not be interrupted by searching for driftwood. Warmth and the appetising aroma of the cooking fish, with bread, would supply for their physical comfort. No question is asked where or how the Lord obtained those fish.

When the Lord commanded to bring of the fish they had caught, again it is Peter who made the first move. The net "full of great fishes, an hundred and fifty three" and heavy with water, must have weighed well over two hundred pounds. Peter, strong of limb and back, pulled it ashore in immediate, personal and full obedience to the Master's word. Was there another lesson here to those "fishers of men"? Did this simple act point forward to that wonderful day when, perhaps in the midst of toil suddenly we shall cry, "It is the Lord" and we shall look on His face to hear Him say, " Bring of the souls which ye have caught in the gospel net and come and dine"? "One day shall the heavenly banquet await the blessed on the eternal shore, while still 'their works' shall 'follow them'-a store gathered by God's help from amid the waves of this troublesome world" (S.G. Green).

It seems to have been a rather quiet meal. After they had dined, the Lord turned to Peter, and addressed him by his old family name, "Simon, son of Jonas". When the Lord and Peter had met alone after the resurrection, clearly communion had been restored. Now the Lord was going to restore the confidence of his brethren, by re-commissioning "Simon" as "Peter" before them.

It had to be asked and it had to be answered, "Lovest thou me". Peter had denied three times, the question must be asked three times. It has been often noted that the Lord used two words for "love", two for "feed", two for the flock and Peter used two words for "know".

"Lovest thou me more than these?", not at all "these boats and nets". Peter had just left the boat and plunged into the water to come to the Lord. Peter's boast had been one of comparison with others, "Though all shall be offended, yet will not I" (Mark 14.29). The Lord's word was *agapaō*, the love of personal and tender affection raised "to the thought of an active and devoted exercise of it on behalf of others" (W.E. Vine). Peter replied, "Yea, Lord; thou knowest that I love thee", but Peter's word was *phileō*, natural affection, an attachment. The Lord responded, "feed my lambs", or as an endearment, "Feed my little sheep".

Again the question, "Simon, son of Jonas, lovest (*agapaō*) thou me?" Peter adhered to his word again, "Yea, Lord; thou knowest that I love (*phileō*) thee". The Lord replied, "Tend my sheep". The third time the question is asked, "Simon, son of Jonas, lovest thou me?" This time, however, the Lord used Peter's word, *phileō*, and Peter was grieved. Not because the Lord had asked three times, but that He should seem to question even Peter's affection. He replied, "Lord, thou knowest (*oida*) all things, thou knowest (*ginōskō*) that I love thee". *Oida* is fulness of knowledge by intuition or perception; *ginōskō* indicates a "relation between the person knowing and the object known" (W.E. Vine, Trench). All confidence in self-accomplishment was gone now and his best confidence would be that his affection would be enlarged to that *agapaō* love and that the Lord would know it as it was evidenced in Peter's life by sacrificial service. The Lord's response to this is "Feed my dear flock" (Tregelles).

The Lord begins with "Feed", then "Tend", or "shepherd" then returns to "Feed". Trench in his *Synonyms* says, "... whatever else of discipline and rule may be added thereto, still, the feeding of the flock, the finding for them of spiritual food, is the first and last; ... How often, in a false ecclesiastical system, the preaching of the Word loses its pre-eminence".

Now follows a distinct reference to the fact that the disciple would follow his Master in being put to death (John 21:18-19), but as a martyr. The first call is echoed, "Follow me". Officially, as it were, reinstating Peter before his brethren in preparation for his significant ministry in the Church.

In the Church (Acts 2:14-40)

The day of Pentecost was "fully come", just how full, for them and the history of the world, those one hundred and twenty gathered disciples had little idea until they heard "a sound out of heaven as of a violent impetuous blowing" (JND). "Not 'wind', but they heard blowing, as of hard breathing, for which it is also used" (JND tr. notes). "Parted tongues, as of fire" appeared and sat upon each one of them and the disciples spoke in foreign languages they had not learned with local dialects they could not impersonate. Then Peter stood up "with the eleven". There is no thought of Peter being out of place. There is no reference to his failure for when the Lord deals with sin it is actually put away and the record is clear.

Peter preached his first sermon in the history of the Church. By this he left on record a clear example of the content of the preaching that is of the Spirit and of power.

He took the word of God, and preached the Christ of God, in the power of God and in fellowship with the people of God. His message was "Christ": Christ on the cross (v.23), Christ in His death (v.24), Christ raised up (vv.24,32), Christ exalted (vv.25,33).

His message was *instructive*, confirming the prophetic Scriptures and the approbation of God's servants (vv.16,33). His message was *effective*, reaching the heart and conscience of his hearers (v.37). His message was *declarative*, as to prophetic declaration (vv.16-21). His message was *affirmative*, as to Christ's personal manifestation (v.22). His message was *descriptive*, as to the Saviour's painful humiliation (v.24). This first message of Peter in the Church was *corrective*, exposing the lie his hearers had perpetrated concerning the resurrection (vv.24,30-32). His message was *directive*, pointing the hearers to the same Jesus whom they crucified, seated now in exalted glory (vv.33-36). Finally his message was positive, declaring that even those who had so grievously sinned against the Lord could have remission of sins and also receive the gift of the Holy Spirit (vv.38-40).

Whole volumes have been written about Peter and the Church. The record of his vision, his words, his works, the miracles performed by him, his fellowships with John and with Paul and others have been the subjects of many writings. His imprisonment and release and his shepherd care for the flock of God are all on ample record.

Tradition has had its hand in it all and, mixing a measure of truth with the religious imaginations of the flesh, has painted all manner of pictures, both by literacy and artistry, of the man called Peter, his life and death.

The site that religious tradition has assigned as Peter's tomb is marked by a magnificent cathedral which bears his name, but could bear neither his approval nor his imprimatur, for he was the disciple who once said, "Silver and gold have I none".

We must look elsewhere for the memorial of the man called Peter, that plain fisherman from Bethsaida, with all his strengths and weaknesses, called, commissioned and conformed by the Lord Himself. We find that memorial in the word of God, a simple unadorned monument, engraved where neither time nor corruption will ever erase its inscription. The words are few but they move the heart of every sinner saved by grace, who has felt within a pulse of Peter's passion, experienced some sad failure and known the pardoning grace of a faithful and loving Saviour. Those words touch the wellspring of our tears and we are deeply moved as we read them, "Lord, thou knowest all things; thou knowest that I love thee".

4. The Outline

I.	*Salutation*	
	1. The Writer	1:1-2
	2. The Recipients	1:1a
	a. Their Location	1:1b-2a
	b. Their Condition	1:1b
	c. Their Disposition	1:1b
	d. Their Election	1:2a
	3. The Request	1:2b
II.	*Salvation*	1:3-12
	1. The Commentary on Salvation	1:3-4
	a. Its Source	1:3a
	b. Its Course	1:3b
	2. The Elements of Salvation	1:3-4

       c. Strength
       d. Grounding

V.   *The Apostolic Doxology*   5:11

       1. Glory
       2. Dominion
               AMEN
VI.   *The Conclusion*   5:12-14
       1. The Faithful Brother   5:12a
       2. The Stated Purpose   5:12b
       3. The Closing Salutation   5:13-14a
          a. The Church   5:13a
          b. The Son   5:13b
          c. The Kiss   5:14a
       4. The Benediction   5:14b
              AMEN

5. Peter's Theology

The following list is only suggestive and not exhaustive, further references and cross-references can be filled in by the student.

1.   *The Bible*
       a. Its Duration   1:23,25
       b. Inspiration of OT   1:10,11,25
       c. Limitations of Bible Writers 1:11
       d. Function of Scripture
          a. The Means of Regeneration 1:23
          b. The Means of Growth   2:2
          e. The Truth   1:22

2.   *God*
       a. Ascriptions of God
          Father   1:2
          Father of our Lord Jesus Christ 1:3
          The Lord   1:25; 2:4; 2:13; 3:12
          The Lord God   3:15 (AV)
          The God of all Grace   5:10
       b. His Power   1:5; 5:6
       c. His Righteous judgment   4:5
       d. His Grace   4:10; 5:5,10,12
       e. His Longsuffering   3:20
       f. His Eternal Praise   4:11; 5:11

	g. The Will of God	2:5; 3:17; 4:2,6,19
h.	God should be	
	Trusted	1:21; 3:5
	Feared	2:17
	Sanctified in the Heart	3:15
	Glorified	4:11,16
i.	His People	1:1,2,14; 2:2; 2:9,10
j.	His Servants	2:16

3.	*God the Father*	
	a. His Omniscience	1:2
	b. To be Praised	1:3
	c. To be Called on	1:17

4.	*Christ*	
	a. The Son of God	1:3
	b. Sanctified Lord in the Heart	3:15 (JND)
	c. Foreordained	1:20
	d. Old Testament Testimony	1:11
	e. His Pre-incarnate Ministry	3:19
	f. On Earth	
	His Great Value	2:7
	His Perfection	2:22
	His Rejection by Men	2:4
	His Approval by God	2:4
	His Suffering	1:11; 2:21; 3:18; 4:1; 5:1
	His Blood	1:2,19
g.	His Resurrection	1:3,21; 3:21-22
h.	His Present Ministry	
	As Great High Priest	2:25
	Overseeing the Believers	1:1; 2:25
	Glorifying God	4:11

5.	*The Holy Spirit*	
	a. In the OT Prophets	1:11
	b. In Noah	3:19
	c. Raised Christ from Death	3:18
	d. Sanctifies	1:2
	e. Helps Believers	1:22; 4:6,14
	f. The Trinity	1:2,3,8,11,17,19,22

| 6. | *Angels* | |
| | a. Interested in the Scriptures | 1:12 |

Women's Adornment	3:1-7
d. Suffering in the Flesh	4:1,12-19
The Old Life	4:3
The New Life	4:9
e. Humility	5:5
Confidence	5:6,7
Courage	5:8,9
f. Love	
to Christ	1:8
to One Another	1:22; 2:17; 4:8; 5:14
of the Brethren	1:22; 3:8
g. Joy	1:6,8; 4:13
h. Peace	1:2; 3:11; 5:14
i. Long Suffering	2:19,20; 3:14,17; 4:1
j. Gentleness	3:8-10
k. Goodness	3:11,13,16
l. Faith	see 8-5
m. Meekness	3:4
n. Self-control	2:1,11,18-20; 3:1,9-10
o. Trials	1:6; 4:12
p. Prayer	3:17,12; 4:7
10. *The Church (see 4-5)*	
a. The Priesthood	2:5,9
b. The Gifts	4:10,11
c. The Elders	5:1,5
11. *Last Things*	
a. Hope	1:3,13,21; 3:5,15
b. Salvation to be Revealed	1:5
c. Judgment Seat of Christ	5:4
d. An Inheritance	1:4; 3:9
e. The Revelation	1:13
f. The Glory	1:7,11; 4:13; 5:1

6. Word List

The following is a list of words in 1 Peter that are not used by any other NT writers as Peter used them. Some are found in the Septuagint and others from some other Greek version of the OT.

Word	AV Translation	Reference
Agathopoiia	Well doing	4:19

Agathopoios	That do well	2:14
Adelphotēs	The brotherhood	2:17
	Brethren	5:9
Adikōs	Wrongfully	2:19
Adolos	Sincere	2:2
Aischrokerdē	For filthy lucre	5:2
Allotriopiskopos	A busybody	4:15
Amarantinos	That fadeth not away	5:4
Amarantos	That fadeth not away	1:4
Anagennaō	Begotten again	1:3
	Being born again	1:23
Anankastōs	By constraint	5:2
Anazōnnumi	Gird up	1:13
Anachusis	Excess	4:4
Aneklalētos	Unspeakable	1:8
Antiloidoreō	Revile (not) again	2:23
Apoginomai	Being dead	2:24
Aponemō	Giving	3:7
Aprosōpolēmptōs	(No respect of) persons	1:17
Artigennētos	Newborn	2:2
Archipoimēn	Chief shepherd	5:4
Bioō	Live	4:2
Gunaikeios	Wife	3:7
Enkomboomai	Be clothed with	5:5
Emplokē	Plaiting	3:3
Endusis	Putting on	3:3
Exangellō	Shew forth	2:9
Exeraunaō	Searched diligently	1:10
Eperōtēma	Answer	3:21
Epikalumma	A cloke	2:16
Epiloipos	The rest (remainder)	4:2
Epimartureō	Testifying	5:12
Epopteuō	Behold	2:12; 3:2
(H)ierateuma	Priesthood	2:5,9
Kleos	Glory	2:20
Krataios	Mighty	5:6
Kristēs	Creator	4:19
Mōlōps	Stripes	2:24
Oinophlugia	Excess of wine	4:3
(H)omophrōn	Of one mind	3:8
(H)oplizō	Arm yourselves	4:1
Patroparadotos	Tradition from . . . fathers	1:18
Perithesis	Wearing	3:3

Potos	Banquetings	4:3
Prothumōs	Of a ready mind	5:2
Promarturomai	Testified beforehand	1:11
Ptoēsis	Amazement	3:6
Rhupos	Filth	3:21
Sthenoō	Strengthen	5:10
Spora	Seed	1:23
Sumpathēs	Having compassion	5:8
Sumpresbuteros	Also an elder (co-elder)	5:1
Suneklektos	Elected together	5:13
Sunoikeō	Dwell with	3:7
Teleiōs	To the end (perfectly)	1:13
(H)upogrammos	An example	2:21
(H)upolimpanō	Leaving	2:21
Philadelphos	Love as brethren	3:8
Philophrōn	Courteous	3:8
Oruomai	Roaring	5:8

8. Bibliography

Books on Peter

Beasley-Murray, G.R. *Bible Guides, The General Epistles.* London: Lutterworth Press. 1965.

Bigg, C. *The International Critical Commentary (The Epistles of St. Peter and St. Jude).* Edinburgh: T. & T. Clark. 1901.

Blum, E.A. *The Expositors's Bible Commentary, 1 Peter.* Grand Rapids: Zondervan Corp. 1981.

Bullinger, E.W. *Selected Writings, The Spirits in Prison.* London: The Lamp Press.

Carson, Tom. *Studies in Peter's First Epistle, Truth and Life Series.* Sydney: Christian Outreach. 1983.

Cook, F.C. (Editor). *The Holy Bible with an Explanation & Critical Commentary.* New York: Charles Scribner & Sons. 1871.

Darby, J.N. *1 Peter (The Present Testimony, Vol 12).* London; R. Groombridge & Sons. 1861.

Darby, J.N. *Notes and Jottings, 1 Peter (Reprint).* Pennsylvania: Believer's Bookshelf. 1971.

English, E.S. *The Life and Letters of Saint Peter.* New York: Our Hope. 1941.

Erdman, C.R. *The General Epistles.* Philadelphia: Westminster Press. 1919.

Fronmuller, G.F.C. *The Epistles General of Peter (Lange's Commentary).* New York: Charles Scribner & Co. 1867.

Grant, F.W. *The Numerical Bible, 1 Peter.* New York: Loizeaux Brothers. 1902.

Green, S.G. *The Apostle Peter: His Life and Letters*. London: Sunday School Union. 18??.

Hastings, James. *The Great Tests of the Bible, Vol 19 (Scribner)*. Grand Rapids: Eerdman's Publishing Co.

Hiebert, D.E. *First Peter*. Chicago: Moody Press. 1984.

Kelly, William. *The Epistles of Peter*. London: C.A. Hammond. 1904.

Kelly, William. *The Preaching to the Spirits in Prison (Reprint)*. Denver: Wilson Foundation. 1970.

Kelly, William (Editor). *The Bible Treasury, Vol 9 (Reprint of 1872 edition)*. Winschoten: Heijkoop, J. 1969.

Lincoln, William. *Lectures on the First and Second Epistles of Peter*. Kilmarnock: John Ritchie.

Lumby, J.R. *The Expositor's Bible, The Epistles of St. Peter*. London: Hodder and Stoughton. 1908.

Macdonald, William. *1 Peter: Faith Tested, Future Triumphant*. Wheaton: Harold Shaw. 1972.

Maclaren, A. *Expositions of Holy Scripture, The Epistles General*. London: Hodder and Stoughton. 1910.

Martin, H. *Simon Peter (The Family Treasury, 1869)*. Edinburgh: Banner of Truth Trust. 1967.

Mason A.J. *The Layman's Handy Commentary, 1 Peter (C.J. Ellicott)*. Grand Rapids: Zondervan Corp. 1957.

Meyer, F.B. *Peter, Fisherman, Disciple, Apostle*. London: Marshall, Morgan & Scott. 1950.

Morgan, G.C. *Peter and the Church*. London: Picketing & Inglis. 1937.

Patterson, P. *A Pilgrim Priesthood*. Nashville: Thomas Nelson. 1982.

Phillips, A.E. *Day by Day Through the New Testament, 1 Peter*. Birmingham: Precious Seed. 1979.

Plumptre, E.H. *Cambridge Bible for Schools and Colleges (The General Epistles of St. Peter and St. Jude)*. Cambridge: University Press. 1910.

Raymer, R.M. *The Bible Knowledge Commentary, 1 Peter (Editor Walvoord-Zuck)*. Wheaton: Victor Books. 1984.

Scroggie, W.G. *The Unfolding Drama of Redemption (Vol 3)*. London: Pickering & Inglis Ltd. 1970.

Selwyn, E.G. *The First Epistle of St. Peter*. London: MacMillan and Co. 1946.

Stibbs, A.M. *Tyndale NT Commentaries, 1 Peter*. London: The Tyndale Press. 1959.

Thomas, W.H.G. *The Apostle Peter*. Grand Rapids: Eerdmans Publishing Co. 1956.

Westwood, T. *The Epistles of Peter*. Glendale: Bible Treasury Hour. 1966.

Wiersbe, W.W. *Be Hopeful*. Wheaton: Victor Books. 1982.

Wolston, W.T.P. *Simon Peter: His Life and Letters*. London: James Nisbet & Co. 1920.

Wuest, K.S. *First Peter in the Greek New Testament*. Grand Rapids: Eerdmans Publishing Co. 1945.

Other books referred to and some useful reference books

Bagster, S. *The Comprehensive Bible*. London: Samuel Bagster. 1829.

Bagster, S. *The Treasury of Scripture Knowledge*. London: Samuel Bagster.

Bernard, T.D. *The Progress of Doctrine in the New Testament*. Boston: Gould and Lincoln. 1867.

Bernard, T.D. *The Central Teaching of Jesus Christ*. New York. MacMillan and Co. 1892.

Berry, H.J. *Gems from the Original*. Lincoln: Back to the Bible.

Binney, Amos. *The Theological Compend: Containing a System of Divinity*. New York: Carlton & Phillips. 1853.

Bruce, A.B. *The Training of the Twelve*. New York: A. C. Armstrong & Son. 1905.

Bullinger, E.W. (?). *The Companion Bible*. London: Oxford University Press.

Bullinger, E.W. *Figures of Speech used in the Bible*. London: Eyre and Spottiswoode. 1898.

Clarke, Adam. *Commentary and Critical Notes (Romans-Revelation)*. Cincinnati: Applegate & Co. 1959.

Cook, M.D. *Biographical Concordance to the NT*. Neptune: Loizeaux Brothers. 1985.

Darby, J.N. *Synopsis of the Books of the Bible, Vol 5, Col-Rev*. New York: Loizeaux Brothers. 1942.

Dodds, Marcus *The Theological Educator, Introduction to the NT*. London: Hodder & Stoughton. 1893.

Kittel, Gerhard. *Theological Dictionary of the New Testament (translated)*. Grand Rapids: Eerdman's Publishing Co. 1964.

Moule, H.C.G. *Outlines of Christian Doctrine*. New York: Thomas Whittaker. 1889.

Patton, William (Editor). *The Cottage Bible and Family Expositor*. Hartford: Case, Tiffany and Co. 1856.

Rienecker, F. *Linguistic Key to the Greek New Testament*. Grand Rapids: Zondervan Corp. 1976.

Robertson, A.T. *Word Pictures in the New Testament, Vol 6*. Nashville: Broadman Press. 1933.

Stock, E. *Lessons on the Life of our Lord*. London: C. of E. Sunday School Inst. 1871.

Strong, E. *Systematic Theology-A Compendium*. New York: Fleming H. Revell Co.

Trench, R.C. *On the Study of Words*. London: John W. Parker & Son. 185 1.

Trench, R.C. *Synonyms of the New Testament (London 1880)*. Grand Rapids: Eerdman's Publishing Co. 1958.

Turner, N. *Grammatical Insights into the New Testament*. Edinburgh: T. & T. Clark. 1965.

Vincent, M.R. *Word Studies in the New Testament, Vol 1*. New York: Charles Scribner's Sons. 1901.

Vine, W.E. *John, His Record of Christ*. London: Oliphants Limited. 1948.
Vine, W.E. *Expository Dictionary of NT Words*. London: Oliphants Limited. 1940.
Ward, R.A. *Hidden meaning in the New Testament*. London: Marshall, Morgan & Scott. 1969.

Text and Exposition

1. Salutation (1:1-2)

v.1 "Peter, an apostle of Jesus Christ, to the strangers scattered throughout Pontus, Galatia, Cappadocia, Asia and Bithynia,

v.2 Elect according to the foreknowledge of God the Father, through sanctification of the Spirit, unto obedience and sprinkling of the blood of Jesus Christ: Grace unto you, and peace, be multiplied.

1. The Writer

la Peter opens the letter with his signature according to the convention of the day. He uses his given name (John 1:42). This does more than establish his identity. By its connotation, it would encourage the readers, especially those suffering as a result of persecution, then or in the future, that "the gates of hell shall not prevail..." (Matt 16:18).

The use of its Greek form rather than the Aramaic *Cephas* could well address a wider audience than Jewish christians only. Rather than his family name, *Simon bar Jona, or Symeon*, the name Peter points beyond the local and temporal to what is of universal and eternal significance.

The authority of the writer is affirmed as "an apostle of Jesus Christ". He did not write "The apostle", claiming a place of primacy. The word is qualifying rather than identifying, since the definite article is not used. "The article is everywhere left out in the original Greek here making it all characteristic and descriptive" (JND, 1 Pet 1, Translator's note d). "Apostle" is from a compound word meaning "to make ready, to send away from" and signifies one prepared and sent forth to fulfil a mission. The word, and therefore the work, is dignified by being associated with the Lord Jesus Christ in Heb 3:1.

While it refers in a general way to others (2 Cor 8:23) Peter uses it in a particular sense as one sent forth by Christ Himself, "an apostle of Jesus Christ", simply and naturally confirming his early confession of Jesus as "the Christ" (Matt 16:16-18). Thus he claims apostolic authority as he writes the epistle which follows.

The requirements for apostleship are set out in the NT: apostles must have companied with the disciples "all the time" from the Lord's baptism by John until the ascension (Acts 1:21,22); apostles must have been eyewitnesses of the resurrected Christ (Acts 1:22); apostles must be chosen by the Lord and not appointed by men (Acts 1:24); apostles were foundational gifts given to the Church by divine selection (1 Cor 12:28) and not by dogmatic succession nor human ordination.

The above scriptural requirements unquestionably exclude all present day claims to apostolic succession and expose them as fraudulent.

2. The Recipients

1b   Three of the provinces listed by Peter were represented at Pentecost (Acts 2:9) as well as "Jews. .. out of every nation" (Acts 2:5). No doubt the gospel was thus carried back by those new believers. Paul had also ministered in parts of Asia and Galatia, so that "all they which dwelt in Asia heard the word of the Lord Jesus, both Jews and Greeks" (Acts 16:6; 19:10,26).

The five locations listed were provinces of the Roman empire situated in Asia Minor, now identified as Turkey. Pontus and Bithynia occupied the northern area forming a southern coastline for the Black Sea. Galatia lay centrally with the province of Asia to the west and Cappadocia to the east. The order of the names is not alphabetical nor provincial but might suggest the path of an intended journey, beginning somewhere in Pontus on the Black Sea coast, travelling southeast through part of northern Galatia into Cappadocia, then cutting back through the waist of Galatia straight west to Asia and turning northward to Bithynia and the coast.

Peter addresses his readers as "strangers". The word is carefully chosen to describe a people, not just living away from where they were born, as we would say, "strangers in a strange land". It is *parepidēmos*, meaning "a temporary resident who does not belong to the area". They were "by" them but not "of" them. In a word, they were "sojourners" away from home but going home, a pilgrim people.

The prevailing influence of the words of the Lord Jesus on Peter may be detected throughout his writings. As he wrote this word, he may well have recalled the prayer of the Lord in John 17, "... the world hath hated them, because they are not of the world, even as I am not of the world. I pray not that thou shouldest take them out of the world, but that thou shouldest keep them from the evil" (John 17:14b-15).

These people were not only sojourners, they were "scattered". Again a specific word (*diaspora*) is used to describe them. Usually translated as "the dispersion" this word came to designate Jews away from their homeland of Palestine (John 7:35; Acts 8:1,4).

However, the signature *Peter* anticipates a wider audience than Jewish believers only. This would seem to be supported by his references to the readers, e.g. as being those whose past is described as "your ignorance" (1:14). In that period they "were not a people" (2:10) but pursued heathen practices from which they had been delivered (4:3,4). By their conversion they "have become" children of Abraham (3:6 JND).

The word *diaspora*, however, is much more illuminating. It is derived from the verb *speirō*, to sow as seed. Again here are echoes of the words of the Master to which Peter had listened: "He that soweth the good seed is the Son of man;

the field is the world; the good seed are the children of the kingdom" (Matt 13:37,38).

Some by persecution and oppression and others by circumstance had been "scattered", but behind the hand of human constraint was another hand, that of the sovereign Lord of the harvest. As Peter will affirm later in the epistle (3:22), all powers have been made subject unto Him.

What a comfort and encouragement this is to suffering saints of every age. The implications of this word reach to the very throne and purpose of God. His people are not scattered by the winds of fate, the hand of an enemy nor the wheels of circumstance. They are neither the result of some chemical coincidence nor some genetic accident. They are not the pawns of providence. They are *what* they are, *where* they are, and *when* they are, by the will and purpose of their sovereign Lord. (See also Isa 43:1-7.)

2a   Just as the sovereignty of God has been seen in the circumstances of His people, so also is it in their salvation. They were not only sojourners, scattered as seed in view of a glorious harvest, but they were "elect" sojourners, selected in view of a glorious purpose.

"Elect" is picked out, selected. Much material, both helpful and otherwise, has been presented over the centuries concerning the doctrine of election.

"Peter, like the other NT writers, enters on no such discussions. Whether amid the full assurance of newly quickened faith the first christians found no room for intellectual difficulties, or whether the Spirit within them led them to feel that such questions must ever be insoluble, we cannot know; but it is instructive to note that the Scripture does not raise them" (J.R. Lumby).

Here, in a verse, are set out the activities of divine persons in the redemptive plan: the sovereign determination of the Father, the sanctifying ministry of the Spirit and the provision and application of the blood of the Son, Jesus Christ.

Election is "according to the foreknowledge of God". The word "foreknowledge" (*prognōsis*) in its noun form occurs only twice in the NT and it is Peter who uses it in both instances (v.2; Acts 2:23). We are not told all that this foreknowledge contemplates, but it is more than prescience, a knowledge of future events. In its verb form it occurs in Rom 8:29, ". . .whom he did foreknow.. .". While God knows about all men, in His elective purpose He does not *know* all men. The Lord Jesus will say to the false professors, at the judgment, "I never knew you" (Matt 7:23). As to His omniscience "he knew all men" (John 2:24). As to the divine election He said, "I know whom I have chosen" (John 13:18). Paul wrote to the Corinthians, "if any man love God, the same is known of him" (1 Cor 8:3). The foreknowledge of God would seem then to include a loving choice.

Any apprehension the readers of the epistle may have concerning their election would be put to rest by the assurance that it was according to the foreknowledge of God the Father. "The choice and the knowledge were not those of an arbitrary sovereign will, capricious as are the sovereigns of earth ... but of a Father whose tender mercies are over all His works. (E.H. Plumptre).

The origin of that great election was in the heart of God the Father. The operation of it comes by the sanctifying ministry of the Holy Spirit, "through [or in] sanctification of the Spirit". "The Holy Spirit is the Agent in sanctification ... it is a divine act. .." (Hogg and Vine). The noun used here, *hagiasmos*, refers to the act of sanctifying, not the perfecting of it in a holy character, which would have employed the word *hagiōsunē*. "The holy character ... is not vicarious, i.e. it cannot be transferred or imputed, it is an individual possession, built up, little by little, as the result of obedience to the word of God, and of following the example of Christ ... in the power of the Holy Spirit" (Vine's Dictionary p. 317). *Hagiasmos* is "the sum and measure of it, the thing as an effect, as a whole, characteristically, not *hagiōsunē*, the quality. .." (JND, 1 Cor 1:30 note). This is the primary work of the Spirit which results in the progressive forming of holy character in the believer so long as he lives and the perfecting of it in the presence of the Lord.

This sanctification is "unto [with a view to] obedience", not the result of obedience. It is not a reward for anything, it is a work of grace upon the individual. The obedience of faith there must be. "The doctrine of election was never meant to destroy man's responsibility for the state of his own soul. The Bible everywhere addresses men as free agents, as being accountable to God. . ." (J.C. Ryle).

The gospel always calls upon the sinner to respond in the will by obedience. This assumes that there is the alternative. So we find the gospel presented in this way, that there are those who believe and those who believe not (John 3:36). There are those who have " obeyed from the heart" (Rom 6:17) and those who "obey not the gospel" (2 Thess 1:8). There are aspects of the divine will which can be resisted. Examples have been left for our warning.

In His own country the Lord Jesus "could there do no mighty work..." (Mark 6:5). The limitation was not as to His person or power but because of the principle of faith. "He marvelled because of their unbelief" (v.6). He wept over the city: "How often would I have gathered thy children ... and ye would not". The loss was not because of His will, but theirs.

This obedience is not a mere assenting to a creed or a set of doctrines, but "unto [the] obedience ... of Jesus Christ". First, obedience to the gospel, leading to a life of obedience. As was the obedience of Christ to the Father's will, so is to be the character and mind of the elect (Phil 2:5-8).

To the elect, sanctified to obedience, are applied all the value and power of "the blood of Jesus Christ". This is not the shedding of the blood, but the sprinkling of it. Of course the blood must be shed before it can be sprinkled, but it may be shed and its efficacy never applied to an individual. The shedding of the blood is the giving up of the life as a sacrifice for sin. It is the provision made. The sprinkling of the blood is the applying of the value and efficacy of the sacrifice. This is the power imparted.

In the OT, the sprinkling of the blood was seen in connection with its power to protect the firstborn in Egypt, its power to purify the priest for service, its power to prepare the way into the holiest, and its power to purge the leper of his ceremonial uncleanness. However it would appear that the reference is to Exod 24 when Moses took the blood of the sacrifice and with half he sprinkled the altar, then the book of the covenant was read in the presence of the people and they responded by a promise of obedience. Moses then took the other half and sprinkled the people and said: "Behold the blood of the covenant.. ." That blood linked the people to the altar of oft-repeated sacrifice. It bound them to the word of their own brittle promise. Its application was limited to the nation. How gloriously different is the portion of the believers to whom Peter was writing. This blood- sprinkling associates the NT believer with a finished work, a sacrifice never to be repeated (Heb 10:11,12). It binds him to the inviolable promise of God (Heb 6:17-18). Its efficacy is unlimited for "whosoever will", Jew or Gentile.

To a scattered company of sojourners having little if anything of this world, having no certain dwelling place and living under the threat of persecution or even death, what cheer and encouragement these words would bring and what hope they would inspire. Like their Lord they were rejected of men, but, O blessed thought, they were chosen of God the Father, chosen for an eternal inheritance, to be before God, privileged above angels to minister to Him as worshipping children in His sanctuary in the heavens. Shunned and excluded from the fellowships of men, they were set apart by the Holy Spirit unto the obedience which takes its character from Christ's own obedience to His Father. Marked men they were, as they moved among the people, yet invisible to the eyes of men, they had been sprinkled with the precious blood of Christ, token of a nobler sacrifice than ever stained the altars of Israel or the plinths of pagan Rome.

3. The Request

2b Grace and peace are uniquely elements of the christian message and blessings of the christian life. "Peace" is the old Hebrew form of salutation (Matt 10:12,13); "grace" is characteristic of the christian community. Of the 160 times the word "grace" is found in the Bible, 128 are in the NT. Grace cannot be defined in a statement any more than can love. Rather, grace is more eloquently conveyed in the life and perfectly expressed in the Son of God, as He lived before men and died for the ungodly.

Many have been the definitions. At least one of these may help us to catch, but faintly, a glimpse of its beneficent beams: "The grace of God is that attribute of God's nature by which He satisfies His own love for sinners and by which He displays His unmerited favour towards them without reference to their deserts".

Peter knew much of that grace towards him and he delighted in it. He refers to it ten times in this brief epistle (1:2,10,13; 2:19-20; 3:7; 4:10; 5:5,10,12). Paul frequently salutes his readers with both grace and peace. Peter characteristically abounds, and adds "be multiplied". This was his desire for those scattered sojourners.

A.T. Robertson points out that "be multiplied" (*plēthuntheiē*) is a relatively rare optative mood in the Greek Testament and is more than a mere wish: "The optative mood in Greek is used whenever a certain action or condition is deemed to be possible without reference to (in this case, regardless of) the existing conditions" (quoted by P. Patterson). He will go on to develop this possibility of joy in spite of sorrows.

Notes

2   Election is a profound subject about which many words have been written and over which many battles have been fought. Man runs into deep problems when he tries to fit the eternal into time and explain the divine mind in terms of his own vocabulary. That God is sovereign is fundamental to the faith. That God in His sovereignty gave to man a will to exercise freely is fundamental to our nature. God will not oppose His own will nor violate the nature He himself designed. He will not conscript the unwilling into heaven nor consign the unable into hell. Endeavouring to reconcile the sovereignty of God and the free will of man or to explain their relationship in human terms is futile and any attempt to resolve the apparent paradox can only fail.

However "Any difficulty in reconciling God's election and man's free will lies in man's mind, not in God's. The Bible teaches both doctrines, and we should believe both. The truth lies in both extremes, not somewhere between them" (W. MacDonald).

Christ is God's elect as the Servant of Jehovah (Isa 42:1). He was chosen to complete a mission and to perform a purpose. By the incarnation He assumed "the form of a servant" (Phil 2:7) that He might fulfil the Father's will on the earth. "He did not wear the disguise of a servant, but took the form (*morphē*) that is the 'nature and essence' of a servant" (Gifford). He was chosen "for the purposes of propitiation" (W.E. Vine).

In this great election there was also a nation, chosen in love (Deut 7:7), to be a "peculiar treasure" to the Lord (Exod 19:5). It was to fulfil a mission and perform a purpose by being the depository of the oracles of God (Rom 3:2) and the vehicle of the incarnation (Rom 9:5). Within and beyond this nation were individuals selected for special ministries and functions such as Moses (Ps 106:23), Aaron (Ps 105:26), David (1 Chron 28:4), Cyrus (Isa 45:1) and others.

Also in this mighty election "in Christ" is a called-out company, the *ekklēsia*, Church or Assembly, chosen in Christ "before the foundation of the world", chosen in love, loved individually, that they might be "before him" and all that signifies of ministering to God for His delight (Eph 1:4; Exod 28). "He will have saints before Him in such a way as God alone could. He will never have what is unworthy of His love and presence" (W. Kelly). Therefore they are chosen to holiness, to blamelessness and to loveliness, being conformed at last to the image of His Son (Rom 8:29).

Their great election is not because of human merit. "God's own mercy, spontaneous, undeserved, condescending, moved Him. God is His own motive. His love is not drawn out by our loveableness, but wells up, like an artesian spring, from the depths of His nature" (McLaren). It is made real and experiential by the sanctifying ministry of the Holy Spirit with a view to the submission of the individual and the application of "the blood of Jesus Christ".

The faith of demons is ineffectual, it is not living. They "also believe, and tremble" (James 2:19). They believe in the identity of Christ, His humanity, His deity, His sovereignty and His authority, but there will be no demons in heaven (Mark 1:24). The child of God has believed "to the saving of the soul" (Heb 10:39). What distinguishes then the faith of the believer in Christ and the faith of infernal beings? The missing element in diabolical faith is obedience. Theirs is the sin of rebellion.

II. Salvation (1:3-12)

1. *The Commentary on Salvation*
   1:3-4

> v.3   "Blessed *be* the God and Father of our Lord Jesus Christ, which according to his abundant mercy hath begotten us again unto a lively hope by the resurrection of Jesus Christ from the dead,
> v.4   To an inheritance incorruptible, and undefiled, and that fadeth not away, reserved in heaven for you,"

3a   Peter, inspired to consider the might of the eternal purpose, the ministry of the divine persons and the miracle of the resulting peace in the hearts of the elect by the grace of God, is moved to praise. Such contemplations of the greatness, the goodness and the grace of God cause him to extol highly the One who is the source of all blessing and the reason for a living hope.

"Blessed" is the translation of that word from which we derive eulogy and eulogise. When we are blessed of God, we are enriched in many ways. When we bless God, however, we speak well of Him by words or actions as being worthy of praise and honour and glory.

Such ascriptions as "the God and Father of our Lord Jesus Christ" may only be uttered by faith. They cannot be understood or explained. Who is this One of whom God is the Father, yet is Himself the Lord? It is "Jesus Christ" and all the elect can delight to address Him as "our Lord".

By employing such language Peter witnesses to that profound mystery, the incarnation, and the unique relationship of divine Persons. To Mary on the resurrection morning this was announced: "I ascend unto my Father, and your Father; and to my God, and your God" (John 20:17). "For Jesus, according to His human nature, God is His God, and for Jesus in His deity God is His Father; His God since the incarnation, His Father from all eternity" (Lenski).

The blessing of salvation flows to sinners by way of God's "abundant mercy" (v.3). Mercy is "the outward manifestation of pity; it assumes need on the part of him who receives it, and resources adequate to meet the need on the part of him who shows it..." (Vine's Dictionary p.60).

God's action in begetting us again is yet another expression of His character, as declared by the Levites in the days of Nehemiah: "but thou art a God ready to pardon, gracious and merciful. . ." (Neh 9:17). Mercy excludes all considerations of worthiness or merit in the recipients (Eph 2:4,5).

When it comes to the new birth of a sinner and the imparting of all the attendant blessings, it is more than mercy that is needed, it is "great" mercy. Not only is the sinner in a place of no merit requiring mercy, he is in the place of utter demerit being in a state of spiritual and moral bankruptcy, even enmity with God (Jas 4:4). Thus his only hope is in the love of God expressed in His " great, abundant, boundless" mercy. Strong in his Systematic Theology describes mercy as "transitive love" (p.289).

"Our regeneration was no sudden capricious favour", it was according to God's mercy. Wuest points out in his commentary that "according to" is more than "in harmony with". The root meaning is "down". "From this we get the idea of domination, thus not 'according to the measure of His abundant mercy' but 'impelled by His abundant mercy'. It was the compelling constraint in the merciful heart of God that made inevitable the atonement for sinners".

2. *The Elements of Salvation*

3b   Salvation is first made real in the experience of the individual by the new birth. Only Peter uses the compound word translated "begotten again". He uses it here and in v.23. Nevertheless the truth of regeneration is found in other Scriptures. It may have been the conversation of the Lord Jesus with Nicodemus that was in Peter's mind as he penned this. The words in John 3:3 however are different. There the word *anothen* is translated "anew" (RV). Certainly Nicodemus understood it that way. However in other places, such as John 3:31, it is translated "from above" (AV), from *anō* meaning "above; a high place".

This spiritual experience then is "not only a new birth (being born again) but also a birth from God, being born from above" (Turner, *Grammatical Insights*, p.182). While those first readers of this epistle were strangers in the provinces of an earthly empire, they had been born from above, children of God the Father. They were away from home but going home, and that home is heaven.

God has never left man without hope, but that hope, to be real, must be in God and in His eternal purpose. Hope is essential to faith as breath is to life. God has revealed Himself as the God of hope (Rom 15:13). The hope to which the individual is born again is not only objective, having to do with something external and beyond, it is also subjective, an inward attitude of joyous expectancy. It is a living hope " like a spring of water, whose waters fail not", and by which many are refreshed.

All hope died in Peter when His Master died. The cold blade of remorse had pierced his soul and he wept bitter tears as he recalled his sad denial of the Lord Jesus. His hope lay buried and a stone sealed the grave. Then came that personal message by the women that the Lord was risen from the dead (Mark 16:7). That message would have a significance for Peter into which perhaps the others could not enter. It was the shaft of light in his darkness, revival for his hope, healing for his heart and new meaning for his life. While he himself had been born again on that happy day when Andrew "brought him to Jesus", his hope was just as surely begotten again by the resurrection of Jesus Christ from the dead.

It is by the resurrection of the Lord Jesus Christ that hope can live and misery can be banished for the believer. "If in this life only we have hope in Christ, we are of all men most miserable. But now is Christ risen from the dead. . ." (1 Cor 15:19,20).

The reality of the new birth depends on the fact of a finished work and a risen Christ. "The resurrection is God's Amen to Christ's cry, 'It is finished' " (quoted by W. MacDonald).

Subjectively then, this joyful anticipation would cheer the suffering sojourners through the wilderness of this world. Objectively, it sees a glorious future. When mingled with the faith that gives substance to things hoped for, it would cheer them on to heaven where an incorruptible, undefiled and unfading inheritance awaited them (v.4).

Israel, sojourning in the wilderness, left the grounded fruit of Egypt behind. They could not yet taste the elevated fruits of Canaan. The only fruit in the wilderness was the promise of the inheritance seen in the pomegranates on the hem of the high priestly garments (Exod 28:33-34).

William Kelly remarks: "The scope of our epistle excludes ... the great truth unfolded in that to the Ephesian saints, that we are already blessed in the heavenlies ... in Christ". They are not viewed in 1 Peter as seated with Christ in heavenly places, but as scattered strangers passing through this wilderness world.

In the dark days of suffering they would need the gleam of a certain hope. This hope of an anticipated event was established, made real and presently enjoyable by the assurance of an accomplished event, the resurrection of Jesus Christ out from among the dead. What lay beyond was an inheritance of indescribable wonder.

4   An inheritance usually comes to the heir by the death of the testator. Sometimes, in the world, the testament is challenged and the outcome can be quite different from the testator's intention. Here is One whose will and testament are inviolable. He Himself has been appointed "heir of all things" (Heb 1:2). He died, but then He rose from the dead and is the Executor of His own will.

His inheritance is described as having three qualities that will ensure its undepreciated value and undiminished glory.

1.   It is incorruptible, that is, impervious to death

2.   It is undefiled, that is, impossible to be dimmed

3.   It is unfading, that is, immune to decay.

This rich and abiding inheritance is thus eternal, celestial and perpetual.

One can almost bear the exulting tones of joy in the words Peter used to describe this inheritance. Their alliteration and cadence is beautiful, but not apparent in English: *aphtharton, amianton, amaranton*. This is indeed a song in the night.

Using again the figure of Israel sojourning in the wilderness, their inheritance was secure in the covenant promise of the Lord even as they wandered those forty years (Exod 3:8; Josh 1:13). So also these sojourners of the dispersion were "heirs of God, and joint-heirs with Christ" (Rom 8:17). Their inheritance was "reserved" for them. This word is from *tēreō*, to guard, keep, preserve, but the perfect passive participle is carefully chosen. "The perfect tense indicates ... the condition and underlines the fact that the inheritance already exists and is being preserved. . ." (Rienecker and Rogers, *Linguistic Key to the Greek NT*). The passive indicates that it is God who preserves it. No earthly inheritance was ever so secure. It is reserved in the place where the thief cannot steal, the moth cannot eat and the rust cannot rot.

Any remaining doubts or fears are dispelled by the assurance that the keeper of the inheritance is God Himself in all His power and authority. What cheer and encouragement this would be to those scattered sojourners whose meagre resources would count for little in the provincial banks of Imperial Rome. Their wealth was a spiritual inheritance kept on deposit in the reserves of heavenly places and secured by the power of God.

3. *The Assurance of Salvation*
   1:5

> v.5   "Who are kept by the power of God through faith unto salvation ready to be revealed in the last time."

5   Not only is the inheritance kept safely in heaven, but the heirs are kept secure on earth. They could not save themselves to begin with and they cannot keep themselves saved. They are "kept by the power of God".

The word "kept" here is different from "reserved" in the previous verse. Here it is *phroureō* which is a military term meaning to keep in ward, to garrison. It is so translated in 2 Cor 11:32: "the governor ... kept the city of the Damascenes with a garrison". "This guard is never changed. It is on duty twenty-four hours a day, year in and year out until we arrive safe in heaven" (Wuest). The present tense is used to emphasise the need for continual protection all the way through the wilderness journey home. The use of this military word would alert the readers to imminent danger. The enemy is ever seeking to attack the people of God. Selwyn points out an interesting comparison between Paul's comment in Gal 3:23 and Peter's view here. In Galatians "the Jews were 'guarded' under a law until faith came, while ... the christians are 'guarded' through faith until salvation comes".

Still, there is responsibility on the part of the sojourners to exercise faith. It is not their faith that keeps them but the power of God. However, this power is appropriated through the exercise of faith. Faith glorifies God and "gives Him His due place, and keeps us in our place of confidence in Him according to His Word" (W. Kelly). Great faith glorifies God. Little faith robs the trembling believer of peace (cf. Acts 27:20,25). Nevertheless the ultimate outcome is settled. It is "salvation ready to be revealed in the last time".

It is the purpose of God to "save them that believe", not just from hell, but all that is implicit in the word "salvation" for the soul, the life and the body. The salvation here in v.5 is a complete thing, contemplated in eternity by the will of the Father, activated in history by the work of the Son, applied individually by the ministry of the Holy Spirit, consummated eventually by the coming of the Lord, manifested universally at the appearing of the Lord Jesus Christ.

To a company of suffering saints it would be comforting to know that everything was "ready". "Christ has so completely wrought redemption to God's glory that nothing calls for delay, save the longsuffering of God that is still bringing souls to repentance" (W. Kelly). This revelation will take place in "the last time".

Two words are translated "time": *chronos*, which denotes a time period, long or short, and *kairos* which is used in v.5 to convey rather a season with certain characteristics, whether long or short. *Chronos* marks quantity, *kairos*, quality (Vine's Dictionary). The fact that the article is left out also emphasises this qualitative aspect.

This reference to "the last time" would impress the readers with the necessity for a hopeful anticipation of deliverance at the consummation of their salvation.

4. *The Accompaniment to Salvation*
1:6-9

v.6 "Wherein ye greatly rejoice, though now for a season, if need be, ye are in heaviness through manifold temptations

v.7 That the trial of your faith, being much more precious than of gold that perisheth, though it be tried with fire, might be found unto praise and honour and glory at the appearing of Jesus Christ

v.8 Whom having not seen, ye love ; in whom, though now ye see *him* not, yet believing, ye rejoice with joy unspeakable and full of glory:

v.9 Receiving the end of your faith, *even* the salvation of *your* souls."

Effectual faith is a living thing. It is intended to grow as a fruit of the Spirit-led life, "the fruit of the Spirit is ... faith" (Gal 5:22). It grows also as a result of a Spirit-fed life, "So then faith cometh by hearing, and hearing by the word of God" (Rom 10:17). In Peter however faith grows as a value of the Spirit-purged life (1:7). Faith is tested and purified in the trials of life.

6 Peter now introduces one of the great paradoxes of the christian faith. While the unbeliever cannot be sad and happy at the same time, it is possible for the child of God to know joy in the midst of sorrow. The word "wherein" in general may point back to the realm of blessing into which the believer is brought. Particularly it may refer to "the last days" and the prevalent conditions then. In either case the word to the readers is "rejoice".

This verb denotes "exulting joy", "enthusiastic and demonstrative joy". Whether in the consciousness of great blessing or in the perplexity of severe testing the believer can rejoice. In this exercise there is great strength for "the joy of the Lord is your strength".

Peter encourages his readers by assuring them of three things.

The Trial is Temporary: It is "for a season". The word *oligos* is otherwise translated "few, little, small, slight, short, briefly". All these convey the temporary nature of suffering. It is not that God in His immensity thinks little of the trials of His own, but He views them in the undiminished light and incomparable values of eternity. Isaiah records the word of the Lord to Israel: "When thou passest through the waters, I will be with thee; and through the rivers, they shall not overflow thee: when thou walkest through the fire, thou shalt not be burned; neither shall the flame kindle upon thee" (Isa 43:2). It is not "into" but "through". Suffering and testing for the child of God is not a destiny but a process. It is not for destruction but for instruction. It is not for punishment but for purging and the perfecting of faith. It will end, and as it was for Jacob, the sun will rise again and dispel the darkness of the night of suffering, separation and sorrow (Gen 32:31).

The Trial is Necessary: " If need be". Suffering at some time or other is inevitable. For the sojourners of the dispersion it was a very present experience but their sovereign God was allowing it for higher and more glorious purposes. The efficacious and permissive decrees of God allow that "all things work together for good to them that love God, to them who are the called according to his purpose" (Rom 8:28). It is v.29 however that tells us what that ultimate "good" is. It is "to be conformed to the image of his Son". Only in God's "afterward" will the purpose of some suffering be unfolded.

The Trials are Manifold: Peter as a fisherman must often have seen the sun rise over the sea of Galilee and watched it spread its radiance across the sky. Many times he must have viewed the rainbow after the storm arching its spectrum overhead. "Manifold" is not a word of fishermen, but a word of the artist as he describes the many hues on the palette of sorrow. It means "many coloured", "multivarious". He uses it later (4:10) to describe the "manifold grace of God", suggesting by this, that for every shade of sorrow there is a complementary hue of grace to relieve it.

7   The word "temptations" (*peirasmos*) can have two meanings: solicitation to evil; or testing to prove value. The context here would seem to indicate the latter since in v.7 the purpose is declared. If the word had meant solicitation to evil then the purpose would be different.

Some commentators suggest that what is "much more precious than of gold" is the approval itself and not the faith approved (Wuest). While this may be so, it is none the less true that as a result of the proving process, the child of God comes forth from the fire of testing purged and proven to be genuine. Job said, "when he hath tried me, I shall come forth as gold" (Job 23:10). So also is the faith of the believer purged and proven to be no counterfeit and therefore "more precious than of gold that perisheth". "The phrase 'the proof' *to dokimion* is problematic. In classical Greek *to dokimion* meant what was 'examined, tested, or approved'. But Peter was not referring to the means of testing ... The expression anticipates the result produced by testing" (Hiebert p.57).

"You cannot compare an act or process with gold, but you can compare 'the genuine character' brought out by the process properly enough" (Ellicott, *Peter* p.13).

When the believer's faith is in the crucible of fiery trial, what comes forth is a treasure more valuable than gold, it is "proven faith" (*dokimazō*).

Calvin observes that there is a two-fold trial of gold by fire, one when it is purified of dross, the other when it is assayed (Isa 1:25). Tested faith then is not only purged, it is also proven to be genuine.

The faith of the individual does not need to be proven to God. He knows where reality lies. Its genuineness does need to be proven to the believer for his present peace and joyous anticipation. It needs to be proven to other believers for their encouragement. It needs to be proven before the world as a witness to its perishing values and the christian's abiding hope.

This tested faith is "more precious than of gold that perishes". Some commentators have raised the question about gold perishing when it is to be found in the new Jerusalem. To perish (*apollumi*) does not mean to become extinct or cease to exist, but ruin or loss. It is to lose the purpose of existence, the reason for creation (cf. Isa 43:7).

It appears in Scripture that gold was intended to glorify and beautify. Almost every reference to gold in the Scriptures is derived from words that mean "shining". Only a few convey the idea of money. To be reduced to the vehicle of materialism and to become the tool of power and the currency of corruption is for gold to miss its purpose entirely. That is perished gold.

It is said that the early refiner would test the purity of the gold by the flawlessness of his own reflection in it. That reflection lasted only as long as the refiner's gaze. Faith tested and approved is "more precious" for the likeness of the divine Refiner remains impressed upon the chastened soul. In responding to that gaze of glory there is a transformation "according to the same image from glory to glory, even as by the Lord the Spirit" (2 Cor 3:18 JND).

Of course v.7 has primarily a prophetic significance and points beyond the rapture of the Church, beyond the Bema and the marriage of the Lamb to "the appearing of Jesus Christ". This would surely strengthen the hearts of those scattered sojourners to whom Peter wrote and to all through the ages who have and will yet suffer for their faith in Christ, suffering not only by pain and distress but also by patient endurance. Those whose genuine faith has been approved will receive "praise", the divine approbation (cf. 1 Cor 4:5). They will be given "honour", the suitable reward. They will be highly esteemed and radiant with the "glory" of rank in the kingdom.

8   v.7 ends with the unveiling (*apokalupsis*) of Jesus Christ. That is when "every eye shall see him" (Rev 1:17). Peter himself had seen Him. Again he may be recalling, as he writes, the words of the Master to Thomas, "blessed are they that have not yet seen, and yet have believed" (John 20:29).

True faith does not depend on the sight of its object before the eyes, either by reality or replica. Yet it is not "blind" faith. "Our Lord has conclusively ruled that believing has a value beyond sight" (W. Kelly). It is Paul who explains the reason for this in Eph 1:18. The believer is given a sixth sense, described as "the eyes of your heart" (JND). Abraham had this eye of faith when "he looked for a city ... whose builder and maker is God" (Heb 11:10). Moses had it when "he endured, as seeing him who is invisible" (Heb 11:27). It is by this spiritual sight the present day believer looks " for that blessed hope . . ." (Titus 2:13).

Some texts read "whom, without knowing Him..." from *eidotes*, instead of "not having seen" from *idontes*. The latter is clearly the meaning since we can love whom we have not seen, but we cannot love whom we have not known.

As true faith does not need the natural eye, neither does true love. Those early readers of the epistle had not seen the Lord Jesus as Peter had, yet they loved Him. They could have sung with us ...

> "Unseen we love Thee, dear Thy Name!
>   But when our eyes behold
> With joyful wonder we'll proclaim
>   The half hath not been told."

This love is the characteristic word for christian love. "The spirit of revelation has used it to express ideas previously unknown. .." (W.E. Vine). This is the word used to describe the love of God, causeless, changeless, ceaseless. It is the word Peter would never forget which the Master used first when questioning him, "lovest thou me?" (John 21:15-17). This is the deepest love of believers for the Lord and for others. It is born in the redeemed heart by Christ's own love, "We love him, because he first loved us" (1 John 4:19).

In v.8 the verb is in the present tense. This "indicates the continual action" (Rienecker and Rogers). It is not an act of love but a constant attitude of the heart.

It is not what but whom, "in whom ... believing". Faith is first in the person.

The faithfulness of the speaker gives confidence to the faith of the hearer. The immutability of the counsel of God depends on the immutability of the character of God (Heb 6: 18). This faith implanted as a grain of seed, watered by the Word, blessed by the sunshine of His love, brings forth abundantly that fruit of the Spirit, the exulting joy of which the unbeliever knows absolutely nothing.

Two adjectives are used to describe the quality of that joy, "unspeakable" and "full of glory". "Unspeakable" (*aneklalētos*) is a beautiful word, used only here, to convey a joy " unable to find expression in words". Some suggest it was a word coined by Peter.

This joy is "full of glory" (*dedoxasmenē*) or "filled with the glory" (JND), glorified. This joy is not a natural exuberance; it is from the realms of glory where the risen Saviour sits whom we love. He spoke to the disciples when Peter was there and He talked to them about "your joy" being full and "my joy" remaining in them. This latter is His glorified joy, a foretaste of heaven, "a present libation of the river of life", in view of the transforming moment when that inner radiance will become an outward glory (cf. 1 Cor 15:40-44).

9   The wise man, under the sun, wrote "Better is the end of a thing than the beginning thereof" (Eccl 7:8). Peter uses this word, "the end" (*telos*) to indicate "the final issue" (W.E. Vine) or "the object to which our faith is directed". Salvation is the goal of initial faith. This is perceived at the beginning as salvation from sin and its eternal consequence, judgment.

The exulting joy comes as the believer "receives" (*komizō*) or, appropriates by faith more and more of the blessings of this so great salvation and apprehends by faith the magnificence and glorious implications of the finished work of the Saviour, loved though yet unseen. That this joy is a present realisation is made clear by the fact that it cannot be spoken out in the present. "Will it be really so in that day, when perfection is come? When we know as we are known, will utterance fail as it does now?" (W. Kelly).

Peter seems to use the word "soul" (*psuchē*) according to the OT usage where it meant the whole person, body, soul and spirit (Exod 1:5), as also he uses it later in 3:20.

5.   *The Anticipation of Salvation*
1:10-12

v.10 "Of which salvation the prophets have inquired and searched diligently, who prophesied of the grace *that should come* unto you:

v.11 Searching what, or what manner of time the Spirit of Christ which was in them did signify, when it testified beforehand the sufferings of Christ, and the glory that should follow.

v.12 Unto whom it was revealed, that not unto themselves, but unto us they did minister the things, which are now reported unto you by them that have preached the gospel unto you with the Holy Ghost sent down from heaven, which things the angels desire to look into.

10   The OT prophets received their revelations from God by visions and dreams, with the exception of Moses to whom God spoke directly, "mouth to mouth" (Num 12:6-8). Revelation was essentially a divine operation: men "spake as they were moved by the Holy Ghost" (2 Pet 1:21). The revelation to their minds did not necessarily include the illumination of their minds. Daniel records: "I heard, but I understood not" (Dan 12:8). Neither did it cancel the operation of their minds, however, for they "sought out and searched out" (JND) the time and the times referred to. Having received the body of the revelation, they made diligent search as to the chronology relating to it. We see Daniel engaged in this kind of search in Dan 9:2. He discovered by seeking to understand a prophecy of Jeremiah (Jer 25:12) "the number of the years" of the captivity.

Man, the time creature, desires to know the future timing of events, the day and the hour. The eternal God however seldom ever reveals this before the fact, since the prophetic chronology is of eternal significance- not so much a schedule linked to solar time, but of moral and spiritual values and conditions. Examples of this can be seen in the words of the disciples. "When shall these things be?" (Matt 24:3) and "Lord, wilt thou at this time restore again the kingdom to Israel?" His reply was "It is not for you to know the times or the seasons, which the Father hath put in his own power" (Acts 1:6-7).

There is an important lesson in this for every sojourner on the way to heaven. God may often show the way to take, the direction to go, the purpose to pursue, but seldom does He show beforehand the calendar of events. This He controls from His heart of love, and by His sovereign hand of power He orders the circumstances of His saints. So they can with implicit trust say with David: "My times are in thy hand" (Ps 31:15).

What did these prophets so earnestly inquire after and so diligently seek? Their inquiry was of the salvation of the soul and the grace of the Saviour. Israel had seen a great work of salvation and will yet see a greater. They had known a mighty salvation of physical and material significance by deliverance from the bondage of their enemies. They had known in their sojourn through the wilderness the consolation of the divine presence and His daily beneficence. But there was a salvation revealed to the prophets that was not immediately related to things physical and temporal, but things spiritual and eternal-a salvation that would bring the Gentile into covenant relationship with God as well as the Jew. This was the salvation possessed by the scattered sojourners to whom Peter wrote, and all the elect, "the salvation of your souls". The "soul" (*psuchē*) is at times considered as distinct from the body and the spirit (1 Thess 5:23). At other times it represents the whole person (Acts 2:41). It would appear it is in the context of the completed work that Peter uses the word, the deliverance of the entire being.

While the grace of God like an underground stream has surfaced here and there in the OT, the full flood of "grace and truth came by Jesus Christ".

It was this message of a coming Messiah who would be both a sufferer and a sovereign that presented such a paradox to the minds of the prophets. The revelation of these two aspects was so diverse that some ancient expositors erred by postulating there must be two messiahs, one who suffers and one who reigns. The suffering messiah they called -Messiah ben Joseph" and the reigning messiah, "Messiah ben David".

Their error was one of "time and times". They should have grasped not two messiahs, but one Messiah and two comings, millennia apart-the first a coming to suffer and the second to reign. The prophets saw the mountain peaks of truth from afar but it was not given to them to perceive the great valley between the ranges.

11 The means by which the Spirit conveyed the divine revelation was both by the spoken word and signs. David said "The Spirit of the Lord spake by me, and his word was in my tongue" (2 Sam 23:2). The Spirit " signified" or "did point unto" (RV) the suffering "which belonged to Christ" (JND). Here is the thought of divine foreordination. Nothing takes God by surprise.

It is suggested strongly by E.H. Plumptre in the *Cambridge Bible* that the grammatical construction demands here that the sufferings and ensuing glory are not "of Christ" but "which pass on to Christ" from the suffering disciples. But the suffering of the people of God and future reward were no paradox for prophets to struggle over. Since they suffered all through the ages it would hardly be the subject of diligent search and earnest enquiry as to what time and what season this would occur. This commentator then reverses the figure by citing: "as the sufferings of Christ abound in us" (2 Cor 1:5). Peter is not referring to the sufferings of the disciples "flowing to Christ", but the sufferings which "belonged to Christ" (JND), or "in store for Christ" (W. Kelly) by the divine decree.

Peter charged the men of Israel concerning Christ, "Him, being delivered by the determinate counsel and foreknowledge of God, ye have taken, and by wicked hands have crucified and slain" (Acts 2:23). On the way to Emmaus, the Lord expounded that glorious subject which fills all Scripture, His sufferings and glories. Just as the sufferings were multiplied so also will the glories be of the greatest number and form. Isaiah noted by the juxtaposition of "as" and "so" the relationship between the sufferings of the elect Servant and the glories of the exalted Monarch (Isa 52:14-15).

This magnificent message, yet mysterious to the prophets, was testified beforehand by the Holy Spirit. Though frequently referred to as "it" in various translations because of the grammatically neuter form of *pneuma*, the Holy Spirit is not an inanimate power but a divine Person. The personality of the Holy Spirit is attested to in various Scriptures (there are seven aspects of real personality attributed to the Spirit in John 16:7-15) and all such demand the personal pronoun "He".

The Holy Spirit is identified here as "the Spirit of Christ". Some suggest by this ascription that the witness of the Spirit was only to those living prophets of the early Church. The problem with this view is that the witness of the Spirit was "beforehand": "[The Spirit] testified of Him beforehand in that character" (W. Kelly). The pre-existent Christ is seen in 1 Cor 10:4 as "that spiritual Rock that followed" the fathers of Israel in the wilderness.

12   As those ancient prophets searched to discover the time and the nature of the times when the prophecies given should be fulfilled, they were somehow made aware that the revelation was not for themselves. While every word of God is profitable and no doubt they derived some benefit from it, yet "it was a partial and so to speak reflected light caught from the far-off dawn . . ." (*The Bible Commentary*, Editor F.C. Cook 1871). David exercised the prophetic perspective in Ps 22:31: "They shall come, and shall declare his righteousness unto a people that shall be born, that he hath done this".

Those ministers of millennia ago were not serving their own interests but those who would live long centuries later. NT believers may sit under the ministry of the mighty Moses, or of David, or Isaiah or Daniel. Things that were a mystery to them can now be seen more clearly by the focus of fulfilled prophecy, the instruction of the indwelling Holy Spirit and the completion of the canon of Scripture. This incorruptible seed of the word of God is seen to have relevance and significance for every sojourner on the way to heaven. Christ, His sufferings and glories are the central and binding fact of both the Old and New Testaments.

The gospel preachers had "now" brought this message of *promise*, the salvation of the soul. They had presented the process by which this salvation is obtained, the grace of God. They had declared the glorious *Person* of the message, Christ, His sufferings and glories. They had witnessed to the power by which they served, the Holy Ghost sent down from heaven.

This message must surely be a wonder to those sinless angels. They minister in realms of radiant glory and in a condition of spotless purity. Yet frail sinners of this planet race briefly living, always dying, sometimes laughing, sometimes crying, are being brought to glory. Their only claim to heavenly realms is the extension of the grace of God, the efficacy of the sufferings of Christ and the expression of the witness and power of the Holy Spirit. Is it any wonder angels have a strong inward desire (*epithumeō*) to look into those things?

The word for "look into" (*parakuptō*) indicates the action of stooping alongside to look in or leaning to the side to get a better view. The angels are spectators, not participants. Being of a different nature from humans (Heb 2:16), they cannot by themselves apprehend the meaning of the grace of God to sinners. This will be unfolded in the ages that are coming by the kindness of God towards the saints (Eph 2:7). The manifold wisdom of God is taught to them by viewing the Church here and now (Eph 3:10). Those sojourning saints to whom the letter was written were servants of God. The angels are servants of the servants of God (Heb 1:14). It is by far a more wonderful thing to be a redeemed human than an angel.

III. Sanctification (1:13-5:9)

1. *Exhortations in the Light of God's Blessings*
1:13-2:10

v.13 "Wherefore gird up the loins of your mind, be sober, and hope to the end for the grace that is to be brought unto you at the revelation of Jesus Christ;

v.14 As obedient children, not fashioning yourselves according to the former lusts in your ignorance.

v.15 But as he which hath called you is holy, so be ye holy in all manner of conversation,

v.16 Because it is written, Be ye holy; for I am holy.

v.17 And if ye call on the Father, who without respect of persons judgeth according to every man's work, pass the time of your sojourning *here* in fear:

v.18 Forasmuch as ye know that ye were not redeemed with corruptible things, as silver and gold, from your vain conversation *received* by tradition from your fathers;

v.19 But with the precious blood of Christ, as of a lamb without blemish and without spot:

v.20 Who verily was foreordained before the foundation of the world, but was manifest in these last times for you,

v.21 Who by him do believe in God, that raised him up from the dead, and gave him glory; that your faith and hope might be in God.

v.22 Seeing ye have purified your souls in obeying the truth through the Spirit unto unfeigned love of the brethren, *see that ye* love one another with a pure heart fervently:

v.23 Being born again, not of corruptible seed, but of incorruptible, by the word of God, which liveth and abideth for ever.

v.24 For all flesh *is* as grass, and all the glory of man as the flower of grass. The grass withereth, and the flower thereof falleth away:

v.25 But the word of the Lord endureth for ever. And this is the word which by the gospel is preached unto you.

2 v.1 Wherefore laying aside all malice, and all guile, and hypocrisies, and envies, and all evil speakings,

v.2 As newborn babes, desire the sincere milk of the word, that ye may grow thereby:

v. 3 If so be ye have tasted that the Lord *is* gracious.

v.4 To whom coming, *as unto* a living stone, disallowed indeed of men, but chosen of God, *and* precious,

v.5 Ye also, as lively stones, are built up a spiritual house, an holy priesthood, to offer up spiritual sacrifices, acceptable to God by Jesus Christ.

v.6 Wherefore also it is contained in the scripture, Behold, I lay in Sion a chief corner stone, elect, precious: and he that believeth on him shall not be confounded.

v.7 Unto you therefore which believe *he is* precious: but unto them which be disobedient, the stone which the builders disallowed, the same is made the head of the corner,

v.8 And a stone of stumbling, and a rock of offence, *even to them* which stumble at the word, being disobedient: whereunto also they were appointed.

v.9 But ye *are* a chosen generation, a royal priesthood, an holy nation, a peculiar people; that ye should show forth the praises of him who hath called you out of darkness into his marvellous light:

v.10 Which in time past *were* not a people, but *are* now the people of God: which had not obtained mercy, but now have obtained mercy."

a. To Spiritual Character (vv.13-25)

It is characteristic of the epistles that, having laid down a doctrinal foundation, there follows that which involves personal responsibility properly to build lives thereupon. Frequently then we read at such new sections the word "wherefore" or "therefore". This points the reader back to what has been under consideration and prepares for a change of emphasis. "The Greek syntax is significant. Peter used the indicative mood in stating the nature of the christian faith in vv.3-12. In this section (1:13-2:5) he changes to the imperative" (E.A. Blum).

Having begun by considering a full salvation, Peter goes on now to show how this is practically expressed in a life of sanctification. It is only by living a life of practical holiness that the sojourner gives evidence of the reality of his salvation and rebukes the slander and innuendo of the ungodly.

Peter would affirm that this practical sanctification is brought about by responding positively to four groups of exhortations:

1. Exhortations in the light of Blessings   (1:13-2:10)

2. Exhortations in the light of Obligations   (2:11-4:11)

3. Exhortations in the light of Sufferings   (4:12-5:7)

4. Exhortation in the light of Dangers   (5:8-11)

The first group of exhortations is in the light of the blessings enjoyed by the elect sojourners. These blessings have been set out in previous verses. There are four given.

1. A Divine Work upon them   (v.2)

2. An Unfading Inheritance for them   (v.4)

3. A Glorious Hope before them   (vv.3-7)

4. An Eternal Salvation to them   (v.9)

In consideration of such wondrous blessings, past present and future, Peter calls forth the first imperative.

13 The thoughts of the Jewish readers would at once be taken to the first Passover and the divine ordinance: "thus shall ye eat it; with your loins girded, your shoes on your feet, and your staff in your hand" (Exod 12:11). The metaphor would be clear to those who were acquainted with the usual wearing of robes.

When energetic action was considered, the skirts of the robe were gathered up and fastened at the belt, removing anything that would hinder or entangle.

Peter applies this metaphorically to the mind. It is the mind the enemy seeks to control. This battle for the mind is part of an ongoing campaign. Paul recognised the dangers of attack against the law of the mind, that is, the way the mind works (Rom 7:23).

In Exod 12 the children of Israel were preparing to move out. Possessions, priorities and plans would all be reconsidered anew. Nothing must be allowed to hinder the walk or clutter the life. The sojourners to whom Peter wrote were already in the wilderness world. There must be "the disentanglement of the christian from all, hindrance to devotedness" (W. Kelly). Repentance is a change of mind that results in a change of life. This mental awakening at conversion is to progress towards the renewing of the mind and the resulting transformation. "The English phrase 'Pull yourselves together' would express the meaning" (Selwyn). Colloquially we might say "Roll up your sleeves". It is a matter of meaning business with God to deal with anything that would impede spiritual progress.

Peter now calls to sobriety. To be sober is not necessarily to be sombre, but as the word suggests, alertness of mind, clarity of speech and steadiness of walk. It is to avoid the heady things that excite the flesh or unnaturally inflame the emotions of the soul. The mind must not be allowed to wander off, out of control, as someone under an alien influence. A disciplined thought-life will lead to an ordered walk.

The life of the sojourner is not all heavy with burdens. It is lightened and brightened with hope. The adverb translated "to the end" means, "fully, perfectly, completely". Just as the trusting soul can have perfect peace about his salvation and destiny, so there can be perfect hope, a hope "without reserve". It is a hope of grace, the shining of the divine favour with no earthborn cloud to come between the soul and the beneficent Lord.

The assurance of that coming grace is emphasised by the fact that the river of grace flows past the door every day. It is "being brought" to us even now. If here in the valley of the shadow that grace is enjoyed, most certainly shall its fulness be the glad portion of the soul when "the clouds have rolled away".

Peter does not speak of the rapture in this epistle, but of the "apocalypse", Christ's unveiling and appearing when His saints will be manifest with Him in glory. While for suffering sojourners the "blessed hope" may be thought of first as the hope of release, of rapture, of reunions, of resemblance, yet the imperative here is the hope of the revelation and all the beneficent favour of God in that day.

Paul reminds the Galatians of the present unveiling of the Lord Jesus Christ which is part of the grace that is "being brought". This is the unveiling of Christ in His own, "...called me by his grace, to reveal his Son in me..."

14   All who are set apart to the obedience of Christ (v.2) are "children of obedience" (JND). This is much more than "obedient children". The latter refers to character, the former to nature. "It is the habitual bent of fallen nature to disobey God" (W. Kelly). This is because by nature they are "the children of disobedience". They derive their manner of life from the spirit of disobedience that works in them (Eph 2:2). On the other hand, those begotten again partake of a new nature from the Father (2 Pet 1:4), a new life from the Son (John 10:28) and a new manner of life by the working of the indwelling Holy Spirit.

The pattern in the life of the disobedient is one of the wrong "fashion". Not the style of dress but the *schēma*, the "scheme". It is that which is outward and changeable, the external "conforming" as distinct from the internal "transforming". The fashioning of the believer is not in itself wrong. We read of "Christ Jesus ... in fashion as a man". What is not to be is the fashioning of the christian after his own sinful past.

The practice of the christian's past was according to "the former lusts". Lust is defined in current English as "sensuous appetite", "animal desire", "lascivious passion". However in Scripture it means any strong desire or craving, whether good or bad. Any dominating force, whether viewed as good or bad that gratifies the old nature is to be avoided as the habit and practice of life.

The participle is in the middle voice: "do not fashion yourselves". It could also be permissive: "do not allow yourselves to be fashioned". One paraphrase carries the same idea in Rom 12:2 where the word is also found, "Don't let the world around you squeeze you into its mould..." (Phillips).

The problem was one of ignorance. While it seems there is some mitigation by reason of ignorance (Luke 23:34), there had to be provision under the old covenant for the sin ignorantly committed (Lev 4) for sin is still sin in the sight of God. Wilful ignorance is another matter (2 Pet 3:5). The period of unregenerate existence is called "the time of your ignorance" (RV). The word "ignorance" is literally "no knowledge", and specifically, no knowledge of God. Eternal life is the vehicle of this supreme knowledge (John 17:3). The knowledge of God is the intent, the content and the extent of that life possessed by every child of God.

15 It is of the very character of God that He is holy. "The word indicates the display of the character of God whose perfect attributes cause Him to be separated from His creation" (W. Kelly). This holy One had called those sojourners to whom Peter wrote. He had called them by the gospel. Now He was calling them to holy lives.

The idea of holiness is often associated with asceticism, with moral rectitude, a higher plane of living. However, the word means simply "set apart" or "separate". For the christian, there is a holiness ("sanctification" RV) that comes about at the time of the new birth. This is a sovereign act of God. This leads, or ought to lead, to a practical separation from all that grieves God, and a closer walk with this God who is holy. This set-apart life is to be diligently pursued until the day of rapture. Then will His work in us be complete, not only sanctified but glorified.

This Scripture would appear to have been taken from three occurrences in Leviticus. There the imperative is definite: "Ye shall be holy". The first is in 11:44 where practical holiness is seen as purity in diet and dress. The second is in 19:2 in a context which has to do with social and family responsibilities. The third is in 20:26, having to do with the spirit world.

A garden is more than the absence of weeds; there must be growth, flowers and fruit. So the holy life is not a negative and passive thing where the only activity is weeding. There is to be the evidence of life.

16   This call for the believer to be distinct in the world rises out of the claim of God upon him as it is found in the Word, "because it is written..." The significance of an OT Scripture is applied to NT believers reminding all that the whole sacred volume is God's word. Because God is holy then His people are to be holy. "In this life we will never be as holy *as* He is, but we should be holy *because* He is" (MacDonald).

This practical holiness is to touch every part of our lives. The "conversation" (v.15) is the whole manner of life, the will, the words and the work.

17   "The first mark of conformity to the holiness of God in believers will be their godly fear. .." (Selwyn). To "call" is from *epikaleō*, "to call a person by name" (W.E. Vine). It is to pray and to "invoke [God] as Father" (JND). The "if" is not to convey uncertainty. Rather it is "since as a fact" (Thomas). Therefore the judgment exercised is first paternal, the judgment as sons.

To be able to address the Judge of the universe as "Father" might seem on the face of it to be a tremendous advantage. However the next thing to learn is that this Judge, while He may have intimates, has no favourites; His judgment is impartial. This is the judgment as sojourners.

Those sojourners however were not tourists. They worked as they went. So the judge assesses every man's work. This is the judgment as servants. Is it any wonder that as they would contemplate coming before such a judge they would know something of the fear of God?

18-19   The fear of God is quite in order when it is realised what it cost Him to provide redemption and how poor in comparison is the noblest response in terms of practical holiness.

The sojourners may have quietly to hope and wait for their release from the body, rapture to glory, reunions and resemblance, but there is one great event for which they never wait, the redemption. It is an accomplished fact. Of this they had a certain knowledge, "ye know" (v.18).

By referring to the tradition of the elders and a ransom price of corruptible currency, Peter directs his readers to remember the offering every man had to give for himself (Exod 30). The purpose was that there might be no plague among them. The price was paid as a ransom for the life. It was paid according to the shekel of the sanctuary. These elect sojourners knew of course that such perishable coin could not pay the ransom for their eternal souls nor deliver them from the plague of sin.

The precious blood of Christ as of a lamb without blemish and without spot, alone could fully pay the ransom price. The figure of the lamb may well look back to the Paschal lamb when the unsheltered firstborn of Egypt died and the sheltered firstborn of Israel lived. Little wonder that the blood of Christ is here called "precious", or "costly". Precious it is to the Father for it is the blood of His dear Son; precious to the Saviour Himself, for it represented His life poured out and offered up through the eternal Spirit. It is precious to the saints for it is the price of their redemption and will be the theme of heavenly song; precious because it is the only acceptable ransom price; precious because it is alone able to cleanse the sinner of his sins; precious because its mighty power and infinite value are undiminished by the passing of centuries and its efficacy is still available for sinners.

20 The impeccable Christ is presented here first in the picture of a lamb. He has been "foreknown" before the foundation of the world. In this, the mystery of His pretemporal existence can be seen. "The gift of His Son to suffer and redeem was ever in the mind of God" (W. Kelly). He was "manifest" or "pointed out at the end of the times". It would be hard, in the light of this word, to avoid John the Baptist as he sees "Jesus coming unto him, and saith, Behold the Lamb of God, which taketh away the sin of the world". This he did "that he should be made manifest..." (John 1:29,31). Here is the mystery of the incarnation. His death and burial are implicit in vv.19-21. His resurrection and glorification are all there, clearly stated.

21 It is by Christ that we come to believe in God-Christ presented in His sufferings, "From Godhead's glory to the shameful tree", and glory, from resurrection to exaltation and all that means. "It is to be observed that the brethren believe in God not because the Son has revealed the Father (Matt 11:27), but because the Father has revealed the Son" (Bigg).

What mighty accomplishments, what magnificent evidences are presented to the sinner to bring him to the place where his faith and hope might be in God! There is the redeeming work of the Son and the rewarding work of the Father, all permeated by the retiring ministry of the Spirit. "Those for whom Christ died have, therefore, double ground for coming to God" (Stibbs). They may come in implicit faith and in certain hope since God raised Him out from among the dead and gave Him glory. "His resurrection eloquently proved that the God of the christian gospel is truly the living God" (Hiebert).

b. To Spiritual Love (vv.22-25)

22   It is not surprising that such exercises of faith and hope as have been considered in this chapter should find their culmination in exhortations to love.

The participle translated "purified" is in the perfect tense, that is "an actual process begun at conversion and going on through life" (Cook). The soul here stands for the whole moral and spiritual being. There is that washing which is subjective and passive and occurs once at the beginning. Then there is that application which is active and participative which is a repeated thing. Aaron at the consecration (Exod 29:4) submitted obediently as Moses, God's representative, applied the water, a onetime washing. Then day by day in his priestly ministry Aaron washed himself at the laver. Peter might well remember the feet-washing and the lesson he learned there: "He that is washed all over needs not to wash save his feet, but is wholly clean" (John 13: 10 JND).

Negatively we have the other side of it illustrated in Daniel and his friends. "In whom was no blemish" was a permanent quality. But he "purposed in his heart that he would not defile himself..." (Dan 1:4,8). That was an ongoing commitment to purity day by day.

The initial cleansing for the christians to whom Peter wrote came about when the gospel truth was obeyed. There is an ongoing cleansing brought about by obediently applying the water of the Word. Its effectiveness however is not our doing but the operation of the Spirit.

Obedience is an evidence of love to Christ: " If a man love me, he will keep my words" (John 14:23). Obedience will also have as an outcome love to the brethren. Yet what we have here is more than "love of the brethren" it is brother-love. "Up to the time of christianity the word was only used of brothers *by blood* ... now it is used for brothers *by grace*" (Thomas). This is not a love as though brothers, but a love because brothers.

Having loved as brothers, Peter calls the saints now to love God (*agapaō*). That is a love that does not come naturally. It "is not an impulse from the feelings ... nor does it spend itself upon those for whom some affinity is discovered" (Hogg and Vine). That love will be characterised by sincerity, an "unfeigned love". The word is "not hypocritical". A hypocrite was one who put on a mask and played a role. Love for the Lord's people must not be masked by sentimental role-playing.

True love is to be with a pure heart, or "out of a heart . . ." (JND marg). As the heart beats spontaneously in good health, so heart-love is spontaneous in its outflow. It is not a calculating, measuring, selective thing, but generous, unselfish and sacrificial.

This love is to be " fervent". The word means to " stretch out" with intensity, or "all out" as we may say. Halfheartedness, bare duty, minimal service mars many a testimony. The antidote is wholehearted love for the Lord first and for His own.

This genuine, intense heart-love is not a product of human nature. It is the firstfruit of the first cluster of the fruit of the Spirit with joy and peace. It is axiomatic then, for that fruit to develop there must be unbroken fellowship with the Spirit and no unconfessed sinning against Him.

23   Is such a life of faith, hope, love and obedience possible? Not by anything that is natural in us. The possibility is there because the christian has been born again, born from above and possesses resources of a life that is imparted by God Himself.

That new life is eternally abiding. It is not the product of corruptible seed but that which issues from the incorruptible word of God. A supernatural love must derive from a supernatural life. That is what every believer enjoys.

24   To the sojourners scattered as seed by the sovereign hand of God, Peter uses a most graphic illustration taken from Isa 40. The brief and transient quality of natural life is presented as withering grass. All the glory of man together is like the flower of grass. Their life is but a brief day. "In the morning it flourisheth, and groweth up; in the evening it is cut down, and withereth" (Ps 90:6).

The same winds and rains and withering heat come upon both the good seed and the fleshly. They look alike in many ways, but the life principle is different. The children of the kingdom, the good seed, have a life engendered by the incorruptible seed. The rest are corruptible, withering, blown and gone forever.

25   The word of the Lord endures. This abiding revelation of the mind of God brings a message of a new kind of life, a heavenly kind of love, and a genuine hope of unfading glory. Little wonder the message is called the gospel, the good news from heaven.

c. To Spiritual Growth (2:1-10)

1   The opening "wherefore" points back to the previous section and the new birth spoken of there. In the light of a new life begun and a new love formed there must be growth and development. However there are certain hindrances to be dealt with. These are evils that affect the spiritual appetite, spoil the taste for divine things and dull the desire for the healthful nourishment essential to the balanced development of the believer's life.

Five of these are listed. The first is "malice", an all-inclusive term for downright wickedness, "badness in quality (the opposite of *aretē*, excellence)" (W.E. Vine). "It is the basic attitude of ill-will towards others" (Hiebert). This malignity is the soil out of which these other evils grow.

Next comes a bitter cluster of three, linked with the word all, "guile, hypocrisies and envies". Guile is the bait by which people are enticed to act trustfully, not realising the danger. The plural "hypocrisies" shows up the many varied ways by which the true nature of a thing is covered up. If guile is the bait to attract, hypocrisy is the blind that conceals the reality. With guile the outward expression is quite different from the inward condition.

Envy, again a plural noun, is described by W.E. Vine as "the feeling of displeasure produced by witnessing or hearing of the advantage or prosperity of others"; it is the feeling "which makes one grudge another something which he himself desires, but does not possess" (Reinecker and Rogers). It is a withering disease, described in the Proverbs as "the rottenness of the bones" (14:30).

Lastly comes "all evil speakings". The verb means to disparage, defame, detract. Though never a shot is fired, many have been the assassinations of character. Victims of outright lies and subtle innuendo have limped through life carrying their scars to the grave. Sad to say, even the truth can be hurtful. It is not enough to speak the truth, it is to be spoken in love (Eph 4:15) and at the right time (Eccl 3:7).

> "The ill-timed truth I might have kept,
>   Oh how it pierced and stung;
> The word I had not grace to say
>   How grandly it had rung."
>
> (A fool's prayer)

All such behaviour as described in v.1 is alien to the new life and love of the christian, and is to be laid aside like a filthy garment (cf. Zech 3:3-4). This is not to be attempted little by little, but by faith, at one fell swoop. It is to be "an act done once for all, as the aorist implies ... not of gradual process" (W. Kelly).

2   The use of this figure by Peter is one of tenderness, not as it is used to the Hebrews (5:12-13) or to the Corinthians (1 Cor 3:1-3) in a tone of rebuke. A newborn infant needs no instruction in nursing. It is an instinct. So it should be instinctive in every child of God to long for the sincere milk of the Word, "the spiritual milk which is without guile" (RV). This longing is the "intense and ever recurring desire ... similar to the desire of newborn babes for their mother's milk" (Fronmuller).

English versions find difficulty in expressing the force of the words "the sincere milk of the word". A literal translation is unhandy, "the genuine mental milk". Darby translates it "the pure mental milk of the word" and adds a translator's note, "No word is satisfactory here for *logikon*; for though it doubtless has the sense of 'suited to the rational faculties' - the mind in contrast with the body - yet I believe there is allusion to the word *logos*. I have added 'of the word' to mark this allusion".

"The milk of which (Peter) speaks is that which nourishes the reason or mind, and not the body" (Plumptre). "It is milk for the saint's intelligence…food to our spiritual understanding" (W. Kelly).

This milk of the Word is "without guile", it is "the pattern of sincerity" (Bigg). The believer having laid aside all guile (v.1) longs for nourishment that is void of deceit and enticement. The word of God is that which informs the mind, quickens the spirit, refreshes the inner man and produces growth. "The word of God must be desired for the sake of life, devoured by hearing, ruminated by the understanding, digested by faith" (Tertullian).

This growth is "up to salvation" (JND) or, as some suggest, "in salvation". Growth relates to the present salvation. Salvation of the believer from the penalty of sin is absolute and in the past; salvation from the presence of sin is consummate and in the future; salvation from the power of sin and all that implies is continuing and in the present. Spiritual health, strength and growth depend on the nourishing of life with the "sincere milk of the word".

"The verb 'grow' is in the subjunctive mood ... indicating a condition that does not exist and may never exist" (Patterson). Observation alone is enough to confirm the fact that stunted believers exist and that because of a lack of nourishment in the Word.

3   "If" here does not imply uncertainty or doubt, rather it is " since ye tasted". It was that taste that first created the longing for the sincere milk of the Word. The words are adapted from Ps 34:8 "O taste and see that the Lord is good". The word translated "gracious" (*chrēstos*), is "good, virtuous, mild, pleasant (in contrast to what is hard, harsh, sharp, bitter)" (W.E. Vine).

Conversely it is by feeding on the Word that the believer is led more and more into the enjoyment of the Lord as the source of life and nourishment. Then as His goodness and sweetness are enjoyed on the spiritual palate greater will be the longing to partake even more fully of the provisions of His grace and find our satisfaction in His fulness. "So the God-given word is to be desired not for its own sake, but because it enables us to feed upon its author, and to appropriate His grace" (Stibbs).

By referring to Ps 34:8 Peter identifies the Lord Jesus with the Jehovah of the Psalm, a most significant reference in Peter's theology.

4   Every believer first comes by faith to Christ. Having thus come he is never to be cast out. That initial act of faith is not what is in view here. This "coming" is the habitual approach of the child of God, not now to derive food as in the previous section, nor to seek blessings, but to minister to God by spiritual sacrifices.

It is one of the gracious revelations of the Lord Jesus, and it was given first to a sinful woman, that God desired to be known as a Father, seeking children who would be worshippers (John 4:23).

The newborn infant is nourished and grows up in his salvation to take his place as a believer-priest in the sacred precincts of the presence of God, to minister to Him.

Peter changes metaphors now and identifies the Lord Jesus as "a living stone". There is no uncertainty in Scripture that the Lord Jesus was raised from the dead, a living Saviour. That mighty resurrection also revived Peter from despair. So he speaks of a living hope (1:3), and a living Word (1:23) and now, paradoxically, of a living Stone. Without the definite article it is character and not identity that is in view. His firmness "is to His followers not hardness, but absolute reliability, truth and faithfulness, that in Him there is nothing of rigidity and death but absolute light and life" (Fronmuller). There is nothing in nature like this. Stones there are and rocks of many kinds and values, but never a living stone. The accretions that gather on these are not evidences of life within. The sculptor may grace his inspiration of a David, a Moses or a Christ from the obdurate block, but he cannot breathe into it the breath of life nor fill the form with coursing blood. It is still, though marvellously formed, a block of stone. But Christ is presented as a living stone.

The word here is not *petros*, a loose stone by the roadside, nor *petra*, a rock, but *lithos* which is " the usual word for a worked stone, whether a stone used in a building or a precious stone" (Selwyn).

Life, when referred to an animal, means so much more than when referred to a tree. "A living dog" and "a living tree" are nourished by different forms of life. Then when we say "a living man" we mean again so much more. When we read of life as it relates to the Lord Jesus we enter a new and loftier realm, that of life-giving (1 Cor 15:45 RV). "Christ is the centre and touchstone and foundation of Christianity" (W. Kelly). To touch the living Christ by faith is to be made alive with His own life. "God hath given to us eternal life, and this life is in his Son" (1 John 5:11).

The newborn babes of v.2 discover that they are now incorporated into a marvellous building. It is founded on the great sub-stratum Rock, and every saint, a living stone, takes character from Christ Himself. Christ as the living Stone was "disallowed" or "rejected after testing" of men. He did not meet the specifications for what they were trying to build for themselves. They "esteemed him not".

By men He was discounted, disapproved and rejected because they considered Him of no value to them, but with God He is "an elect one" dear and precious. Not only is Christ the touchstone for life, He is the test for values. Man esteemed Him as less than a murderer and cried, "Give us Barabbas". They valued Him less than the price of a woman slave and set him at "nought" in Gabbatha. They mocked Him as a king, crowned Him with thorns, anointed Him with spittle and nailed Him through His hands and feet to the only throne men ever gave Him. "I do not seek nor want the world's esteem after that. It tells me how little it is worth, for the world despises what God has chosen, and hates what God loves. So that which is highly esteemed among men, is abomination in the sight of God (Luke 16:15)" (Lincoln).

He was not chosen, one out of many possibilities. There was no other who could be the fulfilment of prophecy nor the foundation of the Church.

> "What think ye of Christ in the test
> To try both your state and your scheme,
> You cannot be right in the rest
> If you do not think rightly of Him."

Not only chosen, He is also "precious", precious not only as to value, but also as to honour. This section has in mind Ps 118:22 and Isa 28:16. It is not His intrinsic worth that is in view so much as His preciousness in the estimate of God, "but with God chosen, precious" (JND).

5   Before the readers can hardly be accustomed to the paradox of a "living stone" they are introduced to the double metaphor of themselves "also" being "as living stones" (RV). Christ is in Himself the living Stone. Now it is revealed that every child of God has derived this same character from Him. They are being built upon Him. The focus of every line and the perspective of every angle in this glorious edifice ever draws the eye to Christ and points to His exquisite loveliness and perfect suitability as the pre-eminent Cornerstone.

Commentators differ as to whether the verb "to build" is in the passive or the middle voice, the indicative or the imperative mood. So some translate "build yourselves up", others suggest, "are being built" or "be ye also built up". Scholars are divided in their view. It would seem that, to the plain reader, the evident sense is best. A building implies a builder with a master plan and the stones would hardly be charged, each individually with the responsibility for constructing so great an edifice. Peter certainly knew who the Builder was to be.

He heard the Master say it, "I will build my church".

This structure is to be a house for God, not as before "made with hands", but spiritual and thus eternal, distinct from material and temporal. The emphasis moves from the individual responsibility to the collective testimony.

These scattered sojourners, far from the city of the great King, may well have felt that they were missing the sacred precincts and the special privileges of the temple there. That was characteristically the place of the presence of God. Now they are introduced to this wonderful truth of a spiritual house built upon Christ. More than that, they themselves were living stones in that sacred edifice. Yet there is more, they themselves formed the holy priesthood of this heavenly sanctuary.

The office of priest had changed through history. From Adam to Noah each man was a priest for himself presenting his offering to God individually. From Noah to Abraham, a man was a priest for his family (Melchizedek, the kingpriest being a unique type). Then God called a nation to be a kingdom of priests, if they would be obedient. They were not obedient, so Israel for these ages has forfeited that national ministry. Out of that nation however God in His grace called a family of priests. Aaron was the high priest and his sons also by succession. This Aaronic priesthood persisted until Caiaphas tore the priestly garment signalling the end of that dynasty which was effectually concluded by the cross.

After the Lord Jesus finished His mighty sacrificial work, He was raised, exalted and anointed the Great High Priest of a new order of priesthood of which every believer in this Church age is a priest requiring no earthly intermediary to act between him and God.

Any establishment today of a caste of priests or ministers, with special titles, distinctive garments, ministering before man-made altars, in earthly sanctuaries, is therefore a great step backwards. It is a failure to distinguish things that differ and confuses the old covenant with the new. It is an endeavour to resurrect what God has laid to rest and to promote that which Christ has finished. It is to divide an equal brotherhood into " clergy" and "laity", be it ever so subtly, which thing God hates (Rev 2:15).

The NT priesthood is first "holy", set apart for the pleasure of God, set apart from all that is offensive to His character. The priority of this sacred office is to minister first to God by offering up spiritual sacrifices. The character of those sacrifices is given in other Scriptures such as Rom 12:1; Phil 2:7; 4:18; Heb 13:15,16. just as God made provision in the old covenant for the - iniquity of the holy things", so also in the new. The holiest of offerings and noblest of sacrifices are affected by "manifold infirmities". Thus they are not acceptable to God on the basis of their own worth, but only as they are offered through the One in whom God is fully satisfied. Fronmuller points out that the construction of the words can show that " not merely the acceptability, but the very existence and possibility of offering of those sacrifices, depends on the mediation of the great High Priest (cf. Heb 13:15)".

The NT priest then is brought into a standing of holiness before God, a bond of relationship with God and the privilege of the acceptable service of God.

6   The writer returns to the subject of Christ as the stone to develop the theme further. He does so by a free quotation of Isa 28:16. His carefulness is seen however in that he does not say "it is written". This would demand a verbatim quote. Rather he says, "it is contained.. ." from a word meaning "to encompass, enclose" (W.E. Vine).

The first thing stated is that it was God Himself who laid this Stone and calls men by His "Behold" to pay attention. While the temples built by men must pass away, here is one that will continue. (There is no structural temple in glory, for every place in that heavenly realm is holy and every word and act a ministry before the Lord, Rev 21:22.)

Secondly, this great Stone was laid in Zion. The geographical entity is called Jerusalem in the Isaiah portion (v.14). Zion is the realm of the new covenant of grace in contrast to Sinai the realm of the old covenant and law (Heb 12:22-24). The NT priest enters salvation by grace (Eph 2:8), stands before God in grace (1 Pet 5:12) and exercises all spiritual gift by grace in the sanctuary of which he forms a part by grace (Rom 12:6). So then the greatly gifted and the greatly privileged have nothing of themselves whereof to boast. All is of grace and in the meantime, for the servant, contained in the earthen vessel of his mortality, "that the excellency of the power may be of God, and not of us" (2 Cor 4:7).

Thirdly, this stone was the "chief corner stone". In Isa 28 it is called "a foundation ... stone". We may call it "the corner stone of the foundation". This was the stone which united the two walls and from which all measurements were taken. So it is with Christ, as the "chief corner stone". He unites the old and the new covenants in Himself. He brings together in a binding union both Jew and Gentile (Eph 2:14-16). In Him "Mercy and truth are met together; righteousness and peace have kissed each other" (Ps 85:10).

Fourthly, this stone is "elect", chosen in the mind and purposes of God before the world was. The temple built by Solomon "was built of stone made ready before it was brought thither" (1 Kings 6:7). Before the magnificent structure of the spiritual temple, perfected in glory, will be seen by creature eyes, the hewing, the forming, the finishing and the fitting of the living stones will all be completed.

Fifthly, this stone is "precious". The word is used of the centurion's servant in Luke 7:2, he "was dear unto" his master. When referring to the Lord Jesus Christ this word carries the idea of being held in great honour, thus "precious" and "valuable" beyond all compare.

Sixthly, Christ is the touchstone of destiny. To all who have exercised the obedience of faith they "shall not be put to shame" (JND). The Septuagint translation of Isa 28:16 is "shall not be in haste". The haste is that of fear and flight in confusion and shame because of the disappointment of misplaced faith. Such a tragedy will never be the portion of any who rest upon the living Stone. Calmly and trustfully they will rest on Him and fulfil the purpose of their election.

> "Often on the rock I tremble,
> Faint of heart and weak of knee,
> But the mighty Rock of Ages
> Never trembles under me."

7   There can be no neutrality with regards to Christ. To the Pharisees He said, "He that is not with me is against me; and he that gathereth not with me scattereth abroad" (Matt 12:30). So there are but two companies here, the believing and the disobedient, those who spurn the truth. This sets aside the spurious arguments about "not being able to believe". Unbelief is disobedience to the gospel call, a matter of personal choice. Those who will know the vengeance of the coming Lord are they who "obey not the gospel".

To the believing, Christ is precious. Yet more, this verse reads "To you therefore who believe is the preciousness" (JND). *The Expositor's Greek Testament* puts it: "The preciousness of the stone is for you who believe.. ." Alternative readings show the Stone as being "held in honour", "the honour and inestimable value of Christ as appropriated by believers, who are joined, as living stones, to Him the Corner Stone" (W.E. Vine).

If as some commentators suggest, the honour is "Unto you therefore which believe", in opposition to the shame of the unbeliever in v.6, then that can only be the special honour accorded to the Lord Jesus Christ in the measure by which it is reflected in His people. This same principle will pertain when He shall come to be glorified in His saints. Then He will be "admired in all them that believe" (2 Thess 1:10). The believer will be "to the praise of his glory" (Eph 1:12). "This honour includes their privileged status here and now and also their triumph over their mocking assailant and their salvation on the last day" (W. Kelly).

The "builders" in Israel were thinking of a visible temple as marvellous as Solomon's and of a king as glorious as he. This Jesus out of Nazareth was not what they envisioned at all, as one on whom to build their religious ambitions. They "rejected" Him (RV). They considered Him as "worthless" (JND). So the Lord exposed the attitude of the Pharisees and the consequence of their choice (Matt 21:42-44). Peter himself had courageously charged those "builders" with their sin (Acts 4:11).

Having been rejected of men, this Stone, exalted by God, is become the chief corner stone of a temple which the builders of Israel could not see nor the gates of hell destroy.

8   Christ is a "stone of stumbling" to the disobedient, that is, a loose stone in the pathway encountered many times in the way. So did the Lord Jesus present Himself to those bent on pursuing the path of destruction. "If heaven is by grace alone, then hell is by works alone and the Christ rejector will have to work his way past every obstacle the love of God can put before him on his downward path to perdition" (R. McClurkin).

Because of their unbelief they stumble as blind men at the Word. The world's principle is " seeing is believing"; the Lord says " if thou wouldest believe, thou shouldest see..." (John 11:40).

Christ is the Great Unavoidable. If we do not meet Him in the way, by His grace, He waits, at the end of the journey; not then as the *lithos* stone in the path but as *petra skandalou*, the high barrier rock around which there is no way of escape. "The genitive 'of offence' points to the calamitous impact of that rock on unbelievers ... Those two designations declare that by rejecting God's Stone, men only bring about their own injury and ruin" (Hiebert).

All such, the disobedient and disbelieving, are appointed to stumble at the Word. Therefore the first step was not to be one of betterment nor improvement but of obedience. There is no thought of reprobation here, that some are appointed to disobedience. "The ungodly are not appointed to be ungodly, but being ungodly God appointed that this should be fully manifest in their rejection of Christ" (F.W. Grant). Peter makes it clear in his second epistle that God does not desire that any should perish (2 Pet 3:9; Ezek 33:11; 1 Tim 2:4).

9   In contrast to the disobedient, Peter focused on the believers with "But ye".

While Peter does not refer to the Church by that term, he does use words of collective description, of which there are four in v.9. These are drawn from the OT Scriptures.

A Chosen Generation This introduces the thought of a new race of people on the earth. Adam was the federal head of a race known as humankind. Christ is the federal head of a new race, "a chosen race" (JND), known as Christ-like, or christians. This expression, more tenderly formed, is found in Isa 43:20, "my people, my chosen". What was directed once to Israel only now refers to Jews and Gentiles also, but not all. The corporate identity is *genea*, "connected with *ginomai*, to become, primarily signifies a begetting, or a birth ... that which has been begotten. .." (W.E. Vine). This new race then is composed of all those who have been "born again" (1:23).

A Royal Priesthood This comes from Exod 19:6 and points back to the desire of the Lord that His earthly people should perform an intermediary work among the nations, speaking to them for God and interceding to God on their behalf. This ministry was conditional on their obedience. They disobeyed and for the time then present and until the millennial kingdom they have nationally forfeited that privilege. Now it is the NT priesthood that is given, in grace, the double privilege of holy and royal service, first to go in to God then out to men. "Priesthood is the common and blessed portion of all believers, so they are a kingdom of priests ... By contrast, gifts in the churches are variously distributed, Rom 12:6" (A.E. Phillips, *Day by Day through the NT*).

The Aaronic order was not a "kingly priesthood". Christ is the great High Priest of the new order. It is after the pattern of Melchisedek, who was both king and priest. Our Lord Jesus Christ will sit as a priest upon His throne and dispense His beneficence to His subjects (Zech 6:13). Those who are His own now are a royal priesthood to "set forth the excellences of him who has called you out of darkness to his wonderful light" (v.9 JND).

It is a most salutary exercise of spiritual intelligence to discern the difference in the directions of the two great ministries of the NT priesthood. There is that highest privilege of going in to the sanctuary to minister to the heart of God by offering up "spiritual sacrifices, acceptable to God by Jesus Christ" (v.5). This is the supreme privilege and highest service into which a believer can enter, in time or eternity. No intervention of man's devising, be it ever so pleasing or popular, should be allowed to divert the Lord's people from this. As the devoted Mary discovered, this ministry will not be taken away from His own.

The other direction is to go out from the sanctuary to set forth the excellencies of Christ and minister to the house of God. This is a privilege not given to angels and a most cherished service of the priesthood. An understanding of the direction of these distinct ministries would preserve God's people from disorder and confusion, especially when they gather at the Lord's supper, that meeting of the church so peculiarly suited for ministering to the heart of God.

An Holy Nation This expression is also from Exod 19:6 and other Scriptures such as Lev 19:2; 20:26; Deut 7:6; Isa 62:12. Aaron and his sons were separated from the people for the ministry of priesthood. As a mark of that separation they were given special garments to wear. Before they could function in the holy office they must be separated to God for it. The NT believer-priest does not wear special garments nor bear special titles as a mark of office. Instead, he is to be marked by his separation to God, an "holy" nation.

The nations of earth are separated by boundaries, and borders. Language and culture and often physical distinctions divide them. This holy nation however knows no such barriers; it overflows all borders; it overlooks mere physical differences; it overcomes culture and language. This glorious unifying victory of grace will be the theme of the new song of praise to the Lamb in glory, "Thou art worthy to take the book, and to open the seals thereof: for thou wast slain, and hast redeemed us to God by thy blood out of every kindred, and tongue, and people, and nation; and hast made us unto our God kings and priests: and we shall reign on the earth" (Rev 5:9-10).

No doubt, such Scriptures will bear a special significance and provide a singular authority to the remnant of Israel brought out of the great tribulation into millennial blessing and service among the nations of the earth (Isa 60; Zech 14:16-19).

A Peculiar People The words are better translated, "a people for a possession". It is the same idea in Eph 1:14, "purchased possession" or, as in the RV, "God's own possession". It is also brought over from the OT (cf. Deut 14:2; 26:18; Mal 3:17 LXX). Mal 3:17 in the AV has "jewels" or "special treasure" (marg). It goes beyond thoughts of "peculiarity" to convey tones of the redemption, of singular value and beauty, and of affectionate possession.

"Peculiar" is an old English usage from "peculium", a personal possession. Its root is *pecus*, cattle (*Oxford English Dictionary*), being the ancient currency of purchase. To this day in parts of Africa the dowry system persists. A young man pays the dowry price for his bride in cattle. These may represent years of wages and by this he conveys his sacrificial love and commitment. The young woman then, in a most personal way, becomes the young bridegroom's possession, not for labour as a slave, but for love and loyalty as a spouse. So God's people are "a people for God to clasp to His heart, to live in His love, to dwell in His presence" (W. Lincoln).

10   This calling then is for the purpose of setting forth the excellencies of Christ. The obligation is upon all who were once in the darkness of the ignorance of God but are now in the light. For the believer that light, spiritually, is the fellowship of God in which to walk. Intellectually, it is the revelation and knowledge of God in which to grow. Morally it is the holiness of God in which to stand. Visibly it is the glory of God in which to dwell forever.

The transition is most remarkable, from darkness to light. It is not only that the unbeliever is in the darkness, the darkness is also in him. It is the transformation from being a child of the darkness, walking in the dark and loving it rather than light, to being one of the children of light, walking in the light, in the path of the just which shines more and more unto the perfect day. The light is more than a mere shaft, a single ray to relieve the blackness, it is "marvellous" or "wonderful light" (JND). Peter never forgot the superlative radiance he beheld that day on the holy mount. The Lord stood before them, His countenance shining as the sun, His garments glistering as sunlit snow, and from His person burst flashings of light. As he beheld the blazing Christ, the record says, Peter "wist not what to say". It was just "wonderful".

Peter draws from the book of Hosea and reflects on the sad history of Israel, pictured in the infant son of the prophet and his wife, Gomer. God instructed them, "Call his name Lo-ammi: for ye are not my people, and I will not be your God" (Hos 1:9). "Yet" (v.10) there was hope. The day will come when "it shall be said unto them, Ye are the sons of the living God". If this is a wonderful transformation for Israel from what they have been and what they are, what shall be said of those of the Gentile nations who, in the past, languished in darkness far beyond the pale of Israel's privilege and blessings, "but" now are the people of God?

Israel as a nation was not able to enter these high realms by law-keeping. The law exposed their sin and called for justice. What was needed was mercy, "The outward manifestation of pity" (W.E. Vine). So of those to whom Peter wrote, he says that in the past they "were not enjoying mercy, but now have found mercy" (JND). "The contrast of the perfect tense with the following aorist tense stresses the contrast between the long antecedent state and the single event of conversion which ended it" (Hort quoted by Rieneker and Rogers).

This section (2:1-10) shows that life to begin with, loving ministry to go on with and marvellous light to dwell in, are each and all possible only in Christ, the elect and precious One. From Him all is derived, upon Him all that is of God is built, and to Him all things converge to be consummated in realms of marvellous light and everlasting mercy.

Notes

5   The epistle was written from Babylon, that city identified with man's counterfeit of God's will and purpose. The spirit of Babylon which is consummated in the false church was spawned in the slime-pits of Babel (Gen 11) and pervades every age of history. The first of five identifying marks of man's alternative is Imitation, they "had brick for stone, and slime had they for mortar". Bricks are imitation stones. Slime is man-mixed adhesive used to hold the edifice together. By contrast, the spiritual house is built of living stones and these are "gathered together", "fitted together" and "builded together" without the adhesion of man's religious ingenuity and organisation (Eph 2:19-22). Any attempt to build up or hold together this glorious edifice by man-made rules or material is to turn back to the spirit of Babylon for help it cannot give to do a work that will not stand the final test.

5   We may see an example of this in the acceptable sacrifice of Rom 12:1. This is often presented as the burnt offering aspect of the believer's life, all on the altar. However this is an offering without blood. It is an acceptance offering and corresponds to one of the three voluntary offerings. Only one of these fits this picture, the meal offering of Lev 2, where there is no blood shed. What then made the meal offering acceptable? It follows and is associated with the burnt offering. So we often read, "the burnt offering ... and ... the meal offering" (Lev 9:16-17; 14:20; 14:31; 23:37 ...). The christian may feel his utter unworthiness even to offer himself to God for holy purposes. Yet that living sacrifice, such as it is, is holy in the sight of God and "acceptable", not on the basis of some noble consecration or personal worth, but on the ground of the great burnt offering of Christ. Therefore it is a most spiritually intelligent act of worship for the believer to present that offering to God.

2.   *Exhortations in the Light of Our Obligations* 2:11-4:11

a. As Strangers and Pilgrims (vv.11-12)

> v.11 "Dearly beloved, I beseech *you* as strangers and pilgrims, abstain from fleshly lusts, which war against the soul;
> v.12 Having your conversation honest among the Gentiles, that, whereas they speak against you as evildoers, they may by *your* good works, which they shall behold, glorify God in the day of visitation.

11   The appeal of the following exhortation is three-fold. First it is based on the response of love. Peter begins, "Dearly beloved", at once reminding his readers not only of his own love for them, but that they were the beloved of God. The joys of love flourish in the duties of love. Some translations give "Dear friends", but this colloquialism is altogether too mundane. It is the trite expression of the politician and speechmaker who would hardly know his audience as friends, far less as "dear". The word Peter uses is *agapētos* and reflects the love of God for His Son, that love extended to a world of sinners and for His own. Here then is the strongest possible appeal for responding to the exhortation to follow.

He addresses the people as "strangers". The emphasis is in the location. The word is *paroikos*, literally, "beside the dwelling". They had not moved in, nor settled down. They were expatriates of heaven, away from their native land, but soon to leave for home. There is about a christian in fellowship with God a certain detachment from the world and a disenchantment with its pleasures. The second appeal to the readers, then, is on the ground of the temporary nature of their residence.

Peter continues to pave the way for the exhortation by the use of the word pilgrims. This is how he described them at the beginning. They were *parepidē moi*, see 1:1b. This is not now residence so much as relationship to the people. They had been delivered from the darkness in which the heathen dwell. They were a holy nation, separated unto God. Now they were to recognise their obligation to the last and God's purpose in sowing them there as good seed; not only by declaring the excellences of Christ but also by displaying the character of Christlikeness in the holy manner of their lives. This then is the three-fold cord of divine constraint: the response of love; the temporary nature of their residence; the obligation of their relationship to the unbelievers, alongside of whom they dwelt in the sovereign plan of God.

The believer in Christ has enemies. Some make frontal attack from without (5:8). Some seek to penetrate and control the mind, invading through the members (Rom 7:23). Still others, like a treacherous fifth column, rise up within and seek to capture the soul. These are "fleshly lusts". While including the immoral and base desires they encompass all "strong desires or cravings" (Arndt and Gingrich). "Fleshly", from *sarkikos*, "means what is inadequate, what is not decisive before God, but in such a way that it tempts man to be satisfied with it. . ." (*Theological Dictionary of the NT*, G. Friedrich). These are "our selfish, indulgent and potentially vicious natural appetites" (A.M. Stibbs). This is the antithesis of all that is spiritual and there is a continual state of war existing between the enmity of the flesh and the Holy Spirit (Gal 5:17).

The believer is to "abstain" from these fleshly lusts. This is not just a passive and negative attitude. Neither is it a cloistered asceticism associated with horsehair shirts, lashes and beds of nails. The word *apechō*, "to hold oneself from" (W.E. Vine). It is with discipline to withstand this persistent foe which ever seeks to subjugate the soul. The graphic picture of this enemy is Amalek. When the flesh in the children of Israel led them to murmur, "Then came Amalek" (Exod 17). It is noteworthy in the account of Deut 25:18 that it was the laggards and the feeble that were attacked first. It was when the people were "faint and weary" they were more subject to onslaught. Egypt was overcome in a night, Pharaoh and his host were overthrown in a day, but Amalek warred against Israel all the desert journey long.

12 Nothing will affect the unbeliever like the high quality of the christian life. More eloquent than words is the testimony of good works with joy and good workmanship on the job. Men with argumentative skill and eloquence may apparently win in contending with a believer. They can overrule his convictions and mock his message, but they cannot gainsay the attractiveness of the christian life, lived in fellowship with God.

The participle "having" "might well be translated 'holding to' or 'persevering in' " (D.E. Hiebert), as though Peter expected the condition to be already existing in the lives of his readers. "Conversation" of course is more than words spoken, it is the manner of the whole life. Honesty should be the hallmark of this life. The present meaning of this is rectitude, sincerity and uprightness in everything. While it means that, the Greek word (*kalos*) conveys much more. It refers to what is "good, admirable, becoming, . .. fair, right, .. . regarded with honour, honourable.. ." (W.E. Vine). "It is the ordinary Greek word for 'beautiful'" (A.J. Mason). The Lord's people should be seen to be the beautiful people by the quality of their lives.

Nevertheless, even in the midst of this kind of honourable life of moral beauty ("wherein", RV), the believers will be slandered. Perhaps we could say *because* of this lovely quality of living they expose, by vivid contrast, the perversion and ugliness of the wicked and draw forth the scourge of the tongue against them. It is an ancient ploy, *argurnentum ad hominem*: if you cannot gainsay the power of the word or the evidence of the life, then try to discredit the character of the witness.

These beloved of the Lord were called by the heathen "evildoers", not surprisingly, since the leaders of Jewry made this charge falsely against the Lord Jesus (John 18:30). In Paul's day the same hierarchy referred to the christians as a "sect ... every where ... spoken against" (Acts 28:22).

They were not to vindicate themselves by goodly words but rather by good works. This was not for personal reasons, but that God might be glorified "in the day of visitation" by those very same who had slandered the saints. This day may refer to a day of grace when the Lord visits to save and to bless (Luke 1:78; 19:41-44). It may be a day of judgment and retribution (Jer 51:18). In either case, God will be glorified as the good works of the believers are examined in the light of eternal values, and the gold of their godliness will be vindicated by "him that judgeth righteously" (v.23).

b. As Good Citizens (vv.13-17)

> v.13 Submit yourselves to every ordinance of man for the Lord's sake: whether it be to the king, as supreme,
> v.14 Or unto governors, as unto them that are sent by him for the punishment of evildoers, and for the praise of them that do well.
> v.15 For so is the will of God, that with well doing ye may put to silence the ignorance of foolish men:
> v.16 As free, and not using *your* liberty for a cloak of maliciousness, but as the servants of God.
> v.17 Honour all *men*. Love the brotherhood. Fear God. Honour the king.

13 Such things as meekness, humility and submission were not considered admirable attributes in Roman or Greek culture; rather were they seen as weaknesses to be taken advantage of. It was the Lord Jesus who by example and exposition showed how excellent and priceless these qualities were in the eternal kingdom. The believer is called to be subordinate to authority, not simply passively or reluctantly to bow the knee, but actively to take a place in the ranks of the subordinate, just as a foot-soldier lines up to wait the command of his superior. It is a word of military significance, remembering the "war against the soul" (v.11). "The verb is not only reflexive, but aorist; and so the meaning is, Be ye those who once for all submitted yourselves" (W. Kelly).

The battlefield is "the soul" (*psuchē*). This word is used to distinguish differently an aspect of being, depending on the context in which it is used (cf. Acts 27:37; 1 Thess 5:23). It is one thing to be in the battle, but another to *be* the battlefield. Job was not only in the battle, he *was* the battle. So do we carry with us an "inner moral nature, the seat and centre of self-conscious human life" which, as long as the believer lives on earth, though saved by grace, needs to be continually saved and preserved from disgrace.

The christian is to submit "to every human institution" (JND). For the ordered structure of society there must be some form of rule and authority to maintain it, both for the reward of the obedient and the punishment of the evildoer; otherwise there is anarchy. That ordained rule may take quite different forms, but the authority comes from God. "Water may be made to assume different forms, in fountains and cascades, and be made to flow in different channels ... by the hand of man; but the element itself, which flows in them is from God" (Wordsworth, quo. J.P. Lange). Paul writes to those under Roman rule, "there is no power but of God: the powers that be are ordained of God" (Rom 13:1). "Indirectly, when one disobeys a human ruler he disobeys God, who ordained the system of human government" (D.W. Burdick, NIV). The Lord Jesus was crucified by the power of Rome (Matt 20:19). Both Peter and Paul were put to death by Rome, yet they preached submission to the Roman emperor.

However there is a qualifying principle. For the christian there is a supreme authority, the Lord Himself, King of kings and Lord of lords. If the state demands what clearly violates a command or principle of Holy Scripture then the believer is to "obey God rather than men" (Acts 5:29; Exod 1:17). This is not merely a matter of personal opinion or political preference, but if by obeying some immoral law the believer must sin to do so, then he is to obey the law of God and suffer the consequences. We all recognise this is easier to write under the rule of a benign government than to carry out in a totalitarian state where prison or death may be the price of conviction.

14 When Peter wrote these words concerning subordination to civil government, he himself was not insulated from danger. The godless and cruel Nero was on the throne and God permitted both Peter and Paul to be put to death under his authority. Whether it is the despotic rule of an absolute monarch, or the delegated authority of the lower echelons of government it is the duty of every christian to be as good a citizen as he can be of the country where he dwells.

It is not given to the christian to change the world or overthrow governments by demonstration, strikes or insurrection. God is not going to clean up this world system, He is ultimately going to burn it. The commission given to His own is to go into the world and declare the gospel and by instruction to make disciples, calling men and women out of the system that they might be put into His eternal kingdom. By this means the hearts of men are changed to live salutary lives under whatever form of government rules the land. There he will be a light in the midst of darkness and salt in the place of corruption.

15 Many times in life, the will of God, in day to day matters, is not always crystal clear and the just really do live by faith. There are however certain things known to be the will of God. Salvation is the will of God (2 Pet 3:9); sanctification is the will of God (1 Thess 4:3). Now here we learn that submission to authority is the will of God.

This willing submission to human ordinance stands in contrast to the charge of evildoing levelled against the christians. It is called "well doing", not so much deeds of goodness, but the whole attitude of a subordinate spirit evident in the midst of a contentious society forever fighting for its rights. This, more than anything, will give the lie to slander and silence the senseless babblings of those who are ignorant of God and His ways. This is not a willing silence, it is forced upon them as a muzzle (*phimoō*) is upon an animal (cf. 1 Cor 9:9). The Lord Jesus silenced the storm, He silenced the spirits and He silenced the Sadducees by the power of His word and His wisdom. It is the obligation of the believer to silence the slander of the senseless by the power of a godly walk in an ungodly world.

16 "Freedom" is a much oversold and little understood word in the world. Man claims to be a "free agent" and sets out to do his own will. The present libertinism and moral collapse of society is the result of an utterly wrong notion of the meaning of freedom. While man is free to choose any course of action, he is not free to choose the consequences of his actions.

As for the believer in Christ, freedom is not an unqualified release from responsibility and constraint. It is freedom from the dominion of sin (Rom 6:14). It is freedom from the yoke of bondage to the law, as a means of obtaining righteousness (Gal 5:1). It is not an exemption from obedience to the laws of the land or exoneration from duty to our fellowman. The freedom of the christian includes a sacred liberty to enter the sanctuary of God in the Spirit, at any time and in any place. This freedom is the liberty to choose a higher service, as "a bondman of God". This is illustrated in Exod 21 by the Hebrew servant. Having the liberty to go out free, he chooses, in love for his master, to remain for life as a bondslave.

H.A. Ironside wrote in the margin of his Bible at Rom 6:16;

"Make me a captive, Lord,
    And then I shall be free;
Force me to render up my sword,
    And I shall conqueror be.
I sink in life's alarms,
    When by myself I stand;
Imprison me within Thine arms,
    And strong shall be my hand."

The freedom in Christ must not be used as a "cloke", or as a cover-up (cf. Exod 26:14 LXX, the covering of the Tabernacle). The paradox is of a christian loudly proclaiming his liberty so that he might cover up the folly of taking again the bondage of sin.

17   A Christlike attitude is to be practically expressed to all in general, to the family of God, to God Himself and to the ruling power.

The command to "Honour all men" is not so much a continual generality as "the act when occasion arises" (JND, note r.) this verb being the aorist tense while the others in the verse, the continuing present tense, conveying "the constant habit of mind". The first honouring is to be "done when called for, not the habitual doing it" (W. Kelly).

It is nonetheless true that every man, woman and child is an object of the love of God, made at first in the image of God as no other creature, and is included in the provision of God when Christ died for the ungodly. All men are to be seen in the light of this and so valued.

"Love the brotherhood" is literally, "The brotherhood, keep on loving" in the assumption that this love already exists. This goes beyond loving those in the brotherhood who love us and with whom we agree on all points. It is again the highest word for love, *agapaō*.

"The brotherhood" is one of Peter's terms which we may apply to the whole Church today. We remember that Peter does not speak of "the Church" by that word, keeping in mind the great significance this epistle will have for the remnant after the Church is taken at the rapture.

If this admonition was obeyed by us all a great many difficulties would evaporate in the sunshine of such a love. Heaven itself would come into the hearts of many hurting believers, assemblies would flourish and the world outside, seeing that love exhibited among the saints, would know they were true disciples of their Lord and not counterfeit (John 13:35).

"Fear God" is not a call to be frightened or terrified of God, but to fear grieving Him, in holy awe and reverence fearing to displease Him. "Holy fear of the majesty of God is peculiarly in place, if you are tempted to abuse your christian liberty" (J.P. Lange).

"Honour the king" is to be a continuous attitude. The admonition is all the more remarkable when we remember that Nero was the emperor in Peter's day. His deeds and words may not be honourable, but as the power ordained of God, he is to be recognised as such.

This is a timely exhortation in a day when men lightly speak evil of dignities and become involved in political haranguing and personal insult against those in authority. The sovereign purpose of God may determine that a malignant ruler be in power to further the divine plan (Rom 9:17; Exod 9:16; Hab 1:6). Here is the perplexity of all who would be involved in the political process. The "best man ... or woman" may not be God's choice for the time.

We may honour the king, or ruler by obeying the exhortation that "supplications, prayers, intercessions, and giving of thanks, be made for all men; for kings, and for all that are in authority..." (1 Tim 2:1-2). The christian has more power to help his country in the prayer room than in the voting booth. Another may cancel his vote, but none can nullify his prayers. Daniel by his prayers affected the government of earth, moved the power of heaven and was known in the gates of hell.

c. As Servants (vv. 18-25)

> v.18 "Servants, be subject to *your* masters with all fear, not only to the good and gentle, but also to the froward.
> v.19 For this *is* thankworthy, if a man for conscience toward God endure grief, suffering wrongfully.
> v.20 For what glory *is it*, if, when ye be buffeted for your faults, ye shall take it patiently? but if, when ye do well, and suffer *for it*, ye take it patiently, this *is* acceptable with God.
> v.21 For even hereunto were ye called: because Christ also suffered for us, leaving us an example, that ye should follow his steps:
> v.22 Who did no sin, neither was guile found in his mouth:
> v.23 Who, when he was reviled, reviled not again, when he suffered, he threatened not, but committed *himself* to him that judgeth righteously:
> v.24 Who his own self bare our sins in his own body on the tree, that we, being dead to sins, should live unto righteousness: by whose stripes ye were healed.
> v.25 For ye were as sheep going astray; but are now returned unto the Shepherd and Bishop of your souls."

18   The servants referred to are domestic helps (*oiketēs*, house servant). This word " is often used as equivalent to *doulos* ... at the same time [it] does not bring out and emphasise the servile relation so strongly as *doulos* does" (R.C. Trench; *Synonyms of the NT*). They were slaves of the household. Peter does not begin by outlining a charter of rights for them. He calls them to be subject to their masters "with all fear". "The reverential fear of God will inspire a constant carefulness in dealing with others in His fear" (W.E. Vine).

Their attitude was not to depend on the conditions under which they served. It was not to be "selective service", whether in the service of the good and gentle, those fundamentally fair, considerate and reasonable in their dealings, or of the "froward", the morally crooked.

19   This lovely submission is an evidence of the grace of God. "Thankworthy"
is *charis*, the word for grace. Submission to a benevolent master is one thing but
to suffer wrongfully and endure grief is an evidence of the grace of God at work
in the sufferer. The word "conscience" may be seen in two ways. Literally it means
"a knowing with", "the witness borne to one's conduct by conscience, that faculty
by which we apprehend the will of God" (W.E. Vine). It is knowing what is right
before God, to submit and suffer the consequences if need be. Grammatically
the word is derived from *sunoida*, meaning "I am conscious". The motive would
then be because of the consciousness of the presence of God, "seeing, judging,
helping, rewarding, His suffering servants" (E.H. Plumptre). Abraham grasped
this truth of living in the consciousness of the divine presence when he said to
his servant, "The Lord, before whom I walk" (Gen 24:40).

20   From the passive "enduring" Peter now moves to the active side of things,
first negatively then positively. If the servant sins (JND, RV) against his master
and is "buffeted", struck on the face with the fist, and takes it patiently, that is not
a cause for gaining fame or a reputation (*kleos*). The blows come from the master
"for neglect of duty towards himself. On the other hand, the *kleos* [good report,
fame, renown] comes from God, in whose eyes the neglect of earthly duty is sin"
(C. Bigg).
    To do well and suffer as a direct result, and to take that patiently, is "acceptable"
with God. "Acceptable" is the same word (*charis*) as in v.19, so we could read,
"this is grace with God". Or as the AV margin has it, "this is thanks with God". It
is hardly conceivable to us that God so appreciates such a submissive obedience
to the point of suffering wrongfully, as a reflection of His own dear Son, that He
considers the servant worthy of thanks. "The apostle does not continue, 'this is
glory' [*kleos*], as we might have expected; a christian is not supposed to care for
such trash as fame. But a christian may well care to win the thanks of God!" (A.J.
Mason). "The contrast is between merited suffering and martyr suffering" (G.F.C.
Fronmuller).

21   The christian rejoices in his holy calling out of darkness into marvellous
light (v.9). He delights that he is called to be a blessing (3:9). He marvels that he
is called to realms of God's eternal glory (5:10). To learn however that this
wondrous calling includes a call to suffer in silent submission for well-doing is
perhaps a more sobering thought.
    The first encouragement for such suffering is subjective, to enjoy the favour
of God. Now the great incentive is objective, the great example of Christ Himself.
"Christ also suffered". It is not here, "Jesus suffered". To the unbelieving Jew a
suffering Messiah is repugnant but to the believing Jew this is a joyous revelation,
"he was wounded for our transgressions".
    More than this, it was "for us", or "for you" (RV, JND). These sufferings are not
His expiatory sufferings, but His exemplary sufferings. Only in these may we

follow His steps, though never in His steps; His walk on earth was unique. How then may the believer follow such an example? There were three significant aspects about Christ in His exemplary sufferings on the way to the cross which we may follow, even though "afar off".

22   *There was no Deviation*: He "did no sin". While He is the impeccable Christ and could not sin, we have a sinful nature still and may sin. God however does not lower His standards to meet our frailty. Sin is never assumed to be the norm in the believer's life: " if any man sin. . ." (1 John 2:1), not " when any man sin". In the context it is the sin of wilfulness that is in view. The Lord Jesus submitted Himself in loving obedience to the Father's will. Here is the great Exemplar we are to follow. We too are to be subject in all things to that perfect will in glad submission and thus be preserved from the sin of insubordination.

23a   *There was no Retaliation*: "He, [the] Lord of angelic legions, did not approve the sword of Peter drawn in His defence, He is spit upon, scourged, mocked. Such long-suffering as His, is an example to all men, but is found in God alone" (Tertullian). Before Pilate, "Jesus gave him no answer". Even under the brutal treatment and mockery at Gabbatha, "as a sheep before her shearers is dumb, so he openeth not his mouth" (Isa 53:7).
     The solemnity of that silence is heightened when we remember who He was as He stood there, mocked as a carnival king. Beneath that thorny crown lay all the authority of Godhood. One word from His mouth and He could have banished His tormentors and the earth upon which they stood to the eternal blackness. But beneath that bloodstained garment there beat a heart full of love. It was for such sinners He came to suffer and die. He wept over the city that refused Him. Judgment is His strange work. The fiat of "the fierceness and wrath of Almighty God" upon this old world must wait till grace and mercy have exhausted their mighty ministries on earth and only the sword remains.
     Retaliation comes naturally to us, but the believer has the sight of the silent Sufferer before him as a sacred example to follow.

23b   *There was no Vindication*: He "gave [Himself] over into the hands of Him who judges righteously" (JND). Before His enemies could deliver Him to Pilate, He had already given Himself over to the righteous judge. The day of His vindication lies ahead and in the long-despised name of Jesus every knee shall bow and every tongue confess His Lordship. He was willing to wait for that day so, He "kept handing Himself over" (W.H.G. Thomas) in every circumstance. "By so doing He provided in principle and in spirit an example to be followed by all who, in following Him, find that they, too, have to suffer unjustly" (A.M. Stibbs).
     William Kelly states, "it has not been shown. .. that the word [committed] admits of the reflexive sense, good as it would seem in itself, that is, of meaning "gave himself over". In the AV, "himself" is in italics, to show that the word is

supplied by the translators. Some commentators feel that since the grammatical object of the verb is not expressed, "it is better not to supply one so definite as 'himself' or 'His cause`. In this view, the Lord Jesus committed absolutely, Himself, His cause, His tormentors, everything and everyone was involved. He passed the whole matter over to the righteous judge, refusing to take any action in self-defence.

Thus, in anticipation of future joy, He endured the cross and despised the shame. This silent Sufferer is set before us as a glorious example that, by His grace and power, we too may be preserved from the folly of vindicating ourselves, but instead, learn to commit the whole matter into the hands of the great Vindicator Himself and wait for the day of righteous judgment.

24   There are companions in suffering and followers in grief, but when it comes to the atoning work of Christ on the cross it is He Himself alone, "who his own self bare our sins". He alone did it because only He could do it.

> "There was no other good enough
>   To pay the price of sin;
> He only could unlock the gate
>   Of heaven, and let us in."
>   C.F. Alexander

It was a sacrificial work, it was for sins. It was a substitutionary work, it was for "our sins". It was a suffering work, He endured it "in his own body". It was a saving work, from the cursed consequences of our sins, He was made a curse for us "on the tree".

Numerous commentators explain the word "bare" as "bearing up to" or "carrying up to" the tree, our sins. However, "unlike the imperfects in v.23, 'bare' is an aorist-a definite event, not a repeated practice" (D.E. Hiebert). "The dark and perilous hypothesis [of Christ's carrying our sins to the tree] would require the imperfect tense to give continuity of bearing our sins ... It is the aorist, on the contrary, which above all shuts out relative duration, continuity, repetition, or action commenced and not accomplished" (W. Kelly). "The AV margin, 'to the tree', is to be rejected. The AV text, 'on', and the RV 'upon' express the phrase rightly" (W.E. Vine).

"Being dead to sins" is not the same as the Pauline doctrine, "dead to sin". Sin is the fact, sins are the acts. Sin has to do with nature, sins to practice. In the Bible, death is not the cessation of existence, as the heathen thinks of it. It is separation of existence`. Being dead to sins, does not mean that we do not exist to them, but that by the work of Christ on the cross we are separated from these as to life, love and loyalty. The word Peter uses here for "death" is not found elsewhere in the NT. It could be literally translated "missing". "When sin comes to seek its old servants it finds them gone" (A.J. Mason). F.W. Grant asks " How is it possible to go on in the sins which the Lord bore upon the tree? "

Having settled the relationship to sins, Peter points to the results, practically expressed, living "unto righteousness". This is the goal of the new life, transitive holiness carried over into righteous living.

The bruise (RV marg) of the Lord Jesus brings healing to the believer; healing from the wounds of sin upon the soul; healing from the disease of sin itself. This healing is an accomplished fact in every believer's life, " ye were healed". This is not healing of the body. That will come, but it must wait the adoption, "the redemption of the purchased possession".

25   Peter has doubtless been thinking of Isa 53 as he penned the previous words. Again he dips his pen into the same sweet well and alludes to v.6 of that chapter, "All we like sheep have gone astray". Few things in nature are more pitiful than a lost sheep away from the shepherd and the fold. Having no homing instinct it can wander to its death. Having neither fang nor claw it is defenceless against its enemies. Such was the picture of the sinner's past, " ye were as sheep going astray". But they had returned, not to the temple nor even to the church, but to the arms of the Shepherd Himself. Neither the temple nor the church can hold the weary and heal the sick. Only the Good Shepherd can do those things. The shepherds of Israel's past cared nothing for the flock. They did not feed the sheep, they ate the sheep! But this Shepherd not only undergirds the sheep with His mighty arm, He oversees (*episkopos*) them all with His sleepless eye.

d. As Wives and Husbands (3:1-7)

> v.1   "Likewise, ye wives, *be* in subjection to your own husbands; that, if any obey not the word, they also may without the word be won by the conversation of the wives;
> v.2   While they behold your chaste conversation *coupled* with fear.
> v.3   Whose adorning let it not be that outward *adorning* of plaiting the hair, and of wearing of gold, or of putting on of apparel;
> v.4   But *let it be* the hidden man of the heart, in that which is not corruptible, *even the ornament* of a meek and quiet spirit, which is in the sight of God of great price.
> v.5   For after this manner in the old time the holy women also, who trusted in God, adorned themselves, being in subjection unto their own husbands:
> v.6   Even as Sara obeyed Abraham, calling him lord: whose daughters ye are, as long as ye do well, and are not afraid with any amazement.
> v.7   Likewise, ye husbands, dwell with them according to knowledge, giving honour unto the wife, as unto the weaker vessel, and as being heirs together of the grace of life; that your prayers be not hindered."

1   As there must be a functional authority in government and in the economy to provide and maintain order, so "likewise" there must be order in the home. It is not submission "like" citizens, nor "like" slaves. "The keyword is subjection" (Selwyn). This submission within the home does not only honour God; it provides also the blessings of order, stability, peace and security for the joy of all its members. Beyond this, the submissive spirit itself becomes a witness of the work of grace in the individual that by beholding such a manner of life, others may glorify God and be won over to the obedience of faith.

The subjection of the wife to her own husband is not exactly the same as that previously spoken of regarding submission to ordinances (2:13). There the aorist is used, to indicate a particular act. Here the present participle indicates rather an habitual state. "This subordination is one of function, within the intimate circle of the home" (*ibid*).

For practical purposes and accountability before God, where there is responsibility there must be an order of authority. Authority without responsibility is autocracy. Responsibility without authority is a mockery. God's order is neither; it is theocracy, the rule of God in effect.

This balance of authority and responsibility is fundamental to the home and family, which is the basic cell of society. If God's order is not recognised nor followed in the home, we should not then be surprised if moral values, economic stability, political integrity and national security disintegrate. It is all one intricate fabric, designed by God and not man (Gen 3:16).

There is no question of rank or inferiority here, but of submission to authority for the testimony's sake. Of course, for the wife, this is not submission to just any man, but each to her own husband.

If this should seem to be difficult in a christian home at times, then the extreme case is presented: that of a wife who becomes a believer in Christ while her husband remains disobedient to the gospel call. "If" that be so, she must seek to win her beloved with the beauty of Christlikeness reflected daily by a submissive spirit, not by preachments of words nor the indiscriminate quoting of "gospel verses". It is not to be the *wearing down* of the stony heart by the continual dropping of the wife's well-meaning sermonettes. It will be the *winning over* of the heart by the "discreet charm of her piety".

It is the worst case that is considered here not involving an ignorant man, but an actively disobedient one. "The word *apeithein*, here rendered "obey not' , is a strong word meaning to disobey, and is probably intended to describe husbands who, far from being won by hearing the gospel preached, deliberately set themselves against the truth" (AM Stibbs).

The wonderful thing here is that even in the most obdurate and difficult cases, there is hope that they "may be won". In the family relationships it is not by what we say, so much, but by how we act and react in the daily vicissitudes of life that the christian message is best expounded. The ungodly husband may win in a contest of words, but he cannot honestly gainsay the loveliness of his partner living a consistent godly life.

2 The life and behaviour of the believing wife is under constant surveillance as she carries out her ministries in each room of the house. No doubt those to whom Peter wrote lived in homes where paganism and idolatry were practised, a most difficult arena wherein to exhibit meekness and chastity.

The "beholding" of the wife meant that the husband was always ' keeping an eye" on her. This is an unusual word, occurring only here and in 2:12. The cognate noun "eye-witnesses" appears in 2 Pet 1:16, referring to the transfiguration which the disciples beheld in wonder, Peter not knowing what to say (Mark 9:6). Historically it has a rather mystic connotation being "applied originally to those who were initiated in the ... highest order of the Eleusinian mysteries" (E.H. Plumptre). To "behold" day by day the loveliness of a chaste life in its submissiveness and meekness, in spite of continual scrutiny, would be somewhat of a mystery to an unbelieving husband, and would do more to win him over than much talking. "His attention to the gospel would be won through the eye rather than the ear" (D.E. Hiebert).

This beauty of life was also to be characterised by "fear", not the terror of her husband, but, in contrast to a bold and haughty spirit, "the dread of offending God or her husband" (W. Kelly).

3-4   However, the wife was not to confuse the attraction of her natural charm, outwardly adorned, with the inner beauty of the heart as a means of winning over her husband to the Lord. Some of these readers were obviously not poor; they had ornaments and gold. There are three verbs of note in this verse: "plaiting", "wearing" and "putting on". These are "intended to convey the notion of elaborate processes in which time is wasted" (Bengel). It is against this inordinate preoccupation with extravagant decoration as a means of attracting attention that is admonished.

While these verses have been used by some sects to legislate the style of women's dress, Peter is not here forbidding "any and every adornment" but he is presenting the comparative values of the outward decoration and the inner ornament of a meek and quiet spirit as a means of winning others for Christ. The more of that inner loveliness that shines forth, the less time, effort and expense will be expended on outward decoration. The most effective and long-lasting cosmetic is prescribed in the Scriptures, "he will beautify the meek..." (Ps 149:4).

"The dress of the christian woman, as all else, should speak of nothing inconsistent with her heavenly and separate character. The very fact that we are not under law should constrain us to more simple obedience. On the other hand, shabbiness or carelessness in dress will never commend the truth" (S. Ridout).

Youth and the blush of natural beauty fade with the passing years. Beauty of character grows more lovely and attractive. It is "not corruptible". As to its intrinsic value in the sight of God it is an ornament "of great price". This is the same word used to describe the "very precious" ointment in Mark 14:3. Peter would not have forgotten that incident and the lesson taught, that the Lord's values and man's are quite different (cf. the twenty- one ornaments in Isa 3:18-23 with the three in Gen 24:22).

5-6   The high fashion models of this world are not to be the pattern for christian wives. Their models are found in the OT among the "saintly women", set apart by God. They trusted in God. They had their hope in God. Their saintliness was a practical thing. "They adorned themselves" as a practice, after the manner referred to, with that ornament of a meek and quiet spirit. Now, meekness is not weakness, nor is it sickly sweetness. It is "an inwrought grace of the soul ... chiefly towards God ... the fruit of power ... Described negatively, meekness is the opposite to self assertiveness and self-interest" (W.E. Vine).

Those saintly women in OT days displayed that spirit by subjection to their own husbands. It was the evidence of great strength of character, a quality it seems most often found in godly women.

Sarah is presented as an example to follow as children partake of the nature and disposition of their mother.   "Just as Abraham is called the father of the faithful, so Sarah may be described as the mother of the obedient" (A.M. Stibbs).

Peter refers to the instance recorded in Gen 18:12 when Sarah, speaking within herself, calls Abraham her lord. We are not told that she addressed him as lord, though she may have, but considered herself in subjection to him, giving him deference. So the believing wives are encouraged by Peter that they had in fact become children of Sarah, (v.6 JND). Her characteristics were reproduced in them (and she was a beautiful woman to look upon, Gen 12:11). They would remain evidently so as they continued in submission, "doing good, and not fearing with any kind of consternation" (JND).

As sojourners they might have feared persecution against themselves or their families. As believers they might have feared the antagonism of their unbelieving husbands. However, their hope was in God, their obedience was to His Word; thus they could with confidence leave their case in His mighty hand.

7   Husbands are now exhorted as to their domestic responsibilities. "Likewise" points back to the whole discussion of submission. The marriage bond is not a dog collar around the wife's neck while she waits to jump at the next command. As to the order in the home there must be a final authority under God. Since the man is answerable to God for all that goes on in his home then he is delegated certain authority as the head. As to harmony in the home there is a mutual consideration as expressed by Paul, "submitting yourselves one to another in the fear of God" (Eph 5:21-23).

The husbands are to "dwell with them". The word is *sunoikeō*, literally, "house together", or "make a home together" in every aspect of a shared home-life. In all this the husband, by taking the necessary initiatives, is to provide for his wife's security. This involves her physical, emotional and material security.

While there is but this one verse addressed to husbands, its implications are deep and far-reaching indeed. Pointing back to the primal union it is significantly stated that it is the man who is to take the lead in the loving, and in the leaving and in the cleaving (Eph 5:25-33). The continuing exercise of home-making is to be "according to knowledge". This is not limited to the physical relationship, but it is a knowledge that seeks ever to know better the object of enquiry (*gnōsis*). As the husband comes to know his wife more fully and to understand her better, early uncertainties and apprehensions should be dispelled as he ministers to her needs, spiritually, emotionally, physically and materially.

The wife is considered as "the weaker vessel", certainly not weaker in any sense beyond the physical make-up. A Deborah leading the armies of Israel, a Mary standing over against the cross of the despised One and a Priscilla opening the Scriptures to the mighty Apollos would never be thought of as weak of will, spirit or intellect. It is a matter of nourishing and cherishing as Paul puts it. The husband is to be the protector of his wife from dangers spiritual, moral and physical, and by his presence to allay her fears.

In the marriage relationship husband and wife, ideally, complement one another. If both are believers, their separate gifts and abilities are brought together to provide one harmonious contribution to the home and beyond. The husband is to give honourable treatment to his wife, considering her precious and of great value. He is to recognise there is a mutual inheritance as heirs together of the grace of life. Here believers are in view. While they will live on earth as husband and wife, there is "a relationship by grace which shall never pass away" (W. Kelly). In that relationship there is no distinction of sex, or of standing. The eternal point of view will add only value to any relationship, lifting it up above the temporal and the transient.

Prayer is the cohesive power that binds a home together; prayer for one another and prayer for one another's burdens and needs. It is most difficult to have unresolved matters between husband and wife when hand in hand they bow to pray. The enemy ever seeks to hinder prayer. He has a thousand devices to use and one of these is to sow discord between partners. Every effort is to be made, led by the husband, the head and priest in the home, in love and appreciation to maintain the family altar.

It is most significant to see the relationship between the prayer life and the love life of husbands and wives. One can affect the other. This whole section shows the importance of a balanced life where there is the following of the divine order in all aspects and areas of daily living.

e. As Sufferers for Righteousness' Sake (3:8-22)

> v.8 "Finally, all of one mind, having compassion one of another, love as brethren, *be* pitiful, *be* courteous:
> v.9 Not rendering evil for evil, or railing for railing; but contrariwise blessing: knowing that ye are thereunto called, that ye should inherit a blessing.
> v.10 For he that will love life, and see good days, let him refrain his tongue from evil, and his lips that they speak no guile:
> v.11 Let him eschew evil, and do good; let him seek peace, and ensue it.
> v.12 For the eyes of the Lord over the righteous, and his ears unto their prayers: but the face of the Lord against them that do evil.

v.13 And who he that will harm you, if ye be followers of that which is good?
v.14 But and if ye suffer for righteousness' sake, happy: and be not afraid of their terror, neither be troubled;
v.15 But sanctify the Lord God in your hearts: and *be* ready always to *give* an answer to every man that asketh you a reason of the hope that is in you with meekness and fear:
v.16 Having a good conscience; that, whereas they speak evil of you, as of evildoers, they may be ashamed that falsely accuse your good conversation in Christ.
v.17 For *it is* better, if the will of God be so, that ye suffer for well doing, than for evil doing.
v.18 For Christ also hath once suffered for sins, the just for the unjust, that he might bring us to God, being put to death in the flesh, but quickened by the Spirit:
v.19 By which also he went and preached unto the spirits in prison;
v.20 Which sometime were disobedient, when once the longsuffering of God waited in the days of Noah, while the ark was a preparing, wherein few, that is, eight souls were saved by water.
v.21 The like figure whereunto baptism doth also now save us (not the putting away of the filth of the flesh, but the answer of a good conscience toward God,) by the resurrection of Jesus Christ:
v.22 Who is gone into heaven, and is on the right hand of God; angels and authorities and powers being made subject unto him."

8 "Finally", Peter comes to the concluding section of the epistle "as if his words were reaching a climax" (C.R. Erdman). It is not so much his intent to end the epistle right here, but to sum up his line of exhortation. Turning from special groups he addresses all christians, in the words, "be ye all. . ."

There is enough opposition from the world, without contending with the brethren. Instead of being protagonists in carnal causes and thereby always being in conflict with others of different mind, Peter exhorts, "be ye all of one mind". This adjective, *homophrōn*, is not found elsewhere in the NT, and conveys " a unity of aim and purpose ", to " mind the same things ". This is not the mindless acquiescence of robots, but "a call for unity of disposition [rather] than uniformity of opinion" (D.E. Hiebert). This oneness coalesces the minds of all those believers who have the mind of Christ (Phil 2:5), thereby displaying that humble and submissive spirit so fully and perfectly exhibited by the Master.

Another beautiful quality of the redeemed nature is called upon, to be "having compassion one of another". This is from one word, JND translates, "sympathizing", to share fellow-feelings in joy or in sorrow, not grudgingly, but with "a readiness to enter into and share the feelings of others" (W. Kelly).

In a world of so much violence and tragedy daily flooding the media, the danger for us today is that of losing sensitivity to the pain of others. The gracious quality of being touched with feeling is seen in our great High Priest who is able to sympathise for us in our infirmities (Heb 4:15). This because He identified Himself with us in our humanity in everything but our sinful nature. It was His simpatico with us that brought forth His sympathy for us.

Moses, the greater man than Aaron, was not called to be high priest. Why not? because he had grown up in the palace. He had never felt the lash of the taskmaster, the blast of the brick kilns, the raw-fingered agony of unrequited toil. He could not be touched with the feeling of their infirmities, but Aaron could, he was there. We may pity from above, but we can only sympathise from beside.

In all this, the believers are to be "loving to the brethren" (AV marg), "full of brotherly love" (JND). That is the love that rises up because of an intimate relationship in the family of God. This familial bond was the basis of Abraham's costly appeal to Lot, "Let there be no strife, I pray thee, between me and thee.. . for we be brethren" (Gen 13:8). This is a love that is developed by divine instruction, "ye yourselves are taught of God to love one another" (1 Thess 4:9). This is a love that easily overflows all natural obstruction between rich and poor, young and old, unlearned and erudite.

Believers are to be " pitiful" towards one another. JND translates this " tender hearted" as it is also in Eph 4:32. The adjective comes from a noun meaning "bowels" and is used in such an expression as "bowels of mercies". While it conveys the idea of "inward affection" it has the additional thought of spontaneity. Many muscles and members of the body are exercised at will, but the inner organs vital to life and health function spontaneously without the will. So is the character of this inner affection for one another. It is not to be a calculating thing, but to evidence itself as spontaneously as the heartbeat.

"Common" courtesy has become rather uncommon in a coarse and calloused world. An exhortation to "be courteous" would be most welcome. However manuscripts present two readings, the other being "humble" or "lowly". An alternative reading then is "[be] humble minded" (JND, RV). This goes along with the context of lowliness and submission one to the other.

Where do we see these lovely qualities scintillating most brightly, but in the radiant beauty of the Lord Jesus Himself as He walked this vale of tears? He was " meek and lowly in heart", loving the unlovely with a compassion that drew forth His pity and His power to relieve. He was gentle with the fallen, gentle with women, gentle with little children. He cared about broken hearts and broken lives and broken homes. Like the river flowing out of Eden, which compassed the whole land and where there was fine gold, His tears traced out His profound sympathy for all. Even when they would not have Him, He went on to the cross to remove the cause of their griefs and make deliverance possible.

9   Some suffering there must be and persecution of the godly, but there is suffering that need not be and we are not to seek it. Anger may be quenched by the soft answer, and opposition turned aside by a gracious spirit. It takes neither gift nor grace to provoke anger. William Lincoln quotes one of the old Puritans, "To return good for evil is God-like; to return good for good is man-like; to return evil for evil is beast-like; to return evil for good is devil-like".

The believer is not to render "evil for evil, or railing for railing". The world system is hostile to Christ, His cause and His own. For its own purpose it often conceals the steel gauntlet with a velvet glove, but if it can, it will render evil against the believer in Christ by deed and by word.

The world's heroes are those who "get even". The violent vigilantes are the stars in their sordid night. These are applauded and they love to have it so. The believer in Christ must not be like them. The natural brute instinct is to return violence with violence (if not in fact perhaps in fantasy). Social mores may restrain the violent response, but give room and license to verbal abuse. The believer however, far from such vengeance, is not simply to " suffer in silence", but is to respond actively by "blessing". This is a present active participle, literally to "eulogise", or to invoke the blessing of God upon the antagonist.

How is this beneficent attitude possible? It cuts clear across the short grain of our old nature. The believers are helped by knowing that they are "thereunto called". This would remind them that they themselves were called by sovereign grace out of that dark realm where the ungodly dwell-and where they still would be but for God's amazing grace. They were called, not only into light, but to be as light and to radiate a beneficent ministry upon men.

The ungodly, if there is no repentance, will inherit the treasures of God's wrath. The people of God will more and more enter into the inherited blessings of God, and a life lived in the conscious joy of the forgiveness of God, as they obey these exhortations and follow the words of the Master, "Love your enemies, bless them that curse you, do good to them that hate you, and pray for them which despitefully use you, and persecute you" (Matt 5:44).

10-11   Men have travelled far, endured much and given lots to find the secret of happiness. Here Peter reaches back into the treasures of the Psalms to find it. By the reference to Ps 34:12-16 he gives a Biblical confirmation of what he has been teaching.

There is a therapeutic value in being contented with our lot in life: "godliness with contentment is great gain". This is for him "that will love life" here and now, not just a future hope, but a present desire, for him "that wills [has a mind] to love life". This is the life which "makes a man glad to live", a healthy and zestful enjoyment of life as it is being lived. This refers to the quality of life in general. To see "good days" is the desire of all men.

Such universal hope is expressed in so many languages by the daily greeting of the peoples, "Good day", "Guten Tag", "Buenas Dias" and the western colloquial, "Have a good day!" To express the wish is one thing, but really to "have a good day" or show how it may be so, requires more than the words and the wish. Ps 34 shows the way. There are certain matters that will require attention if the days are going to be good and a zest for life is to be enjoyed.

The Tongue That little member James warns about, that can bless and curse almost with the same breath, is to be firmly controlled. Evil-speaking must be stopped. "Refrain" is an aorist imperative and implies a forceful act of restraint, making something to cease; specifically here malicious, impure, slanderous, or vile speech.

The Lips While the tongue enables us to speak, the lips can convey a sense to the words. The warning here is against guile, that which misleads. A twisting of the lips, a turning down of the corners of the mouth, a sly smile can all affect the meaning of the words. A disarming smile indeed may be the camouflage that conceals a most deadly snare (*dolos*) and a most virulent poison. Crafty, subtle, deceitful speech can have no place in the conversation of God's people, if they are to live in the sunshine of a guileless life.

The Will When confronted with evil, sordid or subtle, there is to be an exercise of the will to turn away from it. The word *ekklinō* (*ek*, from, *klinō*, to turn, bend, W.E. Vine) pictures an avoiding action, bending away from or swerving aside "to avoid an encounter with evil … [an] evasive action" (D.E. Hiebert). It is to decline the evil suggestion, to say a firm "No" when evil knocks at the door.

In place of the evil avoided, there must be no moral vacuum. That is a dangerous condition. The Lord Jesus warns even the wicked of that (Matt 12:43-45). Instead, Peter says, "do good". Active employment in good works in the fellowship of the people of God is a healthy preservation from evil. It is not just talking about it, forming a committee to plan it, or discussing the proper methodology. It is the doing of good that is urgently needed.

The Pursuit Peace does not always come to stay. We may evict this blessed visitor by failing to be careful in those areas previously considered. Those who would have a zest for life are ever to "seek peace". It is not an automatic blessing. Peace "is to be a matter of diligent search". Every avenue is to be explored, every obstacle surmounted, every door is to be opened both to find peace and to make peace of a godly sort.

Peace is not just an absence of conflict; an armistice can do that. It is the beneficent, positive reign of the Prince of peace in the heart, soul and mind. This tranquil joy may rule in the life of one even under pressure or facing a crisis. In the shadow of the cross the Lord Jesus said, "my peace I give unto you" (John 14:27). Even there He had a deep peace, enough and to spare.

If peace takes flight in the turmoil of life, it must be actively pursued. "Ensue" (AV) is really "pursue". Peace is to be hunted down and captured for the heart. This word implies "both in itself, and by its position in the verse as a climax, the strongest form of seeking" (E.H. Plumptre).

12 There is a strong incentive now presented for the foregoing action. "For" or "because" the believer is not alone. If so, he could only fail in all the foregoing particulars, but because the Lord Himself undertakes the cause of His own, then life can be enjoyed "to the hilt".

The Lord is aware of His people, of their conditions and their needs. His eyes are upon "the righteous". The Lord is also for His people: "his ears [are open] unto their prayers". The picture is more intimate than just a listening God. It is a loving Lord, bowing down with His ear to our lips, to hear our faintest prayer. Some translate the expression "into our prayers". Just as an earthly father stoops down to embrace his child and put his ear to its mouth to hear its lisping tones and convey his love, so does the Lord with His own child. It is not that the Lord cannot hear clearly, but that His interest is so intensely personal.

Further, the Lord is against the enemy of His people, the evil. His face is "upon" (AV marg) them that do evil. What sleepless nights, what cold terror, what wild flights of panic would afflict the ungodly if they but knew how closely their whole lives were being scrutinised by a holy God and with what solemn aspect His face is turned upon them! Many a criminal has mocked the law and escaped its retribution by legal technicalities or lack of evidence. But the supreme court is not yet in session and the Judge of the whole earth has yet to take His seat. Then the ungodly will prefer the rocks and mountains to fall upon them, than just to behold that face (Rev 6:15-17).

13   The bodies of believers may be attacked by the enemies of God, but they cannot reach the soul. They can afflict no ultimate harm to the child of God. "If God be for us, who can be against us?" (Rom 8:31). At the very worst, Nero's executioners could only dispatch those saints home to glory, to rest, reward, and the radiance of the face of Christ.

It is not that followers of the good will be more likely to escape the antagonism of the world; Peter knew better and the Lord prophesied clearly that the righteous would suffer. Though certainly, on occasion, winsome works of goodness may well disarm the worldling.

The "followers of that which is good" are described differently depending on which manuscript is followed. Some read "zealots", or "zealous" (RV), "zealous ardent lovers" (C. Bigg) of that which is good (cf. 1 Cor 14:12; Titus 2:14). Others read "imitators" of that which is good (JND), or "imitators of the Good One" (JND marg). In either case, these ideas are not at variance. Those who would imitate Christ will be zealous of that which is good and, as good disciples, will be followers of Him.

14   The words, "But and if" present to the minds of the readers a possibility, though not a certainty. The particular mood (the optative) "denotes subjective possibility, without any reference to definite time" (Winer). It "envisages a contingency not immediately pressing" (Selwyn). "Having no certainty of fulfilment ... [it means] 'if perchance' " (*Linguistic Key to the NT*, Rienecker and Rogers).

The Holy Spirit, by Peter, carefully selects this mood to indicate that suffering may come later, if not now, and even if it should come, "happy are ye". This is just one word in its plural form, "happiness" or "blessedness". In this word we hear Peter echoing the words of the Master on the Mount of Beatitudes (Matt 5:10-12).

"Be not afraid of their terror" are words taken from the Septuagint of Isa 8:12,13, "neither fear ye their fear, nor be afraid". If suffering should come from the ungodly, face it with courage and not with fear, especially of what they fear, which may allude to the fear of death itself.

Fear breeds unrest and agitation. The believers, if brought into suffering, were not to be "agitated". "The wicked are like the troubled sea, when it cannot rest, whose waters cast up mire and dirt" (Isa 57:20). Agitation brings up the unsavoury dredgings of unbelief. The believer is to rest with quiet confidence in the Lord and let Him work out His purpose.

15 Instead of inordinate fear in the heart, sojourning saints are to "sanctify [the] Lord Jesus Christ" in their hearts (JND). To sanctify the Lord is to recognise His holiness and to set Him apart as the special object of love and loyalty. "To 'glorify' God means ... to recognise His glorious perfections; to 'magnify' Him means to recognise His greatness; to 'justify' Him means to recognise His inherent justice; so to 'sanctify' Him means to recognise, in word and deed, His full holiness, and therefore to treat Him with due awe" (A.J. Mason).

The place of this sanctified presence, for the christian, is" in your hearts". To Israel, God dwelt in the midst of His people corporately. To the NT believer, the Lord dwells in the hearts of His people corporeally.

With the conviction of the indwelling Christ, revered and set apart for love and loyalty, the believer is to be ready to "give an answer". The word here is *apologia*, "a verbal defence". It does not mean that every believer needs to be an apologist, schooled in all the doctrine for the defence of the faith. But every believer should be ready to declare in certain terms, the reason for his own hope and experience with the Lord Jesus Christ and to do it in a spirit of meekness and fear.

In the light of previous exhortations, this can hardly mean the fear of men, nor is it satisfactory to the context to think of the fear of God. Rather, it is that reverent caution and concern "lest through their personal infirmity or lack of restraint the truth of God be brought into disrepute" (D.E. Hiebert).

16 The idea of sheer goodness permeates this section: "good" (v.13); "righteousness" (v.14); "sanctify" (v.15); "good conscience" (v.16a); "good conversation" (v.16b). There cannot be a good conscience if there is something bad going on and things are not right with God. If the conscience is clear before God, it will give the manner of life in Christ a fragrant quality, and the testimony a rare power, that none can gainsay even though false charges be levelled against the child of God.

Contrariwise, "no skill of speech would do the work of the apologist rightly if his life was inconsistent with his profession" (E.H. Plumptre). The words may be right, but the smell will be wrong and even the ungodly will know it.

How important it is to have a good conscience. "A good conscience is free from self-condemnation" (L.S. Chafer). "Conscience in man reveals both the existence of God and, to some extent, the nature of God" (H.C. Thiessen).

"Conscience is the judgment I pronounce on firm, instinctive, and uninfluenced persuasion that such an act is right, such wrong". "A conscience defiled cannot be at its ease before God; and when God enters, there are dark corners that one hides from Him" (W. Kelly). A good conscience is the blessedness of the blessed man in Ps 32, where there is no distance from God, no distress in the night, no drought in the soul.

17   It is this good conscience that proves the accusations are false and that the suffering is not self-inflicted by our own evil-doing. If suffering comes by the scourge of the tongue unjustly applied, it is better than suffering by the law of retribution, where we reap only what we ourselves have sown. Even this is only "if the will of God should will it" (JND). All suffering is not because of our own sin or failure, as Job's sad comforters would claim. In the divine purpose there are deep waters to pass through, flooded rivers to traverse and fierce fires to endure. Having "created" us for His glory, we are "formed" in the flood and in the fire, until we are "made" according to His master design (see Isa 43:1-7). God has a purpose in all things, working them together to one chief end. The things He causes and the things He allows, by efficacious and by permissive decree, are ruled and overruled, all for the ultimate good of the saint and glory to Christ. That ultimate "good" is for the believer to be conformed to the image of His Son (Rom 8:28-29).

18   If the Lord is asking, through His servant Peter, that His people be willing to do good and suffer for it, He is only asking them to do, in their measure, what He Himself has fully experienced. In dark and lonely depths, He plunged to the "bottoms of the mountains" where none other could ever go. We often suffer because of the fact, or the act, of our own sin. When He, the impeccable Christ suffered, it was for the sins of others.

The relevance of what follows and how it fits into the general context of the epistle is important. If God's people, apparently "few", suffer now for righteousness' sake, they are not to be discouraged though the multitude of the wicked seem to win the day. God is sovereign and His government over all cannot be thwarted. His righteous judgment is determined and will be carried out, though in longsuffering patience with the wicked He stays His hand before exercising His strange work. The supreme evidence of this is seen in the solitary suffering of the Lord Jesus for our sins, His death, resurrection and ascension to glory on the seat of all power and authority.

Christ indeed suffered, but that profound suffering for sins was "once", not *pote* ("once upon a time"), but *hapax* (one time only), "once for all ... of perpetual validity not requiring repetition" (W.E. Vine). The great purpose of that suffering was for the unjust "that he might bring us to God". Adam and his sinful progeny were shut out from the presence of God because of sin. Christ suffered to deal with that alienation and "bring us to God". He Himself made a way into the holiest. That is wonderful. He Himself became the very way to God the Father. That is more wonderful. He Himself brings the pardoned sinner by that holy way, to God. That seems most wonderful.

"Various technical meanings have been found in, or read into *prosagō* ('to bring') ... As so often, the simplest interpretation is the most profound: Christ's atoning sacrifice brings us to God" (E.G. Selwyn).

"To God" implies so much more than direction or location. For the unrepentant, to be brought to God at the last and to stand before Him, will be a cause for terror. The Lord Jesus Christ, on the grounds of His finished work, brings the believer to the heart of God, to the house of God, and to stand accepted in the midst of the everlasting burnings of the holiness of God, and to feel at home there. Ultimately the believer will be brought to the heaven of God, but God is more than heaven and the Blesser is more than the blessing. So the christian is not called to the knowledge of heaven, inspiring though it be, but to the knowledge of the God to whom we have been brought. It is difficult in the face of such a revelation of love and grace, to refrain from a note of praise ...

> "Precious Saviour! Great Redeemer!
> Praise, eternal praise to Thee;
> Though so long a wandering sinner
> Thou has kindly welcomed me,
> Even me."
> E. Codner

The Lord Jesus was put to death in the flesh, "He was the victim of a judicial murder". Peter had charged the men of Israel with the death of Him, whom they had taken "and by wicked hands [had] crucified and slain" (Acts 2:23).

He was quickened, that is, made alive, by the Spirit. It is here that we enter an arena of controversy which spans the next few verses. Far greater men than we have differed on the interpretation of what follows. Nevertheless we must present it as we see it, giving the reasons for our convictions. The present readers must be like the noble Bereans, who searched the Scriptures to prove the accuracy of what they were being taught.

There is no difficulty in accepting that the Lord Jesus was put to death in the flesh, though some cults in their self-imposed ignorance even deny this. The testimony however is indisputable. The Roman soldiers marvelled at His death, the centurion in charge of the killing troop confirmed it, the Scriptures declare it and the Lord Jesus Himself affirmed it, "I ... was dead".

Various notions however, have arisen from interpretations concerning His being "quickened by the Spirit" (AV). There is no article in either case and we can read, "in flesh", and "in spirit". However, idiomatically, we supply it in normal usage, "in [the] flesh" and "in [the] Spirit". The problem with doing that in this case is, that "these would be the contrast of the two parts of our Lord's being as man, the outer and the inner" (W. Kelly). This would lead us to the error that it was the Lord's spirit that was made alive, and we know that His spirit never died, but was commended into the hands of the Father (Luke 23:46).

Technicalities of grammar are presented to support the idea that "the Greek is literally 'put to death in flesh, made alive in spirit'". The misconception that grows out of this is seen when we remember the words of the Lord in Luke 24:39, affirming that He was in a resurrected body of "flesh and bone", albeit a spiritual one. "If there is a natural body, there is also a spiritual one" (1 Cor 15:44 JND). William Kelly remarks, "The mere technicality of the schools is sure to err in interpreting Scripture".

The word "quickened" does not mean refreshed, or to remain alive, but made altogether alive from the dead. It is used that way in the NT (see Rom 4:17; 8:11; 1 Cor 15:22 and others). "Quickened" stands in opposition to "being put to death". What was put to death was our Lord's body. What was made alive was also that precious body (John 2:21). "It is impossible to apply 'quicken' to the spirit of Christ any more than to His divine nature" (W. Kelly).

It is germane to this section, that we grasp the implication of "in [the] Spirit". What spirit? Or is it Spirit?

It is suggested by some, that because the article is missing, then it cannot mean the Holy Spirit. It is true that the form of the word without the article points to the character of the acts rather than the person acting. However, it is clear that numerous Scriptures where the article is missing distinctly refer to the Holy Spirit "characterising the action rather than specifying the person. . .". William Kelly gives a list of over twenty of these references including John 3:5; 4:23-24; Rom 8: 1,4,9,13.

"In spirit" cannot mean Christ's human spirit, for "it is not by the human spirit that the body is raised" (F.W. Grant). Referring to the Holy Spirit, we read, "It is the Spirit which quickens" (John 6:63 JND). "He ... shall also quicken your mortal bodies by his Spirit that dwelleth in you" (Rom 8:11). "The Spirit of Christ" is one of the titles of the Holy Spirit, and not the divine Person of Christ (1:11).

19-20   Suffering will end for the believer. There is glory beyond this vale of tears. Christ our forerunner has already entered in. He once suffered, but was raised from the dead by the Holy Spirit. He ascended to heaven in that resurrected body, and is seated in transcendent glory. He is Lord of worlds and Sovereign of the skies, "angels and authorities and powers being made subject unto him" (v.22).

It was by that same Holy Spirit "He went and preached unto the spirits in prison". This difficult Scripture has been used to preach "a second chance" for some, or a universalism, where all at last will reach heaven, some directly, the rest through a kind of purgatory. We must endeavour to answer the questions, Who are these prisoners? and When did Christ preach to them, and where?

We have seen that it was the Holy Spirit that did the quickening work in the body of the Lord Jesus. Then it was "also" by the same spirit that Christ preached.

"The spirits which are in prison" (JND) are described for us as having been disobedient to the message preached and did not hearken to it in the long days of God's patience before the flood. Because of that disobedience and disbelief " the flood came, and took them all away" (Matt 24:39) and their spirits were imprisoned.

It is suggested by some, that when the Lord Jesus died, He went " in spirit" to the unseen world. There He preached to

1.   imprisoned spirits of men long dead, or

2.   to fallen angels, to proclaim His victory, or

3.   to OT saints, whom He released for heavenly realms.

First, we have seen that this cannot be by His human spirit, unless His human spirit could have died. It was by the Holy Spirit He was raised, "By which [Holy Spirit] also he went and preached . . ." It is by this very same Holy Spirit in this day of grace that the gospel is now preached. Wherever the blessed evangel is declared in the power of the Spirit, the Lord is there, for He said in His great commission, "lo, I am with you alway" (Matt 28:20).

This same preaching ministry of Christ is spoken of in Eph 2:16-18. After the cross and after the conquest of the enemy He "came and preached peace to you which were afar off, and to them that were nigh". He did not journey again to earth, but He preached it through His servants, by the power of the Holy Spirit. After the ascension of Christ to the right hand of God, the disciples " went forth, and preached every where, the Lord working with them..." (Mark 16:20).

We must be careful to note that the Scripture does not say that Christ went to the prison and preached to the spirits. Rather we understand it to mean, the Spirit of Christ in Noah, "a preacher of righteousness" (2 Pet 2:5) preached to the antediluvians. They heard this declaration of righteousness, but refused to obey ("believe", see JND marg). Swept away by the flood, their spirits are imprisoned waiting the final judgment.

Fallen angels were "cast ... down to hell, and delivered ... into chains of darkness, to be reserved unto judgment". There is no parenthetical relief taught in Scripture for these once privileged beings. The Lord is known in the legions of hell (Mark 1:24; Luke 8:28). He need not make any proclamation to these wicked beings, they will see Him at the judgment.

Demons are another kind; they are free to roam in the earth for the present, ever seeking a body to inhabit. Even the body of a fly (Beelzebub means lord of the flies, Matt 12:24) or of a pig (Mark 5:12) is better to them than the abyss (Luke 8:31).

It is noted by some that the word *pneuma* standing by itself always refers to a higher order than man and lower than God. Here, they point out, *pneuma* stands alone and therefore must mean some kind of fallen angels. Rotherham shows however that "This clausule is made emphatically prominent ... literally [it is] to the 'in-prison spirits', so *pneuma* does not stand alone here but is predicated".

The longsuffering patience of God with the wicked is seen in the withholding of judgment for 120 years "while the ark was a preparing". Infidels have mocked the record of the ark and the honesty of God. "There wasn't room enough for everyone to be saved by the ark", they claim. These foolish notions arise because of a failure to grasp the significance of the ark.

There are many popular misconceptions about Noah and the ark. The emphasis was not on the sailing of the ark, but the "preparing" of it. It sailed for a year and ten days, it was being prepared for 120 years. Every plank was a sermon, every hammer blow was a warning, and as the structure grew, so did the responsibility of the audience increase.

It was God's object lesson before their eyes, "Repent or perish". It was not built to save the people in the flood, but to save the world *from* the flood. It was not prepared to save the population of the world, but Noah and his family (Heb 11:7), after the world refused Noah's message. The ark is not a picture of Christ, but of salvation and security. The earth is the picture of Christ: the sin of others was on the earth, but there was no sin in it. That which, in itself, was without sin came under the waves and billows of the judgment of God. Noah and his family were saved "through" the waters of judgment.

21   Noah and his family passed "through water" (JND) and were saved. That water forever separated them from their old life in the old world. There was no way back. They were brought into a new life under new principles of rule. The ark "was brought to rest on Mount Ararat with its living freight, in a new world over which the bow without an arrow was spanned" (W. Lincoln). Their new beginning was marked first by offering to the Lord. They were saved through the water from the defilement of the world and its consequences. They were saved to walk in an entirely new life.

Baptism likewise is a figure; it figures death, burial and a resurrection that enables the obedient to walk in newness of life. It witnesses visibly to what has already taken place spiritually and judicially, the believer's identification with Christ in His death, burial and resurrection. The baptism of the cross was the reality. The baptism of the Holy Spirit is the result and the baptism of the believer in water is the representation.

This is not baptismal regeneration. That is error, attributing life-giving power to an ordinance which is first a figure of death. Baptismal water can only touch the skin not the sin. The Scripture clearly states, "Not a putting away of filth of flesh" (JND). "We cannot but be struck with the way in which the Spirit of God guards the subject, by stating that it is not the mere washing away of the filth of the flesh, as by water, 'but the answer of a good conscience toward God' " (C.H. Mackintosh).

The "answer" (*eperōtēma*), better translated "demand" or "appeal", of a good conscience is obedience. "Baptism is therefore the ground of an appeal by a good conscience against wrong doing" (W.E. Vine). The expectation is that "we also should walk in newness of life". The death, burial and resurrection represented by baptism are judicial and factual. The walk is practical, calling for daily obedience. The good conscience interrogates and appeals to the believer on the basis of the commitment expressed by his baptism.

22   The culmination of the suffering of Christ is, for Him, exaltation to glory. The inestimable comfort of this fact to believers in every age cannot be measured. Satanic powers may attack, earthly governments may oppress, the wicked may terrorise and the populace may mock the goodness of the saints and malign their character, but there is One who sits in session at the right hand of God, Jesus Christ, who is their risen Lord and Saviour. He is in control, causing, permitting, moving and ordering all things according to the eternal purpose, and none can stay His hand.

f. As Witnesses in the Conflict (4:1-6)

> v.1   "Forasmuch then as Christ hath suffered for us in the flesh, arm yourselves likewise with the same mind: for he that hath suffered in the flesh hath ceased from sin;
> v.2   That he no longer should live the rest of time in the flesh to the lusts of men, but to the will of God.
> v.3   For the time past of life may suffice us to have wrought the will of the Gentiles, when we walked in lasciviousness, lusts, excess of wine, revellings, banquetings, and abominable idolatries:
> v.4   Wherein they think it strange that ye run not with *them* to the same excess of riot, speaking evil of *you*:
> v.5   Who shall give account to him that is ready to judge the quick and the dead.
> v.6   For for this cause was the gospel preached also to them that are dead, that they might be judged according to men in the flesh, but live according to God in the spirit."

1   The call to arms anticipates a conflict. There is attack which comes from without, by opposition and false accusation. A subtle and much more dangerous one is that which arises from within; that is the evil subterfuge that finds a field of operation in the flesh of the believer (Rom 7:23). Against this, the only safeguard is to be "armed" with the mind of Christ. The cognate noun *hoplon* is used, in the plural, for actual weapons in John 18:3

The "mind" (*ennoia*) signifies "primarily a thinking ... [and] denotes purpose" (W.E. Vine). It is translated "intents" in Heb 4:12. It is the thought, clothed with the intent or resolve. In the context, arming oneself with the mind of Christ is the intent, if suffering for righteousness' sake, to endure it submissively and with patience, recognising God's sovereign purpose will prevail. The mind of Christ is "the temper of patient submission and unwavering trust in the wisdom and love of the Father" (E.H. Plumptre).

Thus the Lord Jesus, "who for the joy that was set before him endured the cross, despising the shame, and is set down at the right hand of the throne of God" (Heb 12:2).

Job suffered; Joseph suffered; Jonah suffered, and vast is the army of the afflicted, but none ever suffered as did Christ. "Christ hath suffered" are words to exhaust the expositor and confound the commentator. We read them in faith and wonder in silence, because we discover it was "for us". Yet the emphasis here is not on the efficacious value of His suffering, to save from the penalty of sin; it is on the exemplary virtue of that suffering in its practical power against sin in the daily life.

"To yield to sin, to go along with the world, is *not* to suffer. It is the resistance to this pressure that entails the suffering, and that ensures the freedom, practically, from the sin. This is most important, in a day of laxity and worldly conformity like the present" (F.W. Grant). Christ suffered for us to the point of death, even death on a cross. By that death He went beyond the reach and realm of sin's dominion (though it never could rule over Him).

Having conceived this the believer with resolve applies the cross daily and walks in newness of life. This is the daily, practical application of the baptism previously referred to and the secret of victory over sin, its claim and its clutches. It is not sinless perfection but "an escape from the dominion and slavery of sin" (P. Patterson). It does not mean that we never sin, but that we *need* not sin.

One day that separation (from sin) will be literal and eternal. The believer will be delivered from the body of this death and transported to glory. For the present time it is judicial and practical, not physical death yet, but that death when we were crucified with Christ (Rom 6:6). If we do sin, "it is our own will that is active to His dishonour" (W. Kelly).

2   While spiritual gifts and opportunities vary, there is one commodity that all possess equally every day, even the ungodly. That is time. It walks hand in hand with life itself and every heartbeat reminds us that "Time ... happeneth to them all". If wasted it can never be recovered, but is as water spilled on the ground which cannot be gathered up again. The first readers of this epistle were reminded, as individuals, that the immediate purpose of Christ's suffering and their following on was not to stop with "resting" from sin (*pauō*, "to take one's rest.... to refrain from", W.E. Vine), but positively and actively to "live ... to the will of God".

3   The Gentile nations were well represented in that part of the world. The deviation and perversion of heathendom worked its way into every level of the social structure. Peter includes himself with them to talk about their "past" (though some manuscripts omit "us"). There is a memory of the past that can only discourage. Some things are to be put out of the mind. "Forgetting those things", said Paul (Phil 3:13). But there is a recalling that, though most humbling, has a salutary effect in the present, making God's will most desirable. On occasion, it is good to "look ... to the hole of the pit whence [we] are digged" (Isa 51:1). The challenge of Peter is the relative value of time. He has pointed to "the rest of [our future] time", now he looks back to the time past, spent perpetrating the will of heathendom. There is an irony here: "Surely that is enough time, more than enough, to give to the world and its perverted will". This rebellious will was manifest in certain moral perversions. A list of six evils is given as representative. Perhaps these were, as Lenski suggests, pagan practices associated with the idolatrous worship of heathen gods. In any case they fall into two classes, impurity and intemperance.

The ungodly walk in that way. Willingly, and even eagerly, they plod their downward course to the hypnotic beat of a diabolical drummer. Paul reminded the Ephesians that the walk of the unbeliever is "according to the ruler of the authority of the air, the spirit who now works in the sons of disobedience" (Eph 2:2 JND). It is the devil that calls the cadence for that solemn downward march.

Apart from the debauchery of the wild excesses listed, the prodigality of squandering irrecoverable time in godless pursuit is most solemn indeed. Peter says, That's enough.

4 It is a matter of wonderment to the ungodly when they see a life transformed by the grace of God. The licentious, bound by habits they cannot break, inflamed by lusts they cannot extinguish, gravitated downwards by a power they cannot by themselves resist, are astonished at the complete change in the lives of those believers whose whole aim in life is now "the will of God".

> "But the master comes, and the foolish crowd
>   Never can quite understand
> The worth of the soul and the change that's wrought
>   By the touch of the Master's hand."
>
>   M.B. Welch

The pace of the perverse ever quickens as they pursue their wicked ways. First they "walk" then they "run" and "run together" (*suntrechō*) like a flock of shepherdless sheep in "the euphoric stampede of pleasure-seekers" (W. Kelly). What is the irresistible bait, the impelling attraction? J.N. Darby translates "excess of riot" as "sink of corruption". Into this cesspool, the effluence of the hearts of the wicked have been poured; hardly a health spa for the child of God.

Lies and calumny are Satan's stock in trade. So it is not surprising that his followers deal in the same coin. When their amazement at transformed lives subsides, then by "speaking evil" they seek to defame and slander the christians for the very prodigality they themselves pursue. Such is the hypocrisy of the human heart. This is a strong word translated "speaking evil". It is that from which we derive "blasphemy" when directed against God; when against men, it is to "defame someone, to injure the reputation of someone. .." (Bagster).

5 There is an accounting to be given. The believer, eternally alive in Christ, will give account of his stewardship at the judgment seat, where his words and works will be assessed. Sin as to its retribution will not be considered at all; its penal consequence has been fully dealt with at the cross. The believer's sin, as to its results however, will be evident to those who suffer loss of reward (1 Cor 3:13-15; 2 Cor 5:10). His faithfulness in respect of stewardship will be rewarded, and "then shall every man have praise of God". In the meantime Peter has already challenged his readers with the same word in 3:15. There it is to be ready, here and now, to give an "answer", an account, to everyone who asks a reason of the hope within.

The wicked dead will stand before the judge at the great white throne (Rev 20:12). To give "account" (*logos*) is to do so by word of mouth. The Lord Jesus warned the Pharisees they would give "account" this way in the day of judgment (Matt 12:36). It would appear however that every voice will at last be "stopped", "gagged" (Rom 3:19). "The word is akin to *phragmos*, "a fence" W.E. Vine). Struck dumb before a holy God, without advocate, without attorney, without argument, without an excuse, it will truly be, for the wicked dead, "Silence in the court!"

The Judge is "ready", that is, He holds Himself in readiness, fully prepared. The day is appointed, the judge is appointed (Acts 17:31), the place is appointed (Rev 20:11). The evidence is already entered in the record (Rev 20:12), and the six-fold principles by which the judgment will be carried out have already been set down (Rom 2:2,6,9,11,12,16). This judgment will embrace all, those who have already died and those still in the body when the judgment call goes forth.

6 Because of the awfulness and certainty of judgment, God in love for His sinful creature sent His message of salvation, "the gospel", to "them that are [now] dead". "The first object of the gospel ministry is the conversion of sinners; for this end was it preached to the generations now literally dead" (W. Patron, *The Cottage Bible* 1856).

In their lifetime, the gospel, called in Rev 14:6 "the everlasting gospel", was proclaimed. Those who responded by faith, suffered at the hands of men. Though judged "according to men in the flesh", perhaps some even put to death for their faith, they now and forever "live according to God in the spirit".

By this affirmation, Peter comforts those scattered sojourners and all who, because of their faith in Christ, suffer. They suffer in respect to sin, as dead to it and separated from it. They suffer the slander and persecution of the ungodly. They pass under the gavel of unrighteous judgment of men. However, that judgment of men will fail and pass away, it will be despised and forgotten. They can rejoice that they have been made alive eternally, to live according to God in the spirit and to pursue His holy will. While they as stewards must give account and receive reward, they will never stand with the wicked dead at the great white throne to receive the penal consequences of their sin.

g. As Watchers (vv.7-11)

v.7   "But the end of all things is at hand: be ye therefore sober, and watch unto prayer.

v.8   And above all things have fervent charity among yourselves: for charity shall cover the multitude of sins.

v.9   Use hospitality one to another without grudging.

v.10 As every man hath received the gift, *even so* minister the same one to another, as good stewards of the manifold grace of God.

v.11 If any man speak, *let him speak* as the oracles of God; if any man minister, *let him do it* as of the ability which God giveth: that God in all things may be glorified through Jesus Christ, to whom be praise and dominion for ever and ever. Amen."

7   God said to Noah, "The end of all flesh is come before me"; here He says, "the end of all things is at hand". Final judgments will never again destroy "all flesh" (mankind). It is "all things" associated with this realm of fleshly pursuit that will be destroyed. The words of v.7 will have profound significance for the remnant living after the Church is raptured. Those will be living "as in the days that were before the flood", waiting for the coming of the Son of man. Since the end of a thing is better than the beginning, we should seek again to emulate the mind of Christ who always had the end in view.

"At hand" is not a chronological expression so much as locative. It is the divine perspective. After all, eternity for us is not as poets dream, in some "Beautiful Isle of Somewhere". It is only one breath or one heartbeat away. So in a special sense this is true for all of us and "therefore" we are to live in the light of it. The believer does this by being "sober" (see 1:13). The word is used to describe the demoniac of Gadara after the Lord delivered him (Mark 5:15). He was unrestrained by authority: no man could bind him. He was unrestrained by moral values: he was naked. He was under an alien influence: dwelling among the dead. Delivered, he sat " in his right mind". "The word connotes a cool head and a balanced mind to exercise self-control..." (Rieneker & Rogers).

Again there is almost an echo of the words of the Lord in Matt 24 with its watchword, "Watch therefore" (v.42). To be awake when we should be resting in sleep is most unwise. To be asleep when we should be awake is most dangerous. This cry also went out from Paul, "Awake thou that sleepest". Did Peter remember his own experience in Gethsemane? On that sad night when, as far as the Lord's earthly sojourn was concerned, the end was at hand, and Peter slept while the Saviour agonised in prayer. Was he recalling those words full of pathos, "What, could ye not watch with me one hour? Watch and pray..." (Matt 26:40-41)?.

The watchfulness enjoined is not a staying awake for fear of the enemy, but with a view to "prayers" (plural), demanding not generalisations but constancy in praying. It is more than praying for good things from the Father, though we do that. Specifically in the context, these are prayers for the consummation of the divine purpose. The last prayer in the Bible is "Even so, come, Lord Jesus". But, we remonstrate, if He is going to come anyway, why pray for this? Well, it is the will of God, and thus we are to pray. Further, God has decreed to work cooperatively with His people in answer to their prayers, in bringing about great matters respecting the Jew (Ps 122:6; Matt 24:20), the Gentile (Luke 10:2) and the Church (Rev 22:20). Thus His people are called to be workers together with Him in the carrying out of His lofty purposes. This lifts prayer into the realm of most sacred privilege.

8   Priority is important, so Peter tells us there is something to do "before all things" (JND), that is to have a fervent, intense love for one another. *Agapē* is the characteristic love of christians. The word "fervent" (*ektenēs*, from *ek*, out; *teino*, to stretch) shows the christian is to extend his love to the other christians, indeed stretching it out to reach all. It is a word of strenuous action, as an athlete stretches himself out to the limit to gain the prize. This love is to be seen in covering a "multitude of sins". This is an application of Prov 10:12. The covering is not winking at sin, hushing it up, or condoning it in the presence of God. There we intercede and advocate on behalf of one another, honestly facing the reality of failure in one another. The believers are not to drag each other's failings out and expose them before all. "As hatred makes the worst of everything, love is entitled to bury things out of sight" (W. Kelly).

9   Hospitality is one of the ways we can practically show love one to the other. When the heart is open, the home is open, open not only to the christians well known to us, but to strangers who arrive among us. This is literally the meaning of the word "hospitality" (*philoxenia* from *philos*, loving, and *xenos*, a stranger, W.E. Vine).

This love is to be shown readily and generously, not with muttering under the breath, grumbling and complaining about the inconvenience or expense of having these people to our homes. Anyone who has travelled, especially in another country, knows the joy and relief of a christian welcome in the home. For the visitor it is rest and refreshment; for the hosts, enrichment for themselves and for their children in enlarging their circle of friends and deriving benefit from the experience of those entertained, perhaps even "angels unawares" (Heb 13:2).

10   Every believer has received at least one spiritual gift. These are given sovereignly by God and the Holy Spirit for the help and edifying of others (1 Cor 12:7-11). The Holy Spirit may be quenched by the disuse of gift, the discouraging of gift in another, or the misuse of gift.

Gift is misused if it is exercised for self-promotion, personal aggrandisement, or financial enrichment. The possession of spiritual gift is no cause for praise to the individual, only honour to Christ. It is by the interplay of the variety of gift, exercised for the benefit of one another and the whole company at large, "every joint supplieth", that there is spiritual increase and loving development (Eph 4:16).

Spiritual gift and natural talent must not be confused. Only a believer can have a spiritual gift but the ungodly as well as believers may have natural talents. These, such as art, music, eloquence, are expressed by the soul and the body while spiritual gifts flow from the spirit. It may well be however, that spiritual gifts are given in harmony with some natural talents (cf. Matt 25:15). In the spiritual believer, all natural talents are in any case yielded to the lordly control of Christ and would never be used to detract or distract the people of God away from the Lord, His Word or His purpose.

Each believer is a steward, having been given a responsibility to discharge and an account to be rendered. Together, the Lord's people are stewards of the multifarious grace of God. Therefore we are to discharge that obligation by the exercise of spiritual gift upon one another and the display of that grace towards one another. Every believer must give account at the Bema as to how faithfully this stewardship has been held in trust.

On the palette of grace there is every colour, shade, tint and hue. These can be blended under any circumstance and applied to the canvas of any individual life or situation. "Manifold" is "many-coloured" and is used only one other time by Peter, that when referring to the trials of the saints (see 1:6).

11   The love and faithful stewardship of the saints towards one another is to be expressed in a two-fold way: by public ministry and by personal service. The speaking ministry may be by "any man" so gifted by God. There is no scriptural warrant whatever for a clergy and laity system in the Church, under whatever guise or name it may appear, overtly or covertly. Some may be gifted especially as teachers, others as evangelists. Within those areas some may be especially gifted to exhort, to comfort, to edify. Then it is in the area of their gift they would be expected to serve.

Those who stand to speak have a most solemn responsibility. They are not to be involved in the mere handling of words, ideas or opinions. Rather, they are to speak "as the oracles of God". The word for oracle is *logion*, "a diminutive of *logos*, a word, narrative, statement, denotes a divine response or utterance" (W.E. Vine). The *logia* refers to Scripture in Rom 3:2. "The teacher or preacher is not to be the purveyor of his own notions, but the transmitter of the utterances of God; the minister [of the Word] must not be setting forth his own competence or importance, but regard himself as acting from resources which God supplies" (E.G. Selwyn).

Most ministries however are not public ones. Not all believers are called to a preaching ministry, but all are called to be "ministers", servants of others. Many acts of loving service are carried on, out of sight of any audience. Paul teaches that it is the hidden members of the body that are more vital to the health, though perhaps not so attractive in appearance (1 Cor 12:23-25). These ministries of that love, spoken of previously, are to be done "as of the ability which God giveth", that is, not halfheartedly, but using the special abilities and resources of strength and supply that God has given to perform deeds of loving service for others.

The motive and express purpose behind it all is "that God in all things may be glorified through Jesus Christ". Not only have these servants of others been saved and set apart for holy living, delivered from the mad rush to the fleshpots of sin, but they pursue the will of God by showing grace to others with a forgiving spirit and a servant's attitude, to the glory of God through Jesus Christ. When we glorify God, of course we do not add any glory to Him. We "magnify, extol, praise ... [by] ascribing honour to Him" (W.E. Vine). We do this by obedient, loving, serving lives in the spirit of the Lord Jesus Christ.

This section concludes on an ascending note of praise in a doxology: "Jesus Christ, whose is the glory and the dominion for ever and ever. Amen" (RV). Since the Lord Jesus Christ is the foundation, the focal point and the fulfilment of the spiritual house, everything that is accomplished for God in it, by it, for it and through it glorifies God. Gladly then do those who, as living stones, form that house, once lost in wicked ways, now enlivened, called, and fitted for holy and royal service, join in ascribing to Him the radiance of glory and the right to reign.

Peter, and no doubt his readers, then and now respond to such thoughts of worthy praise to Christ with their heartfelt "Amen!" This is the expression of the strong assurance of their hearts and this is right.

3.   *Exhortations in the Light of Our Sufferings*
   4:12-5:7

v.12 "Beloved, think it not strange concerning the fiery trial which is to try you, as though some strange thing happened unto you:

v.13 But rejoice, inasmuch as ye are partakers of Christ's sufferings; that, when his glory shall be revealed, ye may be glad also with exceeding joy.

v.14 If ye be reproached for the name of Christ, happy; for the spirit of glory and of God resteth upon you: on their part he is evil spoken of, but on your part he is glorified.

v.15 But let none of you suffer as a murderer, or a thief, or an evildoer, or as a busybody in other men's matters.

v.16 Yet if *any man suffer* as a Christian, let him not be ashamed; but let him glorify God on this behalf.

v.17 For the time *is come* that judgment must begin at the house of God: and if *it* first *begin* at us, what shall the end *be* of them that obey not the gospel of God?

v.18 And if the righteous scarcely be saved, where shall the ungodly and the sinner appear?

v.19 Wherefore let them that suffer according to the will of God commit the keeping of their souls *to him* in well doing, as unto a faithful Creator.

5 v.1 The elders which are among you I exhort, who am also an elder, and a witness of the sufferings of Christ, and also a partaker of the glory that shall be revealed:

v.2 Feed the flock of God which is among you, taking the oversight *thereof*, not by constraint, but willingly; not for filthy lucre, but of a ready mind;

v.3 Neither as being lords over *God's* heritage, but being ensamples to the flock.

> v.4 And when the chief Shepherd shall appear, ye shall receive a crown of glory that fadeth not away.
> v.5 Likewise, ye younger, submit yourselves unto the elder. Yea, all *of you* be subject one to another, and be clothed with humility: for God resisteth the proud, and giveth grace to the humble.
> v.6 Humble yourselves therefore under the mighty hand of God, that he may exalt you in due time:
> v.7 Casting all your care upon him; for he careth for you."

a. To Steadfastness (vv.12-14)

12   Peter assures his readers of their place in his heart, and his deep feelings for them in their trial. He is following the Master's command to shepherd the sheep. More than that, they are in the heart of the Lord as the "Beloved". Circumstances may present a different sense, for in fiery trials it is the enemy who suggests to our trembling spirit, "curse God, and die"! However we are assured that "having loved his own which were in the world, he loved them unto the end" (John 13:1). The fiery trial was not of man's burning. Man's conflagrations are indiscriminate, burning everything. God's fire is selective. In the burning fiery furnace of Daniel's day the flame selected only the bonds of the three young men so that not even a hair of their head was singed while it slew the guards. The fiery trial like that furnace may be ignited by man, but it is controlled by God.

"Fiery" trial describes the fiercest and often the most frightening form of testing. A forest fire runs out of control and is so destructive and hurtful. Perhaps a better rendering for this fire however would be "trial by fire", as in the refining of precious metals. The fire is not for destruction of the precious but for purifying and proving. That kind of fire is most carefully controlled as to both time and temperature. The tested metal is constantly scrutinised in the fire by the refiner and the prover so that it does not burn too hot, nor last too long (see 1:7). This was not a warning of future fire, but of a present trial already ignited. It was "the fire [of persecution) which has taken place amongst you for [your] trial" (JND).

Having been assured of their beloved place in the heart of the Lord, the next thing that would help them in the trial was to have right thinking. There was a danger that the sufferers thought that what they were going through just "happened" to them, an accident of circumstance. They were not to think this experience "strange" or "alien" to the life they had chosen in Christ. It was in fact to "prove" them, to test their faith and prove its reality. When they suffered thus they were not to "be amazed".

How easy for some, who use His name, to believe the false preachers who declare that since Christ is on the throne and all things are in His hand, they should have the best in this world, of health and wealth and place and praise. A follower of that error would surely think it strange if trials came. The refiner need not test stone or clay. It is the gold he puts in the fire, only the dross will burn. That which is pure is indestructible.

13   The safe alternative to amazement is rejoicing. It is easy to quote these words when there is no fire near, but can we rejoice when the fire is breaking out among us? How can the believer do this practically? We are to recognise that when believers suffer in this way, they are "partakers of Christ's sufferings"; not of course of His atoning sufferings, He must bear those alone. To "partake" (*koinōneō*) is to have something in common, and thus to be a companion. It is not a matter of degree, but of kind. When a christian suffers in the trial, it is of the same kind as Christ, but His suffering was infinitely so. When we suffer pain, it is the same experience, though never to the same extent.

We may suffer a pain of severe physical intensity. He could cry by the mouth of the psalmist, "the pains of hell gat hold upon me" (Ps 116:3). If then our single pain so distresses us, what, we may think, were all the pains He endured, from beneath, from around and from above? Thus even by contrast we come to know something of "the fellowship of his sufferings" (Phil 3:10). "Faith realises that the ground for rejoicing does not lie in the sufferings themselves but in the fellowship with Christ that they bring" (D.E. Hiebert).

His sufferings He endured, but now we read that "his glory shall be revealed". The revelation of His glory lies ahead. He is now glorified, but it is not yet unveiled. The hope of the believer is reflected in his present joy in the trial. This joy is *chairō*, the usual word for joy. The joy to come at the revelation is *agalliaomai*, to exult with rapturous joy. The present joy is a shaft of light penetrating the darkness of the trial, pointing our hearts upward to where Christ sits in glory, knowing that we who believe will bask in the blaze of His radiant countenance. Even in the trial the saint can sing a song in the night;

> "Faint not, Christian! Christ is near;
> Soon in glory He'll appear;
> Then shall end thy toil and strife,
> Death be swallowed up in life."

> James H. Evans

14   Right thoughts and a proper attitude mingled with hope of glory can sustain the believer in the trial. But what about those who stand by and watch the sufferer? There must be a witness to others.

There will be reproach for the name of Christ. To "reproach" is to scold, to rebuke, to censure. It is not that we cause that reproach ourselves, but it is for (or "in") His name. If that be so, then "blessed" (RV) is the word from God. That is not the thinking of the world. To them blessedness is freedom from trial, but the believer knows the benediction of God in times of reproach. "To suffer reproach for Christ's sake is not a misfortune to be resented in self-pity but a privilege for which to thank God and to congratulate oneself" (A.M. Stibbs).

That blessing is not just a subjective joy, but a visible radiance in the life brought about by the work of the Holy Spirit, "the spirit of glory and of God". In 2 Cor 3:18 we see how that radiance comes as the believer is occupied with the glory of the Lord and is transfigured "by the Lord, the Spirit" (JND). While it may not be as visible as it was on Stephen's face (Acts 6:15), yet it is often discernible, though not describable, upon the lives of those who have suffered for His name.

The last phrase does not appear in some manuscripts. JND shows it only in brackets as provided by the translator and the RV omits it. Nevertheless it is true that if the ungodly blaspheme the Lord, His people delight to glorify Him.

b. To Worthiness (vv.15-16)

15   This verse likely contains a reference to the false charges laid against his readers. To suffer for the name of Christ was honourable but they were to be free of the violations listed here and all such: murder; theft; evildoing, a general term for any kind of criminality. "Busybody" is an unusual word, occurring only here in the NT, which means literally, "one who oversees another's belongings" or a "meddler". It describes someone who pokes his nose into other people's business, usually because he is critical of the other's person, practice or possession. W. Kelly suggests that the meddling could be even an unwise and "excessive zeal for making converts" among other intrusions into family or business life. Selwyn also suggests "tactless attempts to convert neighbours".

16   It is sad that the world has taken hold of this ascription of believers in Christ and loosely appended it to all manner of persons and things. "The disciples were called christians first in Antioch" (Acts 11:26). They did not at first call themselves that, rather " the brethren" or "the saints". " As applied by Gentiles there was no doubt an implication of scorn ... From the second century onward the term was accepted by believers as a title of honour" (W.E. Vine). It signified a follower of Christ. To suffer as a christian was in Christlike character, with submission and grace and blessing.

If suffering in this name and not for moral failure, then the christian need not ever be ashamed, but glorify God "in this name" (JND) also.

c. To Trustfulness (vv.17-19)

17-18   Great privilege brings great responsibility. In the past this is seen among the angels. For one sin of rebellion they were cast out of heaven into cells of darkness to await judgment. For one sin Adam and Eve were driven out of Eden. The rebellious sons of Aaron for one sin were struck dead. In the NT, Ananias and Sapphira were instantly judged for one sin. Teachers, by virtue of having more light (and influence), come under a heavier principle of judgment (Jas 3:1). Many cases there are where higher privilege brought heavier responsibility (cf. Isa 10: 12; Ezek 9:6; Amos 3:2).

In the AV there is a solemn twofold question in the light of this translation. If judgment first begin at the house of God, "what shall the end be of them that obey not the gospel of God? And if the righteous scarcely [with difficulty] be saved, where shall the ungodly and the sinner appear?" Where indeed? There! at the great white throne with its terrifying conclusion (Rev 20:11-15).

It seems however, while the foregoing is still true, that we may read of the judgment beginning "from" (*apo*) the house of God (JND, W. Kelly and others). The penal consequences of the people of God have been expiated at the cross, so their judgment is not in the sense of condemnation. It is disciplinary, corrective, purgative and instructive. God is holy and He cannot sit by and watch the slow deterioration of a believer or an assembly into worldliness and sin without intervening to save them from moral ruin and loss (1 Cor 11:27-32; Rev 2:4-5).

This judgment as sons will continue till the Church is caught up at the rapture. Then will be, for the christian, the judgment as servants when all accounts must be handed in.

19   "Wherefore" summarises Peter's exhortations to this point. In the light of all that has been considered, those who suffer according to the will of God, by an act of faith are to "commit" (*paratithēmi*) their souls. This is the word used, when it is said of the Lord that He " commended " His spirit to the Father, also of commending disciples and elders to God. It "denotes to place with someone, entrust" (W.E. Vine). This is not death in view for the believer here, but as they continue living lives of goodness amidst evil and opposition, they are continually to trust themselves, the whole being, to God as a faithful Creator.

This commitment recognises that the One we are to trust is the One who created us to begin with. Therefore He understands all the intricacies of our being spiritually, physically, emotionally, psychologically. He knows our chemical composition and our genetic structure. He knows our inherent weaknesses and inborn traits. To this One who knows us through and through and loves us in spite of all, we can safely trust the keeping of our souls.

With adoring wonder at such a God of wisdom love and power, we marvel that He should care for our poor souls and keep us safe to glory. Well may the trusting heart sing:

> "Kept by His power, whatever dangers lower,
>   The strength of God's almighty arm
> Doth shield my soul from every harm,
>   Kept by His power."
>   William Blane

d. To Faithfulness (5:1-4)

1-2 In the local church, plurality of elders, in gift and government, is a safeguard from various dangers. When this divine principle for church government is abandoned, or modified, the flock is thrown into disorder and danger. It was to the "elders" (plural), not "elder" or "bishop" the exhortation was given.

Plurality preserves against error. The test of ministry by godly discernment is taught in 1 Cor 14:29, "Let the prophets speak two or three, and let the other judge". A body of elders seeking the mind and will of God together is less likely to fall into error, or allow it, than if one man should rule and make his own judgments.

Plurality preserves from unbalanced ministry. It is unscriptural to think that all the gifts can reside in one man. It is the variety of gift that provides the well balanced diet of spiritual food required for the health and development of all the flock of God, lambs and sheep.

Plurality preserves from giving undue place or glory to a man. Christendom seeks to honour its leaders with special titles, ranks, and even robes, to mark them out as distinct from the common people (*laos*, the laity). This divides an equal brotherhood into different ranks, which thing the Lord hates (Rev 2:6,15). Religious man has devised these ecclesiastical echelons and invested in them prerogatives that are not theirs to possess. The forgiveness of sins, ordination to special ministries, consecration of persons and places, presiding over the "communion" service, even excommunication and other dispensations are deemed as the sacred preserve of a special caste of religious leaders. These are most solemn prerogatives indeed to be invested in humanly-appointed leaders, especially when their rank, title and position are quite without warrant from Scripture.

Plurality of leadership preserves from the danger of human domination. Diotrephes (3 John 9-10) was a man who loved that place of preeminence. There is no charge of doctrinal error, of moral failure, lack of zeal, gift or industry levelled against him. His error was perverted love. He loved "to have the preeminence". There is an unholy danger to the fellowship, and indeed to the man, when he "loves to be first". There is only One in the Church who can say "I am the first" (Rev 1:17).

Plurality of leadership preserves from disintegration in times of persecution. Oppressive powers seek first to remove or destroy the leaders of any system that opposes their program. Where God's people have gathered around one man and depend on him for their spiritual food and direction, suddenly when that man is gone, like a flock without a shepherd, the sheep wander and scatter. Where the gathering is to Christ and the honour of His name, and the sheep are nurtured and cared for by a body of godly elders, persecution but draws them together.

The Lord in His wisdom has shown that He is in the midst of His people who are gathered in His name (Matt 18:20). The Holy Spirit guides and no man should dare assume the office of president over the church. The government and care of the flock is delegated to a body of elders who will give an account of this stewardship in a coming day (Heb 13:17).

Peter takes his place among the elders as a fellowelder. He did not take a position as a prelate above them, having a special office. He was highly privileged in that he had walked with the Lord and heard His holy teachings. He was "a witness of the sufferings of Christ" and had seen the glory of the Lord on the holy mount. Because of these sacred associations with the Master he might have "pulled rank" over the others had he been a carnal man. Instead in humility he stands beside those elders and claims simply "who am also an elder".

He would never forget either the suffering or the glory he had seen. "A witness" refers not only to what he had observed as an "eyewitness"; that "great sight" had inspired him, in the spirit of his beloved Master, to sacrifice also. "Witness" is *martus*, one who tells what he had seen, heard or knows, or " those who witness for Christ by their death" (W.E. Vine). It was a prophetic designation, for Peter would indeed witness for Christ by his death as a martyr.

Suffering and glory for the followers of Christ are inseparable, as for Christ Himself (Luke 24:26). So Peter, having learned this, anticipates as a "partaker" the "glory that shall be revealed".

Elders: As "elders", those whom Peter addressed were charged with guiding the flock. While some weight of years is in this word, it carries also the meaning of " maturity of spiritual experience" (W.E. Vine). While it ought so to be, it is a disturbing fact that not all who are older are necessarily wiser. It is good for a local church however to be blessed with older men of God, men of experience with God, having learned much in the school of God.

Shepherds: While the actual word "shepherd" is not in the text, the work of the shepherd is clear. These men were in fact under-shepherds with a responsibility to "feed the flock of God". Their ministry was a *giving* one.

The character of God's people as a flock is found in both the Old and New Testaments. David presents it in the Psalms (Ps 23; 79; 100). Isaiah speaks of it (Isa 40:11). Ezekiel refers to it (Ezek 44). John alludes to it in Rev 7:17. Paul uses it in addressing the elders from Ephesus (Acts 20:28-29). The Lord Jesus uses it in John 10 and of Peter himself in ch.21. No doubt Peter would never forget that conversation with the Lord Jesus after the resurrection when he was commissioned to shepherd the sheep and the lambs, feeding them with suitable nourishment.

The shepherds, spiritual leaders, of Israel in the days of Ezekiel (Ezek 34:1-4,8b-10) had a solemn five-fold indictment levelled against them: they fleeced the flock for their own comfort (v.3); they fed not the flock because of laziness (v.8); they fed on the flock (v.10); they failed to guard the flock (v.8); they felt no responsibility to care for the flock (v.4). In a word it was loveless neglect they showed. The Lord had charged Peter to shepherd the flock, both sheep and lambs. Now he was committing to faithful men the same charge.

"Flock" is a singular noun, which bespeaks its unity in spite of diversity. All ecumenical movements designed for the unifying of the Church are spurious even if well-meaning. The Church is already as much one as God can make it in Christ, even though the visible evidence of this is not always apparent. The under-shepherds are viewed as sitting "among" the sheep, hearing every bleat, sensing every danger. They were not to be absent from their post, but abiding where the need was.

Overseers: Again, this word is not specifically used, but it is present by implication. Peter counsels the elders about "taking the oversight" (*episkopos*). Overseers take the oversight. This is the ministry of guarding the flock, watching over them to protect. This ministry was to be wholehearted and willing and "not by constraint". Such a work was not to be the result of pressure or the lust for profit. Instead, it was entered into with a deep sense of the honour and privilege. Money ("base gain" JND) for spiritual service was never to be the motive for that service. Love of gain is unworthy of the servant of the Lord Jesus Christ and must have no part in the ministry of elders.

3   The Lord's people are seen here to be a "heritage" unto God. The sovereign choice of God in selecting and making those believers to be overseers assures their great value in His sight. The elders are cautioned not to lord it over God's heritage; it is most precious to Him. Those leaders were to be "ensamples" to the flock. "Ensamples" or "types" may reflect something of the typology of the OT. Types were visible representations, with a spiritual significance.

When God desired to reveal Himself to His people Israel, yonder in the desert, He called Moses up to meet Him in the mount. God knew the pattern "in the heavens" and He showed that pattern to Moses. Then He told Moses to go down and build a replica of that on the desert sands. While it was not given to the people to understand such a revelation in all its wonder, they could walk up to the replica Moses built, touch and handle it, and by this learn of God.

That is the picture in the word *tupos* as it relates to the elder, the spiritual leader. Leadership is not an ability to arrange meetings, set up programs, organise committees. Leadership is being "in the lead" spiritually. It is walking ahead of God's people in the kind of life that inspires others to follow. They may not be able to grasp the great doctrines outlined in the epistles that relate to the christian life, but they can watch the life being lived out by the elders. They can walk up to one of these men of God and touch that life and draw lessons from him as an example.

4   All is not suffering, sorrow and pain. "The morning cometh" for all believers in Christ. Specifically here in the context, the elders are in view. They will behold the Lord as the Chief Shepherd and those under-shepherds who have cared for the flock of God all through the desert way will receive reward.

The Lord Jesus is the Good Shepherd giving His life for the sheep (John 10:11). He is the Great Shepherd imparting His life to the sheep (Heb 13:20). He is seen here as the Chief Shepherd rewarding the life of the sheep.

There will be the honour of being identified with the Chief Shepherd as under-shepherds. There was even then the certainty of reward. It "shall" be given them. Here is a bright incentive to continuing on, even when the way is hard and seems uphill. There will be a crown of unfading glory. The very radiance of the Lord as the Chief Shepherd will be upon the faithful undershepherds in glory, so that all will see and recognise one of that noble band who cared for the flock of God on earth, pouring out his life for them in toil and tears.

What marvellous grace of God! First He creates us; then He saves the believing soul; then He imparts spiritual gifts; then He opens the way for spiritual service; then He gives the power to serve and the occasions to do so; then when that life of utter dependence on earth is over, He rewards His children as though they had done it all. No wonder they love to sing: "Hallelujah! What a Saviour!"

e. To Lowliness (vv.5-7)

5   Submission is not the strong point in most lives. It must be however if we are to follow the Lord wholly. Peter addresses the younger: they are to submit to the elder and those of advancing years. Possibly the younger are selected because of the natural tendency to bound ahead. If the wills are in agreement there is no need for submission. Only where there is a difference does one need to submit.

Clothing however is often very important. God has provided a garment that fits all sizes, the garment of humility. The word translated "garment" is an unusual one, describing a garment that was tied on around the outer garments, an apron. Was Peter recalling the upper room where the Lord and Master girded Himself with a [servant's] towel and stooped to wash Peter's feet?

The injunction "be clothed" demands a submissive obedience, the younger to the elder and each to the other. The reason is given: "God resisteth the proud, and giveth grace to the humble". If we try to humble someone we usually end up humiliating them also. God gives grace to the humble without humiliating them (cf. Prov 3:34).

What a place to be! Under the mighty hand of God. Yet that implies intimacy, protection, power available and sovereign rights upon our lives.

6   Suffering for His sake here means glory there. That is one of the rules of the kingdom. Subjection is followed by exaltation. This has been shown previously in the epistle regarding the Lord Jesus. That humbling under the mighty hand of God will be seen in all our personal submission to others down here. Here again is an inspiration to the first readers of this letter and all through the ages. Suffering is not waste.

7   The way of peace in a time of humbling and submission is to "cast" our care upon Him. The casting is to do spiritually what the disciples did literally when they brought the colt for the Lord to ride on, they "cast their garments upon the colt". Though this is easier said than done at times, it is the way of peace. Those disciples laid hold of the garments, threw them on the animal and *let them go*.

We can have confidence to do this, "for he careth for you". Our cares ("anxieties") are a burden we would be glad to be rid of. But His care of us is a delight to Him.

4. *Exhortations in the Light of Our Dangers* 5:8-9

v.8 "Be sober, be vigilant; because your adversary the devil, as a roaring lion, walketh about, seeking whom he may devour:
v.9 Whom resist stedfast in the faith, knowing that the same afflictions are accomplished in your brethren that are in the world."

8-9 An "adversary" (*antidikos*) is one who opposes in a legal sense, the antithesis of "advocate" (*parakletos*), one who speaks on behalf of. Here our cruel enemy is seen as one who opposes the people of God in His presence. That right has not yet been stripped from him. It will be one day when he and his hosts are cast down to earth. In the meantime he attacks the brethren. The sad thing is that while he falsely accuses the saints there are times when we provide him, by our sin and failure, with the ammunition by which he assails the throne of God.

"The devil" is the word used to translate the Hebrew word "Satan" in the LXX. It means "slanderer", "a malicious enemy who makes accusations and presses false charges" (AM Stibbs), "the sower of suspicion" (R.O.P. Taylor).

We are no match for this mighty enemy in our own strength. In the picture of the lion we learn that our enemy is cruel, powerful and merciless on the hunt Some foolishly and frivolously at times try to "rebuke" the devil. That is dangerous business; nowhere are we authorised to do so. Even Michael the archangel dared not bring a railing accusation against him, but said, "The Lord rebuke thee".

He roars to strike fear into the hearts of God's people. He "walketh about" in ceaseless agitated activity like a pacing lion. He seeks everywhere whom he may devour with his voracity.

He is pictured in Scripture as a serpent, defiling with the poison of sin; as a lion, devouring with the power of sin; as a wolf distressing with the cruelty of sin. His most frightening aspect may well be, however, as an angel of light, deceiving with the pleasures of sin.

The believer is exhorted to three courses of action:

Firstly, "Be sober". This is to have clear thoughts about the issues at stake and of the enemy not far away. No fuzzy thinking about eternal matters will do. Ignorance is the devil's playground.

Secondly, "be vigilant", wide awake to the dangers and the way of escape. Spiritual sloth and sleepiness is an invitation to attack. Paul cried out, "Awake, thou that sleepest".

Thirdly, "resist steadfast in the faith". It is only in the realm of faith we can resist our powerful foe. If we try to resist him in the energy of the flesh and carnal courage, he will gain a victory over us.

In the fire of fierce attack we are apt to feel like Elijah, "I, even I only, am left". But in all believers at some time or other the same afflictions are performed.

It is not possible for a believer to be demon-possessed, since there is a realm of the spirit where the indwelling Holy Spirit resides. However it is possible for the believer to be demon oppressed. Paul admonishes the Ephesians: "Neither give place (room, opportunity) to the devil" (Eph 4:27). Any area of the believer's life which is not under the control of the Holy Spirit is a target for the enemy. That is why there can be a very fine christian with, say, a very bad temper. That is an area not under the control of the Lord the Spirit.

The man of Gadara was possessed by a legion of demons. A legion is not just a "lot". A legion in the Roman army was a highly trained and specialised force of different ranks, authorities and skills, all disciplined to destroy its opposition. Such an enemy must be guarded against most carefully.

IV. The Apostolic desire (5:10)

> v.10 "But the God of all grace, who hath called us unto his eternal glory by Christ Jesus, after that ye have suffered a while, make you perfect, stablish, strengthen, settle *you*.

10 The basis of Peter's desire for his readers is seen in the lovely title Peter uses now as he draws the epistle to a close, "the God of all grace". What a delightful closing note for those scattered sojourners. They were in the midst of severe trial. There was a cruel enemy snarling at their heels and seeking to shatter their peace with his persecution. Holy and royal priests they were, learning subjection in suffering. But they had a Saviour who has "passed through death and gloriously confounded every foe". He is now seated in the place of sovereign power, angels and authorities and powers being made subject unto Him. Suffering and testing and trials there must be, but their God is "the God of all grace". "All grace" is suggestive of its munificence; however much they will need. "All grace" also insists upon its multivarious spectrum, whatever kind they will ever need.

This God has called His people by the everlasting gospel "unto his eternal glory", that is to the state of glory, the realm of glory. There they will bask in the radiance of "the glory of God in the face of Jesus Christ".

In the time that remains, we must not be surprised when trials come and there is suffering for "a while". Yet in and by that suffering the same God who began the work in us will perfect it, bring it to completion, establish us firmly and provide the strength needed for conflict, suffering and service of the highest kind, and thoroughly ground us on the only sure foundation stone, elect and precious.

V. The Apostolic Doxology (5:11)

v.11 "To him *be* glory and dominion for ever and ever. Amen."

God will not share His glory with another and as Peter concludes his letter with this brief doxology, having contemplated the greatness of His Person, he ascribes to this God of all grace, glory and might for the ages of ages and adds a resounding Amen! Every child of God can add his own Amen!

VI. The Conclusion (5:12-14)

v.12 "By Silvanus, a faithful brother unto you, as I suppose, I have written briefly, exhorting, and testifying that this is the true grace of God wherein ye stand.
v.13 The *church that is* at Babylon, elected together with *you,* saluteth you; and *so doth* Marcus my son.
v.14 Greet ye one another with a kiss of charity. Peace *be* with you all that are in Christ Jesus. Amen.

12   "It is commonly accepted that the 'faithful brother' is to be identified with Silas in the Acts story (cf. 2 Cor 1:19). Peter takes up the pen to conclude the letter and commends Sylvanus for his faithfulness.

The purpose of the epistle as previously noted was to minister to the souls of scattered christians in danger. He cannot close without once more mentioning what was such a constant comfort and encouragement to him, " the true grace of God wherein ye stand".

13   "She that is elected with [you] in Babylon" (JND) some have interpreted as Rome, but there is only conjecture for that. "There is not the slightest hint that Peter was ever at Rome before this, and from the late date of this epistle it is most unlikely that he was ever there afterwards" (F.W. Grant). "Marcus my son" would seem to indicate the presence of John Mark, who had a very special relationship with Peter.

14   A holy brotherly kiss, as was the custom, ever the token of love and affection, would be a fitting symbol between saints as they have listened to this letter so full of comfort, encouragement and wonder at the mighty works of God in Christ Jesus, through the eternal Spirit.

He is loathe to wipe his pen as he thinks of a suitable benediction, "Peace".

Paul usually concluded his letters with "grace". Peter uses "peace". There is no peace to the wicked, said God. What a marvellous possession, more than gold or silver, to have that peace because numbered among that sanctified throng " in Christ Jesus".

Peter adds his last "Amen!" (the RV and JND omit it) and we too say our "Amen!" as we have dipped a very small vessel into a very great river, deep and wide, to draw forth but a taste of the sweet water of the Word.

2 PETER

G. P. Waugh

SECOND PETER
Introduction

1. **General Remarks**
2. **Canonicity**
3. **Authorship**
4. **The Recipients**
5. **Natural Divisions of the letter**
6. **Detailed Analysis**
7. **Bibliography**

1. General Remarks

No one can read this letter without sensing the deep stirrings of the writer's own emotions. His awareness on the one hand of pragmatic pseudo-teachers intent on causing as much damage as possible, and on the other of the vulnerability of saints becomes increasingly evident as we pursue our reading of the three chapters.

Perhaps the diligence (1:5,10) called for by him reflects just where he himself had failed, so we can appreciate the great need for strenuous effort on our part to improve the quality of our personal faith; to hold tenaciously to the Scriptures, and only the Scriptures.

2. Canonicity

The validity, accuracy, and authorship of the epistles are striking, and yet of all the writings in the NT none has had such battles for recognition as this little epistle. It was the final letter to be given a place within the canon of Holy Scripture. Only after protracted debates and discussions was it accepted and in AD 360 the Council of Laodicea approved it and gave it canonicity. Other councils of the fourth century concurred with this decision although in subsequent centuries questions of canonicity and authorship were resurrected.

Reading through early or late relevant history on these two issues can be intellectually interesting. We shall find that well-meaning and able scholars of past and present generations have been, and still are, divided on authorship but most now accept canonicity.

3. Authorship

External evidence is difficult to find to prove that Peter wrote the epistle if we confine our search to the first four centuries AD, but evidence from the epistle itself is illuminating.

1. In v.1 the double name Symeon Peter is a good marker. Symeon was his family and Hebrew name; when James, the chairman at the famous Jerusalem Council (Acts 15), spoke of Peter's helpful contribution, he referred to him by his family name Symeon. It was our Lord Jesus who was responsible for giving Symeon another name which was later used, Cephas or its Greek equivalent *Petros*. This additional name bespeaks a change Peter experienced. He was Symeon the son of Jonas by natural birth, but Peter by divine calling. The use of both names in v.1 clearly identifies this writer and relates him to his Jewish and Gentile friends.

2. The author's use of certain words, e.g. "decease" (1:13,14) is another link with Peter's experience when he journeyed with the Lord before the cross. This special word used in the conversation at the Transfiguration vividly pictures the soul and spirit departing from the body.

3. The detailed and accurate report of the Transfiguration was the account of an eyewitness. Peter was present and 1:16-18 cannot be disregarded as powerful evidence.

4. The method of using OT incidents and personalities is very similar in style to Peter's oral ministry in Acts 2-10, and to his writing in his first epistle.

5. In 3:1 he refers to a first epistle which most scholars accept as 1 Peter, although some think that he may be referring to 2 Peter 1. That as a writer he claims to have produced an earlier document may help us to the conclusion that Symeon Peter, the slave and apostle, is the well known and well loved disciple of the Lord Jesus.

6. Even though the subjects dealt with in each epistle are different, e.g. in the second epistle he makes no reference to the passion or the resurrection, no mention of the Holy Spirit or the House of God, yet he maintains the affectionate expression "beloved" which he uses to describe the saints who received both letters.

7. The reference to our beloved brother Paul and his writings must strengthen the claim that a sympathetic contemporary acquaintance produced this epistle. The Symeon Peter of the Gospels and the Acts must naturally be accepted as the author.

4. The Recipients

Within the epistle there is no mention of any particular individual, group or local church, nor of any geographical area as in 1 Pet 1:1, to whom this letter is addressed. However, there are interesting statements made about the recipients:

1:1	"to them that have obtained like precious faith with us";
1:10	described as "brethren", called and chosen;
1:12	already had been subject to, and appreciated, the truth now being put into permanent record;
2:1	they were afflicted by false teachers;
3:1,8,14,17	they were the "beloved".

These references combine to suggest that the epistle has general application to all the Lord's people irrespective of culture or nationality, and would be useful not only for the first generation christian but for the people of God in all subsequent generations.

5. Natural Divisions of the Letter

The chapter divisions we find in our AV have been well chosen. Each chapter forms a main paragraph of the epistle.

Chapter 1
In ch.1 Peter largely assumes the role of an able scribe of the Kingdom. He serves the King as a good secretary and conveys a preparatory message for the subjects of the Kingdom. What better subject to have in this opening chapter, and who better equipped than an eyewitness to make a report of the majestic glory of the Sovereign.

Chapter 2
Having made mention of cunningly devised myths, now he proceeds in ch.2 to uncover those whom he describes as false teachers. The descriptive language is strong and totally condemnatory of them and their work. His recommendation to use the OT books as truthful illustrations of the nefarious intentions of pseudo-teachers is an indication of the considerable influence of scriptural knowledge upon the penman.
Perhaps in ch.2 we have Peter as the appointed shepherd guiding and guarding the flock, as he travels down the well-trodden historical trail of OT reminders to warn us of lurking and unprincipled enemies.
He unashamedly marks down fables and worthless tales, and with amazing skill he exposes the wolves, lions and bears. The claws they use are damnable and destructive heresies (v.1), their conversation is wickedly filthy (v.7), the

content of their message is evil (v.10), and they constantly bring railing accusations (v.11). These all stand in contrast to the upbuilding doctrine as in ch.1. The need for diligence and a strengthened faith becomes most necessary in order to withstand the repeated onslaughts of the evil one and his emissaries. The promises of a faithful God are great and precious and, when tenaciously held, enable the saint to grow despite the evil intentions of false teachers.

In the resurrection scene reported in John 21, Peter is singled out for the special task of feeding the flock (lambs included), and this he is enabled to do in person and in teaching. He describes himself in 1 Pet 5:1 as an elder, and in encouraging fellow-elders, helpfully draws attention to the coming Lord Jesus as the Chief Shepherd, i.e. chief among the shepherds, Peter being numbered with them. This epistle is the product of the ministry of a true shepherd who engages the enemy and guards the little flock.

The shepherd is aware of the vulnerability of the flock, and he therefore steps forward to combat their enemy. True shepherds have been required in every generation and in every assembly or community of saints; more so today. Today we have a proliferation of false teachers who secretly (using means difficult to discover) lure, snatch and make easy prey of the unwary. Peter therefore uses history to identify and expose the present-day mocker or scoffer. Peter is not a hired shepherd; he is ready to fight and suffer. History had taught him lessons-never again would he deny the Lord who bought him-so he cites the pitfalls and the traps the enemy has and continues to use.

Chapter 3

This final paragraph is the one chapter which spells out in a few verses the calendar of God, taking us from the beginning of creation through to the age of all the ages-the day of God. He wishes to leave us with the conclusion that God is faithful to every great and precious promise. No one, including evil workers or false teachers, can either help or hinder the actual, perfect and detailed, fulfilment of all God has predicted, promised or prophesied. It is in this final paragraph that he directly confronts these mockers, takes them through history and on to prophecy as if it too was a history. He is not baffled nor embarrassed by their question, but rather he uses their question as a platform and, with the Holy Spirit helping him, he teaches (without "maybe" or "perhaps") truth about the promise and the coming of the Lord. Now as a seer or a prophet with extraordinary treasures he brings out both old and new to confirm faith and exhort the saints to greater endeavour whilst silencing the scoffer.

We find that the Peter who received the keys of the Kingdom (Matt 16:19), with authority opens the door to allow us to see the on-going purpose of God, which ultimately will end when God's justice or righteousness forever dwells in the land of fadeless day. His doctrine is in accord with Paul's writings and doctrine, and his concluding remarks are compatible with the advice and counsel given by him throughout this short epistle. He writes as a man of God who knows he has not long to live, and he no doubt has been guided to present the epistle as a last will and testament.

6. Detailed Analysis

I.	*Faithful Teachers Strengthen Faith*	1:1-21
	1. Salutation	1:1-2
	2. Power and Promises	1:3-4
	3. Faith and Fruitfulness	1:5-9
	4. Diligence or Negligence	1:10-14
	5. Fables or Facts	1:15-18
	6. The Dawn and the Daystar	1:19-21
II.	*False Teachers Speak Evil of Truth*	2:1-22
	1. Way of False Teachers	2:1-3
	2. Walk of False Teachers	2:4-9
	3. Wages of False Teachers	2:10-16
	4. Words of False Teachers	2:17-22
III.	*Truth will Gain the Victory*	3:1-18
	1. Value of Scripture	3:1-2
	2. Vanity of Scoffers	3:3-4
	3. Validity of History	3:5-7
	4. Verity of Scripture	3:8-9
	5. Vision of Ages	3:10-13
	6. Virtue of Diligence	3:14-18

7. Bibliography

Brown, Colin (Editor). *Dictionary of New Testament Theology*. Zondervan. 1986.

Jones, M.R. *Cambridge Greek Testament-2nd Peter and Jude*.

Kelly, J.H.D. *Commentary on the Epistles of Peter and Jude*. Baker, Grand Rapids. 1981.

Lenski, R.C.H. *The Interpretation of I and II Epistles of Peter*. Augsburg, Minneapolis. 1938.

Lloyd-Jones, D.M. *Expository Sermons on 2nd Peter*. Banner of Truth. 1972.

MacDonald, William. *Cornerstone Commentaries*. Walterick.

McNab, A. *New Bible Commentary*.

Robertson, A.T. *Vol. VI, Word Pictures in N.T.* Broadman, Nashville, Tennessee, USA. 1931.

Scott, Thomas and Symington, William. *The New Testament of our Lord and Saviour.*

Selwyn, E.G. *1st Epistle of Peter*. Baker, Grand Rapids. 1981.

Text and Exposition

1. Faithful Teachers Strengthen Faith (1:1-21)

1. *Salutation*
1:1-2

> v.1 "Simon Peter, a servant and an apostle of Jesus Christ, to them that have obtained like precious faith with us through the righteousness of God and our Saviour Jesus Christ:
> v.2 Grace and peace be multiplied unto you through the knowledge of God, and of Jesus our Lord,"

1-2 Firstly we note that this introduction is not a copy of 1 Pet 1:1-2, and would therefore demand a thorough investigation of each statement made. We note that there are at least six main items of interest as follows:

1. Dual name of the author.

2. Dual office of the author.

3. Two parties described.

4. Double blessing conferred.

5. Dual role of the Lord.

6. Two important datives-in righteousness, in knowledge.

Each item assumes importance and as we read through this little epistle we can appreciate the wisdom of the author in giving his letter such an instructive introduction.

1. *Dual Name of the Author*

Symeon is of Semitic, whilst Peter is of Greek, origin. Another name is used in other NT writings to describe the author, Cephas, which was of the Aramaic language and is the equivalent of the Greek Petros, or Peter in English. John or Jonas his father gave him the name Symeon at his natural birth and it would be used by other members of his family and friends. Peter, or Cephas, was added by the Lord at their first meeting by the sea of Galilee (John 1); at their second meeting He gave him another occupation. The Jewish fraternity would address him as Symeon as James did in Acts 15:14, whereas in Gentile company he would be called Peter or Cephas.

The reason for the additional name given by the Lord may not have been apparent when it was given but as the years passed it became evident that this man of considerable influence could exercise a uniting ministry. His message, like his name, would appeal alike to Jewish and Gentile christians. Peter would ultimately show the rocklike characteristics of a foundation member laying down basic principles of christian doctrine.

Symeon or Simon was a common name and to help identify him the practical way was to give him an additional name as was the experience of others with the same first name, such as Simon Magus, Simon the tanner, Simon the leper, Simon just and devout, Simon the Pharisee, Simon the zealot, Simeon the father of Judas, etc.

2. Dual Office of the Author

Peter describes himself as a servant and as an apostle. As a servant (*doulos*) he is a bondman and this relates him to a master; in this relationship Peter is under the sole and absolute authority of Jesus Christ. Whilst apostleship was conferred by the Lord, servitude was taken by Peter. Bondservice or slavery was a well established institution in both the Jewish and Gentile manner of life so that those who received this letter would immediately appreciate that the author did not originate the letter, nor would he dare to add to or subtract from its message. The slave in his obedience to, and respect for, his master would address himself with pleasure to every task given to him, and no task would be too menial and no assignment too difficult. As the slave he valued the price paid to purchase him and, to the best of his endeavours, he would promptly obey every wish. In respect to his master he would work to gain approval irrespective of personal cost.

His apostleship bespeaks the authority of a commissioned officer. This is a letter where the writer shows himself to be a responsible servant acting on behalf of the Sovereign whom he serves. The early days of training and disciplining after his selection become invaluable to him: the days when he made mistakes and had them personally corrected by the Lord; the days when he shone above others and the Lord rewarded him with the keys of authority and, on another occasion, put into his care the precious flock that belonged to his Lord.

As an apostle he had the authority of the supreme court of heaven behind him and the resurrected Lord had indicated that in two spheres, heaven and earth, all power was His, so Peter the apostle could and was expected to preach to all kinds of men in every place. Peter was remembered among "the twelve", especially selected and singularly honoured.

As a slave he would work and as an apostle he would direct and supervise work and workers.

3. *Two Parties Described*

The "us" and "them" indicates that there were two groups. The first group would include at least Peter and his companions, or Peter and the other apostles, or Peter and all the Jewish christians. However extensive one may make this group is not so important since when he speaks of "us" and "them" he gives them equality of privilege and position in the faith. The privileges of v.3 and the promises of v.4 which belong to "us" have become also the possessions of "them". The second group, the recipients of the letter, are referred to in very broad statements, the totality of which indicates that there are no class distinctions among God's people.

This second group, like the first, had known of Paul and his writings; now Peter, like Paul, gives no support to elitism having superior claims, but insists that all the people of God today have been elevated to an equal and unique standing in Christ. All human differences are removed in a realm where saints of whatever background are one in Christ Jesus.

In v.1 they had obtained like precious faith in the righteousness of God. They had neither earned nor worked for this faith; then we ask, How did they get it? The verb used by Peter is interesting and reminds us of earlier statements made by him. In Acts 11:17 he stated that God gave to them the same gift; he was definitely speaking of how God had given to the Gentiles. He was not describing how much or how little God gave, but rather the fact. It was this statement of Peter that removed the objections of the other apostles and brethren, and caused them to praise God that God had granted even the Gentiles repentance unto life.

"To obtain" carries the idea of having by lot; the emphasis is on its having been made available beyond the realm of dispute, its being open for possessing. Their experience was like that of Ruth the deprived Moabitess (Ruth 2:2,3) "and her *hap* was to light on a part of the field belonging unto Boaz". She was treated in grace which was already available for Naomi the needy Jewess!

Now this equality of faith, blessing, and privilege, became a problem later to Peter and his colleagues and was fully discussed at the special meeting held in Jerusalem attended by, among others, Paul, Barnabas, Titus, James and Peter. The outcome reached is found in Acts 15:6-29, and Peter, featuring with James, Barnabas and Paul in the discussion, drew attention to the fact that there is no distinction now between Jew and Gentile, and in v.9 Peter asserts that there is no difference between us and them. The council agreed on the equality of privilege and position of the Gentiles with the Jews. Moreover, in Acts 15:11 Peter asserts his conviction that salvation for both parties is through the grace of the Lord Jesus Christ, i.e. salvation is from the same source and comes in the same way and is unto equal blessings.

4. *Double Blessing Conferred*

The double blessing "grace and peace be multiplied" appears often in the salutations of NT epistles and becomes a formal greeting. This, however, should not allow us to lose the freshness or relevance of the truth expressed. Whether we think of grace as God's favour or grace as Peter's disposition and wish for the recipients becomes a matter we must judge for ourselves. If we accept the grace and peace to be primarily God's gifts then there is before us a large inheritance to explore and enjoy. It may be of course the sincere wish of the author, in which case it reveals to us the deep emotions that have only the good of God's people at heart. This is a repeat of 1 Pet 1:2, later adopted as a Rabbinical greeting. It has often been pointed out that the Jewish *shalom* and the Gentile *charis* have been used by NT authors to extend their love to all the churches of the Lord's people.

5. *Dual Role of the Lord Jesus*

The author does not set about proving the absolute deity or the genuine humanity of the Lord Jesus. He simply makes statements of fundamental value: "God and our Saviour Jesus Christ" (v.1); "God and of Jesus our Lord" (v.2).

In v.1 we have the single definite article before "our God and Saviour"; it governs both nouns, telling us of one Person and emphasising a characteristic uniquely His-God our Saviour. Peter is here indicating that Jesus is God our Saviour who always acts in righteousness and is scrupulously fair and just.

The title Saviour is prominent in Paul's last epistles, appearing ten times in the pastoral letters as against only four times in his other ten epistles. It seems that with maturity in christian experience this title becomes more precious. It was a title coveted as a title of honour in the Hellenistic world and of course taken by the Caesars of Rome. Here Peter describes the Jesus he knew in the daily round of everyday life of Galilee, Judaea, and Jerusalem as the "God our Saviour". He is affirming the absolute deity of Jesus, like Thomas who said, "My Lord and my God" (John 20:28) or Paul in Titus 2:13 and of course Heb 1:8 asserts "Thy throne, O God, is for ever and ever". Coupled with "God our Saviour" we have His human name, Jesus, and the office to which He was anointed, Christ. The other four occasions this title is used always refer to the Lord Jesus:

1. He is Lord, Saviour and King, 1:11

2. He is the only Lord and He is the only Saviour, 2:20

3. He superintends the work of the prophets and the apostles, 3:2

4. There is the challenge for us to grow up in the knowledge of our Lord and Saviour, 3:18.

In v.2 his genuine humanity expressed in the human name, Jesus, is coupled with God, and to the name Jesus he adds the title Lord, claiming Him as "our Lord"-his and theirs. Peter guards against familiarity of expression in addressing either God or Jesus our Lord. Never in his epistles would he address Jesus by His human name only, yet who would be closer to Him? There is always a need to have dignity of language when speaking of our Lord or speaking to Him in prayer. In 2:1 this title Lord refers to a despot as in 1 Pet 2: 18. The title emphasises the authority and sovereignty of the Lord Jesus.

6. *Two Important Datives-In Righteousness, In Knowledge*

In v.1 the reception, or obtaining, of like costly faith is said to be in, or through, the righteousness of our Saviour God. We could think profitably of this equal but costly faith as being the result of the exercise of our faith. This would make the righteousness a blessing received from God because of our faith, which would accord with Paul's doctrinal statement of Rom 3:22. On the other hand is not Peter looking at righteousness rather as the basis and not as a blessing of faith? The fact is that God has proved Himself (not that He needed to) absolutely righteous in the method used of blessing Jew and Gentile equally.

It is not only that by grace we are saved through faith (Eph 2) but also that God, in a scrupulously fair and just manner, has elected Jew and Gentile to equal privileges, both having the same precious faith.

Righteousness then is the standard by which equal gift is conferred. No one will be able rightly to accuse God of favouritism for His justice is inviolable; He is beyond suspicion. The righteous judge who returned a verdict of no difference in the guilt of Jew and Gentile (Rom 3:23) is the same Judge who with the same standard has effected the position of equal blessing.

Faith and righteousness are always linked together. God's dealings began from a righteous basis and have continued in such; they will conclude as they began-in righteousness. "Like precious" is a political word describing persons of equal standing, sharing equal rights and in the same relationship to the king or to the state, which leads some to interpret faith here not as the body of truth, but as the principle which brings a person into God's favour. It is the capacity to trust, and is available to Jew, Gentile, slave or apostle. "Like precious faith" is not only common to all but available to all men.

There are others who interpret this faith as a position granted by the edicts of a righteous ruler, a position which every citizen shares equally; each having similar status in matters affecting his freedom within the state.

There are still others who suggest that this faith is the body of truth which has been handed down, committed and entrusted once for all to the saints, originally of course from God Himself. The emphasis on heretical teaching found later in the epistle appeals to those who lean toward this traditional view of the faith. The participle "have been granted" or "obtained by lot" lends support to the idea that the doctrine is not only precious but is the same in content and privilege for Jew and Greek.

If faith is taken as the body of truth, then Jude's comment in the sister epistle to 2 Peter and his use of the word faith "once delivered unto the saints" would strengthen this interpretation. Faith as trust or belief is not handed down, it is not mine by natural birth, but the body of doctrine is committed from one generation of faithful men to the next generation. This of course demands loyalty and accuracy in the transmission of it.

If we relate 2 Peter to 1 Peter then we shall enjoy the objective idea of faith; but if we relate 2 Peter to Jude, then we will accept rather the subjective idea that faith is a deposit to be held and transmitted intact to the next generation of faithful men. Not only can both interpretations be sustained, but better still, both can be enjoyed.

"The knowledge of him who hath called us" is the basis of our call and the bedrock of our faith. The knowledge of Him is essential for the blessing of eternal life (John 17:3) and the expression is used by Peter again in vv.3,8 and 2:20. Apart from Heb 10:26 it occurs only in the later epistles of Paul. Knowledge was "in word" of false teachers and as exploited by them should lead to liberty for all kinds of misbehaviour. Peter would indicate that true knowledge of God and Jesus Christ leads to holiness of life and he positively denounces unworthy practices. The surest safeguard for a successful christian life is to know God and our Saviour Jesus Christ deeply. This "knowledge" (*epignōsis*) is defined by Lightfoot as a larger and more thorough knowledge. Many manuscripts read "in knowledge of our Lord" and probably are correct, fitting the singular "his" of v.3 and being in harmony with the fact that on the other occasions in the epistle it refers to our Lord Jesus Christ.

The call is the way Peter describes how God brought us out to Himself. In 1 Pet 1:15 the nature of the Person who called is emphasised: He is holy. Our call is a challenge to become different in lifestyle from the ungodly around us. In 2:9 our call is out of the darkness of ignorance and guilt and we are expected to live beaming forth the virtues of Christ. He makes further reference in 2:21; 3:9 and 5:10. He hath called us by, or in, glory and virtue: glory to God; virtue to fellowmen as shown by our Saviour. The attractiveness of Christ is the glory and virtue by which He wins the hearts of sinners and holds the hearts of saints.

Peter is not alone in mentioning the glory of Christ. In John 1:14 "we beheld his glory" unique and beautiful. His own glory and excellence bring to us the real impact of His Person. Peter will refer to His glory as witnessed by him when probably at Mount Hermon Jesus was transfigured before them. *Doxē* (glory) and *aretē* (virtue) are found together in Isa 4:8,12 LXX. Peter now sees them both in his Lord. Peter uses this word "call" seven times, but here as an introduction to the treasure-house of His promises, to bring to us the staggering truth that we are partakers of the divine nature. We share His glory and excellence. It may not be apparent yet, and we may not enjoy it as a present experience, but it is true. The glory and excellence can be shared, what an inheritance, what a princely possession-sharer of the divine nature! The traits and characteristic features of Christ Himself can be expressed in each one of us. The life of piety manifested in Christ is now found in us. I am not only a forgiven sinner, but a transformed man or woman. I am a new creation capable of revealing the divine characteristics; that is my real calling. We leave the corruption of this world for the unfading but revealed glory and excellence of God. The visible expressions that we have shared in the divine nature are the evident departure from the corrupting lust of the age, and our attachment to Christ, to live Christ and to die to self and sinful lusts.

2. Power and Promises
1:3-4

v.3 "According as his divine power hath given unto us all things that pertain unto life and godliness, through the knowledge of him that hath called us to glory and virtue:

v.4 Whereby are given unto us exceeding great and precious promises: that by these ye might be partakers of the divine nature, having escaped the corruption that is in the world through lust.

3   What is striking for the scholar is that there is no main verb in this sentence, and so we must either connect it with v.2 and read vv.2 and 3 with an implied verb, "seeing that His divine power" enforcing the fact that grace and peace will be multiplied to them; or, if we reject this suggestion, then we must render the text as follows: "seeing that His divine power has given them ... we must give all diligence", to the end of v.5. Both ideas are tenable and since the early manuscripts are devoid of punctuation, both can be enjoyed. Peter now embarks on opening out the treasures which are possessed by all saints. There are eight features mentioned:

1.	Source	Divine Power
2.	Supply	Has bestowed on us lavishly
3.	Sufficiency	Everything
4.	Special and Spiritual Sustenance	Life and godliness
5.	Simplicity	Through knowledge of Him
6.	Security	His own glory and excellence
7.	Salvation	Called us, having escaped the corruption which is in the world
8.	Sharers	In divine nature.

The saint can never experience a power failure.

The expression " divine power", found nowhere else in the NT, indicates the special treatment from a liberal source to meet every need of every saint. The power is divine in origin and character. Any human weakness is taken care of by His divine power.

The nature of God is revealed not only in the fact of bestowing by His power (v.3) but by what is given, "everything" (v.3) and "great and precious promises" (v.4). God is a giving God, and has enlisted everything to be at our disposal. What an inventory.

The "us" of v.3 must now include all the saints for whom everything is from God without reserve. The life given is sustained in freshness and godliness of character; it is possible and pleasurable to experience.

The way life is sustained and the produce of godliness is very practical; it is "through the knowledge of him". The knowledge we already have is that He called us to be holy, to show forth His virtues, to follow His steps to blessing and ultimately to eternal glory. The One, who calls, enables by supplying our every need. Positively, we participate in the divine nature; negatively, we escape the corruption that is in the world by lust. Noah and Lot escaped the corruption as we shall find in 2:5,7. Both had not only miraculous escapes but they had every provision to sustain life and godliness.

The promises of God never fail, despite the excessive number of them. What He promises, He fulfils. He is faithful that promised (2 Tim 2:13). The promises are rightly described by Peter firstly as great; secondly as precious; and thirdly as a heritage for those who are called (cf. Heb 9:15).

They are "great" because of their *source*: He that called. They are "great" because they satisfy: pardon is full and complete; free from the world's judgment and its corruption. They are "great" because they *separate* me from the state of sin and make me a new creature in Christ. Many other reasons could be added that would justify Peter's appreciation of them as great.

They are also "precious". This is a special word to indicate they were costly to bestow. We get them simply for faith, but they were costly to God. They become "precious" to us-they cannot be found except in Christ. They are rare, and the soul is encouraged to feast on them. The lust and corrupting sin in the world can hold no appeal to those who enjoy and make them their very own: these great and precious promises are all given gratuitously to us, but all paid for by God. These great and precious promises are included in the "everything" that originates and sustains life and godliness. The ultimate of the exceeding great and precious promise must be the blessed hope of the appearing of the great God our Saviour. Then the last bit of corruption that could possibly affect us shall put on incorruptibility; then this body of humiliation shall be eternally changed. Our escape or emancipation will be absolute. We shall be perfect and perfectly suited absolutely for companionship with God.

> "Meet companion then for Jesus,
> From Him, for Him made;
> Glory of God's grace for ever
> There in me displayed."

The main features for our consideration are:

1. The Fact of His Power

2. The Features of His Promises

3. The Fellows of Divine Nature

4. The Foulness of the World.

Peter having experienced this divine power in his early days of preaching in Jerusalem could write with authority. He would remember that meeting on the mount (Matt 28: 18) when the Lord indicated that He had power in two spheres, heaven and earth. This power was ever at the disposal of the saints. Peter so explains the miraculous healing of the lame man (Acts 3,4) not by his gift or power, but by the power of the name of Jesus Christ. The word "great" (*megistos*, the superlative of *megas*, which is found 150 times in our NT) always describes bigness of either form, degree, quality, or quantity, and would indicate that all the promises excel, and cater for every circumstance. The verb is in the perfect tense and emphasises the fulness and permanent freshness of the promises of God. They have a guarantee, being underwritten by God, and made good to us in Christ. The promises relate to the present and the future.

3.   *Faith and Fruitfulness*
1:5-9

> v.5   "And beside this, giving all diligence, add to your faith virtue, and to virtue knowledge;
> v.6   And to knowledge temperance., and to temperance patience; and to patience godliness;
> v.7   And to godliness brotherly kindness; and to brotherly kindness charity.
> v.8   For if these things be in you, and abound, they make *you that ye shall* neither *be* barren nor unfruitful in the knowledge of our Lord Jesus Christ.
> v.9   But he that lacketh these things is blind, and cannot see afar off, and hath forgotten that he was purged from his old sins.

5   This verse is a plea for diligence by an extraordinary sequence. Peter has in these verses followed a logical order. He made doctrinal and fundamental statements in vv.1-4, now he proceeds to encouragement in the use of what has been given to us by God.

vv.1-2   Faith is appreciated
vv.3-4   Faith is acknowledged
vv.5-9   Faith with additions

vv.1-4   What had God done
vv.5-9   What we should do.

Peter is indicating that progress is possible and desirable. In fact it is expected but cannot be achieved without serious effort. We require to be diligent to increase the quality of faith in v.10, to confirm to ourselves and others the manner of entrance we make; in v.15 to endeavour when Peter is absent to continue (3:12) until the final day is reached.

Initial faith can be strengthened and preserved in freshness, fragrance, and fervour. So he sets out what we should mix into our faith. The active verb "to add- simply has the idea of furnishing, but we must add diligently, or wisely, certainly not rashly, not even slowly, but in a businesslike fashion with earnest care constantly and progressively mixing into our faith these additives. This same word in v.11 is translated in the AV "ministered". This takes effort on our part which will pay dividends now and certainly in the future kingdom.

The additive, "virtue", a word used sparingly in our Bible, would refer to manliness and courage. It is found four times in Peter's letters and only once elsewhere in Phil 4:8. Faith with virtue is reasonable, praiseworthy and pleasant.

"Knowledge" is to be added next. A man or woman of faith has an intelligence that exceeds that of their worldly contemporaries. Of course we might be ignorant of this world's ways but we cannot afford to be ignorant of God's ways. The word *gnōsis* simply refers to knowledge that can grow and develop with practical wisdom. It would help to make judgment of what is right or wrong; it would expose the bad and reveal the path of righteousness. This knowledge is not harmful, but rather indispensable. We should grow in the grace and in the knowledge of our Lord and Saviour (3:18). To help us to pray intelligently and to have our requests answered we should, as 1 Pet 3:7, help each other to increase in the knowledge of God. Christian character and spiritual ignorance are not twins. The cure for false knowledge is knowledge of Christ. Knowing Christ is to live in godliness. Stoics and gnostics boasted in their knowledge, and they could deceive many, but not the saint who adds the knowledge of Christ to an active faith.

6   Going up the ladder of faith we find that "temperance" is essential. In this form we discover this word "temperance" in three places in our NT: Acts 24:25; Gal 5:23; and twice here in v.6. In another form it is found in 1 Cor 7:9; 9:25; Titus 1:8. The main idea is of a person in control of himself who never allows his passions to take over but keeps all in subjection. This was one of the three points that Paul preached to Felix when Felix trembled. To the

Galatians Paul indicates that temperance is included in the fruit of the Spirit, and Paul adds "against such there is no law" or limit. To Titus Paul again indicates that a bishop should have this quality of being master of himself, but under subjection to God. It does not only refer to matters of food, drink, or exercises for our bodies, but in the realm where faith is active there must be godly control. Peter here breaks with stoicism. The stoics taught that knowledge removes restraint and gives licence to be free to excess passions. Peter says knowledge does not divorce itself from ethics and any teaching system which disunites ethics from knowledge is basically wrong. Our tongues must be bridled, our minds hedged around, our lips be able to close, our ears open or shut when necessary. The choice of company, the places frequented, practices indulged must be judged by the happy and contented christian for he or she is under law to Christ.

Then comes "endurance" (patience). The christian quickly discovers he is not immune from days of distress and difficulty, from persecution and opposition. He will develop in his faith a disposition to stand firm in his christian belief and practice. True faith does not break under test. Real christians do not quit but steadily, consistently continue to show forth the praises of Christ. Faith is tested for its reality and even though a cross lies across the path it can endure (Heb 12:1,2). This steadfastness of purpose becomes perseverance in practice and does not give up easily. Let trial come as it will; let others be discouraged and give up; the diligent saint is disciplined and never gives way to his feelings or gives up in defeat. This kind of patience develops the quiet calmness of strength. It will muzzle improper impulses, disallow carnal uprisings, and will choke at source the weeds of belligerent badness. Patience goes for gold; nothing but the highest and the best will it pursue in an unassuming and an uncompromising manner.

Next in the ladder of faith comes godliness. The mockers and scoffers are ungodly (3:7), but this growing faith has this characteristic of unselfishness, of being immovable yet constantly abounding in the fear of God. The deep respect for God induces the desire to be like Him. The truth will be defended but with extreme piety. Saints will be defended and encouraged and the truth upheld tenaciously.

7 "Brotherly affections" (*philadelphia*, "kindness") as in 1 Pet 1:22 explains the normal relationship of members in the same family. There should be an evident partnership, sharing responsibilities and privileges. Abraham's advice to Lot and the herdsmen "we be brethren" gives the meaning of this word. It is made of two Greek words: *phileō*, I love, and *adelphos*, brother. There should always be evident a caring love for each other so that when differences arise, as they inevitably will, there could not be any rise in temperature, no giving off steam, no biting and backbiting. There is a family tie which is stronger in the spiritual than in the natural. It begins with the Father's affection and is distributed, or shed abroad, to every family member. It will be above everything else intensely practical as is discerned by John in his epistles.

Finally we read the seventh of these additives, " love", *agapē*, as in 1 Pet 1:22. We move from the exclusive brotherly kindness to the unlimited and deep love. Faith has developed and now we have reached the apex. The growth in quality is perfected in this big, broad but deep love. The stages are concurrent and supplementary; whilst distinct they quietly mesh together to effect a smoothness as faith operates and grows.

8-9   Now in vv. 8 and 9 Peter discusses the issue of this growing faith. The negative effect is in v.8 and the positive in v.9.

Failure to add into our faith these seven qualities can be disastrous. "Blind" (*tuphlos*) is often used in this metaphorical sense of those who are afflicted lacking "insight" (John 9:39-41; Rev 3:14) and cannot see afar off. Such "blind" lack "long sight" and are only occupied with the here and now; they live for the present age and forget the coming age; they are "blind" to the heavenly and short-sighted with the earthly.

Muōpazōn can have the idea of defective sight and also describe the blinking of the eyes. Blind by shutting the eyes to the knowledge of the Lord Jesus Christ, these had forgotten (deliberately) by putting out of their mind the fact "he (or she) was purged from his old sins".

"Old sins" refer to the defiling practices of pre-conversion days. The sacrifice of Christ now means nothing to this person, so the old sins can again be freely practised. Stoicism and gnosticism professed knowledge, but freely practised sin. The christian knows the transforming power of Christ and does not practise sin. The world is corrupt from the inside out, but the saints are not of the world though living in the world. Worldliness as practised today is out of bounds to the christian, so we live righteously and godly in this present age (Titus 2:12).

4.   *Diligence or Negligence*
1:10-14

> v.10 "Wherefore the rather, brethren, give diligence to make your calling and election sure: for if ye do these things, ye shall never fall:
> v.11 For so an entrance shall be ministered unto you abundantly into the everlasting kingdom of our Lord and Saviour Jesus Christ.
> v.12 Wherefore I will not be negligent to put you always in remembrance of these things, though ye know *them*, and be established in the present truth.
> v.13 Yea, I think it meet, as long as I am in this tabernacle, to stir you up by putting *you* in remembrance.
> v.14 Knowing that shortly I must put off *this* my tabernacle, even as our Lord Jesus Christ hath shewed me."

10   "Wherefore rather, brethren, be on your guard", so Peter repeats v.5 again, using the aorist imperative tense to give weight to his plea and strengthening his appeal on the ground of relationship-he addresses them as "brethren".

"Make your calling and election sure", history and eternity meet for electing choice is in foreknowledge (1 Pet 1:1) but the call by grace is in time. The fact that we are asked to make them "sure" is interesting, since both are works of God.

The "election" was the deliberate antecedent choice of God in eternity, becoming history and evident in time's ages. It was in line with His foreknowledge (1 Pet 1:1). It was in accord with His purpose in grace (Rom 9:11). It was to express His pleasure, not by majority vote but by unanimous decision of the Godhead. No charge can be sustained against the elect (Rom 8:33). We are not only beyond the reach of enemies, but beyond a suspicion of any charge. Legally, sacrificially, and finally, God has lifted us to be His special gift to His beloved Son: then without spot (sinless); without wrinkle (ageless); or any such thing (internally, externally, and eternally fresh and beautiful for Christ).

What does it mean then: "Make your calling and election sure"? The verb is interesting, it is in the middle voice which leads us to the idea that Peter expressed. The calling and election is beyond doubt, but make them sure to yourselves. So then fill out your faith, enjoy your calling and election.

The first result is immediate: "ye shall never fall". We should not rest content with a shallow or starved faith, but rather with greater effort help faith to grow and develop and we shall be healthy christians. Two results will be evident: ye shall never fall and stay down in disgrace of failure, but if and when christians stumble, they will soon be on their feet again, and be as surefooted as a mountain horse. Peter is drawing from his personal experience; he has stumbled but has never turned against the Lord in apostasy.

11   The fact of the entrance is not under discussion, but rather the manner of the entrance into the kingdom. The growth of the saint today is important now and very important for the future. There is no doubt about us reaching the heavenly kingdom; we live now in the knowledge that our entry is assured but it could be with an abundance of fruit from an active and obedient faith. The word "ministered" has already appeared in v.5 when it is translated "add" so that added to us is an abundant entry, like a ship returning to its home port in full sail. The phrase "everlasting kingdom" does not recur elsewhere in our NT and perhaps Peter is contrasting in his mind the powerful kingdom of Caesar with the everlasting kingdom of our Lord Jesus Christ.

The kingdom is everlasting. Today it is in mystery, but soon in manifestation. It will fill the universe of God forever. It has always been in existence but not always evident. God has never been dethroned. He still rules in the kingdom of men (Dan 4:32).

Here the kingdom is seen as future, in its public manifestation. When Jesus was amongst men He indicated He had a kingdom but also said "My kingdom is not of this world". His first coming was not to reign but to redeem. No person should be surprised at Pilate asking "Art thou a king then?" when he had before him a prisoner, despised and rejected. But the crown is for the prisoner. He will come again, not in lowly guise but in flaming fire, taking vengeance (2 Thess 1:7,8).

But it is *His* kingdom (Matt 16:28; John 18:36; Ps 2:6). Ps 24 has many questions about the king but they are answered in the Lord Jesus Christ. He has the right to rule, He is Creator (vv.1,2); He has character (v.4); His is the conquest (v.8).

12   Two main points are in this verse:

1.   Peter's intentions-strong because of great issues.

2.   Saint's interest-knowledge received and built upon.

The teacher of divine truth must not hold back the truth because it is well-known. If it is genuine truth it will bear repetition. It would be profitable and useful even though they had received it and remembered it. Because certain truths are well-known by the saints, this does not give licence to teachers to neglect teaching them. The value of repetition is not always appreciated but the truth is always needed.

13   Peter in this verse indicates that it was needful for him to restate the truth in the light of his soon departure. The truth outlives the minister. It is interesting to note how Peter speaks of his body (during the days of his responsibility). He was still in it, but the vacating of his body would be speedy and violent when the time arrived. This apparent shortage of time inspired him to write now. His body is "a tent", a temporary dwelling. His body is expendable, but in v.14 he still describes it as "my body " or "my tabernacle". The putting off of his body would be speedy; his end would not be dragged on by his murderers. He would go as Jesus had "signified" in John 21:18,19.

Paul in 2 Cor 5:4 indicates the temporary nature of his body just like Peter. So long as he was in this (earthly and temporary) dwelling he would stir up the saints. Then when he would vacate this body (his own tent) he would be expecting to have a new kind of body which could be a permanent dwelling.

Notes

The Calling is Heavenly (Heb 3:1) indicating that our profession is not earthly, is not connected with earth's religious houses, we are members of the heavenly house over which Jesus is in control.

The Calling is Holy (1 Pet 1:15). It is God who hath called us into His family so that as sharers of the divine nature we might make evident in our testimony that we have something of God not only in us but demonstrated by us. We are therefore different and set apart to lead sanctified lives.

The Calling is of Hope (Eph 1:18). The future that God has reserved will be enjoyed eternally, not only by us by also by God Himself. Think not only of what our inheritance is to us but also of what God gets out of it for eternity. The gifts and calling of God are never recalled or rescinded. The inheritance is reserved in heaven for you (1 Pet 1:4).

The Calling is on High (Phil 3:14). Paul exerts the weight of his body and mind and personally pushes aside every earthly advantage or disadvantage and just presses straight ahead for the great prize, the "calling on high" (Phil 3:20). We await the Saviour (not the Judge), the Lord Jesus Christ who shall change our limited body and fashion it to the unlimited body of glory. What a blessed future awaits every saint!

5. *Fables or Facts*
   ## 1:15-18

> v.15 "Moreover I will endeavour that ye may be able after my decease to have these things always in remembrance.
> v.16 For we have not followed cunningly devised fables, when we made known unto you the power and coming of our Lord Jesus Christ, but were eyewitnesses of his majesty.
> v.17 For he received from God the Father honour and glory, when there came such a voice to him from the excellent glory, This is my beloved Son, in whom I am well pleased.
> v.18 And this voice which came from heaven we heard, when we were with him in the holy mount."

Peter again uses an expression to describe his outgoing from life as his "departure"-his exodus, indicating that he viewed death not simply as vacating a temporary earthly tent, but as the end of his earthly work. As to the point in time when he would leave earth he was not sure. But Peter had no doubt about the way he would leave this world-by death. Death to him was an exodus or a departure; a release from a kind of bondage and he anticipates an abundant entry into the life to come. He would be completely emancipated from earth and discover heaven literally. The purpose of his reminding them was just the first link in a chain and he expected they would pass on the truth to others. Truth often repeated will be truth heeded. This burden of relaying the truth to succeeding generations was shared by Paul (see 2 Tim 2:2).

The truth in v.12 is "present truth", not now for the saints but for himself. The diligence he exhorted others to have he himself practised. This is a worthy example for all teachers. Peter uses the future tense and may be referring to his input into the Gospel of Mark to leave a permanent record of teaching of the life of Jesus. He indicates that he would continue to help until the moment of death.

16 There are two conflicting accounts before Peter in this verse:

1. "Cleverly devised fables"
2. "Present truth"

The strenuous opposition of false teachers had been suggesting that the transfiguration story was but a fable. Peter now embarks on his account of the transfiguration. The fables had been artfully spun and well presented. The truth will be clearly stated and will remove all credence or foothold for error. This account would be from an eyewitness and must be taken as authentic. After all, the truth needs no embellishment and is not the speculation of active imagination.

Peter in 1 Pet 5: 1 states that he witnessed the sufferings of Christ; here he claims to be an eyewitness of the power and glory of Christ. Fictitious prophesies or old wives' tales (Titus 1:14; 2 Tim 4:4) have been dressed up and given the appearance of truth; they have upset many and have deceived the simple and unwary. Peter now therefore speaks not of the sufferings of Christ (that he does in each section of his first epistle), but is occupied with the majesty of Christ. He is clearly defending the truth of the second coming of the Lord. First, he refers to the undeniable experience of the transfiguration which is a preview of the appearing in, and with, glory. The description given by Peter of the future event is striking, he refers to the power (*dunamis*) and coming (*parousia*). Some commentators combine the power in the coming, but most translate as in the AV which naturally could be linked with the future event as in Matt 24:30 (coming with power and great glory). When in resurrection glory the Lord took His own to the mountain He informed them that all power in two spheres had been granted to Him, i.e. all power in heaven and on earth was His. With that power unexhausted He will come again. No one will be able to withstand Him. Paul in 2 Thess 1 speaks of this coming with flaming fire, taking vengeance, in other words displaying His power.

The other word "coming" (*parousia*) means simply "presence", and indicates that personally He will arrive. He will not send a substitute, He will come Himself, and the weight and influence of His majesty will be universally felt. "Majesty" (*megaleiotēs*) is a rare word in our NT and refers to the majesty of the divine.

Peter, referring to his companions James and John, says, "we were eyewitnesses". The false teachers may make claims but they were never eyewitnesses of the majestic Christ. The word itself *epoptēs* was commonly used in the mystic cults to describe the members of the privileged inner circle. Peter states "we were in the inner circle". Peter destroys any sense of the mystic power claimed by the myth tellers and now he exposes them for what they really are.

Peter's memory of the transfiguration brings together a cluster of words extolling the greatness of Christ which he had made known already:

His power   Divine in origin and operation and destroying all opposition.

His coming   Not mystical, but personal.

His majesty   Telling of His mighty power (Luke 9:43); the magnificence of His
               Person; emphasising the pre-eminence of the royalty of Christ.

This preview of the coming again of Jesus was and remains the subject of the vicious attack of false teachers and foolish scoffers. Peter is saying: Jesus shall reign and Jesus must reign.

17   Peter now turns from the vision to the voice; from the visible to the audible. In referring to Christ, "Having received honour and glory from God the Father", Peter links two words "honour and glory" often found together in Scripture. God crowned Adam with glory and honour (Heb 2:7). Because He had given Adam a task to perform, God supplied the enabling to do it. Alas Adam failed; the last Adam was also given and received glory and honour (Heb 2:9) but He shall not fail. Dominion and rule will be in His safe custody and God spoke out from heaven confirming His confidence in the Lord Jesus. The formula used was well known, taken from David's Ps 2, and from the prophet Isaiah (Isa 42) bespeaking the pleasure of God. The glory received probably refers to kingship, the honour to the Servant who delighted Him. This display of honour and glory might lead us to discuss Dan 7:14 where, as Son of man, there is an outshining presented before God, before He is revealed to men of all nations.

The voice brought a message to Him not from but by, or in, the very excellent glory-an Hebraism meaning God Himself. The bright cloud which overshadowed the mountain was like Exod 16:10; Num, 14:10; Ezek 1:4, God coming down on each occasion for a special purpose. Here God makes the proclamation of His King. John Baptist proclaimed Him as "he that cometh", God is saying "He has arrived".

The Gospels' record of the transfiguration message have the addition, "Hear him", which is a quotation from Deut 18 where Moses is intimating the coming of another leader like himself who would speak for God and all should listen to Him. Then holiness will fill the world and not just a mountain. This mountain itself was holy ground just like Moses' experience as he investigated the bush burning but not consumed; or when he ascended Sinai and was filled with fear and exceedingly quaked (Heb 12). The holiness of God will be felt and respected during the reign of God's King on earth, not only on one particular spot, but the whole earth will be filled with His glory.

18   We heard this voice plainly and it came from heaven for we were with Him on the holy mount, is Peter's witness. He stresses

1.   the fact of the voice

2.   where it came from

3.   to whom it referred.

His testimony was clear and unmistakable: it was from God the Father to the

Lord Jesus, but for the benefit of Peter, James and John to hear. God indicated His close association with His Son and His extreme pleasure in Him. This evidence witnessed to the unique glory of Jesus and emphasises the certain hope for the future. This account is not only authentic but is independent of the Gospel records, yet agreeing in the essential features.

6.   *The Dawn and the Daystar*
   1:19-21

> v.19 "We have also a more sure word of prophecy, whereunto ye do well that ye take heed, as unto a light that shineth in a dark place, until the day dawn, and the day star arise in your hearts:
> v.20 Knowing this first, that no prophecy of the scripture is of any private interpretation.
> v.21 For the prophecy came not in old time by the will of man: but holy men of God spake as they were moved by the Holy Ghost."

19   The transfiguration, in addition, would give weight to the prophetic word of the sacred writing. This experience of the three disciples stamped on their minds the genuineness of OT writings. If ever they required assistance or proof then this revelation would be useful. The prophecies of old are permanently valid and they truthfully and unerringly are fulfilled. Peter, when he preached Christ, saturated his message with OT quotations. The OT could not be made more sure, except in the minds of learners and disciples. The prophets were as trustworthy as the apostles of the NT.

The metaphor of Scripture as a torch of light giving rays of light to a dark, murky room was well known; cf. Ps 119:105. The light shows up the dirt, and removes the darkness; therefore we must use the Scriptures and walk in the light of their truth.

"Until the day dawn, and the day star arise" helps us to appreciate the darkness of this present age and the light of the age to come. OT prophets continuously pointed forward and the final book in the OT (Mal 4:2) speaks of the Sun of Righteousness rising to dispel the darkness of night. So, until that event, we must draw our hope from the Scriptures and await the daystar heralding the new day of full light. The OT Scriptures shine like a torch in the dark, and the dawn of the new era is when Messiah comes in power. The image of the star is well known in the OT (Num 24:17), and the NT continues with the same image; cf. Luke 1:78; Eph 5:14; Rev 2:28; 22:16. Our AV suggests that the day dawns and the daystar arises in our hearts. It is better not to spiritualise the event as if it could be contained in our puny hearts. The phrase "in your hearts" should be attached to the effort of taking heed or paying attention to this coming event. Whilst it is true that the transforming moral miracle takes place in our hearts when we rightly use the OT as a torch, this cannot replace the true fulfilment of the return of Jesus. This verse spells out what the OT Scriptures are, why they were given and how they should be used.

20   Guidance is available and rules of interpretation have been used and should still be used. No word of Scripture is to be interpreted to suit the various notions of men-false or true-since no Scripture originated from man. Highly individualistic theories must not be forced. Scripture compared with other Scriptures is the way to discover their true meaning. Do not allow obscure or difficult-to-understand verses to nullify plain truths taught in many passages of Scripture.

21   The origin of the OT is now emphasised. They are not the production of men, but men were borne along by the Spirit as they spoke for God. Heb 1 indicates that God spoke in the prophets, and the fathers who were addressed became responsible to obey the word. No writer or reader can therefore rightly interpret without the help of the Holy Spirit. The inference is clear-the false teacher used human genius and corrupted or hucksterised the meaning o Scripture. Scripture was being misused and misinterpreted when theories were propounded with verses being quoted out of context. No author of the OT or the NT can write or interpret his own writing without the help of the Holy Spirit. The Holy Spirit is not only the Originator but the Interpreter of Holy Scripture. This is what makes the Book different: it is the word of God. The principles of writing and interpretation apply not only to unfulfilled prophecy but to general doctrine. Careful handling of the Scriptures is imperative and binding on teachers.

II. False Teachers Speak Evil of Truth (2:1-22)

1.   *Way of False Teachers*
   vv.1-3

> v.1   "But there were false prophets also among the people, even as there shall be false teachers among you, who privily shall bring in damnable heresies, even denying the Lord that bought them, and bring upon themselves swift destruction.
> v.2   And many shall follow their pernicious ways, by reason of whom the way of truth shall be evil spoken of.
> v.3   And through covetousness shall they with feigned words make merchandise of you: whose judgment now of a long time lingereth not, and their damnation slumbereth not.

1   Having at the end of ch.1 indicated the way of the true and genuine teacher, he now proceeds to deal with the way of the false teacher. The true prophets of the OT guided by the Holy Spirit have left an inheritance in the sacred writings of OT books. Those prophets were harassed and opposed by false prophets and now, says Peter, the genuine teacher is counterfeited by false teachers. This chapter deals with the character, conduct, condemnation and consummation of the false teacher. False prophets of the OT times have things in common with all false teachers of today. False prophets may lay claim to be genuine as to their call, or at times claim divine authority for their teaching. V.1 indicates the sphere of their movement-in or among the people-so Peter states that false teachers are not remote but are in and among you. The little preposition *en* indicates the sphere of their ministry; then in common with the false prophets of OT times they bring in stealthily their heresies or sects; these are destructive. Note

1. The sphere of their movements   -in and among the people of God

2. The subtlety of their manners   -stealthily bring in

3. The schism of their matter   -damnable heresies

4. The subverting of the Master   -denying the Lord

Their sphere: To be effective they must first gain the ear of the people and in 2 Tim 4 Paul in charging Timothy indicates how the false teacher gets and holds the attention of the people. They seek first to gain the confidence of the unsuspecting and unwary. Initially they are inoffensive, caring and loving, so that even elders and shepherds are deceived by their skill. I suppose Peter with the other disciples never suspected Judas Iscariot was a traitor.

The subtlety of their manners: The pedlars of poison never introduce themselves as such, but gain a hearing by novel and acceptable homilies; they make themselves sociable, acceptable. False teaching is not given in large doses at a first attempt; it is injected in small doses after the pedlar has been accepted. They creep in unawares (Jude 4). They operate from inside which of course gives them the freedom they want. The Gibeonites did work wilily and imposed deceitfully on Joshua and Israel with dry mouldy bread, old worn out garments, and empty bottles; so they wormed their way into the hearts of Israel (Josh 9); finally they were accepted within the ranks of the Lord's people. The false prophets do likewise, and must be tested with all prophets, says Moses, as Deut 13:13; 18:22 indicated. The sad history recorded in 1 Kings 22 shows the true prophet Micaiah speaking the word of God and he is not only despised, discredited but imprisoned and starved whereas the false are applauded and accepted. God of course vindicated the true prophet but at what a cost to the people of God. Again the false prophet had got the ear of the people and had filled their minds with what they wanted to hear rather than with God's word. The false teachers are dangerous in that after getting in themselves, they will smuggle in heresies of destruction. The verb "privily bring in" (*pareisagein*) is interesting, occurring also in Gal 2:4; it suggests underhand methods of bringing in heresies with the intent of bringing people into bondage. Paul stood against the false brethren and stood firm for the Gospel when even Peter was influenced wrongly. We must beware of the friendly approach of false teachers and like Paul stand as a sentry on the watchtower to preserve the health of the people of God.

The schism of their matter, of their damnable heresies. We need to be like the Bereans and abide by the rule: "to the law and the testimony". The divisiveness of false teaching poses the question of genuineness. The heresies have a twofold description

1.   Damnable

2.   Denying the Lord

The word heresy (*hairesis*) is a natural term with the simple meaning of choice, a principle thought out, a sect, or a school holding similar views. Three examples are given where the word is found elsewhere in the NT.

Acts 5:17	The Sadducees who were upset at the influence of Peter and the rapid growth of the church were a sect for the group who were of like mind with the high priest.
Acts 26:5	Paul speaking of his manner of life from his youth called on Pharisees to testify that at that time he was of the straightforward sect of the Pharisees, in other words, of that particular school who thought and taught the tenets of strict Pharisaism.
1 Cor 11:18	Paul announcing what he had previously heard, that in Corinth when the church gathered there were different groupings, rightly asserts that there would be amongst them sects, so that there could not be a worthy remembrance at the Lord's supper.

These "heresies" are "damnable", literally "of destruction". How dangerous.

The subverting of the Master: As a group, these false teachers were united in that they denied the Lord. This now indicates the falsity of their belief and the underlying blasphemy. This charge of Peter is similarly made in Jude 4. There is no denial that Christ is the Master and that He has paid the full price of purchase. Their denial of the Master is in their doctrine and practice. They deny Him His right of ownership now and His right to reign as Lord in the future. The touchstone to reveal error is to discover what is thought of Christ and what hope for the future is held.

The damnable heresy, self-destruction in itself, and the scandalous behaviour allowed and practised lead us to appreciate how serious is this matter. Examples of denying the Master could include besmirching His purity, denying His holy birth, sinless life, perfect sacrifice effecting eternal redemption, bodily resurrection in accord with Scripture, glorious ascension, future glory and power.

They thus bring upon themselves swift destruction. The destruction twice referred to in these verses indicates first in v.2 that which inevitably falls on the false teacher, then what also awaits the many who fall victim to their teaching. The swiftness of it describes what will suddenly envelop them. *Tachinos* (swift) has already been used in ch. 1:14. When the moment strikes there will be no delay in dealing with both leader and disciple of this blasphemy.

2   In v.2 we have two ways stated:

1.   Destructive ways   -pernicious and licentious

2.   Way of truth   -pure and lovely.

Many will follow their destructive ways. Peter now thinks of the victims who fall foul and follow the false teachers. The converts of the false teachers are many, thus describing the considerable success of their efforts. The word "destructive" could well be "licentiousness" which refers to the permissive way of life associated with false teaching. It is true that wrong and sinful habits are produced by wrong doctrine. Paul in his pastoral epistles stresses doctrine that is healthy and health-giving and if our doctrine is wrong our manner of life will turn to ungodliness. Peter is indicating that the love of money, Of illicit sex, and of self-centred power stems from the false teaching. There is no connecting highway from the path of evil on the way of truth. We must know the power of Christ as Lord to be lifted from the evil road to the way of truth. To follow error is to experience not only in thought but in life the licentiousness of the false. Because those who do this have a colouring of religion the way of truth is not esteemed by the poor worldling. The religionists who live in sin bring dishonour and disrespect on the way of truth.

Among the examples of the OT we must cite Jer 23:14. There the prophets commit adultery, walk in lies, and strengthen the hand of evil doers etc.; "they are all of them unto me as Sodom and the inhabitants thereof as Gomorrah". To this Scripture we could add Ezek 13. These samples show that heretical dogma and loose living are twins. The attack on the way of truth is made by the false teacher using any unprincipled but clever arguments to discredit the simple clear christian life.

The "way" was an early descriptive tag for the first century church - Peter knew it well as the "way of truth". The contrast of the two ways is emphasised: the pernicious as against the pure, the destructive as against the delightful, the many ways as against the way of truth.

The idea of many travellers going down the licentious way tells us of how easy and attractive it appeared; it has appeal, captures and of course caters to the delicate but baser lusts. The way of the truth is despised, not simply neglected but deliberately attacked, blasphemed and counted as railing. "Evil spoken of" (*blasphēmeō*, bring a railing charge) is found four times in this chapter: vv.2,10,11,12.

Today as never before the battle for the Bible continues. Opposition to its inspiration from within the so-called christian community has increased. Today those who profess christianity plainly indicate that the Bible should be updated and brought into accord with modern thinking. This of course is blasphemous and outrageous. The way of truth is Christ Himself and if teaching or practice denies Him or His doctrine it must not only be wrong but must be avoided. The evil doctrine itself will bring destruction to its adherents. The way of truth will remain whilst the way of error and all who propagate it and become followers of its evil teaching will perish. Ps 1 states that the way of the ungodly will perish but that the Lord acknowledges the way of the righteous. It is sad to note that many try to unite these two opposite and opposing ways and of course make shipwreck. The way of truth will remain untarnished despite the railing and the blasphemy. God will vindicate His Son though many deny and despise Him.

3   In v.3 the method employed by the false teacher is highlighted by Peter:

1.   through covetousness-internal and private

2.   through feigned words-external and public.

The covetous principle generates the action and conceals the greed of the errorists. What they do is for personal gain but that is made evident in the words they use, although the message is camouflaged to hide the lust for personal gain. The phoney arguments are designed specifically to exploit the people of God, who are treated as merchandise from whom easy money can be taken. In 1 Tim 6:5 christianity is looked upon as another source of financial gain-"gain is godliness" becomes their standard, in their eyes, so the more gain the more godly. The craving for more of this world's good dictates the message and its manner of delivery. How different is Paul: "I have coveted no man's silver ... these hands have ministered unto my necessities and to them that were with me" (Acts 20:33,34).

This is the only occurrence of "feigned" in our NT. "Feigned" indicates that their words have been well spun and fitly chosen to suit and give people what they want to hear. In Jer 6:14 the false prophets said "Peace, peace; when there is no peace", and again in Ezek 13:16. When Zedekiah the false prophet said that Israel would push back the Syrians Micaiah the true prophet told of disaster. What Zedekiah said pleased the king and the people but of course was not the truth. It made him popular but how tragic the result. Hananiah the false prophet said the opposite to Jeremiah's message-what Hananiah said was acceptable but it was not true. It was Micah who said that the priests teach for gain and the prophets seek money. Today, says Peter, false teachers are goaded by the lust of gain. In ch.5 of his first epistle he states that elders must not be interested in filthy lucre; Paul writing to Titus in Crete informs of those who teach for filthy lucre's sake. Woe to them who make merchandise of the Lord's people. Remember for that reason Eli and his two sons (1 Sam 3) Hophni and Phinehas were suddenly destroyed in the disgrace of a national disaster; the worst feature was that the glory departed. The prophet who goes after the god of personal gain must be mercilessly destroyed (Deut 13:1-5; 18:20).

The summary of these vv.1-3 leaves us with the identifying marks of false teachers.

1. They wish to be popular.

2. Their language is choice but deceptive.

3. Their interest is personal gain.

4. Their lifestyle is a pursuit after worldly lusts.

5. They have natural ability and are socially acceptable rather than spiritual and godly.

And these verses also expose the method used and the manners employed:

1. Not open but concealed in mystique.

2. Stealthily introduced.

3. Wisely presented with cunning skill.

4. Biased to love and a forgiving spirit.

5. Appearing as truth having been well mixed with Scripture quotations.

Their manner encompasses:

1. Claiming authority of apostleship.

2. Friendliness of disposition.

3. Plausibility and loud asserting of their link with religion.
The effect of their teaching is disastrous:

1. Their immorality is blatant.

2.   Their covetousness is dishonest.

3.   Their teaching allows them to sin freely specially when they have gained a position of authority, for they have no sense of shame and their graces become licence to sin.

2.   *Walk of False Teachers*
   2:4-9

> v.4   "For if God spared not the angels that sinned, but cast *them* down to hell, and delivered *them* into chains of darkness, to be reserved unto judgment;
> v.5   And spared not the old world, but saved Noah the eighth *person*, a preacher of righteousness, bringing in the flood upon the world of the ungodly;
> v.6   And turning the cities of Sodom and Gomorrah into ashes condemned *them* with an overthrow, making *them* an example unto those that after should live ungodly;
> v.7   And delivered just Lot, vexed with the filthy conversation of the wicked
> v.8   (For that righteous man dwelling among them, in seeing and hearing, vexed *his* righteous soul from day to day with *their* unlawful deeds
> v.9   The Lord knoweth how to deliver the godly out of temptations, and to reserve the unjust unto the day of judgment to be punished:

4   Peter now draws examples from history: angels (v.4), antediluvians (v.5), Sodomites (v.6). Each illustrates Peter's assertion that punishment awaits false teachers, for God is not to be mocked by inhabitants of either heaven or earth. Little is said in the canon of Scripture as to when and what was involved in this reference to angels who had sinned. Certainly the enormity of their sin must have been great (the retribution is just and related to the sin) since they were consigned to *Tartaros* which in the Greek world was the lowest hell-far worse than *Hadēs* and reserved for those who wickedly despised their position and unscrupulously infected the innocent. God did not have regard to their influential position but judged the sin righteously. Reserved to pits or chains of darkness, they would be unable to continue in their unclean and vile sin which had caused such havoc in God's creation. In this writer's judgment this is not the event described in Gen 6. The sequence of the examples shows that Gen 6 is the second example. This reference to angels and the damage done by them takes us back rather to the entrance of sin at Eden. The preaching serpent was a false prophet with insinuation about: firstly the character of God; secondly man's state being unnecessarily restricted; thirdly false sympathy for the woman in subjection.

The fact that a plural is employed does not affect the story of the serpent's visit to Eden. It rather indicates that the fall of Satan from being the administrator for God to adversary against God was a fall which had occurred and Satan had brought down to destruction many of the unseen powers (cf. Rev 12:4). In Job 1:6; 2:1-7 Satan appears before God with a host of other of heaven's creatures but obviously distinct from them (and he is thus singled out when the Lord speaks to him personally). The sons of God came to present themselves before the Lord for instruction for service. Satan also arrived among them but not to take instructions. In Rev 12:4 too Satan as the dragon has a large following. The wonder is in heaven (v.3); the host who follow him are heavenly, indicating that heavenly powers followed the dragon in his work.

The work of Satan the serpent in Eden shows him to be the leader of every one and everything false and counterfeit. The attack in Eden was geared to deceive Eve and to bring down humanity under sin. The sad result we know. The method used, the manner of approach, and the end result foreshadow the wily movements of the false prophets of the OT and the false teachers of the NT. Arising out of Eden comes the promise of God. In a special way Satan has used not only emissaries from the heavenly host but also men and women on earth as agents to discredit the God of Promise. He has violently opposed the fulfilment of the promise and will continue to. God took action then, for He will not ever condone sin; His judgment will be righteous, the penalty related to the severity of the sin committed, and the final outcome, the fulfilment of His promise. Even when angels sinned including Satan, God did not withhold His condemnation, clear evidence that false teachers using the slimy tactics of Satan should fear their ultimate end.

5 Peter's second example shows that whereas men perished in the Flood, Noah was delivered. The situation described in Gen 6 became intolerable because of sin. God had warned of judgment by the prophetic Enoch, a remarkable servant of God (Jude 14,15). The descriptions given in our Bible tell out his interesting story. Peter does not refer to him by name; Jude, a contemporary of Peter and writing on the same subject, describes his work as prophesying (Jude 14), whereas in Heb 11:5 Enoch is a man of faith who walked (in fellowship) with God. His walk stood in contrast to the accepted way of life. God had made a promise and God would fulfil it: Enoch believed God and pleased Him, walked with Him and never experienced the curse of death for God took him. Peter is concerned with the unsparing character of God and how He destroyed a whole world by water (refer to 2 Pet 3:6). That world is described as the old or ancient world (2:5), the world that then was (3:6)-it finished under the judgment of God; the world of the ungodly will not be spared. Jude tells us that Enoch was seventh from Adam but Peter tells us Noah was the eighth. Whilst Enoch the seventh rests epitomising the Sabbath of Creation, Noah the eighth begins the new cycle of earth's future. It may be, however, that Peter is thinking of Noah as one of the eight persons who were saved (Gen 7:13).

The characteristic that Peter attaches to Noah is that he was a "Preacher of righteousness". The word translated "preacher" is the same as that describing John Baptist as the herald of the coming King. Noah then heralded forth a standard of righteousness from which God cannot, and will not, deviate. God always acts in fairness-His justice is above reproach and in heaven or earth in every dispensation the standard never varies. God is righteous and acts in righteousness.

Noah was a responsible herald and preached the message notwithstanding the lack of results. He was concerned about his own life and the lives of others so he preached. In that day men had a lifestyle of eating, drinking, marrying (obviously to generate children, to continue the human species) but giving no heed to the preaching of Noah until the flood came and took them all away. The message from this example of the antediluvian world is that God is righteous, keeps His promises, destroys the false. As Matt 24:39 indicates, they knew not-not because there was no preaching, not because there was no revelation, but because they shut their eyes, ears and minds to God's word. They would rather listen to other voices than Noah's simple message. The message comes loud and clear-God is righteous and punishes sin, and God is faithful to every promise.

6   The third example concerns not a whole world of ungodly but a selected valley containing at least four cities, two of which are mentioned as representatives of the whole valley, Sodom and Gomorrah. What was once a beautiful lush valley like the going down to Egypt is now a vale of ashes. What was once beautiful, because of ungodliness and complete disregard for God and His word is turned into desolation. The destructive agent used in judgment was not now water but fire; not now drowning but burning. The two agencies are put side by side as instruments under God's control. In Noah's day, the fountains below the waters were let loose by God and the world was drowned. In Lot's day the fires from beneath erupted and rose to pour down, covering the whole valley. Both are used as agencies of destruction and death. God's condemnation of the antediluvians and of the inhabitants of this ungodly valley was preceded by heralds warning of God's intention. Neither the preaching of Noah, the prophesying of Enoch, the praying of Abraham nor the messengers from heaven could prevent the judgment on sin. All the godly efforts of Abraham the man of God could not turn the ungodly, nor silence the false prophets, nor bring repentance; but God is just and righteous and sin is judged. God is no respecter of persons, He always acts in accord with His own character and as in grace so in righteousness He must keep His promise. False teachers beware-God is faithful and righteous.

8   This verse is a parenthesis and is inserted to show us that Lot needed deliverance. He is not described as a herald of righteousness but simply as being righteous-as such he needed deliverance. Isa 33:15 tells us of a man that stops his ears from hearing of blood and shutteth his eyes from seeing evil, just like righteous Lot; seeing and hearing vexed his righteous soul. The Genesis account of Lot's history is simply depicting a christian who lives only for this present age, who had turned away from the simple life of pilgrimage. In Gen 19:1 he appears to have an open door for strangers, but what a display of weakness: his word was not respected in his own house nor yet in the street where he lived. In fact he finally had to be dragged out of Sodom. The life of Sodom had a grip on him; he didn't want to leave. The saint who is out of touch with his God can quickly accommodate the sin and wickedness of a lawless, godless society where he dwells. The only solution for the christian is to escape. Only the goodness of God's justice brought Lot liberty. God had a place where he could be safe but it was far outside of the wicked valley. There was a mountain arranged to house Lot and all who belonged to him. It would have been better for him to go all the way with God than to seek a halfway house. Not to go with God in separation is to put your testimony at undue risk. Lot proved this. Read the last paragraph of Gen 19 to have confirmation. He had left Sodom as a settled place but the life of Sodom still controlled and disgraced him. Despite Lot's failure God is faithful; He cannot deny Himself, so He delivered just Lot. Peter returns with a few sharp words to update the history lessons into present experience. Angels, antediluvians, and Sodomites become examples to those who today live ungodly lives and listen to false teaching of errorists.

9   Two principles are stated:

1.   God knows how to deliver the godly out of temptation

2.   God knows how to reserve the ungodly unto the day of judgment to be punished.

The examples of Noah and Lot declare how God delivers and the experiences of angels, antediluvians and Sodomites tell how God imprisons till the day of perdition and punishment.

V.9 is a summary and a stating of inviolable principles, Peter is concerned with the how of God's arrangement and activity. For Noah's deliverance was sheltering within the ark. Inside the ark was the only safe refuge recognised and provided. Today Rom 8: 1 becomes applicable for us: "There is therefore now no judgment to them which are in Christ Jesus". The Lord Jesus Christ is the only safe refuge recognised and provided by God. Lot's deliverance was required because God would not punish the righteous with the ungodly. The judge of all the earth (not just of the valley of Sodom) shall do right. The saint will never be judged with the world (1 Cor 11:32).

Then as we turn to the second principle, "He knows how to reserve the unjust to the day of perdition to be punished", we note that in the case of the angels their sin was judged, they were condemned and then reserved in pits or chains, whichever picture is accepted. (The pits would contain and the chains retain in the deepest abyss until the day of perdition.) They are in prison, in safe custody with no hope of reprieve, finally to be punished.

Then examples 2, the flood victims, and 3, the fire victims, show that God intends to punish root and branch every one above or below who has rebelled against Him. He will be righteous and fair in all His dealings and this fact will be publicly manifested. The flood took them all away; the fire destroyed every living thing in the valley. But God preserved Noah and delivered Lot.

3. *Wages of False Teachers*
   2:10-16

v.10 "But chiefly them that walk after the flesh in the lust of uncleanness, and despise government. Presumptuous *are they*, selfwilled, they are not afraid to speak evil of dignities.

v.11 Whereas angels, which are greater in power and might, bring not railing accusation against them before the Lord.

v.12 But these, as natural brute beasts, made to be taken and destroyed, speak evil of the things that they understand not; and shall utterly perish in their own corruption;

v.13 And shall receive the reward of unrighteousness, as they that count it pleasure to riot in the day time Spots *they are* and blemishes, sporting themselves with their own deceivings while they feast with you;

v.14 Having eyes full of adultery, and that cannot cease from sin; beguiling unstable souls: an heart they have exercised with covetous practices, cursed children:

v.15 Which have forsaken the right way, and are gone astray, following the way of Balaam *the son* of Bosor, who loved the wages of unrighteousness,.

v.16 But was rebuked for his iniquity the dumb ass speaking with man's voice forbad the madness of the prophet."

10-15 Peter returns to the denunciation of the false teachers. Like the rebellious angels, the flood victims and the men of Sodom, they too had sinned. They were disrespectful to God denying the Lord and Master and had no fear of dignitaries. They themselves were guilty of the sin of anarchy. He then details clearly what marks the false teachers.

1. They walk after the flesh in the lust of polluted things — -are unrestrained in lusts.

2. They despise Lordship — -question all authority and the final authority in particular.

3. They are pompous, proud and obnoxious — -have no respect for any person.

4. Self-willed and daring — -will do anything to please self (*tolmētēs*, audacious: *authadēs*, self-pleasing, from two words, *autos*, self, and *hēdomai*, please).

5. Lack respect for authority — -show no honour for the office of rule.

6. Guilty of railing — -maliciously discredit with lies the Righteous One.

7. Live like unintelligent animals — -become easy prey to bondage of sin.

8.   Seeking unrighteous rewards   -are guilty of bribery and trickery.

9.   Drunk with pleasure   -night and day continually intoxicated.

10. Spots and blemishes   -internal and external badness evident,
                                          they remain uncaring.

11. Luxuriating in deceit, feasting   -never satisfied and experts in
     to sin more and more   deceiving.

12. Eyes filled with sexual immorality -Sodomy let loose and unsatisfied.

13. Causing others to sin and   -discredit the true word of God,
     having a craving for sin   totally sold to sin.

14. Cursed children   -Lot's daughters and their offspring
                                          an example of Sodom's life.

15   Four downward steps are taken by such evil men:

1.   Forsaking the right way

2.   Going astray

3.   Following the way of Balaam

4.   They love the wages of unrighteousness.

The four features in this verse are like the four steps taken by false teachers. They become like Balaam (Num 24-26).

Firstly, there is a right way with which they were acquainted but by a definite decision they had forsaken it. Paul refers to some who turned aside to vain jangling (1 Tim 1:6,7), and to some who shall depart from the faith (1 Tim 4:1). There is a definite turning away from the simple truths of the gospel, of church practice, and of godly living.

Secondly, they go astray; they abandon the truth; they accept error rather than healthy doctrine; they practise evil dressed up in religious robes and teach contrary to the faith causing others to stumble and fall.

Thirdly, they follow the way of Balaam, pose as spokesmen for God (Num 22:33) and encourage others to sin (Rev 2:14).

But worst of all, fourthly, they use the ministry as a source of financial enrichment, being willing to be hired by the enemy of God's people. How different from the real prophet Moses who refused the palace life and would rather have affliction now and look ahead for the reward in the coming age.

He has moved out of the book of Genesis and through history to the last enemy that attacked Israel just before they entered Canaan. In this last attack two men featured: Balak a king and Balaam a false prophet. Since Peter is dealing with false prophets and teachers, he makes no mention of Balak. Balaam, was a prophet and he had followers (*exakoloutheō*, used by Peter in 1:16 and 2:2). In 1:16 Peter indicates he was not a follower of cunningly devised fables-but in 2:2 he states that many had and would follow out pernicious ways. Here in v.15 he states that there is a right way in contrast to the false but also that it has been forsaken in favour of the way of Balaam.

16   This verse refers to the astonishing occasions in Balaam's life when pursuing his evil way he was rebuked by a dumb ass speaking in human language forbidding the mad prophet. Balaam whipped the ass when he should have whipped himself. God not only had taught him what to do but also what not to do. He persisted in his course, clinging to his love for gain. How often today a simple despised but humble believer can just momentarily stop one of these professionals who are trained and accepted as teachers or prophets but are in reality false. The Balaams of today do not readily accept a word from God, especially from sources whom they think are ignorant and inferior. But in v.16 Peter indicates the dumb ass was wiser than the false prophet. These word pictures indicate the filthiness and foolishness of those who deceive themselves and bring swift destruction to themselves and their followers.

4.   *Words of False Teachers*
2.17-22

> v.17 "These are wells without water, clouds that are carried with a tempest; to whom the mist of darkness is reserved for ever.
> v.18 For when they speak great swelling *words* of vanity, they allure through the lusts of the flesh, *through much* wantonness, those that were clean escaped from them who live in error.
> v.19 While they promise them liberty, they themselves are the servants of corruption for of whom a man is overcome, of the same is he brought in bondage.
> v.20 For if after they have escaped the pollutions of the world through the knowledge of the Lord and Saviour Jesus Christ, they are again entangled therein, and overcome, the latter end is worse with them than the beginning.
> v.21 For it had been better for them not to have known the way of righteousness, than, after they have known *it*, to turn from the holy commandment delivered unto them.
> v.22 But it is happened unto them according to the true proverb, The dog is turned to his own vomit again; and the sow that was washed to her wallowing in the mire."

Leaving history Peter now culls three illustrations from nature:

1.   Waterless springs on earth

2.   Waterless clouds on high

3.   The fog of darkness.

Waterless Springs: Poor, thirsty, weary pilgrims longing for a cold drink of spiritual refreshment are just as thirsty after their encounter with a false teacher-he cannot refresh their souls. He is a spring shut up, dry and barren.

Waterless Clouds: Being carried by the tempest, with plenty of noise drawing attention to them, they give no dew nor rain. Empty clouds only bring disappointment and leave the ground arid and bare.

Mist of Darkness: They themselves are in a whirl of speculations, holding out the promise and suffering from drought. Their tongues are parched for they have no gospel of salvation. People turning to them for bread get a hard dry dead stone. They themselves are in the fog of confusion and in the mist of dark deception. Balaam's dying words haunt them: "Let me die the death of the righteous". It was impossible for him and his followers.

The conclusion to all this debauchery, a catalogue of dissipated revelling day and night, summer and winter, is that physically, morally, spiritually they have become worthless wrecks. There is nothing to salvage; already they endure a taste of hell's punishment before the time. The seed of corruption has budded, blossomed and brought forth sour fruit. These verses then present to us a vivid and comprehensive view of what sin can do with a man or woman who rebels against God. The three metaphors are used by Peter in v.12, v.22, v.22:

        v.12 Irrational animals -wild and untamed
        v.22 The dog   -the scavenger of the rubbish heaps
        v.22 The sow   -the unchanging nature wallows again in the
                                  mire.

18   Knox translates the great swelling words as "fine phrases that have no meaning". No one could deny but that they were accomplished orators, that they could hold people spellbound by the forced, dogmatic presentation, but then afterwards in quiet moments of reflection the result would be unprofitable. It would all be empty. The methods employed in the conduct of meetings would be alluring- appealing to the flesh and to desires of nature, allowing lust to go unchecked and sin to be unrestrained. Permissiveness would be encouraged and even sinful lusts could be given religious approval.

So we have their speech and strategy: what is said and how it is presented. The emphasis is on the presentation to catch as ready prey those who turn to religion for relief.

19   What is promised is liberty, yet they are slaves of corruption. Probably liberty to them is to be free from the authority of God, to have liberty to live in sin. They become bondmen, bound by evil lusts and wicked habits and powerless to break from the bondage.

20   Here the victims who have been misled by false teachers are referred to by Peter. They had followed the true message preached, escaping the corruptions in the world; having found a knowledge of the Lord and Saviour Jesus Christ they had turned from a life of sin to the liberty promised. Now they found the message of the false teachers "defective" and the purveyors of error, deliberately abandoning themselves to a permissive lifestyle, had become worse than they ever were.

21   To turn from the knowledge of Christ to a life of sin is worse than to have never known Christ. To sink down to a level of utter sin, having rejected the requirements of holiness, is to accept the filthiness of every kind of wickedness.

22   How sad the metaphors which describe two dangers of the false teachers and their victims. The dog having rejected what it has taken in returns to his own vomit; what it rejected as foul again becomes its food. Obviously they are marked by internal pollution. The sow (a domestic unclean animal) cleansed by external washing turns again to the mud which had soiled it; it is marked by *external filth*. The history of a sick dog and the sad picture of a muddy pig indicate that these unfortunate animals had not changed their nature-they were still both unclean animals. Peter sadly but faithfully indicates that false teachers with a false gospel can do nothing to help sinners; rather they deceive them, damn them and destroy them, but don't change them. An empty vain message however presented is useless to change a man's nature, appetite or appearance.

This passage does not deal with true christians: a believer can never be lost. He is born again and as a sharer of the divine nature can never be in bondage; Christ makes him an overcomer. The proverbial statement of Peter may have combined current sayings of his day or perhaps borrowed from the OT, from Prov 26:11, or the LXX version of Jer 45:6. In Matt 7:6 the Lord Jesus links dogs with pigs and likens them to men out of touch with God.

In this sad chapter we must ask ourselves why Peter deals at length with false prophets and their victims. One can only suggest that Peter at heart loves the Lord and His people and as a true shepherd; he warns and directs the saints away from such poisonous teaching. Is there not a need today to teach positively the knowledge of Christ and the requirements of holy living compatible with godliness? Do we not live in an age when religionists preach another gospel, dilute the plain truth of repentance from sin and faith in our Lord Jesus Christ? Would that we could see that lying, permissiveness, gluttony, lust, licentiousness, immorality and disrespect for authority already in an outside world without Christ has insidiously entered the habitation of the saints. Therefore be extra careful of the ministry given from platforms or pulpits. True shepherds should be outspoken against the false teacher. Teachers and preachers should be careful in the extreme as to the doctrine and how it is presented.

III. Truth will Gain the Final Victory (3:1-18)

1. *The Value of the Scriptures*
   3:1 -2

> v.1   "The second epistle, beloved, I now write unto you; in *both* which I stir up your
> pure minds by way of remembrance
> v. 2 That ye may be mindful of the words which were spoken before by the holy
> prophets, and of the commandment of us the apostles of the Lord and Saviour"

Before the writer resumes his principal theme, he states his authorities for his corrective and edifying doctrine. The first authority he cites is the inspired writing of OT prophets; it is buttressed by the second authority-the commandment of NT apostles as received from the Lord Jesus Himself. In any moral or spiritual discussion it is always safe to refer directly to the Holy Scriptures. If any other source of information conflicts with the plain teaching of the Bible then discard it as rubbish. The reference made to the Scriptures should always have regard to the principles of interpretation as in 1:12,13.

1   There are at least three main issues in this verse:

1.   the fact of at least two epistles from Peter

2.   the fervency of the author

3.   the sincere minds of the recipients approving things that are excellent (Phil 1:10).

The common purpose of writing two letters is to strengthen and alert the faculty of thinking. There is such an ever-growing mountain of religious trash and poisonous error that there is need to put ourselves on sentry duty and be ever watchful. This becomes the main thrust in 2 Peter. 1 Peter is an epistle which, with its truth geared to inspire confidence, thus helps the saints in times of suffering. The suffering of Christ and the suffering of saints were real; their faith was severely tried and in many ways becomes similar in their experience. The victories of Christ in the midst of suffering become the pattern for the saint to follow. For this the mind of the believer must be girded, balanced and optimistic (1 Pet 1:12,13).

Objections have been raised to identifying the first epistle referred to here with the 1 Peter of our Bible. There are those who suggest that Peter is referring to a book which did not find a place in the canon of Scripture, whilst others suggest that this epistle itself was originally two letters; the first comprising chapters 1 and 2, and the second epistle chapter 3. There may be some value in these suggestions, but it is a simpler and in all probability correct view that he is referring to the letter known as 1 Peter in our NT as the first epistle.

The purpose of this letter is now stated, to "stir up your pure minds by way of remembrance"; before doing so Peter addresses them with deep affection: "Beloved, I now write to you". The tenderness of a pastor or shepherd can be easily appreciated in his address. "Beloved" is a word Peter is wont to use, and we may think of the saints, the recipients of the letter, as beloved by God and by Christ. How it would strengthen their faith to remember that they are the objects of the deep and abiding love of God. Somehow I feel that Peter is also expressing his own affection for them. Now he lets us see into his own heart and we find he loves the sheep (John 21). He repeats this word twice in the first epistle (2:11; 4:12) where it becomes not only an endearing term of address, but possibly an inspired punctuation mark dividing the first epistle into three large paragraphs, each paragraph reflecting one aspect of the three-fold commission which he received direct from the risen Lord: "feed my lambs, feed my sheep, feed my sheep"; the paragraphs do just that. It is not surprising that in Heb, 6:9 the writer who has been dealing with matters similar to 2 Peter also uses this affectionate term: "But, beloved, we are persuaded better things of you". In our epistle it is used six times; in 1: 17 the reference is to the Son of God. The other five occasions are found in 3:1,8,14,15,17 where its constant use in this final chapter emphasises the deep love and the high appreciation of Peter for God's dear people. To him they were the excellent of all the earth. It is good to be able in truth to address the Lord's people as the beloved. The present aspect of the letter spells out that the time and circumstance demand it: "I *now* write". The ministry was timely in that day, but is just as relevant today.

In saying, "your pure minds" the faculty of thought and not the disposition is obviously being referred to by Peter. In 1 Pet 1 he refers to the need for having minds girded, or tightly enclosed; only what will be helpful and healthy should be entertained in it. It could easily be defiled and diverted from engaging in the higher occupation of heavenly delights. The battle for the mind of the Lord's people continues today. The pushing of error by attractive means to gain a place in minds is engaged in by the false teachers or mockers or scoffers in an ever-increasing and concentrated manner. We need to gird our minds and make no access available for error to enter.

Peter then describes their minds as "pure". Paul uses this word once only in Phil 1:10, where it is translated "sincere". The word carries the idea of being pure without mixture; unadulterated and without a flaw; pure in the light of the sun. In ancient times when a sculptor at work inadvertently cracked the marble, he would sometimes hide the crack by infilling it with wax. Of course if exposed to the sun the wax would readily show. It thus becomes a compliment that Peter should speak of them as having sincere or pure minds-free from any wax which, although coloured to resemble the real thing, was not genuine. The "way of remembrance" could lead us to think of their minds as storehouses already filled with the good word of God. Many of us are indebted to godly elders, like Peter, who constantly encouraged the younger folks to fill their minds with Holy Scripture. To read it, memorise it, and reflect on it, were the habits they enjoined. There is no better advice for any of us, young or old, than that we should feed constantly on the Holy Scriptures.

2 Having cited the faculty of thought in v.1, now he moves to its use in v.2. To be "mindful" is to turn over in our minds, to process the material we have put there. He indicates that we should get to work on what we store in our minds. Paul assures us that in this we are guaranteed the valuable help of the Holy Spirit of God (1 Cor 2:10-16).

The sound material already garnered in these storehouses include:

1.   words spoken by the holy prophets

2.   the commandments of the apostles of the Lord Jesus Christ.

Two acceptable ideas are presented: firstly, that 1. is a reference to the OT and 2. to the NT; secondly, that the words of the holy prophets are from NT prophets and the commandments of authority from NT apostles. The time of writing might readily supplant the second idea since the canon of Scripture was not complete and canonised. NT prophets were not necessarily dealing with subjects relating to the future, but probably most of their work consisted in bringing the word from God orally to the saints of their own generation. These words would be in contrast and in opposition to the error of false teachers.

The commandments of "your apostles" (see JND) would be stamped with authority as doctrine. The teaching of the apostles became the foundational truth for their generation in particular, but is of course of permanent relevance for future generations. The fact that Peter says " your apostles" suggests that he is thinking of the Lord as the source and the apostles as suppliers of their doctrines. I suggest that he includes Paul with the other true apostles known to the saints.

If we accept that the holy prophets are those from OT times then of course this is in harmony with the OT references in ch.2, and would encourage all to acquaint themselves with their ministry, ministry which would not only counter the error propagated by false prophets, but which would guide our conduct positively towards holy living. Probably Peter is thinking of the last mountain scene of Matthew's Gospel when the Lord commanded them to teach what He had personally given them (Matt 28:20).

The titles used of the Lord and Saviour are repeated from 1:11, here instructing the saints of the common source of the teaching by the holy prophets and the apostles.

The references to the word of God in these two verses are supplemented throughout the chapter with different descriptions of it to show its variety with its value:

1. this second epistle-an additional letter to stir up their hearts and minds (v.1);

2. the spoken words-by the holy prophets, guided by the Holy Spirit (v.2);

3. the commandments-by the apostles, officially selected by the Lord (v.3);

4. His actual promise, also in v.9 and v.13, probably the ultimate in promise (v.4);

5. the word of God-creating, without prophets or apostles; operating before the work of creation began (v.5);

6. the same word of God-sustaining creation, without prophets or apostles, after the work of creation was complete (v.6);

7. writings of Paul-enlightening, yet profound, misinterpreted but remaining equal with and complementary to other sacred writings (v.7);

8. other Scriptures-sacred writings, probably the OT (v.8).

2.   *The Vanity of Scoffers*
   3:3-5

> v.3   "Knowing this first, that there shall come in the last days scoffers, walking after their own lusts,
> v.4   And saying, Where is the promise of his coming? for since the fathers fell asleep, all things continue as *they were* from the beginning of the creation.
> v.5   For this they willingly are ignorant of, that by the word of God the heavens were of old, and the earth standing out of the water and in the water:"

3   The complementary ministry of the holy prophets and the original apostles of our Lord Jesus Christ unite to combat the erroneous words of the mockers or scoffers. Firstly, they give us foreknowledge of the arrival, activity and impure aims of the false teachers. The verse also indicates how arrogant and blasphemous these errorists have become. Secondly, they inform us that these false teachers will increase in their numbers towards the close of these days. This particular period is just prior to His coming again. It is not difficult to discern the upsurge in our day of false teaching. Those referred to here are with us today. Thirdly, we are informed that the scoffers or mockers or false teachers now openly live a permissive type of life; they are well-established and have taken licence to remove the standards of holy living. Purity of life to them is old fashioned and outdated, and so with gay abandon they fearlessly indulge in the base appetites of fleshly lusts. They totally reject the coming again of the Lord, therefore they can disregard the fact of coming judgment. They repeat "let us eat, drink, for tomorrow we die" (1 Cor 15:32). These are mockers, mockingly taunting the real and genuine teacher and deliberately deceiving the unwary saint. Some who gathered with the saints at Corinth suggested that there is no resurrection of the dead, and with no life beyond death they had enthroned sin and had rejected the righteous way of life. Fourthly, they repeat the method used by those who opposed the true OT prophets (Heb 11:36) with trial of cruel mockings, scourgings.

4   Message of false teachers or the scoffers suggest that:

1.   The promises of the Lord Jesus Christ are unreliable.

2.   All things continue unchanged from the beginning of creation. They say: Nothing has changed. The cycle of nature just goes on. This is basic to the theory of uniformitarianism.

3.   They lay claim to the "fathers", probably referred to a group who were responsible leaders in their own generation (cf. Acts 3:13; Rom 9:5; Heb 1:2). Now the false teachers and their victims assume the role of the fathers.

The "coming" (*parousia*) was the subject of enquiry by the disciples when they were with our Lord Jesus on the Mount of Olives (Matt 24:3). The question of the disciples then was What shall be the sign of thy coming?" They were accustomed to the *parousia* of eminent ruling officials, and knew well that before their actual arrival there were numerous preliminary preparations and the arrangement of spectacular events to mark the visits. Heralds immediately preceded the arrival in person (*parousia*) indicating who was coming and the purpose of the coming. The Lord graciously indicates in Matt 24 and 25 the signs preceding His coming: "wars and rumours of wars"-political disorders; "famines, pestilences, earthquakes"- natural disorders; "false prophets", deceiving, causing iniquity to abound under a cloak of religion-moral disorder.

5   Peter answers the scoffers' question of v.4. They are looking for visible proof with their eyes shut, says Peter. Nobody is so blind as the man who wills to be blind. The ignorance of the scoffer is occasioned by neglect of the word of God. Thus v.5 is a concise statement of the work of God in creation. Peter quotes in v.4 the prime truth under attack, "Where is the promise of his coming (*parousia*)?" or simply "when will be its fulfilment?

In 1:16 and in v.12 of this chapter Peter uses this particular word *parousia*. It is absent from his first epistle; it simply means His presence. He has stated clearly that He will personally come, but this is denied by the scoffers.

1.   They not only doubt His word, but deny His coming again.

2.   They manufacture their own doctrine from two assumptions:
     a.   For since the fathers fell asleep all things continue as they were.
     b.   For of this they willingly are ignorant-closed their minds to truth.

Doubts and Denials. The coming again of the Lord Jesus was doubted by some in Corinth; in Thessalonica some were confused; here it is denied, so Peter sets out the main features of the future programme relative to Christ.

The false teacher who denies the personal coming again of Christ claims that seeing all things have continued from the beginning of creation without change, they shall abide without any change. This has been designated the Doctrine of Uniformitarianism. It has been formalised to show that the existing natural processes have always acted with uniform intensity throughout the eras of time. The sister theory of evolution, declaring a natural but progressive development of living organisms from pre-existing types, depends on the supposition that conditions have always been uniform. Variants of these theories appear from time to time and as subsequent discoveries in nature come to hand the theories are modified. The word of God needs no modifications.

If therefore it can be proved from history that this earth has undergone cataclysmic changes, then of course the scoffers' arguments and reasonings are untenable. Peter simply states in lay language the programme of God. It might not be classified as scientific, but it does not need to be modified or updated. It can be easily understood and by just quoting facts supported by earlier inspired writings he demolishes the changing theories of men and the false teaching based on them. There is no element of doubt in Peter's statements. Faith can readily accept the validity and value of the promise.

3.   *The Validity of History*
        3:5-7

v.5   "For this they willingly are ignorant of, that by the word of God the heavens were of old, and the earth standing out of the water and in the water:
v.6   Whereby the world that then was, being overflowed with water, perished:
v.7   But the heavens and the earth, which are now, by the same word are kept in store, reserved unto fire against the day of judgment and perdition of ungodly men."

Peter having judged that they were willing to be ignorant then proceeds to answer the scoffers' question.

He begins with the work of creation and attributes it fully to the word of God. "He commanded and it stood fast". But how it stood is miraculous, enveloped in and produced by water. The heavens were "of old" (as in 2:3), i.e. for a long time, is descriptive of their duration. Heavens (plural) indicate all the spheres beyond and above the land mass of earth in cosmic totality. Wherever heaven is in the singular it refers to the inner sanctuary of God's dwelling. In Matt 6:9 heaven is singular indicating the dwelling of "Our Father", whereas in v.10: "Thy will be done in earth as in the heavens" the word is plural referring to the various layers of the ethereal part of the universe containing the celestial bodies Paul refers to in 1 Cor 15:40. Again in Phil 3:20 "our conversation is in heaven" employs the plural, but "from whence" is singular indicating the sanctuary in which our Saviour now is and from which He shall come.

Not only were the heavens created, but the earth (land mass) "standing" or consisting (Col 1:17) through or in the water and out of the water. This, of course, is a miracle. Ps 24:2 tells us that He hath founded it upon the seas and established it on floods. He gave the sea its bounds and controlled the waters; so that Asaph, the sweet singer of Israel, indicates in Ps 77 the controlling power of God in using the clouds above to gather up and pour out water, the troubled depths of the waters beneath to roll at His command: "Thy way is in the sea, and thy path in the great waters". Yet it is amazing that with all this divine power God gently leads His people like a responsible Shepherd.

6-7   The world (physical but orderly creation) that then was (v.6) is contrasted with the world that *now* is (v.7). That world was overflowed with water, submerged but never out of His control. It was subject to His word. Some scholars suggest that this event took place between Gen 1:1 and 1:2; others relate it with the deluge reported in Gen 6. Both were cataclysmic but since Peter has already mentioned the deluge of Gen 6 in 2:5 I would suggest that he is again referring to it.

That a world should perish could never be wiped out of the history of man; but these scoffers deliberately neglect the evidence.

Peter then indicates that this present creation is also a moral sphere and just as ungodliness was judged in the ancient world, so it will be judged again. The element used in this judgment will not be water but fire. As God destroyed the old world by flooding it with water, which was already in it and out of which it had emerged, so God has other elements and He will employ them to purge the present world. The worldwide calamity of the flood proves the instability of the world and makes the mockers' theory untenable. What was formed out of, and sustained by water was destroyed by it. The voice of history loudly proclaims the truth and exposes the lie of the false teachers. When men refused the message of Enoch and of Noah they perished. Peter now argues that the same word of God foretells of a judgment by fire. The word, His word, the power of which created and removed the old, established the present order of creation and will judge it too but with (in) fire.

The present world is kept in store, treasured up in custody. Here the keeping in store is attributed to God, whereas Paul in Rom 2:5 attributes the storing up to unrepentant men with hard hearts who despise the grace of God. They will receive back their store of impiety in the day of wrath and revelation of the righteous judgment of God.

But Peter is saying that God has stored up; see Col 1:17: "In him all things hold together". Today He is restraining the elements with their amazing arsenal of energy. The explosive potential of the elements was there before the discovery of splitting the atom. It is available for use in the day of judgment for the destruction of ungodly men. Today God is acting in grace; then He will act in judgment.

4.   The Verity of the Scriptures
   3:8-9

> v.8   "But, beloved, be not ignorant of this one thing, that one day *is* with the Lord as a thousand years, and a thousand years as one day.
>
> v.9   The Lord is not slack concerning his promise, as some men count slackness, but is longsuffering to us-ward, not willing that any should perish, but that all should come to repentance."

There are three facts about the Lord that are constant:

1.   the Lord is unaffected by time;

2.   the Lord cannot be deflected from fulfilling His promise;

3.   the Lord has a day which must come, which is His day. This present day of patience will end and give way to the day of the Lord.

8   This verse loudly expresses the timelessness of the Lord. Peter is stating a fact about the eternity of his Lord. He does not dwell in nor is conditioned by an ageing or changing world. He is not subject to a diary or calendar of time. One day of time is as a thousand years; He can expand the hours of day to years of a millennium, and He can do the reverse; He can put a thousand years into one day. He can expand or compress as He desires to suit the fulfilment of His promises. His promises decide the days or years of the ages of time.

"But, beloved" is an affectionate appeal by Peter as if to say, Do not be blind (1:9) or ignorant like the scoffers of v.5. One day rests with the Lord as a thousand years or the reverse. So then, what men count a delay is not a delay. God is never late or early. Time is His and so also is eternity.

9   This verse becomes a statement expressing a characteristic of One who is eternal and not bound by days, or years of time. He will as He promised end the history of the godless with His judgment. If we imagine that it is time for God to act in government, then remember He is patient, not slack, He will fulfil His promise; He does not want any to perish. The day of salvation (2 Cor 6) has become almost two millennia. In Isa 61:2 the prophet speaks of the year that is acceptable, being full of grace and longsuffering in contrast with a day of vengeance. He waited more than a hundred years before He sent the flood in Noah's day, today He has offered grace for hundreds of years before the destruction by fire. Delay is not in His vocabulary. He is patient and waits, suffering all this time, giving men space to repent and not to perish.

This verse not only talks of the negative side of the Lord: He is not slack, but also emphatically states the positive. He is longsuffering, not willing that any should perish. When Paul wrote to Timothy in 1 Tim 3:15 he says, "But if I tarry long"-if I delay my coming to you. There is no delay in God's vocabulary. He waits in patience. This enduring grace of the Lord is presently evident. In Matt 18:21-35 the question of Peter to the Lord relative to his attitude to the disagreeable brother allows the Lord Jesus to unfold His patience and forgiving grace. In the parable which He relates of the servants who were heavily in debt to the king and who were asking for time to repay, the king graciously allowed them time; but the story ends sadly with the king, although patient, punishing the servant and giving him over to the tormentors. Despite the patience and forgiving grace of the king, the day of judgment arrived.

Paul in 1 Tim 2 states that God wills all to be saved and provision had been made for all. But also all do not accept God's salvation and presume on His patience and longsuffering. Repentance is offered as the way back to God, and was often preached by Peter in his earlier days of Acts 2:38; 5:31; 11:18 to his own people and to the Gentiles.

But note the longsuffering is "to us-ward"; in a special sense it was for Peter and his colleagues, the saints of that particular age, but of course it is applicable today to all the saints. An unwearied God is dealing in patience with His people. How patient and longsuffering was God to Lot and his family. Ultimately God took him out of the area of devastation and judgment. God will do right by His people.

5.   *The Vision of the Ages*
3:10-13

v.10 "But the day of the Lord will come as a thief in the night, in the which the heavens shall pass away with a great noise, and the elements shall melt with fervent heat, the earth also and the works that are therein shall be burned up.

v.11 *Seeing* then *that* all these things shall be dissolved, what manner *of persons* ought ye to be in *all* holy conversation and godliness,

v.12 Looking for and hasting unto the coming of the day of God, wherein the heavens being on fire shall be dissolved, and the elements shall melt with fervent heat?

v.13 Nevertheless we, according to his promise, look for new heavens and a new earth, wherein dwelleth righteousness."

10   But the day of the patience of the Lord and the day of preaching repentance is now finished; the day of the Lord arrives in this verse. Is this then man's day today? Man today has the right of choice: he can be saved today. But the day of the Lord has arrived-the day when the Lord acts in judgment.

The word "day" occurs often in 2 Peter; describing a cycle of 24 hours: Lot from day to day vexed his soul (2:8); riot in the day time-contrast to night life of sinners (2:13); one day is as a thousand years (3:8 twice). On other occasions it describes a dispensation of years as in 2:9; 3:3,7,10,12.

The expression "day of the Lord" is often found in the OT, usually referring to a day of retribution and judgment. The books of the prophets before and after the Babylonian captivity constantly use the expression, cf. Isa 2:12; 13:6,9; Ezek 13:5; 30:3; Joel 1:15; 2:1,11,31; Amos 5:18,20; Obad 15; Zeph 1:7,14; Zech 14:1; Mal 4:5. The prophets pointed ahead in their ministry to the day when the Lord would reign in righteousness; some indicate how that day begins; others how it continues and how it ends.

The NT continues with references to the day of the Lord as a day of judgment, again like the OT indicating how it will begin, continue and end. The references also tell out clearly that the heavens and the earth will know its influence. Earth-dwellers will be caught unawares. They will not expect it when it arrives. There are reliable texts which in this verse omit the expression "as a thief in the night", but 1 Thess 5:2,4 include it, and there is no valid reason to leave it out. The day is certain though unexpected by the mass of men, but the saints know perfectly that the day of the Lord cometh. "As a thief in the night" it comes, and the poor unsuspecting victims of the false teaching by false prophets and false teachers now discover they have been duped and deceived and ultimately damned.

Those who follow the clear teaching of the OT and NT will not be overtaken, they are not blind, they have the light of Scripture. They know exactly what Peter is saying with certainty. The day *will come*. Certain changes will take place in the heavens and the earth. Peter concentrates on the closing of the age, whereas Paul in 1 Thess 5:2,4, and 2 Thess 1:7-10 refers to the early period of the day of the Lord.

The heavens shall pass away with a great noise. The heavens (in the plural) will come under His judgment. In Heb 1:10 they are said to have been the works of His hands but they shall perish; they shall not escape the judgment. The reference in Matt 5:18 indicates that this passing away cannot occur until every jot and iota of God's promise has been fulfilled. This fact is supplemented in Matt 24:35 to show the faithfulness of God to His every promise: "Heaven and earth shall pass away but my words (plural of *logos*) shall not pass away". They will be honoured and fulfilled perfectly.

The heavens shall pass away with a rushing sound-this description of the noise indicates the excess energy required. "The elements shall melt with fervent heat". There is reference to this again in v.12. The stellar and atmospheric heavens shall perish-the noise will be deafening and the elements (the basic constituents of matter in all its forms) will be melted. This is the final holocaust. Included is the earth; this special planet with all its wonders and works will be burned up. Everything of the old creation is dismissed; it is put away like an old well-used worn garment (Ps 102:25-27; Heb 1:10-12). We take comfort that all this judgment is under the control of the Lord. The heavens and earth with their elements will remain until He has fulfilled every promise. He shall not have an unfulfilled promise nor an uncontrolled holocaust. Just as the introduction of them was orderly and their basic arrangements held intact over the centuries of time, so their change will be with orderly precision.

11   What effect should this have on us now?

1.   Our conversation should be holy.

2.   Our conduct should be godly.

In 1 Pet 1:15 we are invited to be holy in all manner of conversation, i.e., in the way we live daily, we remember our profession to holiness and in every single situation we should be marked by godliness. Now Peter shows up the effects that true knowledge of God produces- holiness and godliness. Here lies the gulf between the true knowledge and humanism, gnosticism, stoicism. True knowledge leads to holiness; humanism, gnosticism and stoicism give licence and lead to sin and lawlessness.

12   If v.11 indicates our present conduct in an impure world, Peter now encourages us to stretch out with the hand of anticipation to the day of God. He has regard for the future. He expectantly looks for the coming (*parousia*) of the day of God. We should live today looking for God's tomorrow. The day of God is the day of His completing the calendar with its ages of time and now begins the state of eternity.
   The word "wherein" is not carrying the thought of "in which" but "on account of which" the heavens are purged with fire, the elements melting in fervent heat. The elements including the earth, all that is involved in v.10, heavens' elements, earth and its works are all dismissed by the fires of holiness. All this holocaust precedes the day of God.
   This is what we look for, and it is to this we hasten, when God's final day shows to us His *parousia*-His excellent supremacy and His ultimate triumph and glory. Our AV version uses the verb "to look" in vv.12,13,14: looking for the "*parousia*" of the day of God (v.12); looking for new heavens and a new earth (v.13); seeing that ye look for such things (v.14). The looking takes us out of and beyond scenes of time and change into eternity and changelessness.
   In the Scriptures we read of man's day; the Lord's day; the day of salvation;

the day of judgment; but now we have arrived at the day of God, the final and permanent rest. The little word "wherein" carries the meaning "on account of which". His work of creation was good (Gen 1). His work of removing the old and introducing the new will be perfect. Peter is now indicating that the release of power in creating will be matched with the evident power in destroying. So the old with all its memorable history is taken away to make room for the unchanging, changeless and unchangeable. However, there will still be heavens and an earth as v.13 states clearly.

13 We look by and in faith for new heavens and a new earth wherein dwelleth righteousness. We look expectantly because it has all been promised. The promise takes in the day of *parousia* of God, the emergence of new heavens and a new earth and righteousness dwelling eternally. In this creation there is no need for involuntary subjection, it is rather the peaceful dwelling with nothing to disturb. It is the Sabbath of righteousness. The heavens and earth then will be perennially fresh-the feeling of newness will always exist. The fulness of bliss for eternity will be enjoyed by all, for all evil will have been destroyed. The profound moral consequence of righteousness dwelling in the day of God describes the ultimate of what God set out in promise, achieved by Him personally and enjoyed by all those included in the same promise. It seems that only righteousness survives, and then we shall understand how He loved righteousness and hated lawlessness. Sin cannot and will not have the final word. Righteousness will prevail.

6. *Virtue of Diligence*
3:14-18

v.14 "Wherefore, beloved, seeing that ye look for such things, be diligent that ye may be found of him in peace, without spot, and blameless.
v.15 And account *that* the longsuffering of our Lord *is* salvation even as our beloved brother Paul also according to the wisdom given unto him hath written unto you;
v.16 As also in all *his* epistles, speaking in them of these things; in which are some things hard to be understood, which they that are unlearned and unstable wrest, as *they do* also the other Scriptures, unto their own destruction.
v.17 Ye therefore, beloved, seeing ye know *these things* before, beware lest ye also, being led away with the error of the wicked, fall from your own stedfastness.
v.18 But grow in grace, and *in* the knowledge of our Lord and Saviour Jesus Christ. To him *be* glory both now and for ever. Amen."

14 "Wherefore" stand still, review the weighty matters discussed, and as we expect them (look for) so let the truth of them shape our lives. This is the summary effect produced. We are the beloved-the objects of divine love and divine promise. No one has a future so bright and glorious, so in this present age "be diligent". Let us not be indifferent, the world hastens on to a fiery judgment, the whole of this present creation will be burned up, but we are subjects of His promise so let us be positive in our testimony now. If false teachers delude men to think that there is nothing but blank negative at the end, then we can understand why men abandon themselves to a gay life in sin. But we look for a future that is bright and glorious. Does it affect us now? John says, he "that hath this hope ... purifieth himself" (1 John 3:3). Paul says, "stand fast in the Lord" (Phil 4:1). Peter here calls for diligence. In 1:5,10,15 (AV has "endeavour"), he invited the saints to be careful, studiously pragmatic and in this final section he emphasises the need to be diligently busy in the things of God as we eagerly await the coming day when the final promise of God will be fulfilled. We must keep ourselves without spot and unblameable by Him that we may be found in peace, having no spot to disfigure christian character, and no blot attached to our christian testimony, whereas in 2:13 false teachers and their followers have both the spot and the blemish. In 1 Pet 1:19 we learn that Jesus had no spot or blemish, internally pure and externally beautiful. These two characteristics in us are for His pleasure. The outcome of such a life is peace. The agitation that sin and error brings belongs to mockers. The deep seated peace is that enjoyed blessing of the saints now.

15-16 The waiting for the *parousia* bespeaks the patient waiting of our Lord. In v.9 he has instructed that what might seem to be delay is in reality a revelation of the longsuffering of the Lord Jesus Christ. This alleged delay is to continue the offer of salvation. He is not willing that any should perish. Having made ample provision for sinners, the Lord waits in the office of Saviour for them to repent.

"Our beloved brother Paul" shows how kind and affectionate is the heart of Peter. Despite the embarrassments of earlier days he appreciates the true worth of this valued servant of the Lord. To Peter, Paul is not just a brother but a beloved brother, this in spite of Acts 15 and Gal 2:11-14: Peter recognises publicly that Paul has the word of wisdom and had written to them. This of course begs the question to which letter or letters of Paul is Peter referring. In our NT we have four sets of letters from Paul and Peter may be referring to them all, for in each set Paul writes about future events. If Peter had all the epistles of Paul then this letter could be dated later than AD 64. Rather than discuss possible dates of writing there is perhaps more profit in reviewing Paul's writings which deal with the promises of God still unfulfilled.

1 and 2 Thessalonians, the earliest writings of Paul, both deal extensively with prophecy relating to the Church and to the coming of the Lord Jesus. A detailed review of the man that is after the working of Satan is given; his appearing and his ignominious defeat. Then the argumentative and doctrinal writings, probably the next set of letters in course of time, Romans, Galatians, 1 and 2 Corinthians, have passages associated with the unfulfilled promises of God and some of them deal fully and doctrinally with the errors of the false teachers and in general outline the future regathering of Israel.

The third set of letters, commonly known as the prison letters of Paul, Ephesians, Colossians, Philippians and Philemon, again have certain statements about the future where the Lord Jesus is Head over all things and headed up in

Him are all things in the dispensation of the age of ages (Eph 1:10). He is the Image (Col 1:15) of the invisible God and the final reconciliation of all things will be effected by Him and for Himself. The futuristic teaching mainly refers to Christ and His Church.

The last set of preserved letters are termed the pastoral letters in which appears the description of the Lord Jesus Christ as God our Saviour, used here in 2 Peter. Both writers relate this title in the same way to the great future glory ahead: Titus 2:13; 1 Tim 1:17; 2 Tim 1:12 ("that day"); 4:8,18.

From the epistles of Paul attention has been drawn not to every reference made by him, but to a few which confirm that Peter and Paul agreed in their prophetic teaching. Peter, in claiming that Paul had a special gift, also indicates that Paul was not always easy to understand. The Thessalonians seemed to be in some confusion not only because of what Paul wrote, but also about others who misrepresented Paul and his teaching. This gave Paul occasion to write 2 Thessalonians. It may also be as some have suggested that the epistle to the Hebrews is being referred to by Peter as one of Paul's epistles. Whether Peter included all Paul's writings or just the writings that had come into his possession, the main point is that both eminent and much-used men of God were in total and full agreement with the teaching that God cannot lie (Titus 1:2), that He fulfils all His promises on time, without any delay. The doctrine of Paul was not misunderstood by Peter, but, says Peter, there are those who have not only misunderstood them but have misused them just as they did the rest of the books of sacred Scripture. In this expression Peter was accepting Paul's epistles with equal respect as the sacred writings. There were those in his day, false teachers, scoffers and mockers, who wrested or twisted the writings to their own destruction. They did it for gain, but actually it turned out to be their own destruction. They had followed the way of Balaam (2:15).

Examples from Paul's letters of such could be "the some" in Corinth (1 Cor 15:12); or Hymenaeus and Philetus (2 Tim 2:17). The unlearned or untaught (*amathēs*), the negative of a true learner; and the unstable and unestablished (*astēriktos*), beguiling unsteadfast souls, cf. 2:14. This description fits these false teachers and their followers, the false teacher ever learning and never coming to a knowledge of the truth, and beguiling or deceiving unstable souls. Their end is destruction (*apōleia*). This word is used six times in the epistle (2:1a, 1b,2,3; 3:7,16), translated in our AV as "perdition", "damnable", "damnation" "pernicious ways" and "destruction". It describes what is waste and useless, what perishes and destroys itself from the inside out; from such nothing is salvageable.

17 Peter speaks directly to the beloved recipients of his letter and repeats a word used in 1 Pet 1:20 (*proginōskō*) and a similar expression in 1:20 and 3:1. He simply draws his letter to a finish by indicating that they know: there was no misunderstanding of Paul by them, and what Peter had spoken and now had written was appreciated by them. They were never in the group of the unlearned or untaught but they should beware lest they be carried away with the error of the lawless. To be led away in error would be their downfall. This reflects on what he indicated in 1:10, but with more severe results; not just that they might stumble (1:10) but even fall from grace.

18 Rather than fall from grace, grow in grace and in the knowledge of our Lord and Saviour Jesus Christ. This is an active imperative- keep on growing in both grace and knowledge.

"To him (the Lord Jesus Christ) be glory now and in the day of Eternity. Amen" is a fitting doxology to end with, perhaps learned by Peter as he listened to the Lord Jesus pray (Matt 6:13).

1, 2, & 3 JOHN
A. M. S. Gooding

JOHN'S EPISTLES
Introduction

1. The Writer
2. The Background
3. Analysis of Epistle
4. Bibliography

1. The Writer

There is very little doubt that these three epistles were written by the author of the fourth Gospel-the disciple whom Jesus loved. His name is not mentioned in his Gospel though it is a document containing many persons. Often names are associated with places and events in order to distinguish them from others of the same name, e.g. Philip of Bethsaida of Galilee, Judas not Iscariot, the town of Mary and Martha and Lazarus; "it was that Mary" etc. It is strange therefore that John never uses the term John the Baptist, always simply John. Is he telling us that he considered himself to be so insignificant, and John Baptist to be so outstanding that it was not necessary to indicate a distinction; the person was obvious; no one else of that name was of any importance. Thus John obscured his identity under this gracious nom-de-plume. He left out his own name, his mother's name and even omitted events where he was a member of the outstanding three!

This self-effacing attitude marks all John's writings except the Revelation where it is evident he had received a revelation of Jesus Christ " which God gave unto him, to show unto his servants things which must shortly come to pass; and he sent and signified it by his angel unto "his servant John" (Rev 1:1) and therefore must mention both his name and the authority with which he spoke. In his first epistle his name is not mentioned, nor the place from which or to which it was written. No greeting with name is mentioned which would identify the locality. He had before him the very serious task of defending the truth and guarding the saints; nothing else was important. In his second and third epistles- unnamed again-he is "the elder"-not some outstanding church dignitary, lording it over others, but simply the last surviving elder of the apostolic band, older than the majority of the saints among whom he laboured-a father figure.

John was the son of Zebedee and Salome. His brother had been martyred at an early date, the first of the apostles to die. John now is the only survivor of that band. As a young man he was both nationalistic and sectarian in his approach to divine things. He and his brother James were designated "sons of thunder" and they, and their mother for them, desired positions of greatness in the kingdom. Now after a half century of fellowship with the Saviour, the prophet of thunder had become the apostle of love. We would gather that John was "one of the two" whom John the Baptist introduced to the Lord (John 1:40). He was the one who leaned on Jesus' breast (John 13:23) at supper. He followed Jesus into the palace of the high priest (18:15), stood by the cross of Jesus (19:25), was early at the sepulchre (20:2). He was following at the beginning (John 1:40) and still following at the end (John 21:20). It would appear that with most if not all the apostles, he left Jerusalem about the year AD 60 before the destruction of Jerusalem and spent the rest of his days at Ephesus. For a quarter of a century the churches of Asia Minor became his immediate concern. He found a fruitful field in the area to which much of Paul's and Peter's written ministry had been sent.

Irenaeus, the disciple of Polycarp, the disciple of John, wrote (AD 180): "The John, the disciple of the Lord, who also leaned back on His breast, he too published a Gospel during his residence at Ephesus". Justin Martyr (AD 150) probably within fifty years of John's death writes: "Among us also a certain man named John, one of the disciples of Christ, prophesied in a revelation made to him, that the believers of our Christ shall spend a thousand years in Jerusalem".

Polycarp, Papias of Hierapolis, Irenaeus of Lyons, Clement of Alexandria, Tertullian, Hippolytus, Cyprian and Eusebius are among the list of worthy names who refer to these writings implying in some small way their association with John. In his Gospel and first epistle one is breathing the same atmosphere; one is in touch with heaven. So many truths, ideas and expressions are common to both. The doctrine taught and the truth defended in the first epistle are the basis of the apostle's concern in the second epistle that this dear sister and her children should not be led away, but should appreciate to the full the truth that "Jesus Christ is come in the flesh" and should not allow into her home, or show fellowship with, those that deny the fundamental truths of which he wrote.

The second and third epistles are twins, both written to individuals: one to a middle-aged widow, the other to a man. Both show love and hospitality to the Lord's people especially to His travelling servants. One shows concern that the sister does not receive and bid God speed to "deceivers who deny" while the other instructs and comments relative to God's servants who walk in the truth. Both have a relevance to children, the one a sister's natural children who bring pleasure by walking in the things of God; the other to John's spiritual children who walk in the truth. One could not divorce these two simple homely letters. The same terms, the same structure, the same concern and care show that they undeniably proceed not only from the Spirit of God but from the same pen. John most likely writes both his Gospel and his epistles at the same time from Ephesus between the years AD 80 and 90.

2. The Background

In the second part of the first century false teachers were appearing among the saints, indeed "many deceivers are entered into the world" (2 John 7). Paul warned that certain would arise (Acts 20:29,30). Indeed the Lord Jesus had forewarned His own that "The kingdom of heaven is like unto leaven, which a woman took, and hid in three measures of meal, till the whole was leavened" (Matt 13:33). This leavening process was advancing rapidly in John's day. Against these various errors the writers of the NT documents defend the saints, particularly Paul dealing with Judaism in Galatians and John dealing with gnosticism (or that which blossomed into gnosticism in the second century) in his Gospel and his first and second epistle.

Gnosticism was the most dangerous heresy threatening the Church in the first three centuries. Gnosticism was built on a false premise that all material was evil and non-material was good. We judge these assertions to be foolish but their effect on the lives and the beliefs of those who held them was far reaching and horrific. Its adherents became either ascetic (who sought to conquer sinful desires) or libertines who engaged in unbridled indulgence of the flesh, taught that matter or the flesh could not affect the spirit, therefore one could engage in whatsoever actions one desired without ill effects on the real self-the spirit especially if in the cause of sinning one was acquiring knowledge. Thus sin was not sin; evil became (in their thinking) good. Thus John writes "let no man deceive you: he that doeth righteousness is righteous ... whosoever does not righteousness is not of God" (3:7,10). Gnosticism had adversely influenced Judaism, and also the religion of Greece. Christianity at its birth was surrounded by this tainted air. Gnosticism while professing no hostility to the gospel proved to be one of its most subtle and dangerous enemies. On the plea of interpreting christian doctrines from a higher standpoint it really demolished them, destroying them by explaining them away. "The two great gnostic principles-the supremacy of knowledge and the impurity of matter produced opposite results in ethical teaching. If knowledge is everything, the body is worthless, then the body must be beaten down and crushed in order that the emancipated soul may rise to the knowledge of higher things ... Alternatively if knowledge is everything and the body is worthless, the body may rightly undergo every kind of experience, no matter how shameless and impure in order that it may increase its share of knowledge-the body could not be made more vile than it is and the soul of the enlightened was incapable of pollution" (Lightfoot).

Gnosticism sought to establish and preserve an intellectual approach to religion. It had its hidden wisdom, its exclusive mysteries and its privileged class.

According to early church writers the father of gnostic heresy was Simon Magus (Acts 8:9-13). Another outstanding gnostic was Cerinthus. It seems that John has him and his teaching in mind in quite a number of places in his first epistle.

Cerinthus. This heretic is said to be originally a native of Alexandria, but pro-consular Asia was the centre of his activity. He lived and taught at the close of the apostolic era, the last ten years of the first century. He was contemporary with John whom Polycarp said denounced him publicly on at least one occasion. It is said by Irenaeus that John wrote to confute this teaching.

The other evil result of their false premise was that it denied the deity and the genuine humanity-the incarnation of our Lord Jesus Christ. If He was indeed God, and they believed that in God there resides the totality of divine powers the *plērōma* or the plenitude, how could He become a real man and possess a material body (seeing that they believed all material was evil)? This posed for them a problem which they sought to solve by teaching that the Lord Jesus was not a real man, had not a real body, was not blood and flesh, was in fact only a phantom-He only seemed to be (hence the word *docetism*). Notice that John, Luke, Paul, and the writer to the Hebrews stress the real humanity of our Lord Jesus. He was, and is, as real a man as any other man. And He is a complete man-body, soul and spirit (sin apart).

"Cerinthus flourished in the province of Asia, accepted the general dualistic world view (including the creation of matter by an inferior power than the God we christians know) and propounded a novel Christology. He distinguished the man Jesus (the son of Joseph and Mary endowed with a greater virtue and wisdom than other men) from the Christ who descended in the form of a dove at His baptism, empowering Him to perform miracles and proclaim the unknown Father but left Him before He died. So Jesus suffered, died and rose again, while Christ remained immune from suffering, did not die, shed no blood since He was a spiritual being" (F. F. Bruce).

John wrote his Gospel that ye might believe that Jesus is the Christ the Son of God and that believing ye might have life through His name (John 20:31). He wrote his first epistle,

1.	That your joy may be full	1:4
2.	That ye sin not	2:1
3.	Because your sins are forgiven you	2:12
4.	That ye know that ye have eternal life	5:13

3. Analysis of the Epistle

John does not follow the usual pattern of NT epistles. Paul commences his with his own name and the names of those associated with him. He next mentions those to whom he writes, the place where they reside and sends to them spiritual greetings. He follows this with thanksgivings for their spiritual progress and prayers for their prosperity in spiritual things. This is followed with the general burden of his message, the first part doctrinal, the later part practical. The whole is brought to a close with various greetings and salutations.

John, however, does not conform to this pattern at all. His epistle almost defies analysis. The same words are repeated over and over again, also the same ideas and expressions. Indeed, some have suggested, almost blasphemously, that the epistle is the muddled thinking of an old man. But we who love God's word could never entertain such an idea. We believe that every letter and every part of a letter in the original document of these epistles are the definite breathings of God, written in words that the Spirit of God teaches.

Professor Robert Law in his excellent work *The Tests of Life* points out: "The almost unvarying simplicity of syntactical structure, the absence of connecting, notably illative, particles, and, in short, the generally Hebraic type of composition have been frequently remarked upon ... One has only to read the epistle with an attentive ear to perceive that, though using another language, the writer had in his own ear, all the time, the swing and the cadence of Old Testament verse ... It is not suggested that there is in the epistle a conscious imitation of Hebraic forms, but it is evident, I think, that no one could have written as our author does whose whole style of thought and expression had not been unconsciously formed upon Old Testament models".

Law also helps by his suggestion that "John's mode of thinking in this epistle is a spiral. The course of thought does not move from point to point in a straight line". It is like a winding staircase, always revolving round the same centre; it is like the flight of an eagle, each circle rising higher than the one before, each circle becoming larger, touching each time similar topics, covering three basic foundation stones: righteousness, love and truth.

4. Bibliography

Barrett, C.S. *The First Epistle of John*. Religious Tract Society, London 19 10.

Blaiklock, E.M. *Faith is the Victory, Studies in First Epistle of John*. Eerdmans 1959.

Bruce, F.F. *The Spreading Flame*. Paternoster Press, Exeter 1958.

Bruce, F.F. *The Epistles of John*. Pickering and Inglis Ltd 1970.

Burdick, Donald W. *The Epistles of John*. Moody Press, Chicago 1970.

Darby, J.N. *Epistles of John*. Geo. Morrish, London.

Hoste, W. and Rodgers, W. *Bible Problems and Answers*. John Ritchie, Kilmarnock 1957.

Lenski, R.C.H. *An Interpretation of Three Epistles of John*. Augsburg Pub. House, Minneapolis, Minnesota.

Lightfoot, J.R. *Epistles of Paul*. Macmillan & Co Ltd 1875.

Lincoln, W. *Epistles of John*. John Ritchie Ltd, Kilmarnock.

Martin, R.P. *Colossians*. Paternoster Press, Exeter 1972.

Plummer, A. *Epistles of St John*. Cambridge Bible for Schools. Cambridge 1900.

Robertson, A.T. *Word Pictures in the New Testament*, Vol.6. Harper, New York 1933.

Stott, J.R.W. *The Epistles of John*. Inter-Varsity Press, Leicester 1983.

Vine, W.E. *Epistles of John*. Gospel Tract Publications, Glasgow 1985.

Walvoord, J.F. and Zuck, Ray B. *The Bible Knowledge Commentary*. Victor Books, Wheaton, Illinois 1983.

Westcott, Brooke F. *The Epistles of John*. Eerdmans, Grand Rapids 1950.

FINAL EXHORTATION - KEEP YOURSELVES FROM IDOLS

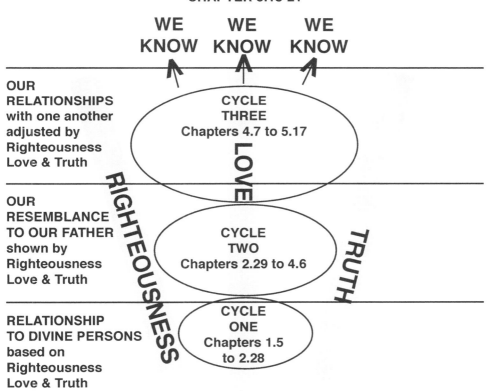

THIS IS THE TRUE GOD
AND ETERNAL LIFE

CHAPTER 5.18-21

WE   WE   WE
KNOW KNOW KNOW

OUR
RELATIONSHIPS
with one another
adjusted by
Righteousness
Love & Truth

CYCLE
THREE
Chapters 4.7 to 5.17

LOVE

OUR
RESEMBLANCE
TO OUR FATHER
shown by
Righteousness
Love & Truth

CYCLE
TWO
Chapters 2.29 to 4.6

TRUTH

RELATIONSHIP
TO DIVINE PERSONS
based on
Righteousness
Love & Truth

CYCLE
ONE
Chapters 1.5
to 2.28

RIGHTEOUSNESS

THE WORD OF LIFE
The Prologue
Chapter 1.1-4

1 JOHN
A.M.S. GOODING

FIRST EPISTLE OF JOHN

I. Prologue (1:1-4)

v.1 "That which was from the beginning, which we have heard, which we have seen with our eyes, which we have looked upon, and our hands have handled, of the Word of life;

v.2 (For the life was manifested, and we have seen *it*, and bear witness, and shew unto you that eternal life, which was with the Father, and was manifested unto us,)

v.3 That which we have seen and heard declare we unto you, that ye may also have fellowship with us and truly our fellowship *is* with the Father, and with his Son Jesus Christ.

v.4 And these things write we unto you, that your joy may be full."

1 It seems strange to commence the epistle with the word "that" instead of "He". "That" should be connected with the expression at the end of the verse "concerning the Word of life" (RV). It is evident that the "Word of life" is a person who could be heard, seen, looked upon and handled. "That" may therefore refer to the message, but the subject is without doubt the Lord Jesus. It could be suggested that "eternal life" is manifested in the Lord Jesus and secondly in the lives of those who receive Him. As Bruce comments: "The epistle is justly called 'the epistle of eternal life'. It shows how and in whom that life was uniquely and perfectly manifested, it shows how the presence of that life in men and women may be recognised".

"From the beginning" reminds us of Gen 1:1 and John 1:1. The former signifies the moment when the work of creation began; the latter looks back beyond that, to what might be called "the unbeginning beginning" where one's mind staggers at the contemplation of the endless, unmeasured past. "The Word was", always was, with no beginning (and equally with no end). It is impossible to have eternity past without God, and impossible without the Word. Both are co-existent and co-eternal. Does not Micah say, "whose goings forth have been from of old, from everlasting" ("from the days of eternity" RV)? Col 1:16 attests His creatorship, "in him were all things created" (as to design), and "through whom were all things created" (i.e. in creation He was the active agent of the Trinity); but more, v.17 picks up and amplifies Micah's distant echo, "he is (not was) before all things". (See also John 17:5, "before the world was"; John 17:24, "before the foundation of the world"; Eph 1:4; 2 Tim 1:9, "before times eternal" (RV).) Lenski's comment is apposite: "The verb *estin* ('is', not 'became', not 'has been') leaves all eternity open to that which already then 'was' the *logos* long before His manifestation in the world".

Here, however, the expression is "That which was from the beginning". This unique person has come from that beginning. His movements have been towards the occupants of the world that He has made, "Then I was by him ... rejoicing always before him, rejoicing in *his habitable earth*" (Prov 8:30,31 RV). He came from the remoteness of an unbeginning eternity and was manifested unto men. From the words "heard", "seen", "looked upon" and "handled" some have suggested the picture of a person gradually approaching from a distance: first heard, but not near enough to be seen; then seen, undoubtedly but indistinctly; then coming nearer so that features can be clearly seen; finally being near enough to be handled. This they have likened to the gradual revelation of Christ in the OT Scriptures from the promise of the seed of the woman, until, crossing the silent years between the testaments, Mary and Simeon received Him into their arms, handling the Word of life. The idea is sweet but I rather think that John is taking his place with his fellow apostles as common witnesses of what they had personally experienced. Witness and testimony are favourite words in John's vocabulary. Is it not more probable that John is establishing for his readers the real humanity of our Lord Jesus Christ? John is writing when gnosticism is beginning to raise its ugly head. He writes his Gospel "that ye might believe that Jesus is the Christ, the Son of God", whereas he is writing his epistle to confirm that the Son of God is Jesus-a real man, as much a real man as any other man (sin apart). In his Gospel he is defending the deity of Christ; here he is confirming truth that is equally fundamental-the perfect humanity of Christ.

John commences his witness not so much with the incarnation, though that is involved, but at the point where he and his fellow apostles had personal contact with the Lord Jesus. This probably refers to John 1:35 and the complete period that followed. John does not speak as a single witness, but as the last remaining representative of the apostolic band. Those who were opposing the truth of our Lord's genuine humanity had not heard, seen or handled Him. They are not genuine eye witnesses. John writes at this late date to confirm the truth while residing in the very area where Cerinthus is actually spreading his errors. John is most severe on many occasions in his contradiction of him.

The gnostics might argue that the Lord Jesus was nothing more than a phantom, a ghost, that He only seemed to be, that He was an intangible appearance similar to the appearances (Christophanies) of the OT. Had not Abram, Moses, Joshua, Gideon and Manoah heard and seen appearances that eventually passed away?

John proceeds therefore: "we have heard, we have seen with our eyes . . this being the personal testimony of many witnesses. "John has two perfects and two aorists. The perfects convey the thought that 'what we have heard' and 'what we have seen' has its continuous effect upon us; the two aorists the fact 'we did actually behold', 'we did actually handle' " (Lenski). They had heard His voice, they had seen Him with their own eyes, they had had opportunity to examine Him carefully for a prolonged period of time and they had handled real solid flesh. They were convinced by personal investigation that He was a real man and the wonder of it still remained with them. Jesus was most truly and fully man. No writer in the NT holds with greater tenacity the reality of the incarnation. John teaches that "we have seen with our own eyes", "handled with our own hands". "The tense teaches that they still heard and saw at the time of writing" (Burdick).

"We beheld" (*theaomai*) may imply we "penetrated beyond what was accessible to outward vision to discern inward glory" (Bruce); beheld with "careful contemplation" (Vine); others suggest viewed attentively; with wondering regard; with a careful and deliberate vision that interprets its object; we beheld "a spectacle that broke on our astonished vision" (D. Smith).

What John and his fellows had heard, seen, looked upon and handled was a real human form, a real man, but He was far more. Absolute Godhood is enshrined in perfect manhood: God is manifested in flesh. He is here designated ',the Word of life"; this reminds us of another of the unique words of John's vocabulary. The Word (*Logos*) is used only by John in this particular way:

"In the beginning was the Word" etc	John 1:1
"The Word was made flesh"	John 1:14
"His name is called the Word of God"	Rev 19:13
"The Word of life"	1 John 1:1

The designation Word (*Logos*) attracts our attention. What does it mean? What picture does it convey of the Lord Jesus? Let me illustrate: I might have all kinds of ideas, thoughts, suggestions in my mind, all kinds of emotions in my heart, but unless there was some way, some means by which I could convey them to others, they would not know them. This is where words derive their value. Words are vehicles for conveying thoughts to others, and if it is true that "as a man thinketh in his heart so is he" then my words will be vehicles for conveying to others what I am. The Lord Jesus is the Word, the conveyor to men not only of the thoughts of God and the wisdom of God, but the conveyor of what God is. He is the vehicle to reveal God to men, thus "no man hath seen God at any time; the only begotten Son, which is in the bosom of the Father (who has His being in the bosom of the Father), he hath declared him" (John 1:18). As the "Word" our Lord Jesus revealed God in His power in the creation (John 1:3) and upholding of the world (Heb 1:1-3). He has revealed Him through incarnation (John 1: 14) and redemption to the guilty sons of men. Did He not say: "He that hath seen me hath seen the Father" (John 14:9)?

2 The expression "Word of life" is the climax of v.1 and this following verse is a parenthesis explaining the expression. V.1 is about the humanity of Christ; v.2 is a statement of His deity. He is the Word of life and the life was manifested.

Compare the facts stated here with John's Gospel:

JOHN 1	*1 JOHN 1*
In the beginning was the Word	Word of life
In Him was life	The eternal life
The life was the light of men	God is light
The light shineth in the darkness	Some walk in darkness
The darkness comprehended it not	Others walk in light

JOHN 3:16	*1 JOHN 4:8,16*
God so loved the world	God is love

It is interesting to note that divine revelation is first of all "God is light" (see above with Gen 1:3) and afterwards "God is love". Men would reverse the order, to their eternal undoing.

The verse reaffirms the statements of v.1 and intimates John's desire to communicate these facts to the saints. To quote Wescott, "The reality of the incarnation would be undeclared if it were said, 'The Word was manifested'; the manifoldness of the operations of life would be circumscribed if it were said, 'the life became flesh'. The manifestation of the life was a consequence of the incarnation of the Word, but not co-extensive with it".

That which was manifested was the *eternal life*, "the life, the eternal" (RV)-the Life of eternity, the Life of the ages. One thinks back into the eternal past (Col 1: 17; Heb 1:2) and He is there, gazes forward into the eternal future (1 Cor 15:22; Rev 21:3-6) and He is there: "from everlasting to everlasting, thou art God" (Ps 90:2); "They shall perish; but thou remainest ... they shall be changed: but thou art the same" (Heb 1:11,12). These lovely words are addressed by the Spirit of God to the Son of God-the Life of eternity.

That "eternal life" was "with the Father". "The word *pros*, with, as in the first verse of the Gospel, signifies not merely an accompaniment, but a living active relationship to, and communion with the Father" (Vine). This living active relationship was with the Father before manifestation, prior to incarnation; it belongs to eternity past and shows the fellowship that existed between divine persons before ever the world was. What delightful, perfect, untarnished, flawless, fellowship was this, with nothing to mar or defile!

3   Thus we are introduced to the widening aspects of the fellowship of our chapter:

1.   *The fellowship of divine persons*
      "The eternal life, which was with the Father" (v.2).

2.   *The fellowship associated with "we", "our", "us"*

3. *Fellowship embracing all the redeemed of this age*
"Ye also may have fellowship with us" (v.3).

It is important to distinguish between the pronouns of the opening section of this chapter. *"We", "our"* and *"us"* refer to John and his fellow apostles and the experiences mentioned were the common experiences of them all, both during the life of the Lord Jesus and in the forty days after His resurrection. The second person pronouns *"you"* and *"ye"* in the clauses, "declare we unto you, that ye also. . ." are the saints to whom John is writing who, for the most part, had not heard, seen or handled Him. To these Peter wrote "whom having not seen, ye love" (1 Pet 1:8). It could be that John is thinking of the words of the Saviour: "Go to my brethren, and say unto them, I ascend unto my Father, and your Father; and to my God, and your God" (John 20:17). A new threefold relationship now existed on resurrection ground: "my brethren", "my Father, your Father", "my God, your God".

The fellowship of eternity had been one of divine Persons exclusively. The eternal Life enjoyed "living, active relationship and fellowship with the Father"-a fellowship connected with the relationships of deity. How marvellous, however, that now, on resurrection ground in new creation, men were brought into relationship with that same Father and His very same Son, Jesus Christ. What matchless grace! Being brought into this new relationship does not, of course, suggest that they had become deity, had ceased to be finite and had become infinite, for that neither they nor we shall ever be. Through sovereign grace alone they had been introduced into a living active relationship with the Father and His Son. "The phrase marks emphatically the distinction and equality between the Son and the Father" (Plummer). "Both he that sanctifieth and they who are sanctified are all of one: for which cause he is not ashamed to call them brethren" (Heb 2:11). "The use of the title 'His Son, Jesus Christ' . . . perhaps contains a side glance at the heretics who denied that the man Jesus was the Christ, the Son of God" (Stott).

4 John is anxious to communicate this truth to his readers; the old man was speaking from personal experience to younger saints who had not known the Lord Jesus "after the flesh". Versions differ as to the tradition of the pronouns here: should it be "these things write we unto you, that your joy may be full" (AV), or "these things we write, that our joy may be fulfilled" (RV)? If the AV be correct John is longing that the joy that filled his own soul when he apprehended this truth might grip their hearts. If the RV is followed, the very fact that he was able to communicate this tremendous truth to them would be the consummation of his joy-his cup would "run over". His readers, of course, were already in this fellowship, although they may not have been aware of the truth of it. John found joy in enlightening them.

II. The First Circle (1:5-2:27)

Subject: Relationships with Divine Persons
Based on Righteousness, Love and Truth

1. *The Message and Its Implications*
1:5-2:2

v.5   "This then is the message which we have heard of him, and declare unto you, that God is light, and in him is no darkness at all.

v.6   If we say that we have fellowship with him, and walk in darkness, we lie, and do not the truth:

v.7   But if we walk in the light, as he is in the light, we have fellowship one with another, and the blood of Jesus Christ his Son cleanseth us from all sin.

v.8   If we say that we have no sin, we deceive ourselves, and the truth is not in us.

v.9   If we confess our sins, he is faithful and just to forgive us *our* sins, and to cleanse us from all unrighteousness.

v.10 If we say that we have not sinned, we make him a liar, and his word is not in us.

2 v.1 My little children, these things write I unto you, that ye sin not. And if any man sin, we have an advocate with the Father, Jesus Christ the righteous

v.2   And he is the propitiation for our sins: and not for ours only, but also for *the sins* of the whole world."

a. The message (vv. 5-7)

5   Here is a link back to v.1 "we heard". They had heard such an abundance of teaching from the person of Christ and they had seen in Him and in His life the living exposition of all that He taught. The central impression that gripped their souls was "God is light, and in him is no darkness at all". What the apostles taught they heard directly from the Lord Jesus; they did not receive it from others. One would have thought that from an apostle commonly called the "apostle of love" the message would have been "God is love", but one has to wait until 4:8,16 before John uses this expression. There he does not call it "the message". Indeed, "God is light" (1:5), "God is love" (4:8,16), "God is Spirit" (John 4:24 RVm). Is this not in accord with the whole body of divine revelation? In Gen 1 God said: "Let there be light" (v.3) and the remainder of the chapter reveals God in sovereignty. Ch. 2 shows the kindness of the Lord God in His care for man, but in ch. 3 in God's attitude to the sinful pair we learn that God is love. Again in John's Gospel we read "In him was life; and the life was the light of men" (v.4). Shall we not say that we have to wait until the great gospel text of 3:16 to learn that "God so loved", that "God is love"? The order is thereafter life, light, love in both Gospel and epistle.

Notice now how John deals in extremes; there is no middle ground, there are no shades of grey, only black and white. It is light and darkness, no twilight, no dawn, no shades of evening. The blackness of midnight is contrasted with the brilliance of noon ("at midday ... I saw ... a light from heaven, above the brightness of the sun" Acts 26:13).

Light suggests:	*Darkness* suggests:
Splendour, Glory	Kingdom of Darkness
Self Revelation	Hostile to Light
Righteousness	Deceit, Lies
Holiness (Absolute)	Error, Immorality
Authority	Life cut off from God

"Light symbolically stands for righteousness. Those who have fellowship with God do righteousness, as 'He is righteous'. Sin is spiritual darkness and is utterly incompatible with fellowship with God" (Vine). He is a God "dwelling in light unapproachable; whom no man hath seen, nor can see" (1 Tim 6:16 RV). "A God that is not infinitely above finite comprehension is not God. The very being of God is absolute light" (Lenski). "God is light, and in him is no darkness at all". The compound word *oudeis*, literally meaning "not one", allows Burdick to paraphrase "In God there is no darkness, not even one bit". This is the message associated with the fellowship into which we have been brought. It is a fellowship with the God who is light and in whom is no darkness at all. Every child of God, every born-again person is in this fellowship; none is excluded. We are in living, active relationship and communion with Himself, the God who is light. How awe-inspiring is this, how awful, that each of us, saved by grace, stands exposed to the blaze of the light of the divine being (see Isa 6:1; Luke 5:8). The all-seeing, all-piercing eye of God, who is the centre of our fellowship, searches and exposes every sin, every stain, every shortening. I am not referring to unsaved men and women, but to believers, to those who are in the fellowship and therefore in the light. They are saved, forgiven (judicially), justified and sure of heaven, but they still have sin within and sins in their lives; positionally they are right for eternity; alas, so often they sin. If the seraphim cover their faces and their feet as they cry "Holy, holy, holy is the Lord of hosts" before the revelation of such a God, how much more should we, before the God to whom we have been brought nearer by far than they. The light of the divine Being shines upon us. In the light of such extreme holiness we are completely exposed. Does not this remind us of the words of Jacob, "Surely the Lord is in this place ... how dreadful is this place!" (Gen 28:16,17)?

6   In the light of this revelation John now introduces three of his "tests of life", tests by which the gnostics with their false claims could be tested and found wanting, tests by which we indeed may test ourselves relative to our profession of being born of God.

1.   "If we say that we have fellowship with him, and walk in darkness, we lie, and do not the truth" (v.6).

2.   "If we say that we have no sin, we deceive ourselves, and the truth is not in us" (v.8).

3.   "If we say that we have not sinned, we make him a liar, and his word is not in us" (v.10).

'If we say'-these false claims each being followed by an appropriate antidote" (Bruce).

It seems evident that John has in mind certain persons, well-known as false teachers who professed to enjoy the highest possible spiritual experiences, but their way of living was not consistent with their claim. "In this passage the distinction is between walking in darkness and walking in light; the former is the condition of the unregenerate, the latter of those who are related to Him who is Light" (Vine). The word rendered "walk" suggests one's normal way of living. Notice, it is not *how* we walk, but *where* we walk. "I remember for many years I was in a great deal of confusion of mind about this. I read it as though it said, If we walk *according to* the light, the blood of Jesus Christ His Son cleanseth us from all sin. I thought that if I was very punctilious about obeying every command of God, that if I walked according to all the light I have, He would cleanse me, which was really only saying that I was cleansed when I did not need cleansing" (Ironside). The converse would likewise then be true: when I need cleansing I should not be cleansed!

Two opposing spheres are before us-*the* darkness, *the* light. Believers have been " delivered *out* of the power of *darkness*" and made "meet to be partakers of the inheritance of the saints in *light*" (Col 1:12,13 RV); again, "Ye are all the children of the *light*, and the children of the *day*: we are not of the *night*, nor of *darkness*" (1 Thess 5:5); Again, "Ye, brethren, are not in *darkness*" (1 Thess 5:4), and again "For ye were sometimes *darkness*, but now are ye *light* in the Lord: walk as children of light" (Eph 5:8). We are not exhorted to walk in the light, but walk as children of light. We have to walk in a way that is consistent with where grace has placed us. A believer is in the light; he walks in the light, and cannot walk anywhere else. He may walk carelessly, stumblingly, staggeringly, even sinfully, but he will walk in the light, for being in the fellowship of which John has spoken, he is eternally, constantly in association with the God who is light. If a person's normal habitual way of walking is contrary to the light, if it is evident that his manner of life is not in keeping with the character of God, John declares that he lies and does not the truth. His profession is false; he lies. He does not do the truth, for his walk is contrary to the truth. John does not say he is a backslider, or a disobedient child. His habitual walking in darkness proves he is a false professor. He has never been born of God-solemn and searching truth. As Burdick asserts: "Fellowship with Him, that is, claiming saving relationship with God, professing to know Him personally, the person who is in fellowship with God will display the characteristics of God. Such a person must walk in the light. If, however, he is walking habitually in darkness there is no basis for his claim". Lenski is equally clear: "To think that we can remain in darkness, and yet be in fellowship with God in whom there is no darkness whatever, is the height of delusion, the saddest contradiction. . . 'What communion hath light with darkness?' (2 Cor 6:14; John 3:19-21). None who are in the darkness, who only lie by claiming fellowship with God, are in fellowship with us, they are without".

7 "But if we walk in the light" is not introducing an "if" of doubt, for a believer cannot walk anywhere else. It is an "if" of argument, and we could well paraphrase the sentence "Since we walk in the light as He is in the light". God is light and in fellowship with Him we ever walk in the light of what He is. Could it be that an illustration from the Tabernacle is before us here? In the holiest of all was the ark of the covenant with its lid called "the mercy seat"; above it were cherubim, and between the cherubim " the shekinah", the light that signified the divine presence (there was no other light there). Into that place only the high priest came once per year within the veil, into the presence of God who is light. In our day the veil is removed-a way is opened up into the divine presence, so we enter there. We have then in picture

1.   God who is light,

2.   Christ who is in the light-our great Priest over the house of God (Heb 10:21),

3.   we (the priests) walking in the light in perfect fellowship one with another.

To complete the picture reference is made to the blood; in the type was it not sprinkled upon and seven times before the mercy seat? So He (our great High Priest) "through his own blood, entered in once for all into the holy place, having obtained eternal redemption" (Heb 9:12 RV). "On this day shall atonement be made to cleanse you, that ye may be clean from all your sins before the Lord" (Lev 16:30). Thus Christ has entered in through His own blood; its efficacy is effective in the presence of God, allowing us to walk there in the blazing light of the divine eye. To think of being in the light, exposed completely to the innermost depths of our beings, every part penetrated, and every sin exposed, not according to our standards or our reckoning of what sin is, but according to His standards, whether deliberate sins or sins of ignorance, things we did not think were in any way sinful, things we even thought were virtuous (He will tell us were but sin!). The light of the being of God exposes all-what an exposure! I might well cry with Isaiah, "Woe is me! for I am undone" (Isa 6:5) or with Paul say, " In me (that is, in my flesh,) dwelleth no good thing" (Rom 7:18). Surely in such a situation I could expect nothing but the swift judgment of God in whose eyes all this sin is abhorrent. But wait, there is the blood, its efficacy ever fresh in the divine presence: "The blood of Jesus Christ his Son cleanseth us from all sin" (every sin, JNDm). Every sin exposed by the eye of infinite holiness and judged according to divine standards-"the blood of Jesus Christ his Son cleanseth us from all sin". Note the tense, *cleanseth*; not that there has to be repeated, constant re-applications of the blood, but the efficacy of that precious blood is perpetually available to cleanse from every single sin. I am so glad that the exposure is so penetrating and exhaustive; it gives me the assurance that every single sin is completely searched out, none has been missed. Instead of being filled with fear my heart rejoices at the amazing truth that, every sin that light exposes, the blood of Christ cleanses. Indeed "The verb suggests that God does more than forgive, He erases the stain of sin" (Stott). "Walking in the light with God makes possible fellowship with one another and is made possible also by the blood of Jesus (real blood and no mere phantom, atoning blood of the sinless Son of God for our sins). John is not ashamed to use this word; it is not the mere example of Jesus that 'cleanses' us from sin" (Robertson). It is blood!

b. A Denial that Sin Exists in our Nature (vv.8-10)

8   "If we say that we have no sin" (singular) should be contrasted with the similar expression in v.10 "If we say that we have not sinned". The first is the principle of sin, the thing, the root; the second has in view the practising of sins, the things we do, the fruits. Being in the light exposes sin both in nature and practice. To claim that the root is not within is an evidence that the person is not exposed to the light and shows a lack of awareness of what sin is. The gnostics who had no time for the precious blood of Christ (seeing that they taught the Christ did not shed His blood) would surely say, "What is it to us if the blood of Jesus is not available to cleanse us from sin? We have no sin" (Bruce). The holiest of men are the most conscious of the presence of sin. To say that one has no sin (that the root has been eradicated) is self deception (no one else has been deceived) and is an evidence that the truth (the body of christian doctrine) is not within. "When the truth is not in us we are by no means empty, but are full of fictions, fables, myths, self-made fancies, notions of things that are not so" (Lenski); these things the gnostics had.

9   In contrast one who is in the light, exposed to the light recognises both the principle and the practice of sin in the life, recognises that while nothing can break the fellowship, sin and sins can, and do, mar the enjoyment of it. Sin is ever grievous to God, ever brings a cloud between us and God. The exercised heart will not be content to know only that blood cleanses from all sin, but will want to know how that which is troubling the conscience may be removed. The person of v.8 denies the presence of sin; the person of v.10 denies the practice of sin; but the believer who is before us in this verse recognises the existence of both and desires the restoration of the joy of fellowship, to know again the smile of the Father against whom he has sinned. In Ps 32 David has sinned and for a while has sought to hide his sin, with the unhappy results described in vv.3,4; however when convicted by the Holy Spirit through the words of the prophet, he says, "I acknowledged my sin unto thee, and mine iniquity have I not hid. I said, I will confess my transgressions unto the Lord; and thou forgavest the iniquity of my sin" (v.5). The whole of the psalm should be meditated upon prayerfully, as also Ps 51. In these we may learn what true confession is.

"If we confess ... he is faithful" implies that the confessing is to God. It is the confession of specific sins, hiding nothing. The word means "to say the same thing as another" and "thereby admit the truth of an accusation". The light exposes, the eye of God sees, the conscience accuses, the confessor does not deny, cover or excuse. "The acknowledgement of specific sins gives evidence of sincerity" (Vine). Generalisations will not suffice.

The Forgiver is described as "faithful and just". "Righteous is the state of being right; In his faithfulness He is consistent with His character, in acting righteously He is faithful to His own nature" (Vine). He does not look lightly upon sin, does not gloss over our transgressions. He is faithful to the allsufficient sacrifice which is the effective basis for the putting away of sin.

Our sins (i.e. believer's sins) are already forgiven judicially (see 2:12, "because your sins are forgiven you for his name's sake"); we already have "redemption through his blood, the forgiveness of sins" (Eph 1:7). This blessing we received the moment we believed. Forgiveness is total and entire; it embraces past, present and future sins; it is absolute, complete and eternal-make no mistake. In the judicial court of God sentence has been passed upon us and we have died in the death of Christ; justice has been satisfied. In that sphere therefore we no longer live. We are in a new sphere. God is not now our judge but our Father and as such delights to forgive His children. We do not confess to One who grudges forgiveness, but One who delights to pardon abundantly. Note that sin (*hamartia*, v.8) is missing the mark; unrighteousness (*adikia*, v.9) is the negation of what is consistent with God's character.

Having been forgiven by our Father (paternally) we need His help that in the future we may not fall again. Therefore the One who forgives us will cleanse us from all unrighteousness, preventing us from committing again those things which are inconsistent with His character, grieving to His heart. Therefore the One who forgives us henceforth leads us away from unrighteousness into righteousness: "He restoreth my soul: he leadeth me in the paths of righteousness for his name's sake" (Ps 23:3). David, having found forgiveness through confession, also found a hiding place and songs of deliverance, and was assured, "I will instruct thee and teach thee in the way that thou shalt go" (Ps 32:8), so that we may well say, "Lead me, O Lord, in thy righteousness" (Ps 5:8). While remission has to do with sinful acts, cleansing from unrighteousness has to do with the personal character of the saint. "The object of this forgiveness is to remove that which has hindered the believer's enjoyment of fellowship with God. In 1 John 2:12 it is legal forgiveness, here it is paternal" (Burdick). In v.7 the cleansing is by the blood of Jesus Christ, His Son. Here the cleansing is by the washing of water by the word of God (Eph 5:26; John 13:10; 15:1-3).

10   Here is the third "if we say"- "If we say we have not practised sins". No one who is in the light could intelligently say these words. The light exposes, the Spirit pierces the conscience; but should a person say this he is making God a liar, for God has said, "All have sinned, and come short of the glory of God" (Rom 3:23). Moreover, God's word is not in him, for Paul had already written these words many years before, and they were circulated and recognised as part of the Holy Scriptures (2 Pet 3:16). The gnostics claimed that the superior knowledge into which they had been initiated made it impossible for them to sin.

c. Sin Not (2:1-2)

1   John uses the first person singular, "My little children ... I write"; he does not say *our* and *we* (as in 1:1). *Teknia* (born ones) is used seven times in this epistle but only here with "my". John is writing as an old man, older than the main part of his readers, and looking on them from that angle he uses a term of endearment, a title indicating loving care. This word should be distinguished from *paidia* (infants) used twice in the later part of this chapter to show the difference between babes in Christ and their more mature fellows. Here *teknia* embraces all the children of God.

"These things write I unto you" refers to the previous statements in 1:5-10. He now anticipates the cavils of opponents of the truth who could well say, "No christian is without the thing called sin, no christian can say that he does not practise sins, and since the blood of Jesus Christ, God's Son cleanses from all sin, and confession is such an easy way to obtain forgiveness, is there any need to strive against sin, may we not indulge in sinning? Since remission is so easy, why not let God remit a few more sins? " (See Rom 6:1,2, "Shall we continue in sin, that grace may abound? God forbid".)

John would not allow his readers to look lightly on sin. He is not permitting them to believe that sinning is unimportant, or that they may live carelessly. "Horror, hatred, fear, repudiation of sin pervade this whole epistle" (Law). John does not want them to be led astray by the antinomianism of the gnostics; his word is clear and unambiguous "that ye sin not" or "that ye may not sin" (RV). His words were to preserve them from sinning; they were both preventative and prohibitive. Believers are not expected to sin, it should be an exceptional, unusual occurrence-oh that it were true of us! Here is a sinless perfection at which we should aim and to which we should seek to attain. Alas how we fail!

"And if any man sin", if he actually does sin, "we have an advocate with the Father". Hebrews deals similarly with Christ as our High Priest: "we have a great high priest" (4:14); "We have such an high priest" (8:1); He has passed through the heavens, "now to appear in the presence of God for us" (9:24). He is in permanent session in the presence of God: "he ever liveth to make intercession for them" (7:25). In the same way "we have an advocate with the Father". (Note: High Priest with God, Advocate with the Father.) We do not need to search for one, to find one, to ask for one or to appoint one-we have one in permanent session in the Father's throne room; "with the Father-face to face with the Father, in the presence of, He acts in our Father's court" (Lenski). It is a face to face encounter. *Paraklētos* ("one called alongside") is elsewhere used only in John's Gospel (14:16,26; 15:26; 16:7 translated "another comforter") of the Spirit of God called alongside to help us in the pilgrimage below. The subject is comfort and Paul confirms the idea in Rom 8:26: "the Spirit also helpeth our infirmities" etc. The fact that the Saviour said "another comforter" indicates that He Himself was a comforter- alongside the disciples to support them. Here, however, the reference is not to One on earth, but to One in heaven, called alongside to represent us, permanently briefed to take up our case with the Father. The word stresses capability and adaptability for giving aid in a court of justice; it denotes a legal assistant, a counsel for defence, an advocate, one who pleads another's cause, an intercessor; "One called on one side in order to give aid, one who speaks on another's behalf" (Lenski). "With the Father" depicts Him standing alongside us, as it were, before the Father. "Sin interrupts communion, which is restored through His Advocacy" (Vine). Certainly our Lord Jesus pleads our cause against the accuser of the brethren (Zech 3:1,2; Luke 22:31; Rev 12:10), but here it is because sin robs of the joy of fellowship and must be removed. Christ is not an advocate with God as a judge, but with a Father who is longing to forgive. "Justice pleads with love for our release" (Findlay). "If he (a believer) should sin he does not need another justification from a divine judge, he is a child of God; he needs a Father's forgiveness" (Stott). This Advocate is Jesus (His human name), Christ (the anointed of God), the righteous (His character). Note the association of the two names Jesus Christ in opposing gnosticism. Both the Father (1:9) and the Advocate are righteous and together they deal with an erring christian's sin. The Advocate once suffered in the erring one's place: "Christ also suffered for sins once, the righteous for the unrighteous, that he might bring us to God" (1 Pet 3:18 RV).

This Advocate does not excuse sin, explain it away, try to justify our actions, or argue extenuating circumstances. He is righteous, He deals righteously, and He has a sacrifice as a righteous basis for His advocacy.

Is it not true that immediately a believer sins, our Advocate says to the Father "Father, that man, that woman has sinned"? He does not wait until we are conscious of having sinned, or are sorry we have sinned, or until we repent of our sin. Left to ourselves we might never reach that point; but immediately (or even before, see Luke 22:31) He takes up the matter with the Father and as a result the machinery of heaven is put into motion for the recovery of the erring one. He moves independently of us to put our case, to plead our cause, before the Father who is longing to fall on our neck and kiss us.

2   He, *He Himself*, the Advocate, is also the *propitiation*; the propitiation is not His cross but Himself. We are not pointed back to Calvary but to the One who offered Himself a sacrifice there; as such He *is* (not "was") the propitiation, continually in the presence of God in the full efficacy of His Calvary work.

"Propitiation is not something which men must do to please God, but something God has provided in His grace to bring man into His presence with the assurance that they are accepted by Him, since He has removed the barrier that has kept them at a distance, guilt with its attendant retribution, the punishment which is banished by perfect love (Eph 2:13)" (Bruce).

"The word *hilasmos* used here and in 4:10 denotes the ground on which God shows mercy to the guilty. Christ alone is this through His death, in the shedding of His blood in sacrifice. Two things are necessary for this, 1. the finished work of the cross, 2. the value of the living Person. He is not only the propitiation by offering Himself, He is Himself the propitiation, thus His advocacy is based on the abiding efficacy of His atoning sacrifice" (Vine).

"It is the divine judgment upon human rebellion which makes the barrier to fellowship with God, and there is no expiation of man's guilt without propitiation of God's wrath. God's holy antagonism to sin must be turned away if sin is to be forgiven and the sinner restored. Propitiation is the appeasement of the wrath of God, by the love of God, through the gift of God" (Stott).

Sin is an offence to God; it calls for righteous condemnation and wrath. His indignation must be turned away; that wrath must be placated, and man could do nothing to placate the wrath of God on his own behalf. God therefore in love provides the placator in the gift of His Son: "Herein is love, not that we loved God, but that he loved us, and sent his Son to be the propitiation for our sins" (4:10). Man has sinned; God's wrath is revealed; God's righteous indignation must be placated, yet man cannot placate or find a placator, so God (against whom sin is an offence) provides a placator, His Son-the propitiation of our sins. Propitiation has reference to persons-God is propitiated. Expiation has reference to things-sin is expiated.

"The whole idea of propitiation is lifted out of the realm of pagan thought when we remember that though there was something in the nature of God that demanded propitiation, there was also that in His Nature that led Him to provide the propitiation" (Curtis Vaughan).

"So far from propitiation and love being unreconcilable, propitiation is the work of love" (Barrett).

"It is God who is "propitiated" by the vindication of His holy and righteous character, whereby through the provision He has made in the vicarious and expiatory sacrifice of Christ, He has so dealt with sin that He can show mercy to the believing sinner in the removal of his guilt and the remission of his sins." *Hilasmos*, "expiation, is a means by which sin is covered and remitted". He Himself through the expiatory sacrifice of His death is the personal means by whom God shows mercy to the sinner who believes on Christ as the One thus provided" (Vine). "And not for ours only, but also for the whole world" ("the sins of" in italics in the AV should be omitted) does not imply that all men's sins are automatically forgiven because of the sacrifice of Christ, but that all men *can* have their sins forgiven. The propitiation is available for all, for the whole world. There is no limited atonement here. God does not offer everlasting life to whosoever believeth in Him (I speak reverently) with His tongue in His cheek. The Lord Jesus is an infinite Being of infinite worth. His sacrifice was one of infinite value. He has therefore provided a salvation that is as infinite in value as He Himself. If all the inhabitants of the earth, throughout the whole time, had put in their claim for forgiveness on the ground of the sacrifice of Christ, they would not have exhausted its value. Yea, if there had been a thousand worlds of sinners the sum of their populations would still not have exhausted or equated with the value of that infinite sacrifice offered by such a person of infinite value. How ever many debts of finite value incurred by finite persons are added together they do not add up to infinity! He is infinite; His sacrifice is infinite. What a wonderful Saviour; thank God He died for me! He is available to the whole world, but of many it can be written, "Ye will not come to me, that ye might have life". "It is a patent fact that thou too art part of the whole world, so that thy heart cannot deceive itself, and think, The Lord died for Peter and Paul but not for me" (Luther).

Notes

2

Eternal light! Eternal light!
   How pure the soul must be
When, placed within Thy searching sight,
It shrinks not, but with calm delight
   Can live, and look on Thee!

The spirits that surround Thy throne
   May bear the burning bliss;
But that is surely theirs alone,
Since they have never, never known
   A fallen world like this.

Oh, how shall I, whose native sphere
   Is dark, whose mind is dim,
Before the Ineffable appear,
And on my naked spirit bear
   The uncreated beam?

There is a way for man to rise
   To that sublime abode;
An offering and a sacrifice,
A Holy Spirit's energies,
   An Advocate with God!

These, these prepare us for the sight
   Of holiness above;
The sons of ignorance and night
May dwell in the eternal light;
   Through the eternal love.

2. *His Commandments and the New Commandment*
2:3-11

v.3 "And hereby we do know that we know him, if we keep his commandments.
v.4 He that saith, I know him, and keepeth not his commandments, is a liar, and the truth is not in him.
v.5 But whoso keepeth his word, in him verily is the love of God perfected hereby know we that we are in him.
v.6 He that saith he abideth in him ought himself also so to walk, even as he walked.
v.7 Brethren, I write no new commandment unto you, but an old commandment which ye had from the beginning. The old commandment is the word which ye have heard from the beginning.
v.8 Again, a new commandment I write unto you, which thing is true in him and in you: because the darkness is past, and the true light now shineth.
v.9 He that saith he is in the light, and hateth his brother, is in darkness even until now.
v.10 He that loveth his brother abideth in the light, and there is none occasion of stumbling in him.
v.11 But he that hateth his brother is in darkness, and walketh in darkness, and knoweth not whither he goeth, because that darkness hath blinded his eyes."

a. His Commandments (vv.3-6)

3 W. E. Vine renders the opening clauses: "Hereby we constantly have the experience of knowing that we have come to know Him". Notice that it is not that we have come to know Him by keeping His commandments, but the fact that we do habitually keep His commandments is the evidence that we have come to know Him. The word here translated "know" (*ginōskō*) is to learn by experience. Keeping His commandments, walking in holiness, obeying His word, are to us and to Him evidence that we really know Him. "John teaches that loving obedience to the divine will, far from being optional, is the only way of showing that we love God" (Vaughan). "The word for 'keep' (*tērein*) expresses the idea of watchful, observant obedience" (Lenski).

4 This is the first of three occurrences of the phrase "He that saith" (see vv.6,9). What is positively treated in the previous verse is now looked at negatively. What a man professes may be tested by what he does. His profession may be impressive, but if his actions contradict his words, he is a liar, for his words are not true and the truth is not in him. "He does not say that those who wholly satisfy the law keep His commandments (and no such instance can be found in the word) but those who strive, according to the capacity of human infirmity, to form their life in obedience to God" (Calvin).

5 "Whoso keepeth his word" (whosoever keeps on keeping) involves observing not only his commandments separately, one by one, but His word in general, in totality, the whole book, regarded as a single, complete, final revelation of God's will. See John 14:21: "He that hath my commandments"; v.23 "He will keep my word" (RV) for similar usages. In such a heart the love of God is perfected, i.e.

"hath been perfected and remains so" (Plummer)-an ideal state of things. "This emphasises not some personal trait in the believer, but rather the work of divine love in him and through him as a sphere of its operation" (Vine). Is this a reference to the love of God objectively or to love *for* God subjectively? The word can embrace both ideas. Love finds its source in God and, as shed abroad in our hearts, radiates towards God and our fellow men. "Hereby know we that we are in him" may refer back to previous expressions or forward to the second "He that saith" (v.6). "Him" is without doubt the Lord Jesus, for He only among the persons of the Godhead has literally walked on earth so that we may imitate Him. Peter says "leaving you an example, that ye should follow his steps" (1 Pet 2:21 RV), and thereafter describes our Lord's conduct on earth.

"To be (or to 'abide' v.6) in Him is equivalent to the phrase to know Him (vv.3,4) and to love Him (v.5). Being a christian consists in essence of a personal relationship with God in Christ, knowing Him, loving Him and abiding in Him as a branch abiding in the Vine (John 15:1ff). This is the meaning of eternal life (John 17:3; 1 John 5:20)" (Stott).

6   He that makes such a claim to be abiding in Him ought also to walk even as He walked. If one really were "in" another person (if that were possible in the natural sphere) one would have to walk wherever and however that person moved. The same principle must apply in this spiritual realm. "Ought" (*opheilō*) suggests the thought of debt and so of moral responsibility on the part of the one who makes the profession to walk even as (suggesting the closest possible imitation of His character and ways) He walked. His walk from first to last was in complete accord with the mind of God.

b. The New Commandment (vv. 7-8)
7   "Beloved" is the correct title (not "brethren" as in the AV); it is the first mention of this title in the epistle (others are 3:2,21; 4:7). The term corresponds with the previous clause "the love of God perfected" (v.5) and appropriately introduces the subject: "love one another". Notice the change from commandments to one commandment (vv.3,4 and 7,8). He has been talking about keeping His commandments-now he draws attention to just one. We are not told what the commandment is in these verses but by comparison with 2 John 5,6 we are sure that it is that we love one another. He has been urging them to walk even as He walked-He walked in love. "New" (*kainos*) signifies what is fresh, new in quality and extent (in contrast to that which is familiar and well known), but not novel or new in kind. The "old commandment" is old in time (*palaios*, "old in teaching as Cain and Abel, but new in practice", Robertson). Mosaic law said: "Love thy neighbour as thyself"; Jesus said: "Love your enemies" (Matt 5:44). "Which ye have heard from the beginning-, i.e. from the date of their conversion, emphasises that it was an essential part of the message they had received: "The old

commandment is the word which ye heard" (RV) ("from the beginning" should be omitted this second time). The emphasis is on the word, not the time.

8 "Again" (i.e. from another point of view, in another sense) it is a new commandment, old in teaching, but not antiquated; new in authority, in standard, in practice and in application; new in fresh sanction because the Lord Jesus has confirmed it and the Holy Spirit gives power to perform it. "Which thing is true" perceives its fulfilment; it is made good "in him and in you"; note the preposition *in* in both places; true in perfection in Him, gradually being produced in them. Here is the commandment from the lips of the Saviour: "A new commandment I give unto you, That ye love one another; as I have loved you, that ye also love one another" (John 13:34). It was true in Him, He was its living exposition, and would be true in them as they obeyed His commandment. In the phrase "the darkness *is passing away*", the voice of *paragetai* shows the darkness "being caused to pass away" (Wuest). The example and teaching of the Lord Jesus made the old commandment new. Passing away means leading by, passing slowly, passing by like a procession, changing from darkness to light as a process; so darkness has not entirely gone, but light is already shining, the true light, now shineth, has been shining already, "the light, the true light is already shining" (lit.). The light is true, *alēthinon* not true as opposed to false, but real differing from unreal, the substance in contrast to the shadow, genuine, reliable, no false flicker" (Robertson). Dawn is here! "There were new-fangled speculations and novelties rushing in like a flood, but the apostle recalls them to what had been an essential element of christianity ever since they and their fathers heard of Christ" (Ramsay).

The question now arises: "what is the *old* commandment and what is the new? Various suggestions have been made:

1.   The old commandment dates back to Gen 4 where the principle of loving or hating one's brother is introduced. Ch. 3:11 reads: "This is the message that ye heard from the beginning, that we should love one another, not as Cain" and is quoted in support of this view. We can see the connection, but the incident is part of an argument relative to loving the brethren in contrast to "the world hate you". It hardly contains a commandment and we do not think this suggestion deserves much consideration.

2.   The old commandment is a reference to Lev 19:18 "thou shalt love thy neighbour as thyself.. I am the Lord". We are reminded that the Lord Jesus said: "The second is like ... Thou shalt love thy neighbour as thyself" (Mark 12:31). All the practical requirements of the Mosaic law are summed up in this statement, indeed James writes, "If ye fulfil the royal law ... Thou shalt love thy neighbour as thyself, ye do well" (2:8). Those who interpret in this way cite John 13:34,35: "A new commandment I give unto you, that ye love one another; as I have loved you, that ye also love one another. By this shall

all men know that ye are my disciples, if you have love one to another". This view has much to commend it.

3. John 13:34 is the old commandment that came from the lips of the Saviour; that commandment, now recorded as John is being "moved by the Holy Spirit" to record Holy Writ, becomes the new commandment, witnessed to by the Spirit of God. This is an interesting suggestion and may have a measure of truth in it.

c. Love and Hate (vv.9-11)
9   This is the third "He that saith". The first was "He that saith, I know him" (v.4), the second "He that saith he abideth in him" (v.6) and the last "He that saith he is in the light". Each time the mere professor's claim is put to the test and is found to be wanting. Here he claims to be in intimate fellowship with the God who is light and yet he hates his brother. In this passage "hateth" or "loveth" is, for the person concerned, his habitual way of living, his fixed pattern of life. "Walking in light, in truth, in love constitutes fellowship with God" (Vine). "The true christian, who knows God and walks in the light, both obeys God and loves his brother. The genuineness of his faith is seen in his right relationship to both God and man" (Stott). The man who hates his brother is in the darkness until now; "now" is emphatic and implies up to this moment. This is in contrast to the previous statement "the darkness is passing away, the true light already shineth"; this man has not seen the light, he is in no way influenced by it, he has not received it (or indeed Him who is the Light). He is in the darkness, away from the God in whom is no darkness at all.

10   He that loveth his brother abideth in the light; he who loves his brother is always in the light; indeed only the man who loves his brother dwells in light. John speaks of light and darkness, not of twilight, hence also of love and hatred and nothing in between: walking in the light (1:7); being in the light (2:9); abiding in the light (2:10). "Walking speaks of conduct; abiding speaks of the condition which determines the conduct" (Vine).
    John adds: "There is none occasion of stumbling in him". *Skandalon* is a stumbling block in the way of others (Matt 18:7) or in one's own way. It might suggest that there would be in his walk nothing that would stumble others, either by intent or by bad example, nothing to trip up or hinder. If we love people, we shall avoid sinning against them. It is, however, more probably, that John is saying that there is no occasion of stumbling in the claimant himself; see John 11:9,10; "If any man walk in the day, he stumbleth not, because he seeth the light of this world. But if a man walk in the night, he stumbleth, because there is no light in him"; again, "I am the light of the world: he that followeth me shall not walk in darkness, but shall have the light of life" (John 8:12).

11   " 'He that hateth his brother is in darkness' (where he is) 'and walketh in darkness' (what he does) 'and knoweth not whither he goeth' (how he walks). His conduct matches his character; he cannot act otherwise than he is, or walk in any other region than that where his habitation lies" (Findlay). Such are "in darkness". But are not true believers translated out of the kingdom of darkness? Have they not an inheritance with the saints in light (Col 1:12,13)? To walk in darkness is to be apart from the children of God. "Hatred distorts our perspective. We do not first misjudge people and then hate them as a result; our view of them is already jaundiced by our hatred. It is love that sees straight, thinks clearly and makes us balanced in our outlook, judgments and conduct" (Stott). "Hath blinded his eyes" shows the blinding effect of being in the darkness; it leads to a permanent state. "There is direct opposition: where there is not love there is hatred. It may be latent but it is there" (Bengel).

3.   *Messages for the Family*
   2:12-28

> v.12   "I write unto you, little children, because your sins are forgiven you for his name's sake.
> v.13   I write unto you, fathers, because ye have known him *that is* from the beginning. I write unto you, young men, because ye have overcome the wicked one. I write unto you, little children, because ye have known the Father.
> v.14   I have written unto you, fathers, because ye have known him that is from the beginning. I have written unto you, young men, because ye are strong, and the word of God abideth in you, and ye have overcome the wicked one.
> v.15   Love not the world, neither the things that are in the world. If any man love the world, the love of the Father is not in him.
> v.16   For all that is in the world, the lust of the flesh, and the lust of the eyes, and the pride of life, is not of the Father, but is of the world.
> v.17   And the world passeth away, and the lust thereof but he that doeth the will of God abideth for ever.
> v.18   Little children, it is the last time and as ye have heard that antichrist shall come, even now are there many antichrists; whereby we know that it is the last time.
> v.19   They went out from us, but they were not of us; for if they had been of us, they would no doubt have continued with us: but they went out, that they might be made manifest that they were not all of us.
> v.20   But ye have an unction from the Holy One, and ye know all things.
> v.21   I have not written unto you because ye know not the truth, but because ye know it, and no lie is of the truth.
> v.22   Who is a liar but he that denieth that Jesus is the Christ? He is antichrist, that denieth the Father and the Son.
> v.23   Whosoever denieth the Son, the same hath not the Father: (but) he that acknowledgeth the Son hath the Father also.
> v.24   Let that therefore abide in you, which ye have heard from the beginning. If that which ye have heard from the beginning remain in you, ye also shall continue in the Son, and in the Father.
> v.25   And this is the promise that he hath promised us, even eternal life.
> v.26   These things have I written unto you concerning them that seduce you.
> v.27   But the anointing which ye have received of him abideth in you, and ye need not that any man teach you: but as the same anointing teacheth you of all

things, and is truth, and is no lie, and even as it hath taught you, ye shall abide in him.

v.28 And now, little children, abide in him, that, when he shall appear, we may have confidence, and not be ashamed before him at his coming.

a. A Message for the Whole Family (v.12)

12 "Little children" is used to translate two different words in this chapter, *teknion* (v.12) and *paidion* (v.13). "If any distinct flavour is preserved between them, *teknion* emphasises the community of nature between the child and its parent, while *paidion* refers to the child's minority, as one under discipline" (Stott). *Paidion* differs from *teknion* "by emphasising the idea of subordination and not that of kinsmanship" (Westcott). *Teknion* is used to embrace all the children of God. As an old man John affectionately views them all as his beloved bairns. *Paidion* is used however to distinguish new born, newly saved persons from young men and fathers (the more mature). "Little children" (here) links with v.1 and is associated with the apostle's instruction "that ye may not sin", i.e. is linked with the divine provision for the recovery of a sinning saint; but it is followed by a clear statement true of every saint: "your sins are forgiven you for his name's sake"; "because your sins have been put away permanently from you because of His Name" (Wuest). In 1:9 John is speaking of paternal forgiveness, involving the Father and the erring child. Here it is judicial forgiveness by the God against whom we had sinned. Our sins forgiven: Peter declares that "through his name whosoever believeth in him shall receive remission of sins" (Acts 10:43), and Paul says "we have. . . the forgiveness of sins" (Eph 1:7; Col 1:14). The forgiveness of sins is a complete and entire forgiveness; past, present and future sins are all forgiven! Remember that all our sins were future and uncommitted when "Christ died for our sins according to the scriptures". Peter declares, "who his own self bare our sins in his own body on the tree" (1 Pet 2:24); Isaiah exults, God "hath laid on him the iniquity of us all" (Isa 53:6); God in righteousness says, "their sins and their iniquities will I remember no more" (Heb 8:12). It is important to distinguish between judicial and paternal forgiveness. John assures us it is for His name's sake (see Acts 10:43).

b. Messages for Different Stages in the Family (vv. 13-27)

13 Introductory messages are sent to each stage of spiritual development:

1. *Fathers*, "because ye have known him that is from the beginning": maturity and authority are seen in them; they have reached the apex of spiritual growth.

2. *Young men*, "because ye have overcome the wicked one"; theirs are the abiding results of past victories.

3. *Little children (paidia)*, "because ye have known the Father" through new birth; for it is thus one recognises that one belongs to the Father.

14   Now the full message to each group seen in v.13 is given:

Fathers: It is noteworthy that the message is precisely the same as that addressed to them in v.13. Is there not here a sense of finality, or arrival? There knowledge is gained by experience; this is maturity. He is the Amen, the All, the Finality. Knowing Him involves learning about Him, meditating upon Him, and imitating Him. This was Paul's urgent desire: "Who art thou, Lord?" (Acts 9:5); "that I may know him" (Phil 3:10). "Know" is again *ginōskō*: "Because ye have come to know experimentally the One who is from the beginning" (Wuest). John seems to have an appreciation of, and satisfaction with, the spiritual state of the fathers. He has no commendation to add, no fresh instruction to give.

Young men have three commendable features:

1.   ye are strong;

2.   the word of God abideth in you;

3.   ye have overcome the wicked one.

They have desired earnestly "the spiritual milk which is without guile" (1 Pet 2:2 RV), they have grown strong and the cause of their strength is the word of God abiding in them, being part of them, guiding, controlling them, regulating their lives. As a result their living has been victorious: they have overcome the wicked one; they have gained a victory over the pernicious one and at the present moment were still victorious. "Victory in the past leaves its permanent effects, but it is not in itself sufficient to ensure victory in the future" (Vine). "Evil" indicates what is pernicious, acts that are detrimental to others, positively bad and actively harmful. It would appear that there had been a battle and the young men had gained a victory over the evil one, but the old strategy of the devil is first to attack and if that fails, to beguile; hence he will present an attractive world to these very young men to beguile them where his attacks against them have failed. So John warns, and spiritually young men who have fed on the word, become strong and can look back on past exploits for God, should heed his words.

15   "The world" is not here *gē* (the earth), nor *oikoumenē*, (the inhabited earth) nor *aiōn* (the age or generation) but *kosmos* (the adorned thing), signifying in an ethical sense the sum total of human life considered in its alienation from, and hostility to, God (as Vine suggests). The system is viewed first in the aggregate, and then as made up of a multitude of -things that are in the world". No true believer would surely love the whole system in its hostility and hatred of everything that is of God. Hence "If any man love the world, the love of the Father is not in him". The world hated the Son, the Father loves the Son. Love for the Father and love for the world are mutually exclusive.

But may we not love some of the things of the world - even "the little world I know, the innocent delights of youth", etc? If there were any little part of the world that is of the Father we could indeed love and enjoy it, but v.16 dispenses with that question. Findlay says of the world: "it is not made up of so many outward objects that can be specified; it is the sum of those influences emanating from men and things around us which draws away from God. It is the awful down-dragging current of life". It is the "society of the unspiritual and godless" (Erdman). "An evil system, organised under the dominion of Satan and not of God is not to be loved" (Stott).

16   "All that is in the world ... is not of the Father", and therefore v. 15 is an absolute prohibition: to love the world is the act of a traitor. Does not James likewise condemn, using a different metaphor: "Ye adulterers and adulteresses, know ye not the friendship of the world is enmity with God? whosoever therefore will be a friend of the world is the enemy of God" (4:4,5). The "all (a singular including every aspect) that is in the world" is resolved into three constituents which make up the world system:

1.   "the lust of the flesh";

2.   "the lust of the eyes";

3.   "the pride of life".

"Lust" (*epithumia*) is essentially strong desire. "The flesh is the seat of sin in man"; the strong desires of the flesh stand for the temptation that proceeds from our fallen nature which is corrupt and opposed to everything which pleases God. These temptations come from within: "every man is tempted, when he is drawn away of his own lust, and enticed" (Jas 1:14).

"The lust of the eyes" underscores that temptation from without, the eyes being the main means of communication between the things apparent in the world and the inward passion of a fallen nature. Some things seen may be considered to be good, artistic, aesthetic, beautiful, or charming, but if they alienate the heart from Christ, rob me of my love of the Saviour, or cause me to turn aside from Him, then they are but the devil's tool to allure me from "the simplicity and the purity that is toward Christ" (2 Cor 11:3 RV).

"The pride of life" is that vainglory, empty display, proud reliance on one's own ability, ostentatious pride which is characteristic of a system alienated from the mind of God. One could profitably notice the similarity between these three lusts, the threefold description of the tree of knowledge of good and evil in the serpent's temptation of Eve, a temptation in which she fell, and the threefold temptation of our Lord Jesus, in which He triumphed (Luke 4). Note Eve's misquotation of the word of God which did not abide in her as it should have done.

17   The world after all "is being caused to pass away" (Wuest). The new thing has arrived, that which has held sway so long is doomed, it has been superseded; like the darkness (v.8) it has no future. But when the world as a system has ceased to be, one group will remain-"he that doeth the will of God abideth for ever". Did not the Lord say, "Whosoever shall do the will of God, the same is my brother, and my sister, and mother" (Mark 3:35)?

18   This is the final element in the series of messages to the three stages in the family. He has addressed the fathers twice (vv.13,14), the young men twice (vv.13,14) and the little children (*paidia*) once (v.13). The introductory sentence is this time divided into two parts. We may reconstruct the sense thus: "Little children" (v.18), "I have not written unto you because ye know not the truth" (v.21); "ye have heard the antichrist shall come". One would have thought that prophetic truth would have been more appropriate to the fathers but John addresses infants in Christ. Paul in the same way makes it evident that he has taught prophecy to babes; see 1 Thess 5:1,2, "of the times and the seasons, brethren, ye have no need that I write unto you. For yourselves know perfectly. . ."
    "It is the last hour" suggests the brevity of time. John speaks as though the Lord's coming is imminent, certainly within the lifetime of those addressed (see v.28). "The antichrist cometh" identifies a distinct person "whom the Lord Jesus will consume with the spirit of his mouth, and destroy with the brightness of his coming" (2 Thess 2:8-12). The antichrist will seek to usurp the authority of Christ and oppose Him. This "man of sin" should be distinguished from the many antichrists which have arisen, who display the spirit of antichrist (Mark 13:6,22; Matt 24:5,11,24; 2 Pet 2:1). "Antichrist" may mean a substitution for or imitation of Christ, or in opposition to Christ; he takes the place of and is antagonistic to Christ. All exponents of gnosticism were really antichrists. Even now there are many antichrists.

19   These antichrists" went out from our membership" (*exēlthan*), for" they were not of us in spirit and life" (*oukēsan*). They had lost the inner desire and voluntarily broke the outward link. Their departure was their "unmasking" (Law). "The heretics went out of their own volition, but behind the secession was the divine purpose that the spurious should be made manifest (*phanerōthōsin*) lest the elect should be led astray" (Stott). Notice Paul warns the Ephesian elders, "after my departing shall grievous wolves enter in among you ... of your own selves shall men arise, speaking perverse things" (Acts 20:29), " who ... bring in damnable heresies" (2 Pet 2:1) The next stage is "they feast with you" (2 Pet 2:13); "they feast with you, feeding themselves without fear" (Jude 12). Paul says they are coming in; Jude and Peter confirm they were in; John says they went out from us. The reason for their departure in person was evident; they had never been one with the saints in heart; they had "never been thoroughly imbued with the knowledge of Christ but only had a slight and passing taste of it" (Calvin).

Notice the RV "that they might be manifest how that they all are not of us", i.e. "there was not a single genuine believer among them". These were without doubt apostates. Continuance is the evidence of reality and their going out was the evidence that they were false. They had been in actual fellowship with (*meta*) the saints without being born again. It was in keeping with the divine will that these false teachers should be thus exposed.

20   "Ye", in contrast to those false teachers who thus had been made manifest, "have an unction (anointing) from the Holy One". Vv. 18 and 19 speak of the antichrist and the antichrists; this verse, by way of contrast, of the Holy One (the Lord Jesus, Acts 3:14) and the anointed ones. True believers receive the Holy Spirit as an anointing at their conversion. Kings, priests and prophets were anointed with material olive oil in OT days for the different offices that they filled. The priests were anointed in the nation of Israel (see Exod 29:7,21; Lev 8:30). In NT days all those who have tasted that the Lord is good (1 Pet 2:5-9) are a holy priesthood, not by natural attainment or even by degree of spirituality, but upon believing (Eph 1:13 RV). The Holy Spirit indwelling the believer is a guide unto all the truth (John 16:13). Hence, in this context, these babes all have the Holy Spirit giving them divine intuition that enables them to distinguish truth from error and thus prevents them from being led astray by error. "Ye know all things" does not mean that they can dispense with God-given teachers who will build them up in the things of God. It would be better translated "Ye all (*pantes*) know it", i.e. the Spirit of God gives them the ability to distinguish between truth and error. "Ye all know it (the truth)" links with v.21 "ye know it".

21   He writes not so much to teach but to confirm what they already knew. He is not inferring that his readers did not know the truth, but that knowing the truth they were able to discern truth from error. "No lie is of the truth" is literally "every lie is not of the truth". God cannot lie, so truth proceeds from Himself. However, Satan is a liar and the father of it. The first lie in the Bible came from the serpent's lips (Gen 3:4). Truth is truth; error is error; there is no halfway house in between. "John does not treat christianity as a religion containing elements of truth, or even more truth than any other religion which had preceded it. He presents it to the soul as a religion that must be everything to it, if it is not really to be worse than nothing" (Liddon). "There is the modesty and the sound philosophy of the apostle. Many of us think that we can put the truth into people, by screaming it into their ears. We do not suppose that they have any truth in them to which we could appeal. John had no notion that he could be of use to his dear children unless there was truth in them, a capacity to distinguish truth from lies, a sense that one must be the eternal opposite of the other" (Maurice).

22   Although the noun "liar" has the definite article, John does not necessarily have a definite person in mind. This person is a representative liar and the denial that Jesus is the Christ is a representative lie. The present participle "the one denying" emphasises that this is this man's habitual attitude. Cerinthus was this type of person. Lenski describes Cerinthus' sin: "Cerinthus dreamed of a heavenly Eon, a fictional being whom he substituted for the Son, who is of one essence with the Father; the Eon Christ was not Jesus who was merely Joseph's natural son. The Eon *Christos* descended upon Jesus at His baptism but left Jesus before His passion, so that the physical son of Joseph died on the Cross. Thus this gnosticism abolished the Son and the efficacy of the Son's blood (1:7)". Hence the gnostics developed the grave error Stott describes: "They made him a mere man invested for a brief period with divine powers, or even adopted into the Godhead, but they denied that the man Jesus and the eternal Son were the same person".

The lie was a denial that Jesus is the Christ come in the flesh. The person who denies that Jesus is the Christ will almost certainly deny the Father and the Son. Did not John write that ye might believe that Jesus is the Christ the Son of God (John 20:31)? The gnostics boasted in the super knowledge of truth but were gripped by the worst of lies.

23   The best manuscripts here confirm that the verse should be as included in the RV: ". . . he that confesseth the Son hath the Father also. Whosoever denieth the Son the same hath not the Father", i.e. hath not even the Father. It would seem that some believed they could deny the Son but retain the Father. But father and son are correlative terms, the one demands the other. If one denies the Son he automatically denies the Father, and if there is no Father the denier robs himself of relationship to and communion with the Father. The two relationships are linked together in Peter's confession (Matt 16:16); they cannot be divorced from each other. All these statements are warnings against the gnostic seducers, but they are equally applicable in our own day to all who deny the fundamental truths connected with the person and work of the Lord Jesus. (See Matt 11:27; John 5:23; 14:6; 15:23.)

24   "As for you" (RV), the genuine children of God in contradistinction to the deceivers, "let that therefore abide in you, which ye have heard from the beginning", i.e. from the very first day the gospel fell on their ears. They are being warned not to be moved away from it. The apostle is emphasising the need to be steadfast in the faith. Notice the reverse order "the Father and the Son" (v.22); "the Son and the Father" (v.24). "Here the thought is that of rising through the confession of the Son to the knowledge of the Father, there the thought is of the issue of denial culminating in the denial of the Father" (Westcott).

25   The promise is sure; it is guaranteed by the identity of the Promiser and by the repetition "promise ... promised". "He" (*autos*) is emphatic, and the promise which He promised us is delineated in three facts which are true of all whose profession of faith is genuine.

1.   The truth will remain in the believer   (2:24)

2.   The anointing of the Spirit indwells the believer   (2:27)

3.   The believer remains in vital communion with Christ   (2:6,24,27,28)

The experience of continuing in the Son is not a temporary abiding. It is the possession of eternal life; thus to have true fellowship with God (1:7), to be in Him (2:5), to abide in Him (2:6,24,27,28) and to have the Father and the Son (2:23) are all descriptions of the same experience. What a contrast between the false teachers, the deniers of Christ who had no eternal life (they perish) and the children of God who have eternal life. "Even eternal life" may be literally rendered "the life, the eternal one"; it underscores the undeniable fact that without the Son there is no life. The Promiser spoke previously in John 3:15,16; 4:14; 5:24; 10:28.

26   "Have I written" is an epistolary aorist, referring back to what he has written in vv.13-15. The participle here (*planōntōn*, those who would deceive you) shows they have not succeeded yet but they are in process of making the attempt; they are trying to deceive that they might lead astray.

27   "The anointing which ye have received of him abideth in you- (remains in you); it is not transient; it is permanently dwelling. The fact that they have not followed the teachers of error is proof that the anointing is still abiding in them. Continuance is always the proof of reality. "The same anointing teacheth you": the Spirit of God has taught them and is continuing to teach them. Against such deceivers we read "that he may abide with you for ever" (John 14:16). There is no suggestion here that these young believers do not need the teachers God has given to His people. There are both general teaching and special teachers in the Church for the purpose of edification (1 Cor 12-14; Eph 4:4). The anointing teacheth you of all things and is true. Note that:

God is true-the only true God	(John 17:3; 1 Thess 1:9 1 John 5:20)
The Lord Jesus is true	(John 1:14; 14:6; Rev 3:7; 19:11)
The Holy Spirit is true	(John 15:26; 16:13)

c. Abide in Him (v.28)
28   John now brings this section to a practical conclusion "and now, little children (*teknia*), abide in him". It is the concluding verse in several senses

1.   the first main division of the epistle, entitled "Relationship with Divine Persons based on righteousness, love and truth" finishes here.

2.   It is also the link with 2:12 where the apostle addresses "My dear children" (*teknia*).

Vv.13-28 are a parenthesis where he has a separate message for each of the three groups who compose the family-fathers, young men, babes (*paidia*). In the following verses he returns to the word *teknia* and is concerned with the whole family of God: all need the exhortation to abide in Him. This immediately draws our attention to our Lord's words concerning the Vine with their insistence that we bear fruit, more fruit, much fruit and that our fruit remain. Fruit cannot be produced except we abide in Him. It is evident that John is impressing upon the saints the need to abide in Christ in the deepest possible communion in order that luscious fruit might be produced for display in a coming day. For " when he shall be manifested" the RV reads "if...", but the "if" does not imply any doubt as to the fact of the coming of the Lord but as to the time. The word "manifested" is used in various ways relative to the person of the Lord Jesus.

1.	Manifested at His Incarnation	1 Tim 3:16; 1 John 1:2; 3:5,8
2.	Manifested in Words and Works	John 2:11; 17:6
3.	Manifested in Resurrection	John 21:1-4
4.	Manifested in Glory	Col 3:4

The Lord Jesus will be manifested to His own at the Rapture ("heaven; from whence also we look for the Saviour", Phil 3:20) and to the world at the Appearing ("Behold, he cometh with clouds; and every eye shall see him", Rev 1:7). Here it is the Judgment Seat of Christ when He shall be manifested to the saints, when they will appear before Him. Yet "we may have confidence" or boldness, literally, freedom in speaking, readiness to say anything, frankness, intrepidity, a fearless attitude in which the faithful saints appear before the Lord. "And not be ashamed before him" is literally "be ashamed from him" or "be ashamed away from before Him" (Lenski); "strikingly indicating the averted face and shrinking form which are the results of shame" (Plummet) (see Matt 10:28-do not shrink away in fear of them). "His coming" (*parousia*) is the only place in the Johannine pages where this word is used. A *parousia* is a period of time, the stay that follows an arrival. "Where the word is used prophetically, the *parousia* refers to the period beginning with the descent of the Lord into the air (1 Thess 4:16,17) and ending with His revelation and manifestation to the world" (Vine). During this period two main events will take place as far as the saints of this age are concerned: 1.

the Judgment Seat of Christ, 2. the Marriage of the Lamb. John is thinking of the first of these. During the *parousia* of the Lord Jesus in the air with His people John and his readers, yea all of us, must stand before the Judgment Seat of Christ, in order that "every one may receive the things done in his body, according to that he hath done, whether it be good or bad" (2 Cor 5:10). John therefore desires that his readers may so abide in Him in order that the fruit in their lives might be pleasing to the Lord and that he himself, as a workman, might not be speechless and ashamed when their response to his labours amongst them are revealed. The rewards to the saints will be made at the Judgment Seat of Christ, and each will be displayed at the appearing of Christ in glory.

Note

13   "When the apostle says 'I write' he is speaking of his being there and then engaged in the act of writing the epistle. The tense of the verb rendered 'I have written' is the epistolary aorist. In letter writing among the Greeks it was customary for the writer to project his thoughts to the time when the recipient, or recipients, would be reading the letter. From their point of view he 'wrote' it a considerable time before they received it . . ." (Vine).

III. The Second Circle (2:29-4:6)

Subject: Our Resemblance to Our Father
Evidenced by Righteousness, love and Truth

1. *Features of Righteousness*
   2:29-3:10

v.29 "if ye know that he is righteous, ye know that every one that doeth righteousness is born of him.

3 v.1 Behold, what manner of love the Father bath bestowed upon us, that we should be called the sons of God: therefore the world knoweth us not, because it knew him not.

v.2 Beloved, now are we the sons of God, and it doth not yet appear what we shall be but we know that, when he shall appear, we shall be like him; for we shall see him as he is.

v.3 And every man that hath this hope in him purifieth himself, even as he is pure.

v.4 Whosoever committeth sin transgresseth also the law for sin is the transgression of the law..

v.5 And ye know that he was manifested to take away our sins; and in him is no sin.

v.6 Whosoever abideth in him sinneth not: whosoever sinneth hath not seen him, neither known him.

v.7 Little children, let no man deceive you he that doeth righteousness is righteous, even as he is righteous.

v.8 He that committeth sin is of the devil, for the devil sinneth from the beginning. For this purpose the Son of God was manifested, that he might destroy the works of the devil.

v.9 Whosoever is born of God doth not commit sin, for his seed remaineth in him and he cannot sin, because he is born of God.

v.10 In this the children of God are manifest, and the children of the devil: whosoever
doeth not righteousness is not of God, neither he that loveth not his brother."

2:29 "If" is not an "if" of doubt, but of argument; it should be rendered "since". Note too the two words for "know" in this verse: "If ye know" (as a fact, intuitively, *eidēte*) "that God is righteous", "then you will know" (*ginōskete*), perceive experimentally by observation) "that everyone that doeth righteousness is born of him". That children display the character and features of their parents because they possess the parent's nature-like father, like son-is confirmed by John 3:6, "That which is born of the flesh is flesh, and that which is born of the Spirit is spirit". This is the principle that governs this section of the epistle. If you know the features of the father you will be able to recognise the children from their possession of identical features.

"He" in the verse is undoubtedly the Father. We are not said in the Scriptures to be born of Christ; we are born of the Spirit and the Word (John 3:5; 1 Pet 1:23); "the Father of lights ... begat he us" (Jas 1:17,18); "born of God" (1 John 3:9; 5:1 etc). Up to v.28 the person in view is the Lord Jesus, in "he shall be manifested", "ashamed before him at his coming", but in v.29 the Spirit is bringing before us the Father. In many of these verses it is difficult to decide whether it is the Father or the Son who is being spoken of. A precious thought one would gather is that if the Father and the Son can be talked of in the same breath, as it were, and the things attributed to the Father are equally true of the Son, it shows the absolute equality of the Son with the Father in the Godhead. We do know, then, intuitively that God is righteous, no true believer would doubt that; even when we cannot understand His ways we would say: "Shall not the judge of all the earth do right". He cannot be unrighteous. We know this is an undeniable feature of the Father's being.

We know then by observation that the people who habitually practise righteousness are born of Him; they have the features of the Father. This does not mean that the true believer will never think or say or do anything unrighteous but that the general bent of his life will display this feature that will show that he has been born of God. This is the first time in the epistle that John uses this expression "born of" God. Does his mind travel back to the occasion of which he speaks in John 3:7? Those memorable words "Ye must be born again" and the wonder of them seem to flow in all their sublime beauty over his soul. "Born of God"! Does the wonder of this truth cease to cause our souls to worship? In this day when so much empty profession goes under the title "born again" we who know the wonder of this expression should never cease to be moved to deep adoration, that we "were born, not of blood, nor of the will of the flesh, nor the will of man, but of God" (John 1:13).

3:1 It seems to me that John pauses here to meditate and worship, and maybe lays down his pen and says "Stop! Step aside and wonder"; "Behold!" Like Moses in Exod 3:3: "I will now turn aside, and see this great sight". "What manner of" (Matt 8:27; Mark 13:1; Luke 1:29; 7:39; 2 Pet 3:11) always indicates astonishment. Different translators and writers almost tumble over each other in the variety of ways they express this: "What amazing love"; "What glorious sublime love" (Luther); "What unearthly love"; "What foreign love"; "What alien love"; "What heavenly love"; "a love foreign to this world"; "love alien to our race" etc. Surely this is a love beyond human description, the very love of God, the love "the Father hath bestowed upon us". "In the Greek these words are in striking juxtaposition; to us miserable sinners the Father hath given this priceless right" (Plummer). Notice not God, but the Father is the giver; the words which follow will tell us that the Father has now become our Father. It is the Father who has bestowed this upon us; all of His grace, it is a pure gift. There was nothing in us to merit it, or call it forth. Maybe the expression should be "what love has given to us the Father" (Lenski) for this love has given to us the Father to know Him and have Him as our very own. He was and is the Father of our Lord Jesus Christ, but through grace He is our Father and He in His love has bestowed it, made it to dwell and He has declared it-we should be called the children of God. We often hear of kindly couples, possibly denied children of their own, who adopt children and bring them up and rear them as their own; all their love, devotion and care are lavished upon them, but all their love cannot really make up for the one vital essential thing- they did not beget them, they are not actually their own children. And is that what we are? Has God in His kindness brought us to Himself, lavished upon us His love, given to us through Christ His riches in glory and merely called us His children? Notice that most of the best MSS rightly add the words "such we are" because as children we have not merely been adopted into the family of God we have been born into it: we are not children of the devil who have been adopted into the family of God. We have been born again, born from above, born of God. God has begotten us and He has said it- "such we are"! We shall eternally praise Him for that.

"Therefore the world knoweth us not, because it knew him not". Again the question arises: Who is the "Him"? The immediate context would suggest "the Father who is righteous". Hence John may be thinking of "O righteous Father, the world hath not known thee: but I have known thee, and these have known that thou has sent me" (John 17:25); or again of "because they have not known the Father, nor me" (John 16:3); or "Ye neither know me, nor my Father: if ye had known me, ye should have known my Father also" (John 8:19); "Ye have not known him; but I know him" (John 8:55). It is evident that the Jews did not know the Father and therefore did not recognise the features of the Father in the person of Christ. It is equally true to say they deliberately would not recognise in the Son the evidences that the Father had sent with Him. Both are true, but we must recognise that "begotten of him" (2:29) (R.V.) is of the Father, and the expression "we shall see him as he is" (3:2) is relative to the Son; in the intervening verses the expressions are gradually moving from the Father to the Son. The

point is clear however that they did not know the Father and had therefore failed
to recognise the Son. The world still did not know the Father and having failed
to perceive in the Son the features of the Father, so they failed to recognise
those same features in the children. This characteristic of righteousness was seen
in the Son for "Thou hast loved righteousness and hast hated lawlessness" (Heb
1:9 JND).

2   The fact that the world had not, and did not, recognise the Son did not
alter the fact that God had already set His Son as King upon His holy hill in
Zion (Ps 2:6). Equally, the fact that the world does not recognise us as God's
children does not alter God's eternal purpose concerning us. It is true: "now
are we children of God" (RV), this is not an empty title; we were born of God.
It is not yet manifested: we look the same, we are the same blood and flesh,
unknown to the world, unrecognised. The world would merely laugh and
mock at our claims to be the children of God; as He was unrecognised so are
we. There are two possible translations of the next phrase: "but we know
that, when he shall appear" (AV) and ". . . it is manifested" (JND); because it
will be manifested when He appears the two ideas are linked. He will appear
to the saints at the Rapture, to the world at the appearing. At the former we
shall be changed to be like Him; at the latter we shall be seen by the world to
be like Him. The day is coming when it will be evident that we are the children
of God. "These first two verses of 1 John 3 celebrate the accomplishment of
God's eternal purposes concerning man . . .'let us make man in our image,
after our likeness'. In other words, He declares His intention of bringing into
existence beings like Himself, as like Himself as it is possible for creatures to
be like their creator ... Gen 3 tells how man, not content with the true likeness
to God which was his by creation, grasped at the deceptive likeness held out
as the serpent's bait: you will be like God, knowing good and evil. In
consequence things most unlike God manifested themselves in human life ...
In the fulness of time the image of God, undefaced by disobedience to His
will, appeared on earth in the person of His Son. 'To this end was the Son of
God manifested that He might destroy the works of the devil' (1 John 3:8)"
(Bruce). God's ultimate purpose is that the redeemed people of God will be
like Him. What does it mean? "When He (it) shall be manifested we shall be
like Him for we shall see Him as He is". Is this physical or moral likeness? We
believe it will be both physical and moral.

Notes

1   THE REDEMPTION OF OUR BODY (Romans 8:23)

The undernoted references show the physical change to take place in the saints at the Rapture:

a.   "We look for the Saviour, the Lord Jesus Christ: who shall change our vile body (fashion anew the body of our humiliation, RV) that it may be fashioned like unto his glorious body (conformed to the body of his glory, RV)" (Phil 3:21).

b.   "A building of God, an house not made with hands, eternal in the heavens ... earnestly desiring to be clothed upon with our house which is from heaven" (2 Cor 5:1-5).

c.   "It is sown in corruption; it is raised in incorruption: it is sown in dishonour; it is raised in glory: it is sown in weakness; it is raised in power: it is sown a natural body; it is raised a spiritual body" (1 Cor 15:42-44).

2   THE REVELATION OF THE SONS OF GOD (Romans 8:19)

The physical change to be manifested at the Appearing is referred to in the following verses:

a.   "When he shall come to be glorified in his saints, and to be admired in all them that believe" (2 Thess 1:10).

b.   "When Christ who is our life shall be manifested then shall ye also appear with him in glory" (Col 3:4).

This will indeed be a wonderful and glorious change when we shall be physically like Him. One would suggest however that the moral change will be more wonderful and more glorious. To change me physically is an act of creatorial power, but to change me to be morally like God and like His Son needed the atoning work of Calvary!

Notice please, that our verse says "we shall be like him". Let me ask: In the context what is He like?

1.   He is righteous   1 John 2:29

2.   He is pure   1 John 3:3

3.   In Him is no sin-and we shall be like Him   1 John 3:5

1.   "*He is righteous*". We are at present, in Christ, reckoned righteous before God: "For he hath made him to be sin for us, who knew no sin; that we might be made the righteousness of God in him" (2 Cor 5:21). Now I am reckoned righteous in Christ, then I shall be actually righteous myself (through what Christ hath done), never to be guilty of an unrighteous thought or word or action again. I shall be "like him". What a marvellous change!

2.   "*He is pure*". We are at present "holy and without blame" before Him in Christ, clean every whit, but needing constantly the use of the laver for the washing

of our feet; but then there will be no more defilement; we will be delivered from the love of sinning, no longer having to confess that "in me (that is, in my flesh,) dwelleth no good thing" (Rom 7:18), to be as pure as God is! Do not I now know, with all my fellow saints, the awful experience of unholy thoughts flashing into my mind even in my holiest moments? but then that will never occur again-I shall be like Him!

3. *"In him is no sin"*. John has already taught in ch. 1 that as long as you and I are in the body, the thing called sin, i.e. the root, will remain in us, and the fruits, sins, will sadly be evident in our lives. While John's teaching is clear "that ye may not sin" (RV) yet we so often do. But then the root of sin will be removed; the fruits of sin will never be produced. I shall not sin, shall not want to sin, shall not be able to sin-I shall be like Him! What wonder! What glory! "We shall see him as he is"; we are those who have never seen Him, but have the blessing of those who have not seen and yet have believed.

> "What will it be in Thy presence when first
>   The visions of glory upon us shall burst;
> Those eyes, flames of fire, which so searching we prove,
>   Shall beam on us, then, inexpressible love".

3   The AV "And everyman that hath this hope in him" is strengthened by the RV *"set* on him". Is this expression to be viewed subjectively or objectively? It is not "in him" as though implanted in the believer, but "on" (the pronoun following *epi* must denote the object of the hope, Bruce). It is the hope of seeing Him, of being like Him. If when we see Him we shall be like Him, it is evident that the more we are occupied with Him even now, the more we shall become like Him. Thus Paul writes: "We all, with open face beholding as in a glass the glory of the Lord, are changed into the same image from glory to glory, even as by the Spirit of the Lord" (2 Cor 3:18). Notice that this verse is not an exhortation, but a statement of fact: everyone that has this hope on Christ is in constant process of purifying himself even as Christ is pure. What a challenge to our hearts! Surely the measure in which I am constantly endeavouring to purify myself is the measure in which I really believe that He is coming, that I shall see Him, that I shall be like Him.

4   It seems to me that the wonder of being born of God caused John to pause and digress from his direct line of reasoning to meditate upon the glorious truths recorded in vv.1-3. Now he returns to the main subject of practising righteousness being an evidence of being born of God: "Every one that practises sin practises also lawlessness; and sin is lawlessness" (JND). The AV "sin is the transgression of the law" (from the Geneva Bible) is an unfortunate translation immediately suggesting the breaking of the Mosaic law. This expression has no reference to the Law of Moses. It is the general idea of lawlessness. On the one hand there is righteousness and on the other lawlessness. Our Lord loved righteousness and hated lawlessness. In this section of John's epistle a man either practises righteousness or practises lawlessness; he that does the one is born of God, who is righteous; he that does the other is of "that wicked one". Sin is doing as I like without regard to the will of God, thus expressing a lawless attitude towards God.

5 "Ye know (absolutely, intuitively) that he was manifested to take away our sins"; this reminds us of John 1:29 "Behold the Lamb of God, which taketh away the sin of the world". But there are things to be distinguished

1. "*our* sins", "the sin *of the world*";

2. "sins", "sin".

Here we have the reason for His coming into the world, for His becoming flesh. He lived, suffered, died, rose again in order to take away our sins-our personal sins. He has taken away our sins, but the root of sin is still in us. It is true, God has said, because of the efficacy of the work of Christ: "their sins and iniquities will I remember no more" (Heb 10:17). John 1:29 is a statement of fact: the Lord Jesus is the Lamb of God, having in view Calvary and His sacrifice; who "taketh away the sin of the world" is the ultimate of what He came to do; as a result of His Calvary work He will eventually take away the sin of the world. In other words sin the thing, the root will be completely eradicated out of the whole creation. So "For it was the good pleasure ... that in him should all the fulness dwell; and through him to reconcile all things unto himself ... whether things upon the earth, or things in the heavens" (Col 1:19,20 RV). "*Apokatallassō* signifies to reconcile completely, that is, to remove enmity and leave no impediment to unity and peace, thus restoring to a condition from which sin had caused a falling away" (Vine). Praise God He has taken my sins away-they are gone forever. Looking on into the future I share the joy of God that sin with all its consequences will eventually be forever removed. The statement here is for my present assurance and personal joy. In order to do that He must Himself be a worthy victim for sacrifice so with regard to the sin offering (dealing with sin) "it is most holy" (Lev 6:25) and the trespass offering (dealing with sins) "it is most holy" (Lev 7:6). Thus the NT deals with the sin offering in 2 Cor 5:21: "he hath made him to be sin for us, who knew no sin"; and the trespass offering in 1 Pet 2:22-24: "who did no sin ... who his own self bare our sins". So John in perfect keeping with these truths stresses that " in him is no sin" which goes further than both Paul and Peter and declares that the root of sin was not found in Him, the presence of indwelling sin was not in His heart. The root of sin present in us was never in Christ: "The sinlessness of Christ belongs neither to His pre-existence, nor to the days of His flesh, nor to his present heavenly condition, but to His essential and eternal nature" (Stott). Thus He was the perfect sin-bearer at Calvary. Therefore, because "he was manifested to take away our sins" and because "in him is no sin", it is inconsistent if a believer practises the very things Christ came to take away.

6 The one who abides in Him is not here a spiritual christian in contrast to a carnal christian; this is a born-again person in contrast to one who is not saved. The born-again person is seen as one who habitually abides in Christ; that person does not habitually practise sin. This does not suggest that the believer never commits one single act of sin (this would be a contradiction of 1:10). He may (and does) commit individual acts of sin but he will not habitually live a life of sin. A sinful life does not mark a child of God. "Whatever high claims may be made by one who indulges in sin, that indulgence is sufficient proof that he has no personal knowledge of Christ" (Bruce). "Whoso sinneth hath not seen him, neither knoweth him" (RV). Notice the tense again here as in the whole of this section. The eyes of the true believer are ever on the Lord Jesus. The eyes of his understanding have been enlightened, but whoever sinneth (habitually sins) hath not seen Him, neither known Him. "To see and to know Christ, the sinless Saviour of sinners is to outlaw sin; to sin is to deny Christ and to reveal the one is not abiding in Him. Sin and Christ are irreconcilably at enmity with each other" (Stott).

7 "My little children (*teknia*), let no one lead you astray", reads the RV, warning against seduction into error of a strange kind. "The tenderness of the address is called out of the peril of the situation" (Westcott). The gnostic false teachers were seeking to deceive the saints, but their high profession and low living were contrary to each other. They claimed that, although they were living lawless lives, nevertheless because of their superior knowledge this was righteous but of course "righteous without a determination to practise righteousness". John would have the saints to know that profession and practice must correspond; the profession on the lips must be consistent with the movements of the feet. "Genuine knowledge would be accompanied by righteous living. Because the gnostic claimed spiritual knowledge while living in sin, John insists that righteousness and knowledge of Christ cannot be divorced ... He who knows Christ will be like Him" (Burdick). It is "the one who practises righteousness who is righteous" (see also 2:29). "Even as he is righteous" here refers to Christ (in 1:9 it refers to God): "*the righteous one*; of whom ye have now become betrayers and murderers" (Acts 7:52 RV); "ye denied the *holy and righteous one* and asked for a murderer" (Acts 3:14 RV); "the *righteous* for the unrighteous" (1 Pet 3:18 RV).

8 John develops the idea of two families with features entirely opposed to each other-there are the children of God and the children of the devil. If you know the father you will be able to recognise the children: "He that committeth sin is of the devil". "John does not say 'is or has been born from the devil'; such a verb would not be apt because 'to be born' implies life, and all that comes from the devil is death. Yet the devil is the father of all those practising sins (John 8:44), they are 'the children of the devil' (v.10)" (Lenski). He who habitually, continually practises sin is of the devil. He possesses the characteristics, the features of his father. What is his father like? the devil sinneth from the beginning".

We have come across the word "beginning" before. Which beginning is before us here? Not the unbeginning beginning of eternity, for the devil is not eternal; he was created, he had a beginning. Neither is it the beginning of the human race, though it is true that he has been sinning ever since that date, but he was created long before that. Under the title "king of Tyrus" we read in Ezek 28:15: "Thou wast perfect in thy ways from the day that thou wast created". So he was created and he was not a sinner from the day of his creation: rather he was " full of wisdom, perfect in beauty, perfect in thy ways". But he became a sinner and he has been sinning ever since. It is of this point that our verse speaks: "till iniquity was found in thee" (Ezek 28:15). It was when his heart was lifted up with pride that he said: "I will be like the most High" (Isa 14:12-15). Then he sinned. "The devil sinneth", it has been his habitual way of living ever since. His children therefore have the same features and the same history: they habitually sin from their beginning. "Here the antithesis is between the family of God and the family of the devil; in either family the children may be known by their moral likeness to the head of the family" (Bruce).

"For this purpose the Son of God was manifested, that he might destroy the works of the devil": that He might undo, unloose, dissolve them, says John. This is one of the chief reasons for the coming into the world of the Son of God. It was of course to save me from hell and to ensure that I spent eternity with Christ in glory, but it was for far more than that: "He was manifested to undo the works of the devil". God worked for the six days of Gen 1, and "saw every thing that he had made, and, behold, it was very good". "And God did rest the seventh day from all his works" (Heb 4:4). His creation rest was marred, His work was undone, so that we read "My Father worketh hitherto, and I work" (John 5:17). Divine persons are working in harmony toward the day when every result of Satan's working will be removed; they are working toward the eternal goal-a "new heavens and a new earth, wherein dwelleth righteousness" (2 Pet 3:13). "When all things shall be subdued unto him, then shall the Son also himself be subject unto him that put all things under him, that God may be all in all" (1 Cor 15:28). "And he that sat upon the throne said, Behold, I make all things new" (Rev 21:5). Then every result of the devil's work will be eradicated; sin and all the tragedy connected with it will be removed. Things in heaven and things on earth will be reconciled completely. In individual lives we see the Lord Jesus doing this as the perfect Servant on earth, e.g. in Mark 1:29-31. A woman is meant to serve Him, but a fever hinders her-"He took her by the hand, lifted her up, the fever left her and she ministered unto them". In Mark 3 too a man had a hand with which he was meant to work for God, but his hand was withered. Jesus said "Stretch forth thine hand"; thereafter the man could work for God. In Mark 7 "they bring unto him one that was deaf, and had an impediment in his speech". He had ears, but could not hear God, a tongue but could not praise God. Jesus undid the work of the devil. In Luke 13:16 "a daughter of Abraham, whom Satan hath bound, lo, these eighteen years"; He loosed her. And so one could continue, for the mighty works of the Lord Jesus were the undoing of the works of the devil, a foretaste of the glorious days yet to come. What are the " works of the devil"? "Morally, this work is enticement to sin; physically, the infliction of disease; intellectually, seduction into error" (Stott). "How can one in whose life sin has manifestly not been destroyed or taken away claim to dwell in Christ?" (Bruce).

9 "Whosoever is begotten of God doeth no sin" (RV) emphasises that such an one has become and therefore remains a child of God; he cannot commit sin as a practice, as a habit. It is not here a contrast between the old nature and the new, but a contrast between the child of God and the children of the devil. "The new birth involves a radical change in human nature; for those who have not experienced it, sin is natural, whereas for those who have experienced it, sin is unnatural-so unnatural, indeed that its practice constitutes a powerful refutation of any claim to possess the divine life" (Bruce). "His seed remaineth in him" recognises "his seed" to be "the divine nature", "the divine seed". "The new birth involves the acquisition of a new nature through the implanting within us of the very seed or lifegiving power of God. Birth of God is a deep radical, inward transformation. Moreover, the new nature received at new birth remains. It exerts a strong internal pressure towards holiness" (Stott). "Therefore the person who is born of God cannot continue practising sin, he is not able habitually to sin, because out of God he has been born" (Wuest). "John 3:5-8 would lead us to interpret seed as meaning the Holy Spirit" (Plummer).

10 "In this" refers back to what has gone before, the doing or not doing of righteousness, but the statement is so placed between the preceding verses concerning righteousness and those that follow concerning love. This chapter as we have remarked deals with the features of righteousness and love showing our resemblance to our Father. Here the two characteristics are brought together and the existence of righteousness and love on the one hand shows that one is the child of God, and the existence of lawlessness and hate on the other hand is the evidence of one being a child of the devil. The term "children of the devil" occurs nowhere else in the NT. We have " ye are of your father the devil" (John 8:44); "children of wrath" (Eph 2:3); " sons of disobedience" (Eph 2:2 RV). A man's principles are invisible but the way he lives manifests what he really is, manifests to which family he belongs. God is righteous and God is love are two inseparable features in the character of God and will both be equally evident in those who are born of God. There are none who are half and half. John only knows extremes: light and darkness, righteousness and lawlessness, love and hate, and therefore only two families-of God or of the devil. There is no middle place; the tree will be known by its fruit.

2. *Features of Love*
     ## 3:11-18

v.11 "For this is the message that ye heard from the beginning, that we should love one another.

v.12 Not as Cain, *who* was of that wicked one, and slew his brother. And wherefore slew he him? Because his own works were evil, and his brother's righteous.

v.13 Marvel not, my brethren, if the world hate you.

v.14 We know that we have passed from death unto life, because we love the brethren. He that loveth not *his* brother abideth in death.

v.15 Whosoever hateth his brother is a murderer: and ye know that no murderer hath eternal life abiding in him.

v.16 Hereby perceive we the love *of God*, because he laid down his life for us: and we ought to lay down *our* lives for the brethren.

v.17 But whoso hath this world's good, and seeth his brother have need, and shutteth up his bowels of *compassion* from him, how dwelleth the love of God in him?

v.18 My little children, let us not love in word, neither in tongue; but in deed and in truth."

11   "For this is the message that ye heard from the beginning, that we should love one another" is reminiscent of 1:5: "This then is the message which we have heard of him, and declare unto you, that God is light". They had also heard this second message from the beginning, from the very first time the gospel fell upon their ears. John had already introduced this subject in 2:7,11 as a proof that one is a child of God. The message would be first spread in the area John was addressing, many years before by Paul (Acts 18:19:1-41), whereas the teaching of the gnostics was a later arrival. The message John is stressing was not merely Paul's, it was the word of the Lord Jesus Himself (John 13:34-35). Thus John says "Let that . . . abide in you, which ye have heard from the beginning" (2:24).

12   John now uses the two first brothers to be born into the world as illustrations of the truths he is teaching; both were by the nature the children of Adam and Eve, but one is of the evil one "out of the pernicious one and killed his brother" (v.12). Compare this with "because his works were pernicious and those of his brother's righteous" (v.12). A brother's love (which is of God) suggests a brother's hate. First of all Cain was of a particular father, the devil. He correspondingly had a nature that was like his father's. "Ye are of your father the devil, and the lusts of your father ye will do. He was a murderer from the beginning" (John 8:44). Cain was of that wicked one, had that nature and produced features that corresponded thereto. "The culmination of his evil ways was 'he slew his brother'. This was the evidence of his devilish nature" (Plummer). The original meaning of the word "slew" was "to cut the throat" especially as a victim for sacrifice. It means "to slay with violence", "to butcher" (Law). See Rev 5:6,9,12; 13:8.

"Wherefore slew he him?", asks John. Cain was of that wicked one. He had an evil nature, a pernicious (evil, destructive, injurious) one, which caused him:

1. to bring an unacceptable sacrifice: "Abel offered ... a more excellent sacrifice than Cain, by which he obtained witness that he was righteous" (Heb 11:4);

2. to be very angry (Gen 4:5);

3. to evidence envy and jealousy, resentment because of another's acceptability: He slew him because his own works were evil-his brother's righteous.

God by accepting Abel's sacrifice had given witness that he was righteous, God had testified to his gifts. "Cain showed his spiritual connection with the evil one by the slaughter of his brother" (Vine). The righteousness of Abel "incited the jealousy" of Cain. "The principle of the hostility of the wicked for the righteous is one which John sees operating in the environment of himself and his readers, hence the following words of encouragement" (Bruce).

13 "Marvel not, my brethren, if the world hate you", better ". . . hateth you", for the continual antagonism between the light and the darkness, between God and the evil one, between righteousness and unrighteousness has never ceased from the time of the first sin (v.8) and of the first murder (v. 12). "The moral descendants of Cain and Abel are still in the world" (Plummer). "It is only to be expected that the wicked should continue to regard and treat the righteous as Cain regarded and treated his righteous brother Abel" (Stott). See the warning of the Lord Jesus in John 15:18,19,25; 17:14. Notice John does not here address "my little children" as he so often does, but "my brethren": he is a brother addressing the brotherhood which is therefore the object of the same hatred.

14 We "know" absolutely (emphatic), in spite of all the malicious hatred that the world may show towards us. "The dark world which is full of devilish hate may think and do what it pleases about us; we know that we have left the atmosphere of death for one of life" (Plummer). John does quote the words of the Saviour in his Gospel: "He that heareth my word, and believeth on him that sent me, hath everlasting life, and shall not come into condemnation; but is passed from death unto life" (5:24). In simple faith many of us read this verse and acted on it; we knew that we had everlasting life, that we would not come into condemnation, that we had passed from death unto life because the Lord Jesus said it. God's word said it, we believed it and we were perfectly assured, but now "we know we have passed from death unto life, because we love the brethren". We have an undeniable proof within ourselves. The evidence of being born of God is that we love the brethren. The world hates the brethren, the true believer loves the brethren, and therefore we have evidence that we have passed from a state of being dead in trespasses and sins and have been quickened by the same mighty power that raised Christ from the dead. "We have stepped over out of the death into the life (we know it by this evidence) because we are loving brothers" (Lenski). We have changed masters, spheres, kingdoms; we are under new ownership; we belong to a new family and the evidence is found in this: "we love the brethren". He that loveth not abideth in death, God is love and those who are born again into His family will continually manifest the features of God; if anyone does not show those features it is evident that he has not passed from death unto life; he has not changed over; he is still in the same place; he "abideth in death".

15   "Whosoever hateth his brother is a murderer", a man-murderer. This is the word that the Lord Jesus used relative to the devil in John 8:44: "a man murderer from the beginning". This takes us back to Gen 2 and 3. The serpent did not actually murder our first parents; his hands were not stained with blood, but he knew that God had said: "In the day that thou eatest thereof thou shalt surely die", so he set about enticing them to eat of the tree, so that God, in keeping His word, would have to bring about their death. Thus Satan would murder them, shall we say, by proxy. They did, as a result of their disobedience, die spiritually that day; they became dead in trespasses and sins. They died too in a substitute that must have been provided by God to make the coats (plural) of skin (singular) with which to cover their nakedness, that they might stand before God. They eventually died physically, so the devil accomplished their death. He was a man-murderer, though his hands were not stained with blood. Those who belong to the devil's family, his seed, show the same features-their hands may not be stained with blood either, but everyone hating his brother is a murderer, a murderer morally, a murderer in his heart (see Matt 5:21, 22). It is not a crime in the eyes of the world to hate a person, but in the eyes of God hatred equates with murder, and ye know absolutely, there is no doubt about it, that no man-murderer hath eternal life remaining in, abiding in him.

16   This love is no emotional sentimental love, no love that is only expressed in words; it evidences itself in a practical way. We perceive love in action in the person of the Lord Jesus; here is the divine definition of love, not in words, but in action. Self-sacrifice is the very essence of love: "he laid down his life for us" (notice "for us"), whereas the opposite spirit is seen on the record of Cain: "Cain rose up against Abel his brother, and slew him" (Gen 4:8). Cain's action took away life. The action of our Lord Jesus is that He laid down His life for (on behalf of) us (see John 10: 11,15,17,18; 13:37,38; 15:13). This phrase "seems to imply not so much the laying down as the laying aside of something like clothes, the divesting oneself of a thing" (Westcott). "It is the same word as 'laying aside his garments' (John 13:4)" (Stott). He laid down His life for us, voluntarily: "No man taketh (my life) from me, but I lay it down of myself". For this reason His Father loved Him. The Father found great pleasure in the self-sacrificing love of His Son. Therefore since His love is perceived in His laying down His life for us, it follows "we ought to lay down our lives for the brethren". In this He has left us an example, and we ought to walk as He walked (2:6); "we ought also to love one another" (4:11).

17   In "But whoso hath the world's goods" (RV), "the 'but' suggests that it would be a mistake to regard the manifestation of love as simply consisting of great and noble deeds such as laying down one's life. The greater includes the less" (Vine). Some saints have wished that they had lived in days of persecution and that they had had the opportunity of dying for Christ (it is sometimes more costly to live for Christ than to die for Him), but John brings this self-sacrificing love into the sphere of daily living and applies it to the very ordinary evidences of christian love-his brother being in need. "The world's goods" are the means of living, enough to live on, resources for the maintaining of life. God in His loving kindness has graciously given us abundantly of these things. "Beholdeth his brother in need" is not a superficial casual glance, or being taken in by a "sob-story" but to have opportunity, over a prolonged period of time for "a definite contemplation of a brother's circumstances" (Vine). The observer "deliberately keeps on contemplating his brother constantly having need" (Wuest). This needs real brotherly shepherd care with a genuine exercise to determine need. Here is our opportunity to show our love to the brethren. But how does he react? He "shutteth up his bowels of compassion", the seat of the affections, his heart, locking the door. He "locks his compassion away from him" (Lenski). Notice

1.   he has,

2.   he looks,

3.   he locks.

"Love is the willingness to surrender that which has value for our own life, to enrich the life of another" (Dodd). Notice the change from the plural "the brethren" to the singular "his brother". It is far easier to talk in the terms of humanity in general, than to face up to one's personal responsibility, brother to brother. "It is easier to be enthusiastic about Humanity with a capital 'H' than it is to love individual men and women, especially those who are uninteresting, exasperating, depraved, or otherwise unattractive. Loving everyone in a general way may be an excuse for loving nobody in particular" (Lenski). A true christian will instinctively show the love that has been exhibited in the Lord Jesus and His sacrifice in sharing his goods with those in need. It is one of the features that is characteristic of the children of God. If we should feel in our hearts the urge to help our brother as we discern his need, and we stifle that urge, drown that emotion, spurn the pressure of the Spirit of God in our consciences, then John questions: "How dwelleth the love of God in him? " The love of God gives, sacrifices; "love does not dwell in a murderer, love does not dwell in a miser" (Stott). The love of God is seen in the great giving of Calvary, but that love now dwells within everyone who has come to know the love of God. If it is within us, shed abroad in our hearts, permanently there, it will show itself. As it is seen in Him, so it will be seen in those who are truly born of God. If it is not seen, John puts the question "How dwelleth the love of God in him?"

18   John is thinking upon love seen in Christ and desiring to see it manifested in the saints uses this term of tender affection "my little children". Did he not in his heart embrace and care for them all, and had not the aged apostle spent the years of his life in this way, laying down his life for the brethren? As the Father had loved and given His Son, and as He had laid down His life for us, so John protests that mere words, however loud, are not enough. Love is not merely words; it expresses itself, warmly, fervently, sacrificing, giving itself. It is not mere profession, it is genuine (in truth) and it acts in a deliberate way (in deed).

3.   *Features of Truth*
   3:19-24

> v.19 "And hereby we know that we are of the truth, and shall assure our hearts before him.
> v.20 For if our heart condemn us, God is greater than our heart, and knoweth all things.
> v.21 Beloved, if our heart condemn us not *then* have we confidence toward God.
> v.22 And whatsoever we ask, we receive of him, because we keep his commandments, and do those things that are pleasing in his sight.
> v.23 And this is his commandment, That we should believe on the name of his Son Jesus Christ, and love one another, as he gave us commandment.
> v.24 And he that keepeth his commandments dwelleth in him, and he in him. And hereby we know that he abideth in us, by the Spirit which he hath given us.

19   The mention of the word "truth" (v.18) introduces the third subsection of this division of the epistle-viz. Our Resemblance to our Father shown by our adherence and walking in the truth! We are of the truth. "Truth can only characterise the behaviour of those whose very character originates in the truth, so that it is by our loving others 'in truth' that we know we are 'of the truth' " (Stott). The "hereby" (AV) definitely refers back to the previous expressions concerning the need for loving our brethren in this practical way. If these things are found in our lives we have the evidence (we know experimentally, ginosko) that we are of the truth. Love to the Lord and for the brethren shown in a self-sacrificing way will be an assurance before Him that we really are born of God. The expressions in v.16 "He laid down his life for us" referring to the Lord Jesus, and "we ought to lay down our lives for the brethren" may have been connected in John's mind by the Spirit of God with words written in ch.13 of his Gospel (possibly also written about the same date) when Peter, whose heart was really true to the Lord, used words that he did not turn into deeds, used his tongue to express things that did not come to fruition: "Lord, why cannot I follow thee now? I will lay down my life for thy sake" (John 13:37). The Lord Jesus replied with words calculated to shake his self confidence (John 13:38): "Wilt thou lay down thy life for my sake? ... The cock shall not crow, till thou hast denied me thrice" (v.38). Our blessed Lord knew well Peter's love and devotion and said to him: "The spirit truly is ready, but the flesh is weak (Mark 14:38). When Peter was turned again (Luke 22:32) he was "before" the Lord (John 21:15). Peter was three times questioned by the Lord:

1.   "Lovest thou me more than these?" to which Peter replies "Yea, Lord; thou knowest that I am attached to thee" (v.15 JND);

2.   "Lovest thou me?", to which Peter replies in the same words;

3.   "Simon, son of Jonas, art thou attached to me?" Peter was grieved because He said to him the third time, "Art thou attached to me?" and said unto Him, "Lord, thou knowest all things; thou knowest that I am attached to thee".

Peter had declared he would lay down his life for the Lord, and had failed to fulfil his pledge. Thus John is teaching here that if we have been characterised by this self-sacrificing love and we have expressed that love truly to our brother in his need, then by that we have evidence that we are of the truth and our hearts will be assured (convinced, persuaded) of that fact in His presence: "And shall assure our hearts before him". The order in the original is "and before Him we shall assure our hearts".

20   But like so many of us, Peter was in the Lord's presence as one who had failed in this matter. His heart did condemn him in this matter of love to the Lord. He had failed. And who amongst God's people has not equally failed and far more in the matter of laying down our lives for the brethren? The fact that such yearnings are produced in our hearts by the Holy Spirit, and that we give expression to them on occasions in responding to the needs of our brethren, is an assurance that we are of the truth. For this we are abundantly thankful, but like Peter we so often fail in these matters. Peter's conscience was doubtless probed by the questioning of the Lord Jesus and he was grieved, not only that the Lord asked him three times, but that the third time He changed the question from "love me" to "attached to me". His heart surely condemned him, but he found assurance in the presence of the Lord and expressed himself. "thou knowest all things". John says, "If our heart condemn us, God is greater than our heart, and knoweth all things". It is worth noting other renderings: "Hereby we shall know that we are of the truth, and shall persuade our hearts before him-that if our heart condemn us, God is greater than our heart and knows all things" (JND); "shall assure our heart before him, whereinsoever our heart condemn us; because God is greater than our heart, and knoweth all things" (RV, note punctuation); "and reassure our hearts before Him whenever our hearts condemn us; for God is greater than our hearts, and He knows everything" (RSV); "in his presence shall tranquillise our hearts in whatever our hearts condemn us, because greater is God than our hearts and knows all things" (Wuest); "shall persuade our hearts before Him, if in regard to anything the heart condemns us, that God is greater than our heart and knows everything" (Lenski). Hence, when before Him our heart may condemn us because of our lack of self-sacrificing love we are re-assured, tranquillised by the fact that though our knowledge is so limited even with regard to ourselves God is greater than our hearts and knows all; so Peter said and was assured before Him. He knows our hearts and appreciates our affection, He knows all the circumstances of our failures, nevertheless His blood cleanses from all sin (1:7); His advocacy restores us perfectly (2:1); His sacrifice is eternally efficacious (2:2). Thus we assure our hearts before Him. "It will be noted that the RV continues in this verse the sentence of v.19 making the phrase 'whereinsoever our heart condemn us' depend on the word 'persuade'. That is to say, if we have something upon our conscience by which we are self-condemned, such as failure to exercise love, 'God is greater than our heart and knows all things', and the apostle has already shown how, through the efficacy of the blood of Christ, we may be cleansed from our sin and enjoy fellowship with God" (Vine). "Condemn" is used in the sense of "to know against".

21   "Beloved, if our heart condemn us not, then have we confidence, (boldness) toward God". This sentence is prefaced by the loving address "beloved". John really does love these dear saints. If there is a clear sky between our souls and God, conscious that everything is right with Him, that we are in His presence, we shall have "boldness, face to face with God". Robertson notes that confidence (*parrhēsia*) is "used to indicate contact". "When God, who is greater than our conscience and pronounces a more authoritative verdict, one based on perfect knowledge of us and all the relevant circumstances, assures us of the forgiveness of our sins for Christ's sake we enjoy peace of conscience" (Bruce). "The thought here is of the boldness with which the Son appears before the Father, and not of that with which the accused appears before the Judge" (Westcott).

22   The second benefit which results from a heart that condemns us not is a boldness in prayer, a "boldness to enter into the holiest by the blood of Jesus ... (to) draw near with a true heart in full assurance of faith" (Heb 10:19-22). To draw near with the confidence of our Father's smile with no cloud upon our souls is to be assured not only that He hears us, but that our prayers will be answered: "we receive of him, because we keep his commandments, and do those things that are pleasing in his sight' which is the believer's habitual way of living. The true believer will be careful to keep His commandments as found in the Word and, in a more general way, having the whole book before him will know and do the things that are pleasing in His sight. This requires living close to the Lord, walking in His sight, keeping short accounts with God, obeying all the Spirit of God reveals to us from the word of God. Then we can be assured that "whatsoever we ask, we receive of him". (Cf. "If you abide in me, and my words abide in you, ye shall ask what ye will, and it shall be done unto you" (John 15:7); "What things soever ye desire, when ye pray, believe that ye receive them, and ye shall have them" (Mark 11:24); "Whatsoever ye shall ask in my name, that will I do, that the Father may be glorified in the Son" (John 14:13).) "Every answer to our petitions is the clearest factual evidence that He treats us as children. Blessed are we indeed!" (Lenski). "If ye abide in me, and my words abide in you, ye shall ask what ye will, and it shall be done unto you" (John 15:7).

23   John, having spoken of keeping His commandments now speaks of one commandment which in itself sums up the whole of our Lord's teaching. This is the commandment to which he has referred already in this epistle and to which he will return again. It is one commandment, for "you cannot believe without loving nor love without believing" (Lenski). "This is his commandment, That we should believe on the name of His Son Jesus Christ, and love one another". We ever continue believing and ever continue loving. It is important what one believes. True faith is expressed in right conduct. Right doctrine leads to right behaviour. The phrase "believe the name" (the preposition "in" is not in the original) conveys the thought of believing all that the name implies: His deity, His real humanity, His Saviourhood, His Messiahship, His anointing of God-all these are declared in the expression "his Son Jesus Christ". Belief in the name of such a person will be expressed in a spontaneous "love one another", even as He gave us commandment (John 13:34; 15:12,17).

24   This feature, keeping His commandments (referring back to v.22) by which the believer will be characterised, is the evidence of this most intimate union which is mutual: "abideth in him and he in him" (see John 15:4; 17:23,26). "And hereby we know that he abideth in us, by the Spirit which he hath given to us". This is the first mention of the Holy Spirit by name in the epistle though "an unction from the Holy One" is found in 2:20,27. In 2:27 believers are said to have received Him; here He was given to us, the aorist tense pointing to a particular time, the time when a person believed on the Lord Jesus for salvation. It is at that time the Holy Spirit is received: "having also believed (RV), ye were sealed with that holy Spirit of promise, which is the earnest of our inheritance until the redemption of the purchased possession, unto the praise of his glory" (Eph 1:13:14).

4. *The Spirit of Truth and the Spirit of Error*
   ## 4:1-6

> v.1 "Beloved, believe not every spirit, but try the spirits whether they are of God: because many false prophets are gone out into the world.
> v.2 Hereby know ye the Spirit of God: Every spirit that confesseth that Jesus Christ is come in the flesh is of God:
> v.3 And every spirit that confesseth not that Jesus Christ is come in the flesh is not of God: and this is that *spirit* of antichrist, whereof ye have heard that it should come; and even now already is it in the world.
> v.4 Ye are of God, little children, and have overcome them: because greater is he that is in you, than he that is in the world.
> v.5 They are of the world: therefore speak they of the world, and the world heareth them.
> v.6 We are of God: he that knoweth God heareth us ; he that is not of God heareth not us. Hereby know we the spirit of truth, and the spirit of error."

1 The Spirit of God has been given and received by every believer, but John would now have his readers to recognise that there are two spirits in the world. There is the Spirit of God who has sent forth the servants of God into the world. There is the spirit of antichrist who has sent forth his false teachers into the world. "Beloved" shows John loves these dear saints and therefore does not want them to be led astray by evil men and false teaching, so he warns "believe not every spirit". The unction from the Holy One mentioned at the end of ch.2 has been given to every believer and is a divinely-given Protector, helping them to distinguish between truth and error. The knowledge of this should cause us to use our Spirit-given powers of discernment. The tense of the verb is continuous showing that the habit of our lives should be one of refusing to believe every spirit, but trying (proving) the spirits so that one may accept what is of God, and reject what is not of God. All believers are responsible to exercise judgment concerning spiritual things. We have the Spirit of God and the word of God and we are well equipped so to do.

There are many spiritual influences in the world, and we all will have experience of them; they are not necessarily of God just because they are spiritual. Miraculous powers are not absolute proof of the possession of the truth. They may be delusions of fanatical enthusiasts, uninstructed and self-deceived, or they may be lies by deliberate deceivers. God has given to us the complete word of God; the faith has once for all been delivered to the saints. That which these saints heard from the beginning was indeed the truth; they are warned against those that would go beyond (2 John 9) because many false prophets are gone out into the world, as the Lord foretold and the apostles confirmed would happen: "Beware of false prophets, which come to you in sheep's clothing, but inwardly they are ravening wolves. Ye shall know them by their fruits" (Matt 7:15,16); "Take heed that no man deceive you. For many shall come in my name, saying, I am Christ; and shall deceive many" (Matt 24:4-5); "the time will come ... they shall turn away their ears from the truth, and shall be turned unto fables" (2 Tim 4:3,4); "of this sort ... creep into houses, and lead captive silly women" etc (2 Tim 3:6).

2 "Hereby know ye the Spirit of God", know by experience, by observation, assures of the infallibility of the test. Every believer will be able to recognise the nature of any testimony borne, by its agreement or otherwise with the fundamental doctrines of christianity which were written by the inspiration of the Spirit of God. "Every spirit that confesseth that Jesus Christ is come in the flesh is of God". "Every spirit" indicates that every person who is activated by the Spirit of God and by whose leading he confesses; he will declare that Jesus Christ is come in the flesh. This is a credal statement as it contains the basic truths concerning the deity and real humanity of the Lord. This statement is a standard by which the gnostic errors taught by Cerinthus could be tested. Cerinthus and his followers taught that Jesus was an ordinary man upon whom the Christ came at His baptism because of His piety. The word of God declares that "unto you is born this day in the city of David a Saviour, which is Christ the Lord" (Luke 2:11); this was spoken at His birth, not His baptism. Again, "God sent forth his Son, born of a woman, born under the law" (Gal 4:4 RV); and again, "Christ Jesus came into the world to save sinners" (1 Tim 1:15). Truly "the Word became flesh, and dwelt among us" (John 1:14 RV). The perfect tense "having come" is important; it indicates a coming with an abiding effect. At incarnation our Lord Jesus took on true manhood. He took part of blood and flesh (Heb 2:14 Gk). He took on true manhood permanently and He has taken manhood to the very throne of God. He is now, at this moment, "one mediator also between God and men, himself man Christ Jesus" (1 Tim 2:5 RV) and now "in him dwelleth all the fulness of the Godhead bodily" (Col 2:9). Every spirit that confesseth these things of Christ is without doubt "of God".

3 Many of the best MSS omit "Christ come in the flesh" from this verse but it is obviously the meaning which John wishes to convey. Those that confess not are said to be "not of God". It is therefore a simple thing to try the spirits whether they are of God. "This is the spirit of the antichrist, whereof ye have heard that it cometh; and now it is in the world already" (RV). The antichrist has not yet come-he will in his own time-but the antichristian nature and attitude is already in the world. The word "already" suggests that something more is expected to follow. See "the mystery of lawlessness doth already work. .. then shall be revealed the lawless one" (2 Thess 2:7,8 RV).

4   The purveyors of error are not of God, but John's well-loved children (this term of endearment occurs again) are of God. The two expressions: "every spirit that confesseth that Jesus Christ is come in the flesh" (v.2), and "every spirit that confesseth not" (v.3) categorise those who had gone out into the world-the teachers whether sent by God or by the devil. John's readers had listened to both, had proved the spirits, had accepted the testimony of the former and had refused to be deceived by the latter. Thus John says, "Ye are of God". Notice, "Ye", John's readers, "are of God" (v.4). "We", John and his fellow teachers, "are of God" (v.6). They are of the world (v.5). ("ye" and "we" are emphatic). They had listened to the false teaching and rejected it, had refused to be swayed by it, though it was good words and fair speeches (Rom 16:18); they had "overcome them" (those in whom was the spirit of antichrist) "because greater is he that is in you, than he that is in the world". This expression indicates that he that is in the world is great-we should never underestimate the power of the spirit of antichrist, the spirit of error, the adversary. But He that is in us is greater. This person is the Spirit of God, called the Spirit of Truth and referred to in 2:20,27 as the Anointing from the Holy One; the Spirit of God given to us by the Lord Jesus, acting as a divine intuition, an inward guide, to lead us into truth and to keep us from error. Says 2:27 "Ye have received of him and he abideth in you". Therefore through the word of God (the Truth) and the Spirit of Truth in their hearts they had overcome them, both the false teachers and their adherents.

5   "The world, because of the philosophy to which they endeavour to accommodate the gospel, depriving it of what makes it the gospel in the process, is current secular philosophy, the prevalent climate of opinion ... it is in line with contemporary fashion" (Bruce). These teachers of error belong to a system utterly opposed to the things of God, "therefore speak they (as) of the world". The world in every form rejected Him at the cross, they reject Him still by denying His claim to be the incarnate Son of God. "We are to fight against the influence which permeates that system of human society which lies in spiritual darkness and is organised, socially, intellectually and morally, by the evil one and his hosts, against God and His Christ" (Vine). "And", adds John, "the world heareth them". "Because they come, spiritually and morally, from this evil world system, 'therefore they speak of the world'. By this the apostle does not mean that they are talking about the world ... but their message ... springs from secular and anti-christian orientation" (Burdick).

6   The phrase "We are of God: he that knoweth God heareth us" is set in contrast to v.5. "We" are the apostle and his fellow apostles and teachers-they know God, they were born of God. It therefore follows that everyone that knows God in an experimental way, who has really been born of God will hear, believe, endorse what John has taught. "The change from 'he that is of God' to 'he that knoweth God' suggests at once that the child of God is one who enters on the progressive experience of knowing Him" (Vine). The "one knowing" is a description of habit. "He that increaseth in the knowledge of God heareth us" (Plummet). "He that is not of God heareth us not".

The Lord Jesus said "Every one that is of the truth heareth my voice" (John 8:45-47; 18:37,38). "You can recognise God's word because God's people listen to it, just as you can recognise God's people because they listen to God's word" (Stott). God's people instinctively turn to the word of God, of it they have been born again and to it they turn for sustenance. "Being born again of the incorruptible seed of the word of God ... desire the spiritual milk which is without guile that ye may grow thereby unto salvation" (1 Peter 1:23; 2:2). Those that are not of God have no appetite for the word of God and therefore, John says, hear us not. "By this, we know (by experience, by observation) the Spirit of truth and the spirit of error (of deceit)"-the one from whom all error flows is "a liar, and the father of it" (John 8:44; see 2 Thess 2:9,10; 1 Tim 4:1,2). Let us finish this section with a note of triumph: "The devil that deceived them was cast into the lake of fire ... and shall be tormented day and night for ever and ever" (Rev 20:10).

IV. The Third Circle (4:7-5:15)

Subject: Our Relationships with One Another
Adjusted by Righteousness, Love and Truth

1.   *Loving One Another*
4:7-13

v.7   "Beloved, let us love one another: for love is of God; and every one that loveth is born of God, and knoweth God.
v.8   He that loveth not knoweth not God; for God is love.
v.9   In this was manifested the love of God toward us, because that God sent his only begotten Son into the world, that we might live through him.
v.10 Herein is love, not that we loved God, but that he loved us, and sent his Son *to be* the propitiation for our sins.
v.11 Beloved, if God so loved us, we ought also to love one another.
v.12 No man hath seen God at any time. If we love one another, God dwelleth in us, and his love is perfected in us.
v.13 Hereby know we that we dwell in him, and he in us, because he hath given us of his Spirit."

7   It would appear at first sight to be an abrupt change from a somewhat painful subject to that which is far more pleasing to the reader. It is a transition from

"the spirit of error" to loving one another; yet there is a connection. John has mentioned the Spirit of truth (v.6) and surely the love of God is shed abroad in our hearts by the Holy Ghost. We have been born of the Spirit and thus have become the children of God. Therefore we ought to love one another. The spirit of error evidences itself in those who are of the world and they possess the opposite features, "Marvel not, my brethren, if the world hate you" (3:13). "Beloved", an endearing mode of address, is in keeping with the truth that is now impressed on the saints: He loves then, so they must love one another. While it is true that, in fellowship with God, we must love "the world of sinners lost, and ruined by the fall", what we have here is a mutual love, the special love that the Father has for His children, now shown to one another. "Here the epistle rises to the summit of all revelations" (Law):

"Let us love one another" (v.7);

"We ought also to love one another" (v.11);

"If we love one another" (v.12);

"Love is of God" (v.7).

What kind of love is this? Not love for the world, which we are forbidden to love! Not the love of the world, for the world loves its own, but the love the Father has bestowed upon us. Of this love He is the source for "love is of God" and "ye" (v.4) and "we" (v.6) are of God and therefore the love of which God is the source will obviously be displayed in those who are His children. Everyone that loveth is begotten of God (loveth with the same kind of love that is of God) and loveth God in an experimental way. These are two of the evidences of new birth. "God has revealed Himself to us in Jesus Christ as self-sacrificial love. It is because God is love in Himself (vv.8,16), has loved us in Christ (vv. 12,13), that we must love each other" (Stott).

8 Wuest translates: "He that is not habitually loving, has not come to know God". "The failure of a person to exhibit such love demonstrates that he has never come to know God. He has never known anything other than estrangement from His Maker" (Burdick). After all God is love; that is, God is in essence love. It does not say that love is God but love is of God. "If nothing were said in praise of love throughout the pages of this epistle, if nothing whatever throughout the other pages of the Scriptures and this one thing only were all that we were told by the voice of the Spirit of God, 'For God is love', nothing more ought we to require" (Augustine). Note that "love", "loveth" etc. are found thirty-two times between 4:7 and 5:3. "The christian affirmation that God is love is not sustained by ignoring the cross, in all its stark obscenity, but by setting it in the forefront of the situation" (Bruce). "God commendeth his love toward us, in that, while we were yet sinners, Christ died for us" (Rom 5:8).

9   John has already drawn attention to the perfect manifestation of love: " Herein is love" (4:10); " he laid down his life for us" (3:16). He returns to the subject again by almost repeating the words of John 3:16 concerning God's great love in giving and sending His only begotten Son into the world. Herein was the love of God manifested-God sent-"he was come from God, and went to God" (John 13:3); "I came forth from the Father and am come into the world" (John 16:28). His pre-existence, alongside the Father and His incarnation are here taught, but though being the child of Mary, conceived of the Holy Ghost, He is indeed the Son of God.

The adjective "only begotten Son" links together the thought of "only begotten" and "well-beloved" (used four times in the Gospel, 1:14,18; 3:16,18). The Father sent the Son! but at what a cost: "Last of all he sent unto them his son" (Matt 21:37); "He that spared not his own Son, but delivered him up for us all" (Rom 8:32). Plummer notes that "Christ is the only born Son as distinct from the many who have become sons"; there is no other!

This love is manifested *toward* us and *in* us. We are the sphere in which the love of God is manifested. And it was "that we might live through him". God's purpose in sending the Lord Jesus was that we should "not perish, but have everlasting life". This great self-sacrificing love of God is here introduced primarily to impress upon us the kind of love we must display. "It is not our love that is primary, but God's, free uncaused and spontaneous and all our love is but a reflection of His and a response to it" (Stott).

10   "Herein is love", literally, "in this", pointing out the way in which this love is manifested. It is not revealed in our love to God or drawn out by our love to Him. We should have loved the Lord our God with all our heart and soul and might (Deut 6:5) but we had not. Our attitude to God was rather one of enmity. We neither loved Him, nor did we seek Him (4:10; Rom 3:11). It was not that we loved God, but that He loved us. God is love, and love must find an object. He did not love us because there was anything good or meritorious, or praiseworthy in us. We were sinners, undone, dead in sins, deserving nothing but His righteous judgment because of our sins, but (praise God!) He loved us, just because He is love. He loved us because He would love us! The cause was in Himself; it was according to His own nature to love and He found an object in us. "For he does not indeed take hold of angels (by the hand), but he takes hold of the seed of Abraham" (Heb 2:16 JND). (His taking hold is to deliver.)

He loves us and sent His Son to be the propitiation for our sins. Our sins had offended a holy God and we therefore deserved His righteous wrath. But the same God holy and righteous against whom we had sinned and whose wrath must be appeased, in amazing love sent His own Son-provided Him as a propitiation, from His own bosom. "Here the initiative lies entirely with God: before there was any possibility of our exercising such love He manifested it, when 'He loved us and sent His Son to be the propitiation for our sins' " (Bruce). "Because He is a God of justice, He must demand the payment of sin's penalty. However, the God of justice is, at the same time, the God of love, and thus He Himself provided payment in the propitiatory sacrifice of His Son" (Burdick).

> "Eternal Love! Oh, mighty sea,
>   That hath not bounds, nor shore,
> We gaze upon thy tideless waves,
> We know the Love that loving saves,
>   We worship and adore.
>
> Eternal Love, Eternal Love,
>   That ever shall abide;
> The Love that saves, the Love that keeps,
> What vastness in Thy glorious deeps,
>   Oh ocean deep and wide!
>
> Eternal Love, that loveth me,
>   And loving, made me love,
> That brought my Saviour pain and loss,
> The awful anguish of the Cross,
>   To lift my soul above!
>
> Eternal Love that bore the curse,
>   That else must fall on me,
> Now to the glory of Thy grace,
> Mine eyes shall see the Saviour's face
>   Through all Eternity."

11   "Beloved", says John for the sixth and last time, "if God so loved us, we ought also to love one another". Here "if. . ." is equivalent to "since God so loved us". The "so" is as immense as the love of John 3:16. It covers the truths of vv.9,10.

1.   God sent

2.   His only begotten Son

3.   to be the propitiation

4.   for our sins.

Compare the parallel usage of the words "so" and "also" in John 13:14: "If I then, your Lord and Master, have washed your feet; ye ought also . . ."; so here, "if God so . . . we ought also". What was an exhortation in v.7 is now an obligation, a debt we ought to pay, "we also ought" (RV), i.e. we with God. God so loved us, and we also, we as well as God, like God, in the same giving, self-sacrificing way, ought to love one another. Loving one another is mutual, not one sided: my brother ought to love me, I ought to love my brother. Notice this exhortation is based upon Calvary-the basic example of the ethics of christianity.

12   "No man hath seen God at any time" for God is spirit (John 4:24). He is in Himself invisible, "whom no man hath seen, nor can see" (1 Tim 1:17; 6:16). God said "Thou canst not see my face, for there shall no man see me, and live" (Exod 33:20). See "We shall surely die, because we have seen God" (Jud 13:22); also "Alas, O Lord God! for because I have seen an (the) angel of the Lord face to face" (Jud 6:22). The Christophanies of the OT were pre-incarnate revelations of the Lord Jesus in various ways. The statement in this verse is almost the same as that in John 1:18 (it is the same in the AV). How then can God be revealed? John in his Gospel continues "the only begotten Son, which is in the bosom of the Father, he hath declared him". "The unseen God, who was once revealed in His Son, is now revealed in His people, and when they love one another, God's love is seen in their love because their love is His love imparted to them by His Spirit (cf. v.13)" (Stott). "While men cannot see God, it is possible to see God's character exhibited in His people. God is love and if we love one another it is because God dwelleth in us and His love is perfected, hath reached its goal in us" (Lenski). It is not *our* love that is perfected, but His love revealed in us, so that men see God by his features being displayed in us.

13   "Hereby know we" (experimentally), adds John, "that we dwell in him, and he in us". Our love for one another is evidence that God dwells in us because it is not our love but His love that reaches its goal in us. The divine indwelling is mentioned three times in this passage: "God dwelleth in us" (v.12); "we dwell in him, and he in us" (v.13); "God dwelleth in him, and he in God" (v.15). Each time this indwelling of God is mentioned, the evidence of its existence is added: "because he hath given us of his Spirit" (v.13); "Whosoever shall confess that Jesus is the Son of God" (v.15); "he that dwelleth in love" (v.16). Here the fact that "he hath given us of his Spirit" is the continuing proof that "we dwell in him, and he in us". Every believer has been given His Holy Spirit by God. "If any man have not the Spirit of Christ, he is none of his" (Rom 8:9); having believed "ye were sealed with the Holy Spirit of promise" (Eph 1:13 RV). The Spirit of God is not an influence, though He has an influence. He is a person. He must therefore be given and received as a real complete Person. He cannot be given partially: "For he giveth not the Spirit by measure" (John 3:34 RV); "God gives not the Spirit by measure" (JND); "For it is not by measure that He gives the Spirit"

(RSV); "God does not give the Spirit with limitations" (Weymouth); "For not by measure doth God give the Spirit" (Young's Lit.).

You cannot get more of the Spirit, but the Spirit can have more of you; therefore "be filled with the Spirit" (Eph 5:18). In "he hath given us of his Spirit", "of" cannot therefore mean "a part of". The gift is the complete Person so that "the fruit of the Spirit" are those things that are of Him and from Him which might be manifest in our lives. "The significance of the phrase 'of his Spirit', seems to be, that, while each child of God has the Holy Spirit, the love which we manifest is the outcome of that gift. In other words, the exercise of love is involved in the possession of the Spirit" (Vine).

2.   *The Eye-witness Report*
   4:14-16

   v.14 And we have seen and do testify that the Father sent the Son *to be* the Saviour of the world.
   v.15 Whosoever shall confess that Jesus is the Son of God, God dwelleth in him, and he in God.
   v.16 And we have known and believed the love that God hath to us.
   v.17 God is love, and he that dwelleth in love dwelleth in God, and God in him."

14   "We" (emphatic) is as in 1:1: it has in mind John and his fellow apostles, and while John is the only survivor, he speaks as representing them. "The word must here refer to the actual eye-witness of the life of Jesus on earth" (Brooke). See contrast with verse "No man hath seen (beheld) God..." (to behold is "to have the opportunity of examining carefully for a prolonged period of time"). "As for us, we have deliberately and steadfastly contemplated", translates Wuest. While no man had beheld God at any time, the apostles had opportunity for over three years steadfastly to examine Him (see notes on 1:1) and out of experience they now testified. John the Baptist, relative to the occasion of the baptism of the Lord Jesus declared, "I saw, and bare record that this is the Son of God" (John 1:34) and on Him he declared "Behold the Lamb of God, which taketh away the sin of the world" (John 1:29).

On "the Father sent the Son to be the Saviour of the world", Plummer comments "God Himself no one hath ever yet beheld; but we have beheld His Son". " 'Hath sent' (RV) intimates not merely the historic fact but the abiding effects of the sending" (Vine). In John 1:33,34 already mentioned, John says, "he that sent me": it was God who had sent John to baptise with water; "the same (God) said unto me, Upon whom thou shalt see the Spirit descending, and remaining on him" is both He that baptiseth with the Holy Ghost and the Son of God. What John and his fellows beheld (contemplated-same word as above) was a glory as of an only begotten with a father (John 1: 14 JND). Thus they witnessed and thus they testified that "The Father sent the Son". Notice in these two verses (vv. 13,14) we have the activity of the Trinity: The *Father* sent the *Son*; He hath given us of *His Spirit*, for it is by the Spirit we recognise the truth that the Father sent the Son. The evidence that we have received the Spirit is seen in our exercising the same self-giving and sacrificing love as the One we acknowledge as "the Saviour of the world". As young men John and James would have called fire from heaven on the Samaritans, but as an old man John records in his Gospel from Samaritan lips: "we ... know that this is indeed the Christ, the Saviour of the world" (John 4:42). This title is peculiar to John. "Samaritans who had no interest in promises that were attached to the tribe of Judah but great interest in promises which spoke of a worldwide salvation" (Bruce). Is it not also interesting that John writes these words from Ephesus to which church Paul had written ". . . far off are made nigh by the blood of Christ"? (Eph 2:13).

15   Confessing that Jesus is the Son of God is what the false prophets refused to do. It is, however, a characteristic feature of those that overcome the world (5:5). "This aorist tense (of 'confess') cannot be rendered precisely in English. John is referring neither to a future confession (AV, RV 'shall confess') nor to a present and continuing confession ('confesses' RSV; 'acknowledges' NEB) but to a single and decisive public confession, the time of which is unspecified" (Stott). "The confession is shown to be produced by the Holy Spirit, and involves the same spirit of love that was manifested by Christ, and a life that bears testimony to His saving power" (Vine). Such a confession can only be made as a result of the operation of the Spirit of God. "Confessing conveys the thought, not so much of time, as of decisiveness. This is something that a gnostic teacher of error would never confess (see 2 John 7)."

There could be no closer communion or relationship than what is expressed in the statement "God abideth in him and he is God" (RV). Ch.3 uses this expression of the one who "keepeth his commandments" (v.24). Doctrine and practice are joined together in this epistle and let us remember that "What ... God hath joined together, let not man put asunder" (Matt 19:6). "No man can say that Jesus is Lord, but by the Holy Ghost" (1 Cor 12:3).

16   "To know as John speaks (in this verse) is to believe, and vice versa. No inner realisation can be without a corresponding confidence, no true confidence without such a realisation" (Lenski). "We" does not as in v. 14 necessarily refer to John and his fellow apostles, but to John and his readers (to us). " 'Known' speaks of the understanding of spiritual truth, whereas 'believed' describes the aspect of confidence in and conviction concerning that which is known-spiritual perception leads to heartfelt conviction" (Burdick). "What is here being said about love is no matter of mere theory; it is something which is proved in experience and faith" (Bruce). "We have come to know and have believed, that is to say, we have entered upon the path of progressive knowledge" (Vine). "The love that is eternally in God and was historically manifested in Christ is to come to fruition" (Stott).

John writes not of "the love that God hath for us", rather of the love God hath in us. What God hath done for us is the expression of His love in sending His own Son, but what He has done in us means far more. His love has been poured into us, shed abroad in our hearts by the Holy Spirit and from us flows out to others. "He that believeth on me, as the scripture hath said, out of his belly shall flow rivers of living water. (But this spake he of the Spirit, which they that believe on him should receive: for the Holy Ghost was not yet given; because that Jesus was not yet glorified)" (John 7:38,39). That same love now dwells in all God's people. We know that God is in essence love, and he that abideth in love does therefore abide in God and the God who is love abides in him. "Since God, who is love, indwells the believer, the believer must and will love his fellow believers. Thus love for the family of God is a vital test of one's salvation" (Burdick).

3. *His Love Perfected in Us*
   4:17-21

   v.17 "Herein is our love made perfect, that we may have boldness in the day of judgment: because as he is, so are we in this world.
   v.18 There is no fear in love, but perfect love casteth out fear: because fear hath torment. He that feareth is not made perfect in love.
   v.19 We love him, because he first loved us.
   v.20 If a man say, I love God, and hateth his brother, he is a liar: for he that loveth not his brother whom he hath seen, how can he love God whom he hath not seen?
   v.21 And this commandment have we from him, That he who loveth God love his brother also."

17   The opening clause refers to divine love, not to our love; the following renderings are to be preferred: "Herein has love been perfected with us" (JND); "In this is love made perfect". "Herein" (in this) throws our minds back to the previous verses: we know that we dwell in Him, and He in us, because He hath given us of His Spirit; whosoever shall confess that Jesus is the Son of God, God dwelleth in him and he in God; we have known and believed the love that God hath to us. God is love; He that dwelleth in love dwelleth in God, and God in him. We may summarise their contents as follows:

1.   The possession of the Holy Spirit is the assurance that we dwell in God and God in us.

2.   The fact that we confess that Jesus is the Son of God is an evidence that God dwells in us and we in God.

3.   The fact that we dwell in love (God is love) is the result of our dwelling in God and God in us.

   It is evident from a comparison of these verses that the term "(he) dwelleth in

God, and God in him" is descriptive of *every* believer for they have all received the Holy Spirit; seen and do testify that the Father sent the Son to be the Saviour of the world; confessed that Jesus is the Son of God; and all dwell in love (the love of God). These are therefore facts true of everyone who is born of God. Just as the habitual walk of the child of God is "doeth righteousness", "committeth not lawlessness", so his habitual attitude to his brother is that he loves him (it is a family characteristic) and never hates him (that feature belongs to the children of the devil). John knows nothing between love and hate, so " in this is (God's) love made perfect to us". It is then, "to us", "toward us", " with us", "radiating from us": "in this has this love been brought to its goal with us" (Lenski). "With us" means "in company with us", "in its companionship". Seeing that we do love one another, it is evident that God's love has reached its goal in our lives: "herein love has been made perfect". Love to my brother is evidently one of the proofs that I have been born of God. It is an evidence that I am in Him and He is in me. It is a confirmation that I am one of God's children and that gives me boldness in the day of judgment. We must now enquire as to the meaning of the expression "the day of judgment". Two views predominate:

1.   the judgment seat of Christ;

2.   the great white throne judgment.

Is this the Judgment Seat of Christ? "One of the functions of love in the believer's life is the impartation of a bold confidence that will enable him to stand before the judgment seat of Christ without fear or shame. The judgment referred to cannot be the judgment of the wicked, since only the wicked will appear there" (Burdick). "Now this manifestation of Christ's nature in us is connected with our boldness in the day of judgment, that is boldness with which we shall stand before the judgment seat of Christ. The ground of our boldness is our present likeness to Him. Not the matter of our being acquitted, or cleared of guilt, and so standing without condemnation before God is here in view, but the assurance that, in as far as we manifest the divine nature in our hearts to others, we shall stand blameless, without reproach and without regret before Christ's judgment seat ... the judgment seat of Christ is to be distinguished from the day of judgment of the ungodly which is entirely another and subsequent event" (Vine).

"When I think of love I am happy; but when I think of the judgment, my conscience is not quite easy ... that is what is provided for here 'As he is, so are we in this world'. The love was shown in visiting us when we were sinners; it is enjoyed in communion but it is completed in this, that I am in Christ, and that Christ must condemn Himself in the day of judgment if He condemns me, because as He is so am I in this world. I am glorified before I get there. He changes this vile body and makes it like to His glorious body. When I am before the judgment seat, I am in this changed and glorified body: I am like my judge. If He is my righteousness, as He is, that I am now; because it is Christ's work, and Christ's work is finished, and Christ is appearing in heaven for me. And though I have exercise and trials of heart, yet 'As he is, so am I in this world'. There love is perfected" (J. N. Darby).

"The writer is not referring here to the final judgment in which the final judgment of every believer hangs in the balance. There is no such judgment for the believer (John 5:24) but the believer's life will be assessed at the judgment seat of Christ (1 Cor 3:12-15, 2 Cor 5:10). Yet even on that solemn occasion a believer may have confidence, that God will approve the quality of his life; through love, that believer while in this world becomes like Him. The unloving christian is unlike his Lord and may anticipate rebuke or loss of reward at the judgment seat of Christ" (Walvoord and Zuck).

This view leads to the conclusion that if we display the moral features of Christ and love our brethren then we may be sure that at the judgment seat of Christ we shall have confidence before Him and not shame (2:28).

Is this the Great White Throne Judgment? It needs to be clearly stated that no true believer in the Lord Jesus, no child of God will ever appear before that grand assize. It is the throne of judgment from which those who appear will be cast into the lake of fire: "whosoever was not found written in the book of life was cast into the lake of fire (Rev 20:15). John recorded the words of the Lord Jesus: "Verily, verily I say unto you, he that heareth my word, and believeth on him that sent me, hath everlasting life, and shall not come into condemnation; but is passed from death unto life" (5:24). Paul reaffirmed it: "There is therefore now no condemnation to them which are in Christ Jesus" (Rom 8:1). Upon this rock many of us rest our souls!

Whichever view is adopted, it will be agreed that John sometimes writes things in a general way and truth revealed in the remainder of the NT helps us to understand his meaning. For example, John wrote (the words of Martha): "I know that he shall rise again in the resurrection at the last day" (John 11:24). In the other NT writings we are instructed relative to the first and the final resurrections and the day. Again, he recorded the words of the Lord Jesus: "Of all which he hath given me I should lose nothing, but should raise it up again at the last day" (6:39); "that every one which seeth the Son, and believeth on him, may have everlasting life: and I will raise him up at the last day" (6:40); "he that rejecteth me ... the word that I have spoken, the same shall judge him in the last day" (John 12:48). To what resurrection and to what persons and judgments these verses refer, the Holy Spirit makes clear in further revelation.

To what then does the expression "the day of judgment" refer? Since all believers will stand before the judgment seat of Christ and only unbelievers will be at the great white throne-the Lord's people will not be there!

V. 17 contains three parts:

1. "that we may have boldness in the day of judgment": "The leading idea here
    is 'boldness in the day of judgment'; not boldness prospectively when the
    day comes, but present boldness in view of it now" (Candlish). Lenski
    paraphrases: "We have boldness in connection with the day of judging".

2. the ground of this confidence: "as he is, so are we in this world": "with
    John the grounds of assurance are ethical, not emotional; objective, not
    subjective; plain and tangible, not microscopic and elusive. They are three:
    belief, righteousness, love. By his belief in Christ, his keeping God's
    commandments, and his love to the brethren a christian man is recognised
    and recognises himself as being begotten of God ... it is precisely when it
    deals with the subject at closest quarters that it most rigorously postulates
    love embodied and perfected in actual deeds, as a crucial test by which
    we shall recognise that we are of the truth and shall assure our hearts
    before Him. For this proof that as He is so are we in this world there is no
    substitute" (Law).

3. because " herein is love perfected in us": Candlish elaborates on both the
    tense and the preposition: "the verb . . . is so used as to denote a work or
    process brought to a full or final issue; the perfecting of His love with us, as a
    treaty or transaction of some sort. . . Love then, or the love before indicated
    (God's love) is perfected with us; and the perfecting of this love with us is
    bound up with our having boldness in the day of judgment. . . It is God's love
    so shared by Him with us as to constitute a love relationship or love fellowship
    between Him and us. This is indispensable to our having boldness in the
    prospect of the day of judgment".

We conclude that when we love our brethren (because the love of God has
come to us, is in us, has reached its goal in us, and is with us) we have sure
evidence that we are born of God. Alluding perhaps to the Lord's words in his
Gospel (5:24), John has said: "We know that we have *passed from death unto
life*, because we love the brethren" (3:14). Here he takes up the remaining part
of John 5:24, viz. "shall not come into condemnation"; this assurance gives us
the confidence, as we see in the future the certainty of a day of judgment for
those who are not born again, that we shall not come into condemnation, we
shall not be at the great white throne judgment, we have already passed from
death unto life. Thus we have a double assurance because we find in ourselves
the evidence of divine life. Loving the brethren "we know that we have passed
from death unto life" (3:14) and we have confidence relative to the day of
judgment (4:17).

While the author believes that the day of judgment here is the great white
throne, these two possible interpretations are submitted for the prayerful
consideration of fellow-children of God. The Lord help us in our meditations.

18   "Fear is expelled by perfect love, and love is prevented by fear from being perfected ... that must be so because of the impossibility of the co-existence of love and fear in the way mentioned here" is Vine's comment on the verse. "Not only is there nothing in love that produces fear; it banishes fear where it exists" (Law). "There is no place for fear in this love of God for us ... God does not let those who have been born from Him, the children of God, quake with fear at the thought of the judgment day" (Lenski). That fear has torment, "torturing punishment" (Lenski). "Fear towards God is the product of a self-accusing heart" (Law). "Fear has to do with punishment, which is quite alien to God's forgiven children who love Him" (Stott). "Fear has in itself something of the nature of punishment" (Law, Brooke). "Once assured that we are God's beloved children we cease to be afraid of Him. It is evident, therefore, that he that feareth is not made perfect in love" (Stott).

19   For "We love him" (AV), JND has simply "We love"; this is the better rendering. We love, without any expressed object. It is not an exhortation so to do, either to love God or to love men, but a statement of fact. That we do love is the evidence of our having been born of God. We love, we do not fear. All true Godlike love (*agapē*) is a response to His loving us and a reflection of His love being expressed in us.

"The words of the apostle show strong contrast: *We* on our part, love, because *He*, on His part, first loved us. His love enables us to love because, as a result of it, He who is love now indwells us. Also we now love because He has become our example, teaching us and persuading us to love. However we view it, love finds its origin in God: and because He is the author of love, He is also the author of assurance" (Burdick). "Our Lord made it plain that the two OT commandments of love to God and love to one's neighbour are two sides of one coin (Mark 12:29-31)" (Bruce). "There is stress on both the pronouns 'we' and 'He'. The word 'first' also bears emphasis, and serves to point the connection with the preceding verses" (Vine).

20   "If a man say" reminds us of the three tests of 1:6,8,10. This man, professedly at least, has confidence or assurance as he anticipates the day of judgment. He boasts, "I love God" but he is presumptuous, morally blind, a hypocrite: "he hateth his brother"; he has Cain features; it is evident he is "of that wicked one". John does not spare him: "he is a liar". It is obviously easier to love his brother whom he has seen (whom he has continually before his eyes) than to love God whom he has not seen. "This indicates that his claim is manifestly contradictory. Love for God and hatred for a brother cannot possibly co-exist in the same heart, thus with Johannine brusqueness, the claim is dismissed as a lie" (Burdick). "To claim to know God and to have fellowship with God while we walk in the darkness of disobedience is to lie (1:6, 2:4). To claim to possess the Father while denying the deity of the Son is to lie (2:22,23). To claim to love God while hating the brethren is to lie also".

21 Some suggest that "him" in "this commandment have we from him" refers to the Lord Jesus, but He is not directly mentioned in the immediate context. This however is the summing up of the teaching of the old and new covenants: loving God with all thy heart and thy neighbour as thyself (Deut 6:5; Lev 19:18) and "A new commandment I give unto you that, Ye love one another" (John 13:34); "that he who loveth God love his brother also". "Man may not separate what Jesus has joined. Besides, if we love God we shall keep His commandments (2 John 3) and His commandment is to love our neighbour as ourselves" (Stott). "This commandment already shows that one who hates his brother cannot love God, for love to God would most certainly keep God's commandment" (Lenski).

4. *Evidences of the New Birth*
5:1-5

v.1 "Whosoever believeth that Jesus is the Christ is born of God: and every one that loveth him that begat loveth him also that is begotten of him.
v.2 By this we know that we love the children of God, when we love God, and keep his commandments.
v.3 For this is the love of God, that we keep his commandments: and his commandments are not grievous.
v.4 For whatsoever is born of God overcometh the world: and this is the victory that overcometh the world, *even* our faith.
v.5 Who is he that overcometh the world, but he that believeth that Jesus is the Son of God?"

1 The AV "is born of God" is in fact a perfect tense, rendered by Stott as "has been born of God"; "Everyone believing that Jesus is the Christ has been born of God" (Lenski). The use together of the present participle *ho pisteuōn* ("believeth") with the perfect is significant. It indicates the believing is the result, the continuous condition, not the cause of being born again. The teachers of error did not believe that Jesus was the Christ. On the contrary, those that did had the evidence that they were the genuine children of God: their belief was the result of their new birth. As children of God they will automatically love their Father. The Father bestows His love on them (3:1) and they reciprocate that love. It naturally follows that they will love all those that are born of Him. One would not expect it to be otherwise. "What is true of the human family is also true of the divine society" (Brooke); it is the begetting, the experience of being "begotten", which establishes an affinity and therefore an affection not only between the parent and the children but between children and children. Plummer notes the sequence of propositions:

> "Everyone who believes the incarnation is a child of God;
> Every child of God loves its Father;
> ... Every believer in the incarnation loves God.

> Every believer in the incarnation loves God;
> Everyone who loves God loves the children of God;
> ... Every believer in the incarnation loves the children of God"

2   Love to God implies obedience, and either of these implies love of His children, which again implies the other two. Love to God and love to the Lord's people are twinned together. One cannot be without the other. Notice "do" (RV) rather than "keep" (AV). This is not a mental assent or a matter of theory but a doing of the warm sacrificial loving that has been seen in the out-going affections of divine persons. A family relationship is expressed in two loves: *agapē* is always both practical and active. "Not to be doing God's commandments leaves you with nothing but the lying claim that you are loving God (4:20) and have fellowship with Him (1:6)" (Lenski). "There are three boxes. The outer one is doing what God wants. Open that, and it is loving God, the Father, and all His children. Open that, and it is loving His children, so you know" (Lenski).

3   Love of God ensures that we love the children of God, but it also results in obedience to His commandments. Love for God is not merely an emotional experience expressed often with a measure of excitement, it is expressed in moral obedience. If we really love God we shall wish to please Him, and if we wish to please Him we shall read His word carefully in order to know those things that are pleasing in His sight. Love expresses itself in loving our brethren, in deed and in truth, in real sacrificial service. The Lord Jesus was the example in this matter: "he laid down his life for us" (1 John 3:16). He also said to His disciples: "If ye love me, ye will keep my commandments" (John 14:15 RV) and "He that hath my commandments, and keepeth them, he it is that loveth me: and he that loveth me shall be loved of my Father" etc. (John 14:21); "and his commandments are not grievous", irksome, burdensome. Did not He say: "my yoke is easy, and my burden is light" (Matt 11:30)? His commandments are in distinct contrast to the traditional teachings of the scribes and Pharisees: "Ye lade men with burdens grievous to be borne, and ye yourselves touch not the burdens with one of your fingers" (Luke 11:46). Note that He gives us strength both to bear and to obey them (Phil 4:12,13) and His burdens are light; they are not heavy, they will not weigh one down. Is not God's will "good, and acceptable and perfect" (Rom 12:2)? Because He loves us so perfectly He always has before Him our highest good: "The law of God was for the punishing and testing of the old man; the word of God is the food and directory of the new man" (Kelly).

4   The commandments of the Lord seem intolerably difficult and burdensome to the man of the world, but with the children of God it is different. First of all we love the Lord and therefore have a real desire to live to be pleasing to Him. The love of God operating in our hearts will not only evidence itself in love to the brethren, but in love to our Father and a desire to be pleasing in His sight. The commandments are to us not burdensome, we want to obey them and having overcome the world (because "whatsoever is born of God overcometh the world") we find it both desirable and easy to obey. "It is not the man, but his birth from God that conquers" (Stott). "He emphasises not the victorious *person* but the victorious *power*" (Plummer). It is not "whosoever" but "whatsoever". "It is not the mere fact of the divine birth that is insisted upon, but the permanent results of the birth" (Plummer). "This is the victory that hath overcome the world, even our faith" (RV). "The victory that overcame the world is this"-a victory won once for all (as the aorist tense shows, pointing back to the blessed moment when we were born of God, when by faith we believed that Jesus was the Christ, the Son of God). The world and indeed the false teachers did not accept that; we through grace have, and by it have overcome the world.

5   "The faith that conquers is no mere vague belief in the existence of God, but a definite belief in the incarnation" (Plummer) (2:22; 3:23; 4:2,3). He believes that Jesus, the real man, who could be heard seen and handled, perfect manhood was indeed "the Christ, the Son of the living God" (Matt 16:16). The world would not accept that testimony; it crucified Him and cast Him out because He claimed to be the Son of God, but in contradistinction to the world, we have accepted that testimony that God hath given of His Son. " Faith is both the victory and the victor. In the faith that has won a decisive victory the believer goes on conquering" (Plummer). "He that overcometh the world" is not Christ as the great victorious One, "who has given to us the victory" (1 Cor 15:57) but the believer in the Lord Jesus.

5.   *Witness to Christ*
5:6-12

v.6   "This is he that came by water and blood, *even* Jesus Christ; not by water only, but by water and blood. And it is the Spirit that beareth witness, because the Spirit is truth.

v.7   For there are three that bear record in heaven, the Father, the Word, and the Holy Ghost: and these three are one.

v.8   And there are three that bear witness in earth, the spirit, and the water, and the blood: and these three agree in one.

v.9   If we receive the witness of men, the witness of God is greater: for this is the witness of God which he hath testified of his Son.

v.10   He that believeth on the Son of God hath the witness in himself: he that believeth not God hath made him a liar; because he believeth not the record that God gave of his Son.

v.11   And this is the record, that God hath given to us eternal life, and this life is in his Son.

v.12   He that hath the Son hath life, *and* he that hath not the Son of God hath not life."

6 "This is he that came" refers to the Son of God; see the previous verse. Here the historic Jesus is connected with His pre-existence. He came from God; He came into the world to save sinners ("This is a faithful saying", 1 Tim 1:15). The historic person is identified with the eternal Son of the eternal God: "the Eternal Life that was with the Father and has been manifested unto us " (1:2). He came! But John stresses here that He came "by means of", or better "through", water and blood. Cerinthus and his followers were teaching that the Lord Jesus was born of an association between Joseph and Mary, born of ordinary generation; they denied the virgin birth. They claimed that because of His piety the Christ came upon Him at His baptism, and left Him prior to Calvary, so that the Christ did not die, He was not nailed to the cross, His blood was not shed. Only the Jesus passed through the suffering of Calvary. John would determinedly contradict this error by stating that the One who came by water (His baptism) came also by blood (Calvary with its sacrificial death). "Faith in the truth is the only faith that can overcome the world and give eternal life" (Plummer). "Water" and "blood" have been understood in a great variety of ways, some of which are these:

1.   Our Lord's baptism in water in Jordan and His death associated with His blood-shedding on the Cross.

2.   The blood and water that flowed from the pierced side of Christ at the Cross: "But one of the soldiers with a spear pierced his side, and forthwith came there out blood and water" (John 19:34). It is worth noting here the order "blood and water" whereas our verse in John's epistle is " water and blood" which agrees with the order of the events we have suggested: water (baptism) first; then blood (Calvary) second.

3.   Sanctification (purification) and redemption, making the water a picture of the word of God: "sanctify and cleanse it with the washing of water by the word" (Eph 5:26). Again this order is wrong; the sanctification by the Word is something that takes place after conversion, after the application of the blood.

4.   The Holy Spirit (see John 7:37-39) is seen as living water, "this he spake of the Spirit, which they that believe on him should receive". But this interpretation inverts the order; see Eph 1:13: "Having believed (and consequently the blood having been applied) ye were sealed with that Holy Spirit of promise" (the water). The "water and blood" are in the reverse order, along with an unwarranted spiritualisation.

5.   The sacraments of baptism and the Lord's Supper (in Christendom christening and the eucharist).

We judge that the first suggestion is the best interpretation.

7   "If there is one thing certain in textual criticism, it is that this famous passage
is not genuine. The revisers have only performed an imperative duty in excluding
it both from the text and the margin ... These words are not found in a single
Greek MS, earlier than the fourteenth century ... The words occur first towards
the end of the fifth century in Latin and are found in no other language until the
fourteenth century". See also JND.

8   "John says 'those who bear witness', not simply 'the witnesses'; they are
not merely witnesses that might be called, but who are perpetually delivering
their testimony" (Plummer). "Moreover 'these three are one', or better, simply
agree or are in agreement! The false witness at the trial of Jesus, seeking to
discredit Him did not agree (Mark 14:56,59); the true witnesses however,
seeking to accredit Him, are in perfect agreement" (Stott). There is no
doubt that John here is referring first to events associated with our Lord's
baptism (as in John 1:31-34) and then to His death, a sacrificial death
with the shedding of blood (see John 19:34 "and forthwith came there
out blood and water").
      John's inspired comments in John 1:31-34 with regard to the baptism of the
Lord Jesus are a witness to the fact that it was Jesus (v.29), a man ("after me
cometh *a man* which is become before me", v.30 RV), at whose baptism the
Spirit of God descended and remained upon Him. John accepts this as evidence
that Jesus is the Son of God. This record is a perfect answer to the error
propagated by Cerinthus and his followers. Jesus is the Son of God, witnessed to
at His baptism.
      But the One who came "in (with, through) water" (His baptism) also came "in
(with, through) blood". That is, the One who was baptised also was the One who
went to Calvary. It was then Jesus (the Son of God, declared so to be by water,
John 1), who "bowed his head, and gave up the ghost" (John 19:30) and whose
blood was shed: "One of the soldiers with a spear pierced his side, and forthwith
came there out blood and water". Notice what John adds: "He that saw it bare
record, and his record is true: and he knoweth that he saith true, that ye might
believe" (v.35).
      Here from John's own pen are the three witnesses-the Spirit, the water and
the blood, agreeing in one (united into one). "The trinity of witnesses furnish
one testimony" (Plummer).

9   "If we receive the witness of men, the witness of God is greater: for this is the
witness of God which he hath testified of his Son". "It is also written in your law,
that the testimony of two men is true" (John 8:17). Here we have a three-fold
cord that cannot be broken. Is this a veiled reference to the words spoken from
heaven on the occasion of the baptism of the Lord Jesus, "This is my beloved
Son, in whom I am well pleased" coupled with the descent of the Spirit of God
on the same occasion?

10 Believing on the Son of God, a formula used nearly forty times in John's Gospel, is used here in this epistle for the first time. Elsewhere in the NT it occurs about ten times. It is indicative of the strongest confidence and trust: faith moving towards and completely resting in calm peace and reliance on its object; "whereas to believe a person need mean no more than to believe what he says (4:1), to believe on or in a person means to have full trust in his character" (Plummer). "Hath the witness" indicates this witness is an abiding possession: "The Spirit itself beareth witness with our spirit, that we are children of God" (Rom 8:16); "God sent forth the Spirit of his Son into our hearts, crying, Abba, Father" (Gal 4:6 RV). This witness of the Spirit in himself (subjective, in his own heart) "carries with it an inward assurance, strong though implicit, that it shall never fail" (J. M. Newman).

The unbeliever has not believed (the perfect tense indicating a past "crisis of choice", Westcott) but has rejected the divine testimony. "Unbelief is not a misfortune to be pitied; it is a sin to be deplored. Its sinfulness lies in the fact that it contradicts the word of the one true God and thus attributes falsehood to Him" (Stott).

11 "This is the record" is the same expression as in v.9 "This is the witness". There it looks back to the witness of the Spirit, the water and the blood. Here it includes the further testimony of the Spirit of God witnessing within the true believer (the witness in himself, v.10). "Eternal life is emphatic in the sentence; i.e. the record is that it is eternal life which God gave us in giving His Son. But the witness is not objective to Christ as the life-giver, but subjective in the gift of life itself" (Stott). As our Lord Jesus Himself taught, "this is life eternal, that they should know thee the only true God, and him whom thou didst send, even Jesus Christ" (John 17:3 RV).

"Gave" (not offered, or promised) refers to a past experience; the believer already possesses this life. It is as sure as God's glorious "hath" in John 5:24. Eternal life has its origin and its seat in the Son, the author of life (John 1:4; 5:26).

12 This verse is the obvious conclusion to which one comes after reading v.11. To have the person of the Son as one's very own Saviour is to possess the life that is in Himself. "Three important truths are taught about eternal life. First, it is not a prize which we have earned, but an undeserved gift. Secondly, it is found in Christ, so that, in order to give us life, God both gave and gives His Son. Thirdly, this gift of life in Christ is a present possession" (Stott). "The wages of sin is death; but the gift of God is eternal life through Jesus Christ our Lord" (Rom 6:23).

6. *Assurance of Eternal Life*
   5:13-17

> v.13 "These things have I written unto you that believe on the name of the Son of God; that ye may know that ye have eternal life, and that ye may believe on the name of the Son of God.

v.14 And this is the confidence that we have in him, that, if we ask any thing according
      to his will, he heareth us:
v.15 And if we know that he hear us, whatsoever we ask, we know that we have the
      petitions that we desired of him..
v.16 If any man see his brother sin a sin *which is* not unto death, he shall ask, and he
      shall give him life for them that sin not unto death. There is a sin unto death: I
      do not say that he shall pray for it.
v.17 All unrighteousness is sin: and there is a sin not unto death."

13 Though this verse commences a new paragraph in the RV and RSV, it is so evidently the closing statement of the previous verses, a fitting conclusion and the explanation of why and what the author has written about the three witnesses. One would naturally link this verse with the similar expression in John's Gospel: "These are written, that ye might believe that Jesus is the Christ, the Son of God; and that believing ye might have life through his name" (20:31). Here he writes: "These things have I written unto you, that ye may know that ye have eternal life, even unto you that believe on the name of the Son of God" (5:13 RV). In the beginning of the epistle John writes: "these things we write, that our joy might be fulfilled" (1:4 RV). Now he explains the reason for his writing: "that ye may know that ye have eternal life"; it is not a matter of hoping so, nor of waiting till the end to see, but of absolute assurance and certainty. Praise God!

14 John now moves to his second assurance-*answered prayer*. This is the fourth time in the epistle that John mentions christian boldness. The contexts are: once in connection with the judgment seat of Christ and the appearing (2:28), once relative to the day of judgment (4:17) and twice in connection with the matter of approaching God in prayer (3:21,22 and here). Here it has special reference to intercessory prayer, praying for others, and so two features of the epistle are now joined together

1. confidence in prayer

2. love of the brethren.

   Real love for the brethren will be a strong incentive to pray for them. Our requests however must be governed by His will, and if they are according to His will the answer will be for His glory and for the blessing of our fellow saints. We might in our ignorance desire something that would not be for the spiritual good of the brother prayed for, but God knows the need and knows what would be best in the circumstances; real exercise of heart is required if we are to be sure that what we ask is according to His will. "Heareth" means hears and answers in the affirmative. "The desire of the righteous shall be granted" (Prov 10:24). The confidence that we have is both in our approach to God (Heb 4:16) and in our expecting and being assured that He answers prayer (Jas 1:5).

15   "And if we know that he hear us, whatsoever we ask, we know that we have the petition that we desired of him" can be paraphrased: if we trust in the unbounded goodness of God we can be assured that He will not fail us; our trust will not be misplaced. "What things soever ye desire, when ye pray, believe that ye receive them, and ye shall have them" (Mark 11:24). The tense used here, "we have" (not shall have) shows our prayers are already granted, we possess the answers in anticipation. "Every one that asketh receiveth; and he that seeketh findeth" (Matt 7:8).

16   All these prayers are qualified by the condition "according to his will" and therefore the Spirit of God proceeds with instructions relative to His will, as to what things we may pray for and what we may not. (For encouragement in the matter of intercession see 1 Thess 5:25; Heb 13:18,19; Jas 5:14.) "A brother" is obviously a professed believer. John so often takes up things on the ground of profession ("if we say", 1:6,8,10; "he that saith", 2:4,6,9). The person therefore in view takes the place of a professed believer. "Sin a sin" or sinning a sin means in the process of sinning, in the very act (see John 8:4). This expression is found nowhere else in the NT (but see Lev 5:6,10,13). "He shall ask" is emphatic: "He will ask". A christian is bound to, must, is sure to, pray for his erring brother "and he shall give him life". "He" may refer either to God or to the one who prays; similarly "him" may refer to the intercessor or to the sinning brother for whom intercession is made (the Greek is ambiguous). Is John thinking along the same lines as James in his last chapter? It seems that James has a sinning brother in mind who is sick and in danger of dying under the disciplining hand of God because of unconfessed sin. James insists on the prayer of faith by others and the confession of the sin by the erring brother, with the glad result "the Lord shall raise him up; and if he have committed sins, they shall be forgiven him" (5:15). Notice the triumphant note at the end of that chapter: "he which converteth the sinner from the error of his way shall save a soul from death, and hide a multitude of sins" (5:20). It is interesting that James, writing the first NT epistle (in order of writing) and John in writing the last epistles are in perfect agreement in this matter. God will give him life, restore him to health, otherwise he would physically die under a Father's chastening hand (see 1 Cor 11:30).

All John's readers were undoubtedly well acquainted with the expression "there is a sin unto death" ; they knew its meaning but expositors have differed on its meaning from post-apostolic days. Various suggestions have been made:

1.   murder

2.   suicide

3.   adultery

4. some specific sin persisted in in spite of discipline (see Amos 4:6-12)

5. blasphemy against the Holy Ghost

6. apostasy.

   Maybe this does not refer to any specific sin. It should read "there is sin(not a sin) unto death". "Sin unto death, therefore is not an act of sin, however heinous, but a state or habit of sin wilfully chosen and persisted in. It is constant and consummate opposition to God. In the phraseology of the epistle we may say that it is the deliberate preference of darkness to light, of falsehood to truth, of sin to righteousness, of the world to the Father, of spiritual death to eternal life" (Plummer). This quotation describing the one who commits sin unto death would be aptly attributed to the ones whom John mentions in 1 John 2:18 onwards, the antichrists, deceivers who had been ostensibly in the fellowship of the saints, but not one with them in heart. Their going out proved that they were "not all of us". This has been made manifest. They had apostatised. They had abandoned their professed belief (only professed) in Jesus as the Christ, the Son of God, they had denied the incarnation and now were exhibiting in their lives the sins that accompany those who turn "the grace of our God into lasciviousness, and denying our only Master and Lord, Jesus Christ" (Jude 4 RV). Cerinthus was one of the leaders and possibly the main teacher of those errors. The gnostic teachers were both doctrinally unsound and morally depraved.
   Relative to the other suggestions: Clement of Alexandria and Origen wrote of forgivable and unforgivable sins. Tertullian listed certain grosser sins, which he considered beyond pardon (murder, adultery, blasphemy, idolatry); this led eventually to differentiation between "mortal" and "venial" sins and the idea of "the seven deadly sins". There is however no suggestion in the NT of such distinctions between one sin and another.
   We judge that this sin unto death is apostasy. The question is asked, Can a christian, one who is born of God, apostatise? The answer is, No!-a thousand times, No! The apostate may have been physically amongst the saints, posing as one of them but nevertheless he had not really been born again! He may have been present at their love-feasts (Jude 12; 2 Pet 2:13) for "certain men crept in unawares, who were before of old set forth unto this condemnation" (Jude 4). The apostates in Hebrews were maybe of a different kind for they apostatised to Judaism: "once enlightened and tasted of the heavenly gift, and were made partakers of the Holy Ghost and tasted the good word of God and the powers of the world to come and then fell away" (Heb 6:4-6); professors who went along for a while professing to be born of God, who hear the word and straightway with joy receive it, yet they have not root in themselves but endure for a while (see Matt 13:20); professors only, never really born of God.
   It is interesting to notice that John does not say: I say that you should not pray for this man, but "I do not say that he shall pray for it". Put in the negative way it

is not a complete prohibition. Is this because it is very difficult to decide when a man is a complete and determined apostate and beyond the possibility of salvation? (see Jude 22,23).

17 All unrighteousness is sin: and there is a sin unto death. Carelessness about one's conduct can lead to all kinds of misdemeanours in ourselves or others. The gnostics might claim that the root of sin had been eradicated (1:8) and that the fruits of sin were absent too; they might even claim that when they committed sin it was merely to increase their experimental knowledge and thus was not sinful but good. John gives the answer: "all unrighteousness is sin" and has already said that it is everyone that doeth righteousness who is born of God. If therefore there is sin that is not unto death, that can be forgiven, what an opportunity then exists for the exercise of brotherly love in praying for another's recovery.

V. The Apex Reached (5:18-5:20)

1   *A Triumphant Triad-"We know"*
   5:18-20a

> v.18 "We know that whosoever is born of God sinneth not; but he that is begotten of God keepeth himself, and that wicked one toucheth him not.
> v.19 *And* we know that we are of God, and the whole world lieth in wickedness.
> v.20a And we know that the Son of God is come, and hath given us an understanding, that we may know him that is true, and we are in him that is true, *even* in his Son Jesus Christ."

18 John has now completed three circles of his spiral, or eagle flight, circling each time over righteousness, love and truth, dealing with

1.   our Relationship to Divine Persons (1:5 to 2:28)

2.   our Resemblance to our Father (2:29 to 4:6)

3.   our Relationships with one another (4:7 to 5:17).

He now stands, as it were, at the top of his teaching, the apex of the truth he has taught and cries three times "we know" (v.18), " we know ... we know" (v.20). Three things the saints know intuitively, of which they have sure knowledge, "Hence we have in these last verses a final emphasis laid on the fundamental principles on which the epistle rests; that through the mission of the Lord Jesus Christ we have fellowship with God; that this fellowship protects us from sin; and that it establishes us in a relation of utter opposition to the world" (Haupt). The real knowledge of the believer is contrasted with the spurious knowledge of the gnostic. Firstly, "whosoever is born of God sinneth not". This is a repetition of the statement of 3:19. It is impossible for one who is begotten of God habitually to practise sin; "a child of God may sin; but the normal condition is one of resistance to sin" (Plummer).

We now encounter a difficult statement: "He that is begotten of God keepeth himself" (AV); "He that was begotten of God keepeth him" (RV). There are two possible ways of translating this expression.

1.   As in the AV: "but he that is begotten of God keepeth himself, and that wicked one toucheth him not". According to this translation, "he that is begotten of God" refers to the person in the previous clause who "sinneth not". The expression "keepeth himself" refers to his own efforts to keep himself. Because he is born of God "His seed remaineth in him", i.e. he is a partaker of the divine nature, and in the power associated with being a partaker of the divine nature (2 Pet 1:4), elsewhere designated "the law of the Spirit of life in Jesus Christ" (Rom 8:2), he " keepeth himself, and the wicked one toucheth him not". "He keeps himself-namely by the strength of the spiritual life that is born in him" (Lenski). Lenski has surprisingly very little comment on this difficult verse.

2.   As in the RV: "but he that was begotten of God keepeth him, and the evil one toucheth him not". According to this translation, "he that was begotten of God" refers to the Lord Jesus; the expression " keepeth him" expresses the fact that the Lord Jesus is the One who keeps him so that "the evil one toucheth him not". This seems more in keeping with such verses as "I kept them in thy name" and " those that thou gavest me I have kept" (John 17:12) and "I pray not that thou shouldest take them out of the world, but that thou shouldest keep them from the evil (one)" (John 17:15); "who are kept by the power of God" (1 Pet 1:5); "kept for Jesus Christ" (Jude 1:1 RV). Did not the Saviour Himself say: "I give unto them eternal life; and they shall never perish, neither shall any man pluck them out of my hand" (John 10:28)? We are told however to "keep yourselves in the love of God" (Jude 21), but the majority of passages that one could quote suggest that we cannot keep ourselves, but are dependent on the power of God to keep us. Thus there is One "that is able to keep you from falling, and to present you faultless before the presence of his glory with exceeding joy" (Jude 24).

Burdick notes: "A superficial reading of v.18 presents several problems:

1.   Is it true that the child of God does not sin at all?

2.   Can he actually keep himself so that he will not sin?

3.   Is he so safe that the devil cannot even touch him?

"*Problem 1*. The child of God does not habitually engage in sin (3:9). He may commit individual acts of sin (2:1-2) but he does not live in sin. This is not because the child of God keepeth himself.

"*Problem 2*. Whereas the verb translated (is born) is the perfect tense stressing the results of the action, the verb 'is begotten' appears in the aorist tense pointing back to a past occurrence. The reason for the change of tense seems to be that the author is speaking of different persons. The perfect tense 'is born' refers to the christian, but the aorist tense 'is begotten' speaks of Christ, the only begotten Son of God. The One who is keeping the child of God, then, is not the believer himself, but is Christ.

"*Problem 3*. The word 'toucheth' is not an adequate translation of *haptetai*-the Greek word literally means 'to fasten oneself to' something or someone. Thus John is assuring us that Satan cannot lay hold on the child of God. He may touch the believer, but he cannot take hold of him and keep him in his grasp" (Burdick).

The perfect participle " is born" emphasises that the new birth, far from being a transient phase of religious experience has an abiding result. He who has been begotten of God remains God's child with permanent privileges and obligations. One of these obligations is expressed in the phrase that he " sinneth not". The AV has "keepeth himself" as also translations from the Codex Sinaiticus and most Greek MSS reading *heauton* (himself); the Alexandrian and Vatican Codices read *auton* (him). "So if the RV as seems probable is the correct reading, then the subject of the verb (viz. he that is begotten of God) is Christ, not the christian, and the truth here taught is not that the christian keeps himself but that Christ keeps him ... observe that the three verbs are all in the present tense. They indicate abiding truths. The devil does not touch the christian because the Son keeps him, and so, because the Son keeps him the christian does not sin" (Stott).

Plummer, preferring the rendering "the begotten of God keepeth him", comments: "The first change depends upon a question of interpretation, the second on one of reading; and neither can be determined with certainty. The latter is the easier question and throws light on the former ... who it is that 'keepeth him'? Not the child of God himself ... but the Son of God, the only begotten. Recipients of the divine birth are always spoken of by John both in his Gospel and in his epistle in the perfect participle (3:9; 5:1,4; John 3:6,8; also the first clause here). In the present clause he abruptly changes to the aorist participle, which he uses nowhere else. The force of the two tenses seems to be thus: the perfect expresses a permanent relation begun in the past, and continued in the present; the aorist expresses a timeless relation, a fact. The one signifies the child of God, as opposed to those who have not become His children; the other signifies the Son of God as opposed to the evil one".

Bruce is in agreement: "Here the reason the child of God does not sin is expressed in different terms; it is because the Son of God keeps him ... The adjective clause 'whosoever is begotten of God' . . . refers to every child of God: the expression 'he that was begotten of God'.. . denotes the one and only Son of God".

John adds: "and that wicked one toucheth him not", i.e. does not fasten himself on him (middle voice). The wicked one is John's designation of the devil (2:13,14; 3:12); he writes "the devil" in 3:8. "The wicked one will try to fasten himself upon him but will not succeed" (Lenski). The christian can only hope to "keep" the commandments of God (3:24; 5:3) if the Son of God keeps him; cf. Jude 24; 1 Pet 1:5. But why does he need to be kept? If he has been begotten of God is he not immune to temptation? No. The devil, that wicked one, is maliciously active; strong and subtle, he is more than a match for the christian, but "the Son of God came to undo the works of the devil".

19   The second triumphant "we know!" is: "We know (this personally affects us) that we are of God, and the whole world lieth in the evil one" (RV). They had faced various "tests of life" and had the features that proved the reality of conversion. "We are of God" is in immediate contrast with the expression "the evil one". *Ek tou theou* (of God) speaks of the source from which the believer comes. It equates with the saying that he has been born of God-out of God. We are therefore in the sphere of the family of God, whereas the whole world is in the devil's sphere; the godless world, the kingdom of darkness, is wholly within his domination, evidently helpless to escape, maybe happy there - warmed, lulled to sleep in the devil's lap. What a contrast to the former verse 1 "the wicked one cannot lay hold of him". "It is in the evil one, in his grip and under his dominion. Moreover, it lies there. It is not represented as struggling actively to be free, but as quietly lying, perhaps even unconsciously asleep in the arms of Satan" (Stott). "Evil one in our versions is not as good as 'wicked one' (*poneros*, actively, viciously wicked). In contrast the idea of passivity which does not even struggle against the devil" (Lenski).

20   And we know that the Son of God is come. Here John confirms and we believe in the incarnation. The Son of God is come. The eternal life which was with the Father has been manifested unto us (1:2). The gnostics with their claim of superior knowledge were bitterly opposed to this truth, believing as they did that our Lord Jesus was born of a natural association between Joseph and Mary, and was an ordinary man; but says John, "we know"-we have a knowledge superior to theirs. We know that Jesus is the Son of God, we know that the eternal Son has come into this scene, born of a virgin: "that holy thing which shall be born of thee shall be called the Son of God" (Luke 1:35). "They shall call his name Emmanuel, which being interpreted is, God with us" (Matt 1:23). And how do we know, how are we perfectly convinced, when gnostics claimed they did not know? He has not only come, but "hath given us an understanding".
   " 'The Son of God has come', 'come in flesh' (4:2), come moreover 'through water and blood' (5:6) and given us spiritual intelligence, a faculty of perception or apprehension which far surpasses the knowledge cultivated by the gnostic

seducers, for through it we came to the personal knowledge not only of truth in the abstract (2:21) but of 'the True One' Himself " (Bruce).

" ' Has come' . . . is another example in the epistle of John's emphasis that the christian belief is both historical and experimental, and not one without the other ... He hath given us as an understanding (*dianoia*) the power or capacity of knowing" (Ebrard); "spiritual sense and ability to understand" (Lenski). "He has caused to abound towards us in all wisdom and intelligence" (Eph 1:8 JND). (See also 1 John 2:20,27.) Again has He not given to us the Holy Spirit? "God hath revealed them unto us by his Spirit: for the Spirit searcheth all things, yea, the deep things of God" (1 Cor 2:10). "There is this divinely-given understanding that the One who has come has given us-that we know Him that is true (real)-the "true" or "real" bread and vine (John 6:32; 15:1) as opposed to baker's bread and the farmer's vine which are the shadows of which He is the substance; so God is the ultimate reality" (Stott). John's "that we may know" (AV); "that we know him that is true" (RV) dispels doubt; this understanding makes us intelligent about it and confirms us in it.

2. *The Climax*
5:20b

> v.20b"This is the true God, and eternal life."

There seems to be very little doubt that the matters about which John wrote in John 13 to 17 are always very much before his mind as he writes this epistle. Is there not a close parallel here with various of the statements recorded in our Lord's high priestly prayer in John 17? "And this is life eternal, that they might know thee the only true God, and Jesus Christ, whom thou hast sent" (v.3); there the Son is addressing His Father and calls Him, among other things, the only true God". Here in our epistle His prayer is answered: we know Him that is true and we are in Him that is true, in His Son Jesus Christ. This is the real God, and eternal life. It is the Son who having come has brought us to know, to perceive, to experience Him that is true. We are in Him that is true. This must of necessity be God, the Father of Him who has come. "Even" should be omitted from the phrase "even in his Son Jesus Christ"; it has been inserted in the AV and the RV to make "in him that is true" refer to Christ. The last clause explains how it is that we are in the Father, viz. by being in the Son (2:23; John 1:18; 14:9 17:21,22). "Tyndale boldly turns the second 'in' into 'through'-'we are in Him that is true, through His son Jesus Christ' " (Plummer). Burdick concurs: "That the designation 'him that is true' refers to the Father is indicated by the following references to His Son Jesus Christ".

"Through faith-union with Him His people have their being in 'the true One'. To abide in the Father and to abide 'in the Son' are two ways of stating the one experience: 'If what ye heard from the beginning abides in you',

John has already told them, 'then you will abide in the Son and in the Father' (2:24)" (Bruce).

Notice that in John 17:21 "that they all may be one; as thou, Father, art in me, and I in thee" refers to

1.   the Father in the Son;

2.   the Son in the Father;

3.   the saints in the Father and the Son: and (v.23) "I in them, and thou in me, that they may be made perfect in one";

4.   the Son in the saints;

5.   the Father in the Son;

6.   that they may be made perfect into One (RV).

These complex expressions relative to the Father, the Son and the saints seem in line with John's thinking in these final expressions of the epistle. Bruce comments: "Jesus is characterised as the true God and eternal Life. So truly is the Father expressed in the Son that what is predicated of the former is predicated of the latter".

Lenski is worth quoting in extenso: "This God is the real God and life eternal. As the Father who is made known to us by Him is the only real God (1 Thess 1:9) so also His Son Jesus Christ is 'the real God' and eternal life. If the Son is less, if He is not the real God even as the Father is the real God, then the entire epistle and all that it declared about His blood, expiation and fellowship with God etc., is futile. So John has hitherto called Jesus 'the Son of God' and His (the Father's, God's) Son, and now, here at the end and the climax, John duplicates and calls also Jesus Christ the real God's Son, because He is the real God's only begotten Son (4:9), yea 'the real God'. As the Father is the (genuine) real God, so His Son is the real genuine God, and His Son places us in fellowship with the Father. Need we add the words that Jesus spoke (John 10:30; 12:45; 14:9)". Stott's summary is: "Eternal Life is here defined in terms of knowing God both Father and Son".

This is the climax, the apex of all that John declares in the epistle: "This is the true God, and eternal life"

Notes

18   Griffith Thomas says "Our use of the word 'begotten' must always be safeguarded by the association of 'from everlasting' ".

A. H. Strong writes, "Neither the incarnation, the baptism, the transfiguration, nor the resurrection marks the beginning of Christ's Sonship or constitutes Him Son of God. These are but recognition of a pre-existing Sonship inseparable from His Godhead".

G. H. Handley Moule adds: "The inscrutable mode of the blessed Filiation is named in the theology of the christian church 'the Eternal Generation'. The phrase is due to Origen and was, like the word Trinity, an instance of the happy denomination that at once collects and clears up truths already held. Scripture reveals that Christ is the Son antecedent to Incarnation. It also reveals that He is eternal. Eternal Generation combines these truths in the thought that the Begetting is not an event in time, however remote, but a fact irrespective of time. The Christ did not become, but necessarily and eternally is the Son. He, a Person, possesses every attribute of pure Godhood. This necessitates an eternally absolute being: in this respect He is not 'after' the Father".

"The Son, which is the Word of the Father, begotten from everlasting of the Father, the very and eternal God, and of one substance with the Father took man's nature in the womb of the blessed Virgin Mary, of her substance; so that the two whole and perfect natures, that is to say the Godhead and manhood, were joined together in one Person, never to be divided, and hence is one Christ Very God and Very Man" (Article 2 of the 39 Articles).

VI. A Final loving Exhortation (5:21)

v.21 "Little children, keep yourselves from idols. Amen."

21   How his heart moves out finally towards them in this term of endearment "Little children". He wrote to tell them these things that their joy and his joy might be full (1:4). Now he adds "keep yourselves from idols". The Son of God will keep them and Satan will not be able to lay hold on them, but that does not relieve them of the responsibility of keeping themselves from idols. David Smith says the word is used of guarding " a flock (Luke 2:8), a deposit or a trust (1 Tim 6:20; 2 Tim 2:14) or a prisoner (Acts 12:4)". The knowledge and communion with the true God is inconsistent with anything that has the character of idols, even if they be "untrue mental images fashioned by the false teachers" (Brooke). All substitutes for God are idols. "Since they were for the most part Gentile converts living in the idolatrous cities of Asia this urgent command is no doubt most fitting" (Burdick). "The 'idols' or false appearances (*eidōla*) against which John warns his readers to be on their guard are not material images, they are false conceptions of God. Any conception of Him that is variance with His self-revelation in Christ is an idol ... have nothing to do with counterfeit and refuse all substitutes" (Bruce).

"John is not speaking of common pagan idols, which are then irrelevantly introduced at the very end of the epistle. These idols are the fictional conceptions of God that were held by Cerinthus and by his devotees. By calling these conceptions the idols John places them in the same class with all the pagan images and the imagined gods" (Lenski).

"This emphatic warning against the worship of creatures intensifies the whole teaching of the epistle; the main purpose of which is to establish the truth that the Son of God has come in the flesh in the man Jesus. Such a Being was worthy of worship. But if, as Ebionites and Cerinthus taught, Jesus was a creature, the son of Joseph and Mary, then worship to such an one would only be one more of these idolatries from which John in his farewell injunction bids christians once for all to guard themselves" (Plummer). But He is no idol; He is the true God and eternal life.

2 JOHN
A. M. S. Gooding

SECOND EPISTLE OF JOHN

I. Greetings (vv.1-4)

v.1   "The elder unto the elect lady and her children, whom I love in the truth; and not I only, but also all they that have known the truth;

v.2   For the truth's sake, which dwelleth in us, and shall be with us for ever.

v.3   Grace be with you, mercy, *and* peace, from God the Father, and from the Lord Jesus Christ, the Son of the Father, in truth and love.

v.4   I rejoiced greatly that I found of thy children walking in truth, as we have received a commandment from the Father."

1. *The Writer*

1 "The elder" is without doubt the apostle John. There is insufficient support for the suggestion of another John called John the Presbyter, a fictitious person based on an apparent misreading of Papias by Eusebius: "Irenaeus who also made much use of Papias' work, and independently of it knew a great deal about Ephesus and St. John makes no mention of a second John. Other predecessors of Eusebius, whether they had read Papias or not, agreed in believing in only one John, viz. the apostle" (Plummer).

John was not "*the* elder" for there is no definite article in the original Greek. Elders are called bishops, overseers, pastors, guides in NT writings, but the word elder is not used here in that sense, but rather to indicate that he was a teacher of a venerable age, much loved, and loving all the saints as his dear children; he was the last surviving member of the apostolic band. The idea of one person being called "the elder" is contrary to the whole of NT teaching. Peter says "the elders which are among you I exhort, who also am *an* elder" (1 Pet 5:1). He was a fellow elder, one among many, not elevated above them. One elder over a local assembly or one elder over a number of assemblies rapidly appeared early in the second century. The letters of Ignatius contain constant reference in words like, "Let us take heed, brethren, that we set not ourselves against the bishop, that we may be subject unto God ... it is evident that we ought to look upon the bishop as we do on the Lord Himself" (to the Ephesians). The late Dr H. Moule writes, "The title 'bishop' does not in the NT denote a minister ruling over other ministers

... he is the *episkopos* not of the shepherds but the flock". "One local church might have several bishops" (W. Hoste). The apostle Paul warned that such things would come, thus "Of your own selves (the elders at Ephesus) shall men arise" (Acts 20:30). Peter warns "neither as lording it over the charge allotted to you" (1 Pet 5:3 RV) and John speaks of Diotrephes who loveth the preeminence (3 John 9). John could have been (and possibly was) a fellow elder like Peter in the locality where he lived, but he is not using the word in that way here. He is writing a letter to a sister living in another place, doubtless in another assembly in which he would not be an elder.

2.   *The Elect Lady*

Much has been written about this "elect lady"; who was she? Was she an individual lady known to John, or is "the elect lady" a term indicating a local assembly? "Unto the elect lady" may possibly be read "an elect lady", there being no definite article. The reading "to the lady Electa", which some have suggested, may be dismissed, seeing that *eklekta* is used again in v.13, and if it is a proper name it would be extraordinary to find two sisters of the same name in one family. (For "elect" see 1 Pet 1:1 RV, " to the elect", and 2 Tim 2:10 "for the elect's sake".) Every truly born again person is "elect according to the foreknowledge of God the Father" (1 Pet 1:2) and that description would include this sister. Various suggestions have been made as to her identity:

1.   The whole church;

2.   An unnamed local church;

3.   The church at Babylon;

4.   The church in Rome;

5.   The Virgin Mary;

6.   Martha;

7.   Lady named Electa;

8.   Lady named Kyria;

9.   An anonymous woman (this is the most probable suggestion).

Nothing in the epistle suggests or demands that the recipient must be interpreted as a local church. It is unnatural to suppose that such an individual figure of speech should be employed in a little family-type letter of this kind, concerning such ordinary things as children and their progress, worthy guests and unworthy guests and how to treat them. It is far simpler and more profitable to take the word of God as it stands, "the elect lady". She is not said to be a relative or a special friend, but the relationship mentioned is purely spiritual; it is based on sovereign grace. Sovereign grace and election always go together. There is a bond that unites the saints, brings them into a union where they love one another with a pure heart fervently. Would not this apostle who impresses upon the saints the commandment " that we love one another" be exemplary in this matter. Seeing however that there were those who turned the grace of God into lasciviousness (and John was writing to warn this sister against these) John is extremely careful as a servant of God to guard against words in his letter that would be considered indiscreet.

It could be inferred from the letter that she was a middle aged widow. No husband is addressed or mentioned and it would be very impolite and improper to address her and ignore him (even if he were not converted). I suggest she is a widow with at least four children. John addresses children (sons) with her and also states that he found of her children (sons) walking in truth and he writes to her about them too.

3.   *John's Discretion*

2   John says "whom I love in the truth". "The Greek phrase translated 'in the truth' lacks the article. It could therefore be an adverbial expression 'whom I love in truth' (as in 3 John 1) or 'truly', that is in christian sincerity" (Plummer). But the context, with two subsequent references to the truth, with the article (vv.1,2) surely justifies the AV and RSV translation "whom I love in the truth" (Stott). It was the truth that bound John in love to the dear saints and it was in the sphere of the truth that John loved this sister. The love of the Lord's people must be fervent and real and abounding, but their love must be controlled by the word of God. John is going to insist that her love is to be controlled by the word of God relative to the deceivers who would knock on her door. Before he brings this fact before her, the expression of his own love is a model of discretion. Notice too that further to safeguard himself he addresses also her children and they are equally the object of his love. This is not natural love, secret or special for her in any way, but the kind of love wherewith John loved all the saints, and all the saints who knew the truth would love her in the same way. Thus very discreetly he indicates the kind and quality of this love and he becomes a unique example to all the Lord's servants in their relationships with members of the opposite sex.

It is interesting to notice how careful John is throughout this epistle relative to the terms he uses. Notice the absence of the word "beloved". In the first epistle, addressing all the dear children he uses it in 2:7; 3:2; 3:21;4:1;4:7;4:11. In the third epistle to a man he uses it three times (vv.1,2,5,11) but he omits it entirely in the second epistle, lest its use should be misconstrued.

Why did John and all those who knew the truth love this lady and the members of her family? Because of the truth that "dwelleth in us, and shall be with us for ever". As christians we are bidden to love our friends and even our enemies, but we love our fellow believers because of the bond that there is between us. We believe in the same person. We believe the same truth about Him; it is therefore the truth that joins us together. We do not love fellow saints because they are like ourselves, or because they are attractive, or kind or have lovely characters; not even because they love us, but because of the bond of the truth.

This sister and her children had done and were doing something because of the truth, and this had earned the love of the Lord's people. One would gather from the letter that they engaged in a ministry of hospitality to the Lord's servants, brethren, and other strangers and were well known and appreciated because of their work. John expresses his love and the love of all the others. Maybe he could say of her as Paul could of Phoebe: "She hath been a succourer of many, and of myself also" (Rom 16:2); and of Priscilla and Aquila "unto whom ... I give thanks, but also all the churches of the Gentiles" (16:4). (See also in that chapter Mary (v.6), Tryphena and Tryphosa and the beloved Persis (v.12), also Rufus, his mother and mine (v.13) and join in the thanksgiving for the noble army of sisters who thus minister unto him of their substance.)

The repetition of "the truth" in the phrase "the truth's sake" is perfectly in keeping with John's thinking. The truth of God "abideth in us" (RV), i.e. it remains the active principle in us, hidden in our hearts controlling our lives. The truth given in the power of the Spirit is not passing; it will not change. It has been committed once for all unto the saints. Of the Spirit it is said " that he may abide with you for ever; even the Spirit of truth" (John 14:16,17). Here similar words are used of the truth: it "shall be with us for ever".

4.   *The Greetings*

3   Paul had a customary way of opening his letters to christian churches, viz. "Grace be unto you, and peace, from God our Father, and from the Lord Jesus Christ" (1 Cor 1:3). When however he was addressing individuals in the pastoral epistles he says "Grace, mercy, and peace" (see 1 Tim 1:2; 2 Tim 1:2; Titus 1:4). This is the expression that John uses here, and is not this letter for an individual primarily and is it not pastoral in content? The greeting is not a greeting for a local church. The salutation is not part of a request but a direct affirmation of divine blessings on the recipients. "Grace" is not the grace of initial salvation (they were already enjoying that), but the unmerited favour of God everyday which will culminate when

"Grace all the work shall crown through everlasting days
It lays in heaven the topmost stone and well deserves the praise".

"Mercy" is added because of our continued great need. Thank God we have a throne of grace where we can obtain mercy (Heb 4:16). "Peace" too is necessary, not peace with God (that they had, made "by the blood of his cross"), but that calm unruffled peace that the Saviour knew and bequeathed to His own (John 14:27). These three come from God the Father as the source, and from Jesus Christ the Son of the Father as the channel. Notice that the word "God" applies equally to the Father and to Jesus Christ, the Son of the Father, proving the equality of the persons of the Godhead. Also the repetition of the "from" relative to Jesus Christ marks the distinct personalities of the Father and the Son and anticipated the exposing of wrong teaching in vv.7 to 10. Again John seems to have gnostic error in mind as he stresses the Son/Father relationship between the God who is light and the Lord Jesus Christ.

5. *Her Children*

4 Commentaries are meant for the head; this verse is meant for the heart. It is full of pathos and emotion. I am convinced that when it was read by the elect lady for the first time it was accompanied by a flood of tears of gratitude and joy. Imagine this dear widow receiving the letter from the aged apostle: "I was rejoiced greatly (aorist passive) that I found of thy children walking in truth". What a recompense for a mother's faithful sowing of the seed, for her careful nurturing in the things of God; she had seen them saved, baptised, received into fellowship among the saints and going on. Now they have left the family nest to face all the temptations of the world. Think of the anxiety of a mother's heart, and now the thrill of this news: they are still going on, walking in truth. Did she shed many a tear as she read it over and over again-my children! Let us to whom God in His grace has given children pause with thankfulness and praise if God has in His mercy saved them; and in these wicked days let us like job pray for them, "It may be that my sons have sinned, and renounced God in their hearts. Thus did Job continually" (1:5 RV).

It has been pointed out that John says "of thy children" not "all thy children" and some have suggested that this implies that there were others who were not walking in truth. I hardly think so. John found those who were at some place where he had visited in the course of ministry; there were others at home (they were loved for the truth's sake) who were also walking in truth. He would hardly have rejoiced if he had found others who were not, he would have expressed grief because of them.

John describes their behaviour: "as we have received a commandment from the Father". Were these babes in Christ? If so "I write unto you, little children, because ye have known the Father". He (the Father) would care for them as a Father, now they were removed from the care of their mother. As their Father He had given commandments which they were obeying. They were walking believing all that they had been taught relative to the Father and the Son. In belief they were doctrinally right (not lead astray by gnosticism). Walking according to the Father's commandments, their habitual way of living was doing the Father's will.

May I say to all young believers who have or hope to have children to rear for God. What a privilege! What a responsibility! Shall we rear them for this world or the next? Shall we put before them an example of godliness. Would it not be better for them to sweep the roads and in their lives bring pleasure to God, than sit in a professor's chair in time and at the end spend eternity in the lake of fire? May the God of all grace grant to readers this widow's joy!

II. The Danger of False Teachers (vv.5-11)

v.5   "And now I beseech thee, lady, not as though I wrote a new commandment unto thee, but that which we had from the beginning, that we love one another.
v.6   And this is love, that we walk after his commandments. This is the commandment, That, as ye have heard from the beginning, ye should walk in it.
v.7   For many deceivers are entered into the world, who confess not that Jesus Christ is come in the flesh. This is a deceiver and an antichrist.
v.8   Look to yourselves, that we lose not those things which we have wrought, but that we receive a full reward.
v.9   Whosoever transgresseth, and abideth not in the doctrine of Christ, hath not God. He that abideth in the doctrine of Christ, he hath both the Father and the Son.
v.10 If there come any unto you, and bring not this doctrine, receive him not into *your* house, neither bid him God speed:
v.11 For he that biddeth him Godspeed is partaker of his evil deeds."

1. *The Message*

5-6 I am requesting you (*erōtaō*). Here are both dignity and formality. Having expressed his joy relative to the walk of her children, he now expresses his anxiety with regard to those who may visit her home. The verb "beseech" (*erōtaō*) suggests that he begs an equal or superior. "Not as though I wrote a new commandment unto thee ... that we love one another" (1 John 2:5) reminds us again of the words of the Lord Jesus "That ye love one another; as I have loved you, that ye also love one another" (John 13:34). John recognised that this is what this lady had been expressing in her kindness and care of the saints, and for that he would commend her and indeed impress upon her the commandment. There were however dangers about which he would warn her. She must realise that there was one commandment: "that we love one another", but there were also other commandments. Obedience to the one must not violate the others. Her love must "abound yet more and more in knowledge and all discernment" (Phil 1:9 RV). "Love that is genuine reveals itself in obedience. If we love one another we will treat one another in accordance with God's commands" (Burdick). "Obedience prompts love, love prompts obedience. Love divorced from duty will run riot, duty divorced from love will starve" (Plummer). "Christian love is not an involuntary, uncontrollable passion, but an unselfish service undertaken by deliberate choice (faith and love are both commandments, 1 John 3:28). Christian love belongs rather to the sphere of action, than to the emotions"

(Stott). Experimental knowledge and moral discernment must be exercised by this lady if she were not to be found showing christian kindness to those who were false and undeserving.

2. *False Teachers*

7   John knew and would acquaint her with the fact that there were travelling preachers of various kinds, those who were genuine and those who were false, true servants of God and servants of Satan, true apostles and false apostles. "Deceivers" is derived from a verb meaning to wander, to rove, to mislead, to lead into error; corrupters, deceivers, imposters. They have "gone forth ('entered', aorist) into the world" (RV) like the swarming of a pest, for false teachers suddenly burst upon the saints. "Perhaps the implication is that as the apostles were sent forth into the world to preach the truth, so these false teachers had gone forth to teach lies as emissaries of the devil, the father of lies" (Stott). "Not content to be deceived themselves, these men cannot rest until they have deceived others ... they do not bother pagans, their prey are true christians" (Lenski). Some of these might arrive at this lady's door (maybe she was well known in the locality as one "given to hospitality") seeking food and shelter as the servants of God, so she must be warned of them. But how should she detect them? They would not introduce themselves by saying "I'm a servant of Satan on a mission of deceiving the saints". They are deceivers, "for such are false apostles, deceitful workers, transforming themselves into apostles of Christ. And no marvel; for Satan himself is transformed into an angel of light. Therefore it is no great thing if his ministers also be transformed as the ministers of righteousness; whose end shall be according to their works" (2 Cor 11:13-15). Were these men not of that kind that "creep into houses, and lead captive silly women" (2 Tim 3:6). How will she detect the real from the false? The Spirit of God instructs her to listen, not so much to what they say, but to what they do not say: "they confess not". Listen to what these deceivers do not confess. "To confess not" is really to deny (1 John 2:22).

3. *A Credal Statement*

Notice this statement: "confess not, Jesus Christ is come (cometh?) in the flesh". She was to take particular note as to what they did not say in these vital subjects:

"*Jesus*" - His manhood, His Saviourhood: did they believe He was a real man? Did they believe He was the son of Joseph by natural generation?

"*Christ*" - His deity, His Messiahship, God's anointed: what did they confess about Jesus Christ? Cerinthus and his followers taught that Jesus was an ordinary man, born of human parentage and that because of His piety the Christ descended on Him at His baptism and left Him at Gethsemane. But

Jesus Christ was not the Christ superimposed on the Jesus-a dualism, but one person, absolute Godhead and perfect manhood from His very birth.

"*Is come*" demands His pre-existence before and outside of this world of ours: "I came forth from the Father, and am come into the world: again, I leave the world, and go to the Father (John 16:28).

The present participle (*erchomenon*, "coming") may refer to His future coming at the Rapture for His own, or to His appearing when every eye shall see Him. It is evident that at the Rapture He will have a real body, for our bodies will be fashioned like unto the body of His glory. And at His appearing (after the tribulation) His feet shall stand upon the Mount of Olives (Zech 14:4). He has a real body now, having taken manhood to the very throne of God. Now at this moment "in him dwelleth all the fulness of the Godhead bodily" (Col 2:9). He took a real body at incarnation: "it was pleasing that in Him should all the fulness dwell" (Col 1:19). Thus the expression embraces the fact that He came, was here, and is coming again. "The epistles are concerned to assert that His first coming was in the flesh, the latter (coming) is almost certainly in mind here. In this case the present tense is 'altogether timeless' " (Alford). "The incarnation is not only an event in history, it is an abiding truth" (Brooke). Jesus did not become the Christ or the Son at His baptism; Jesus was the Christ in the flesh. "The two natures, manhood and Godhead were united already at His birth, never to be divided" (Stott). "Unto you is born this day in the city of David a Saviour, which is *Christ* the Lord" (Luke 2:11). "Therefore that holy thing which shall be born of thee shall be called the *Son of God*" (Luke 1:35).

These men were servants of Satan, deceivers to their fellow men, antichrist relative to the Redeemer.

Notice the condemnatory names used of the false teachers; liars (1 John 2:22), seducers (2:26), false prophets (4:1), deceivers (2 John 7), antichrists (1 John 2:18,22; 4:3; 2 John 7). The heresy of which 2 John speaks is the identical error refuted in 1 John 4:2,3. "False teachers such as Cerinthus refused to believe that the divine Christ actually came in human flesh" (Burdick).

4. *Looking or Losing*
8   While the lady and her children would need to listen carefully to detect the false teaching they must first look to themselves lest they be beguiled from that simplicity and purity that is toward Christ (2 Cor 11:3 RV). These heretical teachers might rob them of spiritual truth already acquired and enjoyed. The AV and RV give variant renderings of the second half of the verse: "that we lose not those things which we have wrought, but that we receive a full reward" (AV); "that ye lose not the things which we have wrought, but that ye receive a full reward" (RV); some MSS having first, others second, person plural forms of the verbs. The meaning seems to be "take heed that these deceivers do not undo the work

which the apostles and evangelists have wrought in you, but that ye receive the full fruit of it" (Plummer). John and his associates had laboured teaching believers the fundamental truths relative to the person of the Lord Jesus. He is anxious that the elect lady retains these truths, not letting them slip. John has "wrought" (indicating the hard, prayerful toil of teaching the truth) and he now desires that

1.   at the Judgment Seat of Christ he may receive a full reward for his labours

2.   that she may receive a full reward
        a. by fruit being produced in her own life
        b. by fruit being seen for the glory of God at the judgment Seat.

5. *Leaping Forward*
9   There is a line between truth and error. False teachers invariably profess to bring new light, fresh revelation, something new, something unknown before. How many simple folk are ensnared by such plausible talk! Whoso comes with such new teaching is transgressing (crossing the line) going beyond divine revelation, and thus departing from what has been revealed by God. "Flesh and blood hath not revealed it unto thee, but my Father which is in heaven" (Matt 16:17). "Whosoever transgresseth (goeth onward RV), and abideth not in the doctrine of Christ", i.e. the body of doctrine, "the faith . . . once for all delivered unto the saints" (Jude 3 RV).
     John is stern, plain, dogmatic and true in his denunciation of these false teachers: "Leaping forward (*protipo*) from a safe place to one that is wholly unsafe is folly" (Lenski). "There is an advance which involves desertion of first principles and such an advance is not progress but apostasy" (Plummer). "John is almost certainly borrowing from the vocabulary of the heretic. They claimed to have go-ahead ideas, a super gnosis, which enabled them to advance beyond the rudiments of the faith in which the common herd were content to abide. John refers sarcastically to their claim. They had indeed gone ahead! They had advanced so far that they had left God behind them. He who denies Christ thereby forfeits God" (Stott).
     By way of contrast " He that abideth in (that does not go beyond) the doctrine of Christ, hath both the Father and the Son".

6. *Attitude to False Teachers*
10   Having been sent forth by their master to propagate his denials of the Father and the Son, these false teachers were advancing in their evil work and would eventually, John fears, arrive at the door of this lady's house. He has told her the way to discern the true from the false, and if she perceives that "he bringeth not this doctrine" her instructions are clear: "receive him not into your house" (the house). Which house? The house in which she has responsibility and authority, not the local church, but literally her own home. This suggests again that she is

a widow; no mention is made of a husband to be considered in the matter. Her instruction (and ours) are: when he arrives, "Receive him not into your house"; when he leaves, "Give him no greeting" (RV); "Neither bid him God speed" (AV). This, some argue, is unkind, uncharitable, unchristian, but should we receive and harbour and bless those who are antichrist and deceivers, who deny both the deity and the humanity of the Lord Jesus? Surely to receive them is to have fellowship with them in their evil work of denying Him. This is the way we must treat those who have gone forth with the definite intention of deceiving men and denying Him. Those led astray by them are covered by Jude 22: "And of some have compassion, making a difference". But even here simple believers must act with care: " on some have mercy with fear; hating even the garment spotted by the flesh" (Jude 23 RV). Therefore the teaching is clear: no reception of such; for such no provision, no greeting, no support. (Contrast 3 John where Gaius is commended for these very kindnesses to the true servants of God.) " If John's instructions seem harsh, it is perhaps because his concern for the glory of the Son and the good of man's soul is greater than ours" (Stott), or because "the tolerance on which we pride ourselves is in reality an indifference to truth" (Alexander) or is it just cowardice-ashamed of Jesus? Is it a lack of deep seated conviction relative to the claims of Christ?

"In that day when there were no missionary organisations for channelling missionary giving, the simple exercise of christian hospitality towards travelling teachers and evangelists was a primitive form of missionary support" (Burdick). Is it not still the best way, the scriptural way? "John is clearly forbidding the support of any whose teaching denies that Jesus is the incarnate Son of God" (Burdick).

7. No Blessing

"He that biddeth him God speed is partaker of his evil deeds". To partake (*koinōneō*) means to share. By providing shelter, food or sustenance and invoking God's blessing, she would be actually helping, sharing, investing her labour, time and resources in the spreading of his evil teaching, helping the devil in his evil work. To receive such a man into one's home is to provide a centre, headquarters for his false teaching and puts the members of one's own family in spiritual danger. The word for evil (*ponēros*) is that used for the evil one (1 John 2:13,14; 3:12; 5:18,19). We would not like to be an accomplice in such wicked deeds. To bid a person "God speed" suggests that we express the desire that God will bless his mission. The Greek term is the normal greeting (*chairein*, to rejoice). This suggests that the speaker wishes the traveller joy. The AV "biddeth him God speed" is therefore not far from the idea that John intended.

III. Concluding Greetings (vv.12-13)

v.12 "Having many things to write unto you, I would not *write* with paper and ink: but I trust to come unto you, and speak face to face, that our joy may be full.
v.13 The children of thy elect sister greet thee. Amen."

12   John's close acquaintance with the elect lady and her family seems to be evident from the fact that he had many things to communicate to them. He had however mentioned those of immediate importance. Paul uses the same kind of expression in 1 Cor 11:34 where he had dealt with the important things. Other things needed to be adjusted but they could wait until he visited Corinth. Reasons have been suggested for John's brevity both here and in the third epistle:

1.   his old age and the strain of writing

2.   his letter has filled his sheet of papyrus (as distinct from the more expensive parchment mentioned in 2 Tim 4:13)

3.   this length of letter was all that the Spirit of God moved him to write.

He would rather visit the lady and her children as such a meeting is always better for joyful fellowship and clear understanding. He desired that they might speak mouth to mouth (not the phrase used in 1 Cor 13:12 and Gen 33: 10). Our joy may be fulfilled (better "your joy"). "The high association with which the phrase is connected leads us to suppose that it would scarcely have been applied by John to any meeting but one of particular solemnity after a cruel and prolonged separation which had threatened to be eternal" (Bishop Alexander). The " ink " could be a mixture of lamp black and gall juice (the only other places where it occurs in the NT is 2 Cor 3:3; 3 John 13). "Paper" means Egyptian papyrus as distinct from parchment.

The Elect Sister
13   "You" in v.12 is plural and includes the children of v.1. This when contrasted with "thee" here and in v.5 seems to be in favour of understanding the "lady" literally (i.e. not of a local church). "The change from 'thee' to 'you' seems more in harmony with the matron and her family, than with the church and its members" (Plummet). The fact that "the children of thy elect sister salute thee- and not the elect sister herself suggests again that the elect sister is a real person. Was she away from home? living elsewhere? already deceased? All these are possibilities. The local church cannot be away from home; it cannot live elsewhere; it cannot be dead. "Robertson suggests that the elect sister was deceased since only her children are mentioned" (Burdick).

The third epistle, undoubtedly written to an individual, has a conclusion so similar to what we have here that it would also support the suggestion that this was written to an individual.

The "Amen" seems to be a copyist's addition as also in 1 John 5:21.

3 JOHN
A. M. S. Gooding

THIRD EPISTLE OF JOHN

1. The Elder and the Greeting (v.1)

v.1 "The elder unto the wellbeloved Gaius, whom I love in the truth.

1 For "the elder" see our comments on the second epistle. The word "beloved" is used four times in the epistle (vv.1,2,5,11) which contrasts with the twin epistle written to a matron with no mention of "beloved". There has been much controversy as to the identity of the recipient of this letter. Three men bearing the name Gaius are found in the NT writings. "Gaius was perhaps the most common of all names in the Roman Empire" (Plummer). There were Crispus and Gaius whom Paul baptised (1 Cor 1:14; Rom 16:23); Gaius and Aristarchus who suffered in the visit at Ephesus (Acts 19:29); Gaius of Derbe who accompanied Paul into Asia (Acts 20:4). However while various traditions exist, it is quite within possibility that our Gaius is not one of these three. The number of years that had elapsed and the movement of population at that time make all suggestions mere unprofitable guesses. It seems that in whatever place he was, he was associated with the saints in the local assembly, he was greatly respected and beloved possibly because like another Gaius he was on many occasions "mine host". We think of the beloved Persis in a similar way (Rom 16:12). "I" is emphatic in the clause "whom I love in the truth" and may be in contrast to others who did not love in truth. "The AV and RSV are certainly right to translate the expression here not 'in truth' (RV), but 'in the truth', the body of doctrine being the sphere in which the love existed and manifested itself" (Stott).

II. Gaius and the Brethren (vv.2-8)

v.2 "Beloved, I wish above all things that thou mayest prosper and be in health, even as thy soul prospereth.

> v.3 For I rejoiced greatly, when the brethren came and testified of the truth that is in thee, even as thou walkest in the truth.
> v.4 I have no greater joy than to hear that my children walk in truth.
> v.5 Beloved, thou doest faithfully whatsoever thou doest to the brethren, and to strangers;
> v.6 Which have borne witness of thy charity before the church: whom if thou bring forward on their journey after a godly sort, thou shalt do well:
> v.7 Because that for his name's sake they went forth, taking nothing of the Gentiles.
> v.8 We therefore ought to receive such, that we might be fellowhelpers to the truth."

2   Commenting on "beloved", Stott notes: "Three of the first eleven Greek words ... refer to love". The word *euchomai* may express either a prayer or a wish. John is following the standard pattern for introducing a letter by expressing his desire in the form of a prayer. This desire embraces all aspects of Gaius' life: "I pray in (concerning) all things" or "in all respects" (Plummer). "Prosper" (*euodoumai*) strictly means to prosper on a journey, but that shade of meaning has been lost over the years and the word now means to prosper in any way; cf. Rom 1:10; 1 Cor 16:2. To "be in health" (*hugiaino*) is used in its literal sense of physical well-being. It does not necessarily mean that Gaius is in ill health or failing in business but expresses a genuine desire that every material blessing be granted to him. He is prospering in soul; this is evidenced by his love to the saints. One cannot suggest anything better than that his material prosperity equate with his spiritual health. (I wonder if our spiritual health is better than our bodily health and our spiritual prosperity above our material prosperity.) Such requests were in keeping with the kind of service Gaius was engaging in for God. He needed good health in order to maintain his ministry, and he needed to prosper in order to provide hospitality and send forth God's servants in a manner worthy of God. "There is biblical warrant here for desiring both the physical as well as the spiritual welfare of our christian friends" (Stott).

3   He has rejoiced greatly (2 John 4) that the elect lady's children (her natural children) were walking in truth. Here his sentiments are the same (though he does not use the epistolary aorist) but he has before him his own spiritual children, Gaius and all who like him have been brought to know Christ as Saviour through John's preaching. Notice that in the second epistle it was John bearing witness to the elect lady, but here the brethren came and testified "of the truth that is in thee, even as thou walkest in the truth". (Cf. "Thy word have I hid in mine heart", the truth that is *in* thee; "that I might not sin against thee", thou walkest in the truth.) John was not boasting prematurely of a number of professions of faith but of those who had the truth abiding in them with the result that their walk was pleasing to the Lord. The pronoun is again emphatic as if to contrast his walk with that of Diotrephes which was not "in the truth". Two characteristics of Gaius' spiritual life witnessed to by "the brethren" are recorded here: "the truth that is in thee" (v.3), "thy love" (v.6 RV). Should we not desire to live a balanced christian life like this? He held the truth and loved in the truth.

4   "I have no greater joy" is literally "greater joy have I none than this", a rendering which gives greater emphasis. "Joy" should read "grace", the unmerited favour of God in allowing John to be the vehicle for blessing to Gaius and God's grace in his continuance. What grace does God show to His unworthy servants in allowing any of us to be used of Himself. "This" is plural and should be translated "these"; John is referring to the frequent reports that come from travelling preachers. "Nothing exceeds John's interest in and concern for the spiritual welfare of his children" (Burdick). "My children" contains another emphatic pronoun; they are "my own children".

5   "Beloved" manifests again how much John loves this brother. "Thou doest faithfully" is literally "a faithful thing thou doest". His activity sprang from his christian faith. He was a faithful steward. There do not appear to be two different kinds of persons before us here. They were "brethren", the same family, begotten of the same Father. That gave to the saints the responsibility to love them. (Saints are responsible to love all those who are begotten of Him.) They were also strangers, unknown by Gaius and Diotrephes and the members of the assembly. "Whatsoever thou doest" is an expression covering the whole of his exercise, and reminding us of Matt 25:40 "Inasmuch as ... unto one of the least of these my brethren, ye have done it unto me". Gaius had done it to the brethren, but it was unto the Lord, and He would recompense fully. The better MSS read "brethren and that to strangers". This ministry is the privilege of all the Lord's people; "Given to hospitality" (Rom 12:13); "be not forgetful to entertain strangers . . . entertained angels unawares" (Heb 13:2). It is essential in overseers (1 Tim 3:2; Titus 1:8), and essential too in those widows who were to be supported by the assembly (1 Tim 5:10).

6   These brethren and strangers had already visited the assembly where Gaius was. They had been warmly received by him; he had shown them real christian care and hospitality. The brethren returned home (was it to Ephesus?) and bore witness on a definite occasion (aorist) before the church (in the presence of the church). At a public gathering of the local assembly they reported their reception at the assembly where Gaius and Diotrephes were and the condition that existed there. This confirms the principle seen in Acts 14:27 of reporting back to one's assembly: "And when they (Paul and Barnabas) were come, and had gathered the church together, they rehearsed all that God had done with them, and how he had opened the door of faith unto the Gentiles". This was a scriptural missionary report meeting. These brethren were glad to report of "thy love" (RV). Love in the NT is never mere words: "let us not love in word, neither in tongue; but in deed and in truth" (1 John 3:18). It is the same word as used for the love of God: intelligent, deliberate, outgoing, self-giving love patterned according to the love of God Himself. John has looked back on the past and mentioned what Gaius did; now he looks forward to what he is confident he will do when shortly these brethren visit again. "The words 'thou wilt do well' are an idiomatic form of conveying a request ('Please help them on their journey')" (Bruce). "You will please send them off on their journey" (Williams). Notice that the clauses are in a different order in the RV. "Whom thou wilt do well to set forward on their journey" will not only involve accompanying them on their journey for a short distance, but the giving of provision for the journey, both in cash and kind, in a manner worthy of God. These are the servants of God; He has sent them; He is responsible for their food and all their needs-as Paul declared, "My God shall supply all your need according to his riches in glory by Christ Jesus" (Phil 4:19). In the context of that verse God was meeting all the need of Paul while in bonds in Rome. He never fails to meet the needs of His servants who trust Him. He is the best of masters. John is certain that when these servants visit Gaius again he will show them the same love as on the previous visit, and is also sure that when they leave him to continue their journey as they serve the Lord, he will make adequate provision. This is God's way of supporting servants-not by wages or salary or guaranteed honorarium but just trusting a God who is faithful. The servants of Christ should be supported by the saints (1 Cor 9:1-18; Gal 6:6) but not by a fixed salary (Phil 4:11-12).

7   "This epistle does not contain the title Christ, but 'the Name' is a synonym for Christ" (Bruce). The name of course means Christ but always the full revelation that He is the Christ, the Son of the living God. It was for His sake that these forsook the ordinary callings of life and went forth at His call. John experienced this call (Mark 1:19,20) and so did these dear men. The false teachers went forth on their evil business (1 John 2:19; 4:1; 2 John 7). These men also went forth but in Christ's glad service. Blessed are those who hear and respond to such a call, "taking nothing of the Gentiles". They are not Gentiles in contrast to Jews, but pagans in contrast to christians. The Lord is able to finance His own work; He does not need the help of the ungodly. So it is true to say that His servants would not (as a matter of policy) and did not (as a matter of practice) receive support from those who did not know and love the Lord. "These missionaries not only could not expect to get anything from the pagans whom they would win for the Name; like Paul they would not take anything lest their converts and others might think that this was what they were after. The Name dare not be compromised in any way" (Lenski).

8   "We (emphatic) ... ought to receive", welcome, support or undertake for such. There is very likely a play on the Greek here. The Lord's servants were taking nothing from the Gentiles, therefore the Lord's people ought to undertake for them. The word should not be limited to "receive" as in the AV. The final clause is variously rendered: "fellow workers" is better than "fellowhelpers"; "with the truth" (JND, RV) rather than "to the truth"; Plummer translates "their fellow workers for the truth"; and Moffatt "allies of the truth". Obviously the truth is

being personified and regarded as the one with whom we collaborate. The dear sister in the second epistle if she supported and bade God speed to the false teachers would become a fellow partaker of their evil deeds. The Lord's people have the privilege of supporting the Lord's true servants and thus of being fellow partakers of their good deeds (see v.11). "The christian missionaries co-operate with the truth by proclaiming it; we co-operate with it by entertaining them. The christian missionary enterprise is, therefore, not undertaken by evangelists only, but by those who entertain and support them" (Stott). "To harbour a false teacher is to have fellowship with his 'wicked works'; correspondingly to show hospitality to those who maintain the truth of the gospel is to co-operate 'with the truth', and to enjoy the fulfilment of our Lord's promise that 'he who receives a prophet in the name of a prophet will receive a prophet's reward' (Matt 10:41)" (Bruce). These servants have gone forth for the sake of the Name and should be received for the sake of the Name and will be rewarded correspondingly.

III. Diotrephes' Sin (vv.9-11)

v.9 "I wrote unto the church: but Diotrephes, who loveth to have the preeminence among them, receiveth us not.

v.10 Wherefore, if I come, I will remember his deeds which he doeth, prating against us with malicious words: and not content therewith, neither doth he himself receive the brethren, and forbiddeth them that would, and casteth *them* out of the church.

v.11 Beloved, follow not that which is evil, but that which is good. He that doeth good is of God: but he that doeth evil hath not seen God."

9 For "I wrote unto the church". Some variants have "I would have written unto the church". Those who so write believe John wrote to Gaius because he knew that a letter addressed to the church would not reach the church because of the domineering attitude of Diotrephes. Others retain "I wrote" and suggest that the second epistle is in view; of course, these believe "the elect lady" is a term for the local assembly, a view which we reject. Both these suggestions are unacceptable. "I wrote a short letter, a something on which I do not lay such stress" (Plummer). The obvious inference is that John had already written to the assembly in which Gaius was in fellowship. Questions naturally arise:

1. Was it a letter commending the brethren, the strangers (v.5) who had visited the company?

2. Did the letter bear John's signature? and was it by ignoring it that Diotrephes had indicated that he "receiveth us not" (the signatories)? Certainly the RSV "does not acknowledge my authority" and Bruce "he neither accepted, recognised John's authority nor admitted his messengers to the church" point in that direction. Was the attitude of Diotrephes a beginning of the tendency that was beginning to show itself in the second century-the monarchial episcopate?

"The letter in question must, therefore, have been lost, possibly because Diotrephes destroyed it" (Stott). The reason for this unchristian attitude is clearly stated "who loveth to have the preeminence among them" (see Matt 20:26 "whosoever willeth to be first among you", Plummer). "Just as the antichristian teachers claimed to be first in the intellectual sphere (2 John 9) so the unchristian Diotrephes claimed to be first in influence and authority" (Plummer). What a contrast there is between Gaius and Diotrephes: the one walking in the truth, loving the brethren, even those who were strangers to him; the other walking in pride and arrogance, loving himself, refusing welcome to strangers. These two men are found in the same assembly! How often this has been repeated in local church history! Diotrephes "loves to have the first place among them" (JND). One is reminded of the "I will's" of Lucifer (Isa 14:13,14), of the "ye shall be as God" (Gen 3:5 RV), and of the "fall into the condemnation of the devil" (1 Tim 3:6). How different from all this are the words of Phil 2:3,4: "Let nothing be done through strife or vainglory; but in lowliness of mind let each esteem other better than themselves. Look not every man on his own things, but every man also on the things of others". But this man knows nothing of this spirit. He is "the ambitious Diotrephes" (Lenski).

10 Because of this, "if I come, I will remind (them) of his works which he is doing". This is not a supposition, he intends to go and his presence will be decisive. He will come with apostolic authority. "Dodd suggests that the preservation of this letter is an argument of some weight in favour of the view that the elder's appeal was successful" (Bruce).

The word "prating" occurs nowhere else in the NT. It means to " 'talk nonsense", " not only wicked but senseless" (Plummer); "He lays baseless and spiteful charges against us" (NEB); "false accusations in a garrulous way" (Vine); "chiding against us" (Wyclif); "jesting on us" (Tyndale); "babble without sense" (Lenski). His accusations were not only baseless nonsense but they were malicious or with evil words. It is the same adjective as is used throughout the first epistle of the evil one. Sadly Diotrephes was exhibiting features that were not of God but of the evil one. How the words of Peter challenge us: "Wherefore laying aside all malice, and all guile, and hypocrisies, and envies, and all evil speakings. ..". It would appear that Diotrephes was guilty of all these. He:

1.   prated "against us with evil words"

2.   "neither doth he himself receive the brethren"

3.   "forbiddeth them that would"

4.   "casteth them out of the church".

Not content with denying the brethren a welcome and refusing hospitality, he forbids those who would, and if they dare to disobey he was excommunicating them from the church. He could not of course excommunicate from the Church which is His body, but was casting out of the local assembly. To what amazing lengths an unbridled dictatorial spirit will go.

11   "Beloved", how wondrously this word fits here! What a lack of love on the part of Diotrephes! What generous love was being shown by Gaius; how John warms to his spirit-Beloved. Was Gaius being pressurised by Diotrephes with threats of excommunication? Would he be persuaded by fair or foul means to change his attitude to the brethren? John appeals, "follow not that which is evil, but that which is good". This statement, coming as it does between Diotrephes and Demetrius, opens up to question whether or not Diotrephes was really born of God. For Diotrephes was characterised by evil deeds and evil words whereas of Demetrius we read he "hath good report of all men"; he was a good man. "He that doeth good (note the tense, implying his habitual way of living) is of God: but he that doeth evil (the tense likewise implies his habitual way of living) hath not seen God". How solemn and searching. Gaius had two examples before him. The appeal "follow (imitate) not that which is evil" is urgent, for it is common to look to others and follow them. What greater object we have to imitate in our blessed Lord (1 Pet 2:21). "Perhaps in this generalisation John has Diotrephes in mind and thus obliquely indicated that he questions whether Diotrephes is a true christian at all" (Stott).

IV. Demetrius' Good Report (v.12)

> v.12 "Demetrius hath good report of all *men*, and of the truth itself: yea, and we *also* bear record; and ye know that our record is true."

12   Demetrius may or may not have been the bearer of this letter. His identity with Demetrius, the silversmith, who made silver shrines for Diana and who opposed the servants of the Lord (Acts 19:24) has been suggested. If so he must have been converted in the interval and a marvellous change has taken place. It is a happy consideration but there is not a shred of evidence to rest on. The AV "Demetrius hath good report of all men" and Plummer "Witness hath been borne to Demetrius by all men" amount substantially to the same thing. "All men" could mean all the members of the church, but there is no reason to limit its scope-he had a good report among saved and unsaved; every servant of God should have that. His testimony has an impressive threefold witness:

1.   of all men (the tense points to a past report still valid in the present)

2.   of the truth itself

3.   we also bear witness.

He had a good report of all men and of the truth itself. "The truth he professed was embodied in him, so closely did his life conform to it" (Stott). He not only believed it and taught it, but practised it. His consistent life was an excellent testimony. Demetrius walked according to this rule and his conformity was manifest to all who knew the rule: thus the rule bore witness to his christian life. Better still John says, "we also bear record"; the apostle adds his own testimony to corroborate the testimony of all men. "This would be enough for Gaius because, even if he did not know any of the 'all men' who had testified to Demetrius, and had not yet met Demetrius to see in him the witness of the truth itself, he knew and trusted the judgment of John who concludes the sentence by writing: 'ye know that our record is true' " (Stott).

V. Final Greetings (vv.13-14)

v.13 "I had many things to write, but I will not with ink and pen write unto thee:
v.14 But I trust I shall shortly see thee, and we shall speak face to face. Peace be to thee. Our friends salute thee. Greet the friends by name."

13-14   See notes on 2 John 12. Note the difference "ink and pen" (*kalamos*, a reed used by the ancients for a pen) instead of "paper and ink". The quill pen was not in use till the fifth century AD, so is not in view here.

15   "Peace be to thee". What a greeting in an assembly where strife caused by Diotrephes' love of preeminence dominated. Things had been unpleasant in the past, still were and would be in the future, till John came, but in the midst of the storm John would wish them the very peace of God. This would be particularly precious to Gaius (John 14:27; 20:19,26). "Friends" (*philos*) conveys the thought of intimacy and affection. It is one of the titles the Lord Jesus bestowed upon His own: "Ye are my friends" (John 15:13-15):

1.   for them He lays down His life,

2.   they keep His commands,

3.   He reveals to them His purposes.

JUDE
A. McShane

JUDE
Introduction

1. **Authorship, Date and First Readers**
2. **The Purpose of the Epistle**
3. **Special Features of its Composition**
4. **Links with Other Writings**
5. **Outline**
6. **Bibliography**

1. Authorship, Date and First Readers

Jude, the shortest of the so called Catholic or General epistles, has presented many with a problem as to who was its penman. Unlike Hebrews where a similar problem exists, the writer tells us his name and apparently adds his relationship to James in order to make clear his identity, yet in spite of this, opinions are divided as to which one of the Judes mentioned in the NT he really was. Although there are six men bearing the name Jude, only two have been seriously considered as having a claim to be its writer-one the apostle Jude and the other Jude, the Lord's brother. The difficulty is increased by the fact that in the AV both men are said to have a brother named James, so that when "Jude the brother of James" is read in Luke 6:16 and in Acts 1:13 the conclusion many will reach is that this must be the man who wrote this epistle.

However, it must be noted that the word "brother" in these two references is not in the original, so that the reading should be "Jude of James" and the normal significance of this is that Jude was the son of James and not his brother. There cannot be much doubt that the James mentioned in Jude 1 was one of the apostles, for the most prominent one who bore that name was slain early in the Acts period and was likely only a name to many who would first read this epistle. There is another James who is first mentioned in Acts 12:17 and later in Acts 15 where he is seen to have taken an important part in the dispute which arose about circumcision. He was visited by Paul (Acts 21:18) and mentioned by him as one of the pillars of the church along with Peter and John (Gal 2:9). There can be little doubt that in the minds of the saints when the name James was used to denote someone of importance amongst them, he was the man of whom they thought. This James was the Lord's brother and according to the order of the names he was likely the oldest and Jude his brother was either the youngest or the second youngest of the sons of Joseph and Mary born after Christ.

If our conclusions be correct then it follows that we have two epistles written by the brethren of the Lord, that of James and this one Jude. Neither of these men followed Christ during His public ministry. Indeed John makes clear that none of His brethren believed on Him (John 7:5), nor have we any change in their attitude suggested until after His resurrection. The sight of that risen One, seen first by His brother James (1 Cor 15:7), may well have been the means of convincing the whole family of His Messiahship.

We know practically nothing of Jude apart from what is said of him as one of the Lord's brethren. We know he was in the upper room with the apostles (Acts 1:14) and that he travelled about in his service accompanied with his wife (1 Cor 9:5). The earlier part of his epistle gives the impression that he was a man of stern character, but toward its end another side of his character can be discerned for he shows deep sympathy for those who have been misled and encourages the saints to seek their restoration.

There is no way of knowing the whereabouts of Jude when he wrote this epistle, nor does he give us a clue to its destination. It is directed to the saints, but who they were and where they lived we are not told. When we consider the developed state of the evils he denounces we must conceive that it was late in the apostolic age, if not after it, when it was penned. Of course those who think the letter was written by the apostle Jude would assign it to an early period, but we think that somewhere about AD 70 might be the nearest we can go to the date of its composition. As for its first readers, it is impossible to say who they were. It could well be that it was first circulated in Palestine and later distributed to every part where the gospel had reached.

It must have been no small shock to the saints to discover that some of the worst evils of the world were appearing in their midst and being practised by those who claimed to be christians. The strange phenomenon was not confined to any one area, but appears to have been widespread at that time, so the warnings and encouragements of this epistle became necessary in order to fortify the faithful who must have been shaken by what they witnessed.

2. The Purpose of the Epistle
Broadly speaking Jude has two great messages in this epistle: one in which he tells the saints that in view of the evil men who had crept in amongst them, they should contend for the faith; the other is that they should build themselves up so as to be strengthened against the temptations which confronted them. As has often been pointed out, they were called upon to act much like the Jews in the days of Nehemiah, who held a sword in one hand and a trowel in the other.

The saints in all ages have felt much like the psalmist in Ps 73 who was greatly perturbed at the success of the wicked and the apparent lack of any intervention by God to arrest them in their evil ways. The readers of this epistle are clearly shown that there is a day of judgment for all sin, and that God in His own time will vindicate His character. The highest created beings and the most privileged of men alike come under His heavy hand when they sin. The evils that are dealt with in the epistle appear to be:

1. fleshly corruptions,

2. disrespect for authority,

3. pride and arrogance,

4. scoffing, and

5. absence of the fear of God.

It must not be forgotten that Jude does not deal with the evils of the world in general, for it has changed little over the centuries, but rather does he speak of those who were living like the world, yet claiming to have some links with christianity. Nor is he like Paul in 1 Corinthians dealing with matters for assembly discipline, but the wrong-doers he refers to are subjects for divine retribution and are not expected to repent of their evil deeds. Like the tares amongst the wheat, they have infiltrated the ranks of the saints, but they are distinct from them. Satan ever seeks to mar the work of God from within, as well as attacking it from without. All can conceive how depressing it is to be confronted with evil and yet be powerless to deal with those who are guilty of it. On the other hand we can equally comfort our hearts that what we cannot do we can safely leave in God's hands for He is the judge of all.

There is a danger of being unduly occupied with the wrongs of others and becoming cold at heart as a result. This epistle was written to preserve from this evil and to assure the saints that they would be kept from falling even though many, who once appeared to be the Lord's, had proved themselves to be strangers to His grace. While he would not want them to be complacent, yet he would not want them to be despondent.

3. Special Features of its Composition

All who have read this epistle will have been struck with the many triplets which appear in it. It is true to say that the writer whenever possible collects his matter into groups of three. Possibly twelve or so of these can be counted in its twenty-five verses. He is not the only penman in Scripture who does this, for Isaiah also used this form of composition in his great prophecy.

Another feature of Jude is his use of metaphors selected mainly from nature. He speaks of "brute beasts", "clouds without water", "winds", "fruitless trees", "waves of the sea" and "wandering stars". It might be too much to infer from these illustrations that he was reared in rural surroundings, but it has to be admitted that both he and his brother James had an alert eye in seeing in creation around them the object lessons that could be used to drive home to their readers the lessons they desired to teach.

Although Jude is manifestly acquainted with the OT, yet a feature of his writing is the absence of any quotation from its books He uses the language of Scripture, yet avoids citing any passage even when dealing with the subject of it. At times he comes close to a quotation, as when he writes "The Lord rebuke thee", but even then he is not quoting verbatim.

His use of the pronoun "these" when making reference to the evil-workers is another characteristic of his writing. In the RV it occurs some seven times and a careful note of each occurrence is vital in the understanding of the epistle.

We are somewhat surprised at the additional light shed by Jude on some OT passages. For example, we learn from him that there was a dispute over the body of Moses and that two of the greatest spiritual powers were in conflict, also that Enoch was a prophet and that he told of coming judgment. Many will tell us that he learned these things from the Apocryphal books of Enoch and the Assumption of Moses. We will later have a look at the foundation of their assertions.

4. Links with Other Writings

As regards this short epistle, nothing has caused more discussion than its resemblance to 2 Pet 2. Almost all writers claim that the relationship is so close that we must either believe that Peter copied from Jude, or else Jude copied from Peter. Some have suggested that there was a basic document, no longer in existence, from which both extracted their matter. All that can be said for these views is that if this were the case their copying was far from accurate. The fact is that though there is a resemblance between the two writings, yet they differ greatly even in those passages where they come close together. It has been reckoned that the two parallel passages contain in Jude 297 words and in Peter 256 words, and from these they share only 76 in common. If Peter borrowed from Jude he changed seventy percent of the words; and if Jude borrowed from Peter the percentage is even higher. There is little difference in the conciseness of their respective writings, but if anything Jude elaborates slightly more than Peter. One distinction is obvious and must be kept in mind; it is that Peter is stressing evil teaching and teachers, whereas Jude is concerned with evil living.

This question of one writer copying the other is not confined to these two epistles, for the same charge could be brought against the writers of the Gospels. We might ask, did Matthew copy Mark, or Mark Matthew? Did Luke consult the former two when he wrote his Gospel? What is most strange to human thinking is that John, who had access to the Synoptics shows no trace of having copied from any of them. A much more simple view of this similarity between the two writings is to see it as arising from the presence of certain evils in apostolic days which were being constantly condemned by the apostles and others in their oral ministry. Certain language would in that case be commonly heard which would in turn become the "stock in trade", as it were, of all who had concern about the welfare of the saints. Who of us have not been surprised to listen to some speaker preach messages we ourselves have preached, but he was totally unaware of this? The same medicine has often to be prescribed for the same illness. While we must agree that there is a certain agreement between Peter and Jude, yet we must not fail to see wherein they differ. Peter speaks prophetically and tells of the evil teachers who are about to appear, but Jude views them as already present and practising the corruptions warned of in Peter. The judgments threatened in Peter are upon the world, but those denounced in Jude are those who have some profession of christianity. Perhaps this is why he makes no mention of the Deluge, for it was a worldwide judgment.

The issue of Jude having obtained his information regarding the dispute about the body of Moses and his record regarding Enoch's prophecy from the Apocryphal writings of Enoch and the Assumption of Moses is fraught with difficulties. Not the least of these is the date of these writings. Some have no doubt that they were produced after Jude had written his epistle, and that the writers took his statements and built some of their ideas upon them. Until definite proof appears we must be content to know that the source of information is of small moment, for it is what is written in the NT that is inspired. Though Paul quotes a heathen poet, this does not add to the value of that writer's work.

Later we will notice the references to Zech 3 which appear in this epistle, but here we refer to it to show the link this epistle has with that OT book. Just as Zechariah encouraged the Jews to restart the building of the temple by showing them the destruction of all the enemies who would assemble around Jerusalem in a coming day, so Jude encourages the saints to build up themselves in their most holy faith, for their enemies will certainly be destroyed by the coming of the Lord. God's compassion for His high-priest in spite of his defiled garments is an example for the saints to follow in dealing with their brethren who have become defiled. They too should be plucked out of the fire as he was.

5. Outline

III. *Exhortation*   vv.20-25
    1. The Development of Spiritual Life   vv.20-21
    2. Treatment of Defaulters and Distinguishing
       between Them   vv.22-23
    3. Concluding Doxology   vv.24-25

7. Bibliography

Alford, H. *The Greek Testament*. Rivingtons, London. 1857.
Bloomfield, S.T. *Greek Testament*. Longmans, London. 1841.
Bigg, C. *International Critical Commentary*. T. & T. Clark, Edinburgh. 1915.
Coder, S. Maxwell. *Jude: The Acts of the Apostates*. Moody Press, Chicago. 1958.
Darby, J.N. *Synopsis of the Books of the Bible*. Morrish, London.
Green, M. *Tyndale Commentaries*. Tyndale Press, London. 1957.
Huther, J.E. *Meyer's Commentary*. T. & T. Clarke, Edinburgh. 1880.
Jenkyn, W. *Exposition of Jude*. 1652. Reprinted James Nicol, London. 1863.
Kelly, W. *Notes on Jude*. London, G. Morrish.
Mayor, J. *Epistle of Jude and 2 Peter*. Baker, Grand Rapids. 1979.
Plummer, A. *Bible Commentary of C. J. Ellicott*. Longmans, London. 1875.
Plumptre, E.H. *Cambridge Bible for Schools*. Cambridge University Press. 1899.
Wordsworth, C. *Greek Commentary*. Rivington, London. 1879.
Wuest, K.S. *Word Studies. In These Last Days*. W. B. Eerdmans, Grand Rapids. 1944.

Text and Exposition

I. Introduction (vv.1-4)

v.1　"Jude, the servant of Jesus Christ, and brother of James, to them that are sanctified by God the Father, and preserved in Jesus Christ, *and* called:

v.2　Mercy unto you, and peace, and love, be multiplied.

v.3　Beloved, when I gave all diligence to write unto you of the common salvation, it was needful for me to write unto you, and exhort *you* that ye should earnestly contend for the faith which was once delivered unto the saints.

v.4　For there are certain men crept in unawares, who were before of old ordained to this condemnation, ungodly men, turning the grace of our God into lasciviousness, and denying the only Lord God, and our Lord Jesus Christ."

1.　*Address and Greeting*
　　vv.1-2

1　Jude introduces himself to his readers by giving his name, his relationship to his brother James and his relationship to Christ. Although other epistles in the NT commence in almost the same way, such as James and Romans, still they have other statements added which are wanting here. The name Jude is the Greek equivalent of the Hebrew Judah which was originally given to the fourth son of Jacob and was later borne by the tribe which sprang from him. Because this was the royal tribe its name was no doubt chosen for their sons by parents in Israel, in this case by Joseph and Mary, with the ambition that the one who bore it would live up to its dignity. However, the popularity of any name can lead to confusion, so with Jude and James, another popular name, there was often added some other appellative that the particular man might be identified. Thus we have "Judas Iscariot", "James the less" and here "Jude ... brother of James".

　　If the writer had been an apostle, he no doubt would have included this in his address, more especially in view of the stern and serious statements of this epistle. Instead, he speaks of himself as the "servant of Jesus Christ". We cannot help being amazed at such words being used by one of the "brethren of the Lord". Neither he, nor his brother James use the name "Jesus" alone but always add either Christ or Lord to it. Though raised in the same home, obeying the same parents and sharing the same circumstances in early life, yet they show no common familiarity in their reference to Him. Doubtless this was because they now know Him as the risen One. They could use the words of Paul, "though we have known Christ after the flesh, yet now henceforth know we him no more". We would like to know more of the family life of Joseph and Mary, but God has seen fit to allow much of it to be hidden in obscurity. Of this we are sure, none of these brethren were apostles, nor did any of them believe on Him during His public ministry (John 7:5). Their unbelief must have been a great burden upon their mother's heart, more especially if she were left in widowhood, as the absence of any reference to Joseph during the time of Christ's death seems to imply.

When Jude speaks of "bondslave" we must not conclude that he considered his service for Christ was menial slavery. No, he, like every other servant of Christ, knew it to be the most honourable work in which one can be engaged. The chief feature of the bondservant was that he had become the absolute property of his master. During the Lord's public ministry, His brethren like many more were greatly perplexed about His words and works, so we read that His friends attempted "to lay hold on him: for they said, he is beside himself" (Mark 3:21). If, as we may assume, Jude and James were among them, we can be sure they never thought that the day would come when both of them would claim Him to be their Master.

It is interesting to compare Jude with the man after whom he was named, Judah. There was a time when he did not believe in the worth of his half-brother Joseph, and was active in selling him down to Egypt. The time came, however, when he called the one he once rejected his lord and offered to become his bond-slave (Gen 44:33).

With the end in mind of removing all ambiguity as to his identity Jude now says that he is the "brother of James". Obviously his brother was better known, and he was humble enough to play second part to him. We learn from Paul that James was one who saw the Lord shortly after His resurrection (1 Cor 15:7) and no doubt it was then that his conversion took place and all his doubts regarding the Messiahship of Jesus were dispelled. It is possible that he in turn was instrumental in leading the entire family to the same conviction.

After introducing himself, Jude proceeds to describe in a threefold way the addressees:

1.   As beloved of God,

2.   as preserved by Him,

3.   as called by Him.

"Beloved in God" (RV) is a rare statement which occurs nowhere else in Scripture. Our position is usually described as "in Christ", or "in the Lord". Most critics agree that this is the correct text, and if so, then the saints are comforted to know that they are dear to God and that He has set His eternal love upon them. Some have suggested that here Jude is assuring the saints of his love to them as he does in vv.3,17, and 20, but it is better to view God as the subject of all three statements. On no account would the writer allow the terrible corruptions he is about to expose and the consequent judgments upon them to dim in the least the preciousness of divine love. Later he will ask them to keep themselves in the good of it (v.21). All too often occupation with evil workers has a hardening effect upon our hearts, but if we realise that we are loved of God and are dear to Him, then we are preserved from any hardness of spirit. Relationship is involved, for this love is in "God the Father", so the saints are His dear children. In view of this we are not surprised to read the next statement, "preserved in (or for) Jesus Christ". God not only loves, but He also keeps. Again we can see how fitting it is that the readers be set at rest in their minds, and that all dread of the fate awaiting the apostates becoming their lot should be removed. The thunderings of God's judgment are not for His beloved ones, but for His enemies. If we take " for" to be the right idea here, then it follows that the saints are not only kept for their own benefit, but for the glory and joy of "Jesus Christ". If any of them should perish, then He would also be the loser.

They were not only "beloved" and "preserved", but also "called". When divine calling is referred to, it is ever an effectual call. While they responded to it, yet this is not the uppermost thought here. Once called they entered into the good of God's purpose for them. This calling is not a process, but is a momentary experience, and all who have had it are aware of its reality. Although we sing much about the Saviour calling, yet we must realise that in most references to "calling" in the NT it is God who is said to call.

2   In this verse we have Jude's threefold desire for his readers. This is the only greeting in NT epistles where the three words "mercy", "peace" and "love" occur together. In 1 and 2 Timothy we find "grace", "mercy" and "peace", but in most other epistles the salutation is "grace" and "peace". The difference between "grace" and "mercy" appears to be that the former has to do with our unworthiness and the latter with our miseries. There is the thought of pity in "mercy" that is not in "grace". In the terrible conditions prevailing the dear saints would need mercy from God to sustain them and to preserve them from the influences of every evil. His second desire for them is "peace". Perhaps in Scripture "peace" includes more than calm in the soul resulting from salvation, but extends to every form of blessing which delivers from fear and distress. Even though these saints were confronted with scenes demanding God's judgment, yet they could look at them in much the same way as Noah viewed the deluged earth when he was at peace in the ark. His third prayer for them was for " love". He would have them enjoy the love of God and also allow it to flow out in fulness to others. We might well connect "mercy" with being "called", for as regards our experience it began with the mercy of our call; "peace" could equally well be connected with "preserved", for those who are kept have nothing to dread; and of course "love" fits well with "beloved", for the love which we show is but a reflection of the love shown to us by God. Not only does he desire these favours for the saints, but he longs that they might have them in abundance. All that is multiplied is not only increased, but vastly increased.

2.   *The Purpose of the Epistle*
   v. 3

3   Jude discloses to his readers that he was actively engaged in writing to them
on the subject of "the common salvation", but, instead of developing this theme,
he was guided, no doubt by divine intervention, to change his mind and exhort
them to "earnestly contend for the faith". Why this change of plan became needful
we are not directly told, but the following verses would suggest that the rising
tide of apostasy had exposed the saints to grave dangers and made it necessary
that they be warned and instructed so that they be preserved in the solemn
crisis.

It is difficult to decide what aspect of salvation he had before him, whether it
was the initial reception of it or the daily salvation experienced in the lives of the
saints, but this latter aspect is the more prominent one in the epistles which deal
with the last days. In a certain sense he has not wholly abandoned his original
subject, for the closing portion of this epistle does teach us how we can be
preserved, or saved, in the midst of grave dangers.

By addressing them as "beloved" at almost the opening of the epistle he no
doubt assures them of his deep love for them and that it is out of a heart of love
that he is writing his exhortations and warnings to them. He repeats this word
"beloved" in vv.17,20. 3 John is the only other epistle which has this word at its
beginning. Would he have sensed the possibility of his strong exhortations and
bold denunciations being construed by some of the readers as an indication of
his hardness of spirit and even lack of love toward them? It could be that he is
making sure that no such misunderstanding of his heart can arise.

If he dropped the subject of "salvation" this is not because he had lost interest
in it, for he was executing his work with zeal and diligence. It is not difficult to lay
aside something that is of little importance, but when enraptured with some
theme, and its wonders fill the heart, it is painful to be wrenched from it. In this
case the writer's mind was diverted from the grand subject of salvation to the
gloomy one of human corruption and its consequences.

When he describes salvation as "common" he is not implying that it is
something secular, but rather that it is shared by all. The early christians had all
things "common" (Acts 2:44) which meant that they were viewing their
possessions as owned by all their fellow-believers. We might compare the words
of Peter, "like precious faith with us" (2 Pet 1:1). There was no special salvation
for any, not even an apostle, for just as there is no difference in the state and
danger of all men, so God's deliverance is the same for all.

The need to write this epistle arose from his awareness of the onslaught that
the enemy was making against the faith and the responsibility of all who valued
it to rise to its defence. It would never do for the faithful to stand idly by and
allow that which was so dear to them be destroyed. While most references to
"faith" in the NT have to do with the exercise of faith, or faith subjectively, here it

is used objectively and refers to that which is believed. It would appear that by the time this epistle was written the apostolic doctrine had been fully established. The words "once for all" (RV) make this clear. Later he will refer to the "words ... spoken before by the apostles" (RV) which shows that though he himself was not one of them, yet he was conversant with their teaching; and in v.20 he makes mention of "your most holy faith". This same body of doctrine is also called "the truth", especially in the pastoral epistles. The saints are the custodians of this treasure for to them it has been delivered. We read of the " commandment delivered unto them" (2 Pet 2:21), and the things " most surely believed among us", we are told, were delivered "unto us" (Luke 1:1,2). It is our responsibility to "contend" for this vital deposit, but the question may be asked, how are we to do this? Certainly not by physical conflict, for "the weapons of our warfare are not carnal". Those who "earnestly contend" must know the faith for which they contend for no one can defend that about which he stands in doubt. Where conviction is lacking, the contending will cease. We have an illustration of properly earnest contending in the case of Paul when he withstood Peter who was not walking "according to the truth". However, the opponents of the "faith" in Jude were not misguided apostles, but avowed enemies whose only aim was its destruction. In fulfilling the exhortation here the saints would boldly declare the truth in the face of opposition and not refrain from denouncing the evils which had sprung up amongst them. It is ever so easy and pleasant to be tolerant, but the toleration of wrong will eventually lead to its establishment. Had men stood faithfully for the truth of the gospel, the Dark Ages would never have been known.

It could well be that the believers are here called "saints" or "holy ones" because their way of living was in sharp contrast to the corruptions which were abounding amongst those who once claimed to be christians. The custodians of the faith are those who are directed by it, and those whose lives exemplify its teaching.

3. *The Reason for His Writing*
   v.4

4 "For" at the opening of this verse indicates that he is about to tell the readers why he has exhorted them to contend earnestly for the faith. In a condensed statement he informs them that the crisis has arisen because of "certain men". These will be the subject of the main body of the epistle, and will be constantly referred to as "these". Here we have a threefold delineation of them:

1.   They have crept in among the saints;

2.   They are sure of condemnation; and

3.   Their character.

This latter is developed in a threefold way:

a. They are ungodly;
b. They have turned grace into lasciviousness; and
c. They deny their Master and Lord.

These evil workers have penetrated the ranks of the saints by stealth; they wormed their way unnoticed and unsuspected into the society of christians and became numbered with them, and by their corrupt living brought that society into disrepute. Just as the thieves and robbers entered the Jewish fold by climbing "up some other way" (John 10:1), so these men had professed salvation and for a time may have lived like christians, but eventually they manifested their true state and proved themselves to be apostates. Many will ask, Were these men in assembly fellowship, and if so, why were they not excommunicated according to 1 Cor 5? The answer to this is that Jude is writing not to an assembly, though most of his readers were no doubt in assembly fellowship, but to saints in a more general way; hence the judgment in this epistle is not church discipline, but falls directly from God Himself.

The next clause "ordained to this condemnation" may give the impression at first sight that God had pre-determined them for judgment, but this is not the thought here. Rather is it a statement to show that the men he has mentioned, and will later describe, are such as the prophecies of old mark out as subjects of divine condemnation. Presently they appear to escape their deserts, but all the inspired writings make clear that their day of reckoning will come. "Of old" must not be stretched to the eternal past, but must refer to the past of time, nor can it refer to the writings of Peter, for they were too recent. Nowhere in Scripture are predestination and election associated with the lost, but on the other hand, Scripture has left us in no doubt that sin will be punished by God.

In his threefold description of these men, he begins with their ungodliness. Indeed "ungodly" is a kind of key word in this epistle, for it occurs several times and in different forms in v.15. It implies a lack of respect and reverence for God and so marks out these men as those who have "no fear of God before their eyes". The second feature of their character is their wantonness. Because the gospel message tells of God's grace and His forgiveness for the vilest sinners, they assumed that He would continue to show the same grace if they continued to live in sin. This was transforming the whole idea of grace, for as Paul wrote, it was meant to teach us to deny "ungodliness and worldly lusts" (Titus 2:12). They turned liberty into licentiousness, and by their evil ways they brought shame upon the name they professed. The third characteristic of these men is their insubjection to divine authority. They treated with disdain the only Master and the Lord Jesus Christ. Most likely their sins were not in what they said, but rather in how they acted. It is not easy to decide whether "only Master" (RV) refers to God as in the AV, or to Christ as seems to be the case in 2 Pet 2:1. The absence of the article before the second name might suggest that only one person is in the text, but quite often when the Lord and such titles are mentioned alone there is no article, so the meaning cannot be settled by grammar. When "only" is used as here it mostly refers to God as in v.25 and this has led some to see two persons here, so while the AV has not the support of the MSS, yet it does give the true sense. When we think of "Master" we think of "Lord" we think of One who has complete control and our obligation to obey Him.

It will have been noticed that it is in this verse that we begin the section of our epistle which resembles 2 Peter 2, but we must not fetter our minds to the idea that both writings say the same thing, or that one can be interpreted by the other.

Notes

1 Among those who think that it was the apostle Jude who wrote this epistle not all insist that he was a different person from the Lord's brother, for some argue that the "brethren of the Lord" were in fact His cousins; i.e. they identify Jude the apostle with Jude the Lord's brother, and James the less with James the Lord's brother. The chief motive behind their reasoning is to sustain the notion that Mary remained a virgin all her life and never had any children to Joseph. If "the brethren of the Lord" were not His cousins, then these claim, they must be Joseph's children by a previous marriage. Had the writers in the NT wanted to tell us that these men were the cousins of the Lord, they could have used the word "cousin" (*anepsios*) and not the word "brother" (*adelphos*). The obvious conclusion one would reach is that after the birth of Christ Mary and Joseph lived a normal married life and had children. "He knew her not until she brought forth her first-born son" (Matt 1:25), seems to imply that their abnormal relationship ended after the birth of Christ. Jude, Judah and Judas are various forms of the same name which means "praise" as is clear from the words of Leah at the naming of her fourth son when she said, "Now will I praise the Lord" (Gen 29:35). Jacob in his dying song also makes reference to praise when, speaking of Judah, he says "thou art he whom thy brethren shall praise" (Gen 49:8).

The words "servant of Jesus Christ" are used by Paul in Rom 1:1 and in Phil 1:1; Peter also uses them in the opening of his epistles. These writers, unlike Jude, could immediately add a reference to their apostleship. Paul could not do this in Philippians because Timothy, who was linked with him in the address, was not an apostle, but was, like Jude, a "servant". The word "servant" (*doulos*) implies complete submission to the master whose property he is. He could have added that he was "the brother of the Lord", but in modesty, he simply writes, "brother of James".

The change from "sanctified" (*hēgiasmenos*, AV) to "beloved" (*ēgapēmenos*, RV) is well supported, but "beloved in God" is a rare expression. Perhaps Jude views the saints

1.   as regards to God - they are beloved;

2.   as regards Christ - they are preserved.

"Beloved" recurs in vv. 3,17, and 20, and "Preserved" in vv.1,6,13 and 21. Some translations transfer "called"(*klētos*) from the end of the verse and place it before "beloved". Peter does not describe the saints as "called" in either of his epistles, but Paul frequently does.

2 The word "multiplied" (*pléthunó*) occurs in Matt 24:12; 1 Pet 1:2; 2 Pet 1:2. The idea of "peace be multiplied" appears first in Dan 4:1.

3 A different tense is used in the two occurrences of the word "write" (*graphó*) in this verse. The former is the present and suggests a process, whereas the latter is the aorist which implies that it was done at once. There is action as well as earnestness implied in the word "diligence" (*spoudé*). The word "earnestly contend" (*epagónizomai*), only here in the NT, is a strengthened form of "strive" (*agónizomai*, Luke 13:24; 1 Cor 9:25; Col 1:29). "The faith" here is the most notable example of the objective use of *pistis* in the NT. The word "faith" is mostly used for our believing, but here it is used for what we believe. Just as "hope" refers at times to what is hoped for, as in Titus 2:13; Heb 6:18,19, so faith is used here for the body of truth delivered to the saints. There are passages, such as Gal 1:23; 1 Tim 1:4,19; 2:7, where it is doubtful whether faith is subjective or objective but here there can be no doubt. In this we may have a hint that the epistle was written at the end of the apostolic age when the canon was complete, especially when we see that this faith was "once" (*hapax*, "once for all") "delivered" (*paradidómi*) to the saints. We might compare the "holy commandment delivered unto them" (2 Pet 2:21) and "delivered them the decrees" (Acts 16:4). Sometimes the word "delivered" is used in a bad sense, especial in the betrayal by Judas. It is noteworthy that at the end of the epistle some of the same words are used as we have here considered: e.g. "beloved (v.20); "most holy faith" (v.20); "preserved" or "kept" (vv.21,24); "mercy" (v.21); "love" (v.21) and "only" (v.25).

4 The evil men had "crept in unawares" (*pareisduó*) which means that they came in by stealth, or by a side door. The word is found only here in the NT, but we might compare false brethren "unawares brought in" (Gal 2:4). The word "ordained" (*prographó*) means "to write before" (Rom 15:4; Gal 3:1; Eph 3:3). As far back as the days of Enoch God had indicated that such evil workers would be condemned or judged, so it was in truth "of old". The three outstanding features of these men are:

1.   "ungodly" (*asebés*) which indicates that they had no respect for God;

2.   "lascivious" (*aselgeia*) so there was no restraint in their wantonness;

3.   "denying the Lord" (*arneomai*) and they disowned the Lord (*despotés*).

Though "God" is not in the original here, yet the AV, where it is added, may be giving the proper sense. "Only" points in that direction. Those who are guided by 2 Pet 2:1 see only one person here, who is both Master and Lord.

II. Warning and Denunciation (vv.5-19)

v.5   "I will therefore put you in remembrance, though ye once knew this, how that the Lord, having saved the people out of the land of Egypt, afterward destroyed them that believed not.

v.6   And the angels which kept not their first estate, but left their own habitation, he hath reserved in everlasting chains under darkness unto the judgment of the great day.

v.7   Even as Sodom and Gomorrha, and the cities about them in like manner, giving themselves over to fornication, and going after strange flesh, are set forth for an example, suffering the vengeance of eternal fire.

v.8 Likewise also these *filthy* dreamers defile the flesh, despise dominion, and speak evil of dignities.
v.9 Yet Michael the archangel, when contending with the devil he disputed about the body of Moses, durst not bring against him a railing accusation, but said, The Lord rebuke thee.
v.10 But these speak evil of those things which they know not: but what they know naturally, as brute beasts, in those things they corrupt themselves.
v.11 Woe unto them! for they have gone in the way of Cain, and ran greedily after the error of Balaam for reward, and perished in the gainsaying of Core.
v.12 These are spots in your feasts of charity, when they feast with you, feeding themselves without fear: clouds *they* are without water, carried about of winds; trees whose fruit withereth, without fruit, twice dead, plucked up by the roots..
v.13 Raging waves of the sea, foaming out of their own shame., wandering stars, to whom is reserved the blackness of darkness for ever.
v.14 And Enoch also, the seventh from Adam, prophesied of these, saying, Behold, the Lord cometh with ten thousand of his saints,
v.15 To execute judgment upon all, and to convince all that are ungodly among them of all their ungodly deeds which they have ungodly committed, and of all their hard *speeches* which ungodly sinners have spoken against him.
v.16 These are murmurers, complainers, walking after their own lusts; and their mouth speaketh great swelling *words*, having men's persons in admiration because of advantage.
v.17 But, beloved, remember ye the words which were spoken before of the apostles of our Lord Jesus Christ;
v.18 How that they told you there should be mockers in the last time, who should walk after their own ungodly lusts.
v.19 These be they who separate themselves, sensual, having not the Spirit."

1. *Examples of God's Judgment* vv.5-7

5 Since God has predicted "of old" the fate of evil-doers, Jude has no difficulty finding examples of those who had sinned and were judged for their wickedness. The unbelieving Israelites, the fallen angels and the Sodomites are his selection. A thoughtful consideration of the samples he cites will reveal how apropos these three cases are to his purpose, for the apostates he has mentioned in v.4 are seen to be guilty of the sins which brought down the wrath of God in the past. The Israelites who fell in the wilderness were an example of the "ungodly" who have no regard for God; the men of Sodom must ever be a warning against "lasciviousness"; and the angels who rebelled against divine authority "denied" their only Master. All this will become more evident when we reach v.8.

Those who attempt to prove that Jude copied Peter or vice versa find themselves in great straits when it comes to explaining why the two writings differ so much. We can account for a divergence in detail if one is quoting from memory, but for Jude to include the Israelites who fell in the wilderness and overlook the greatest example of judgment in the Scriptures, the Deluge, is not easily explained, especially if he was seeking to copy the apostle Peter. Stranger still is the fact that he does not even follow chronological order, for he mentions the Israelites before the cities of the plain, and the angels which should have come first, he places in the middle. Peter not only writes in chronological order, but speaks of the deliverance of Noah and Lot, whereas Jude is silent regarding any being saved, so neither Joshua, Caleb, Lot, nor the elect angels are mentioned in his epistle. The deliverance of the righteous is not his theme, but rather the dark clouds and thunderings of judgment without a silver lining are before him. Perhaps this explains why he omits all reference to the Deluge, for in that story the ark and the saving of Noah's household occupy a major part.

Jude is sure that his readers were not ignorant of what he is about to write for he is aware that they were thoroughly acquainted with the Scriptures. This appears to be the meaning of the better text which changes "once knew this" (AV) to "know all things once for all" (RV). Not that they had nothing more to learn, but that they were no novices in the study of the OT. All they required for him to do was to call to their remembrance what was already stored in their minds. How often do well-known historic facts take on a new interest when they are applied by the Holy Spirit to present circumstances. Possibly few, if any, who read this epistle would ever have thought of finding in these early examples of judgment a proof that the evil workers of their day were sure to be subjects of the wrath of God. Because He is unchanging in His character, He will ever deal with evil whether in the case of the most favoured people, or the most exalted of His creatures.

No people ever experienced a more wonderful deliverance than that of the Israelites who were redeemed out of Egypt. It affected them socially, religiously and nationally, and was intended by God to be an object lesson to the nations of His power and might. It is difficult to imagine that the sweet singers on the banks of the Red Sea would have within them "an evil heart of unbelief", but when the vital test came this proved to be the case. The reference here is to Num 14 and to the refusal by the nation to enter the land to which they had been journeying, even when brought to its very borders. Their case was not one of mere timidity, or of feeling their helplessness, though they did feel this, but rather one of rebellion against God and one which demonstrated their apostasy from Him. God swore in His wrath that they would never enter their inheritance, but instead would die in the wilderness. In our verse we have two works of God-one of great mercy, and a second one of great judgment, for He is able to save and to destroy (Jas 4:12). Perhaps this is why "afterward" is translated " in the second place" by JND and others.

The application of this disaster to the evil workers is obvious, for they too had professed salvation and for a time at least seemed to enjoy their deliverance, but to the astonishment of many they had proved themselves to be "ungodly". In their hearts they had turned back to what they formerly valued and turned away from God and His ways. They ceased to fear Him and disregarded Him as though He no longer existed. There is a close link between unbelief and apostasy, for of this people it is written "they turned back and tempted God, and limited the Holy One of Israel" (Ps 78:41).

6   The second example of God's judgment is that of the angels which sinned, for they present to Jude's mind a further proof that the evil workers will also be dealt with in due time. Once we enter the realm of heaven and try to establish what has taken place there, we are greatly limited in our information, but it can be understood from a number of references in Scripture that these created beings, in spite of their high position, were capable of sinning. Their chief was undoubtedly Satan and he led the rebellion by attempting to be like the Most High. Pride was at the root of his and their fall, so they were not satisfied to remain in their position, or estate, but left it to reach for something higher, and in so doing fell under divine wrath. Their "estate" may refer to their first position, but the word used here is translated "principality" in Eph 6:12, so it may well describe not only a first position, but a position of high dignity. To suggest that they would give up such a wonderful state of glory to become companions of women on earth, seems to assign to them the grace that was manifest in Christ when He stooped to earth to become our Saviour. No, their sin was not in coming down, but in reaching up, which resulted in their being cast down by God. Their habitation was undoubtedly heaven where they dwelt in the light of God's glory. Once they fell, then they lost their liberty and became bound, and at the same time lost the light of heaven and were confined to darkness. They are described by Paul as "principalities and powers, as world rulers of this darkness" (Eph 6:12 RV). In this bondage of darkness they will remain until the day when they will be judged and consigned to the lake of fire. Like all the wicked they are not yet in their final abode, but are kept without hope of escape until their end is reached. The implication of the verse is that just as the highest created beings were judged for their sin, so surely will the evil workers suffer their just doom.

It is somewhat amazing to read such words as "angels ... kept not their own principality" (RV). This shows that they became discontented with their lot, and at the same time dissatisfied with their Creator's purpose for them. Their sin was not due to lack of intelligence, for they are ever represented as intelligent beings, nor did it arise from an inherited depraved nature, for they were as perfect as the handiwork of God, neither was it because they were allocated an inferior position, for they were much more lofty than man upon the earth. We cannot blame God for creating beings who could sin, for it was never His will that they should do so. However, it has been His purpose to have around Him free and responsible agents who would willingly give Him the glory due to His name. Even we ourselves, who are made in His image, can never find companionship or satisfaction in mere machines. They obey us, but we cannot thank them for this because they can do nothing else. The joy of God's heart is to find obedience, and devotion to Him rising spontaneously from the hearts of His own. He found this to perfection in the person of His Son. Only when freewill steps aside and rebels against God has it ceased to be a blessing to His creatures.

A vast number of writers connect this passage with Gen 6 and claim that it was when angels (sons of God) left heaven in order to obtain wives from the stock of

Adam that they left their own habitation. It is not easy for some of us to believe that sexless spirits would lust after women and that they would vacate heaven in order to gratify their passion. It takes some stretch of imagination to conceive that bodiless beings could be plagued with fleshly lusts. Is it not strange that it took almost 1000 years for them to behold the beauty of women? Why did they not take hold of Eve, for they witnessed her creation, and she must have been the most beautiful of all women? Are we to think that their heavenly abode meant so little to them as to leave it to become subjects of the limitations of a cursed earth?

The second idea propounded from this passage in Genesis is that the giants were the product of this uniting of angels and women and were the evidence of this abnormal relationship. Support for this is supposed to be found in the meaning of the Hebrew word for giants (*nephilim*) which they say means "fallen ones", but according to Gesenius the more likely meaning is "fallers upon". Their treatment of the weaker ones gave rise to their name. It is clear from the passage that the giants were on earth before the "men of renown" and were not the fruit of the imagined relationship. Giants appear in the days of Israel in the wilderness and later in David's day. Are we to believe that there were several falls of angels, and must we believe that every time we learn of any one of massive stature and physique that some angel has begotten him? Even in nature around us God has so overruled that while different species can be crossed and produce such as mules, it ends there, for no mule can reproduce. Strange then if angels and women unite to produce giants, that we read of the sons of giants. All this is so absurd that it is scarcely worthy of an attempt to overthrow it. Angels sinned and were cast down from their excellence, their humiliation followed their sin, but was not the cause of it.

There has been much difficulty understanding the various positions said to be occupied by Satan and his hosts: we read of him as being in heaven and having access to God (Rev 12:10), of his going about as a roaring lion (1 Pet 5:8), of him falling from heaven (Luke 10:18), of his turning into an angel of light (2 Cor 11:14), of his being bound in the pit and of his being cast into the lake of fire (Rev 20:2,10). Much confusion which arises from these various statements is removed when we realise that God can speak of future events as though they were already fulfilled. While Satan is not omnipresent, yet he has agents everywhere and what is done by his agents is viewed as done by him.

7   The third example of judgment is the well-known case of the cities of the plain. They are ever held up as the stark exhibition of divine wrath against fleshly sins. The inhabitants of these cities threw off all restraint and let their passions drive them into the basest of sins, so that to this day sodomy is used as equivalent to homosexuality. The climax of these evil men mentioned in v.4 is here reached, for in the RV they are linked by the words "with these", so the "fornication, and going after strange flesh" describes both the men of Sodom and the evil workers.

This is the first of seven references to "these"; see vv. 8,10,12,14,16 and 19. Some have tried to distinguish this first one from the others and make it refer to the angels, but this is inconsistent with the normal style of the epistle and leads to all kinds of strange ideas. The fire that consumed these cities is viewed here as eternal and displaying the nearest that was ever seen on earth to the final abode of the lost-the lake of fire.

We must notice the development in these examples of judgment. In the first the sinners were destroyed; in the second they were bound in darkness, but in the third, they are undergoing suffering in the fire. The apostates also will be destroyed by physical death, like the Israelites, will be kept in darkness until the judgment of the great white throne, and then finally be cast into the lake of fire. This may be another reason why Jude departed from chronological order.

2. *The Application of these Examples* vv.8-11

8 For the second time we are reminded of the "certain men" of v.4 by the word "these". They are described for us in a threefold way.

1. They "defile the flesh";

2. they set aside lordship;

3. they speak evil of dignities.

In the first charge there is a reference to their minds, for they are called "dreamers", so are living in the world of imagination. It is not alone while asleep that they dream, but they are "day-dreamers" as well as night- dreamers. While there is no word in the original corresponding to the word "filthy" in the AV, yet it is obvious from the context that the substance of their dreams was impure. They were strangers to the "pure mind" mentioned by Peter (2 Pet 3:1), but were at home with the "vain imagination" of the Gentile world. We cannot be too careful of our thoughts, for if they be centred on any object, it will not be long until that object will captivate our hearts. Here these men "defile the flesh" and so are like the Sodomites. They failed to guard the citadel of their minds and were carried away with the lusts of the flesh. How often men make excuses for their sins and claim they are powerless to resist temptation, but if all were known they feasted their thoughts on the evil for a time and then when opportunity came along to commit it they readily responded. Is it not amazing to find those who once professed the name of Christ being linked with the corruption of Sodom? This is implied in the words "Yet in like manner these also" (RV). Instead of grace teaching them to deny "worldly lusts", they assumed it gave them licence to indulge in them, so they gave full rein to the cravings of their fallen nature. It is almost unbelievable the depths to which some have sunk while claiming to be christians. The will of God for His own is their sanctification (1 Thess 4:3), and their bodies are "the temple of the Holy Spirit" (1 Cor 6:19), so it follows that they should seek divine help to overcome every desire of the flesh, and "make not provision for the flesh to fulfil the lusts thereof" (Rom 13:14).

The second charge against these "dreamers" is their setting aside of Lordship. This seems to imply that they have no regard for authority, especially divinely-constituted authority, so they are in essence rebels. In this respect they are like the Israelites who were not only unbelievers, but were also rebels, for they rebelled and would not go over and possess the land. They had no regard for either their leader Moses, or even for "the angel of his presence" who had promised to be with them. It is not easy deciding here exactly what "dominion" these dreamers despised. Some would limit it to spiritual powers, while others think it refers to those in authority in the assembly, and some think that earthly magistrates are alone in view. One thing is clear in the Scriptures and cannot be denied, it is that God ever establishes rule and sets over His creatures those who will control them. Even the heavenly hosts have their superiors; so too on earth, whether we look at the nations or the churches of God, it is His will that there should be those in responsibility. Anarchy has no place in His domain, nor does He condone rebellion against those whom He placed in authority. It has been well said that even bad rule is better than no rule. It might be best in this case to leave open the exact Lordship here involved and not attempt to specify any particular sphere of it, for even the powers that be are ordained of God and all other authority has Him as its origin. Those, who like these dreamers want to indulge the flesh, are usually the first to disregard those who would attempt to turn them from their evil ways.

The third accusation made against these men is their blasphemy of "dignities". Here we can be more specific, for the reference is to created spiritual powers, whether good or evil. In this, their evil speaking, they are more manifest, for this is not a state of mind nor an attitude, but is outward and known to all. The "dreamers" are here seen talking in their sleep, but what leaves their lips is as evil as what is in their hearts. They feel free to use their unbridled tongue in slandering these "glories" and forget that such beings are in a loftier position than the highest of men, so even if they have fallen, as is the case of Satan, they are to be spoken of with reserve and respect. Satan and his agents may slander the saints, and they do, but this gives no liberty for mortal man to blaspheme him or his associates. Although the rebellion of Satan and those who took sides with him have changed his position and diminished his glory, yet he is a powerful being and one which God allows to fulfil His purpose.

9 In sharp contrast to these slanderers of "dignities" Jude cites the case of Michael and his conflict with Satan at the burial of Moses. It is useless for us to enquire where the details of this episode were obtained, for like some other items of information, such as the names of the magicians who withstood Moses (2 Tim 3:8), we know not how they were obtained. It would seem that there was much handed down by tradition that was not put into the Scriptures. Some would tell us that Jude found this story in a book now lost called the *Assumption of Moses*, but we need not think that he resorted to any such source in order to learn what he here writes. Many suggestions have been made as to why Satan was in dispute with Michael over the body of Moses. In the narrative in Deut 34 there is no mention of this contention, nor of the presence of Michael at the burial, but simply, that he died according to the word of the Lord, and that He buried him. The arch-enemy would have slain Moses at his birth, made life difficult for him especially in the wilderness, and now even at his death the same opposition is manifest.

We might well ask: What claim had Satan on the body of Moses, or for that matter, on any human body? It would appear from the wording here that Satan claimed to have a legal right to the body, for it is in fact the proof of death, and he has the power of death (Heb 2:14). Obviously he was opposed to the secret burial of it, most likely because the Israelites would have embalmed it and turned it into an object of worship. However, we must give them credit, for not making the bones of Joseph an idol, for though they carried them with them, they apparently did nothing other than bury them as he requested them to do. Had they known of the whereabouts of the body of Moses, they would have been anxious to carry it over with them into the land. We must leave the matter there, and concentrate our attention on the main reason for this reference to the body of Moses which is to demonstrate how respectful even the archangel Michael was when in dispute with Satan. Although he was in a superior position and had greater power than Satan, yet he refused to exercise either his strength or his speech to belittle him, but left the matter in the Lord's hands and said, "The Lord rebuke thee". These same words appear in Zech 3:2 where Satan is seen standing to resist Joshua the high priest. The filthy garments in which the priest was clothed may have given Satan a basis for attack, for well he knew that such attire would not be allowed in the presence of God. Doubtless in the prophecy Joshua represents the nation, but that are no grounds for thinking that the body of Moses is to be understood figuratively as representing the people of God.

It is interesting to note that the time is coming when Michael and Satan will again be in conflict. The war in heaven will bring into collision these two mighty powers, but then Michael will not be meek and yielding, but he and his hosts will expel Satan and his associates from their present position and cast them down to earth (Rev 12:7-9). Even the highest of God's servants know to wait His time to deal with their enemies. We might be tempted to exert our strength against those who are doing Satan's work, but we must ever remember the words of Scripture, "Vengeance is mine; I will repay, saith the Lord" (Rom 12:19). It is not unusual to hear people calling Satan all kinds of derogatory names and depicting him in grotesque forms, but the saints must not become involved in such matters, for they know something of the extent of his power and influence. It would appear that even when angels or men fall from their high station they are still to be treated with the same respect as though they were unchanged. David always treated Saul as the "Lord's anointed", and while all in Israel knew that the king was rejected by God and would soon lose his throne, yet he was still to be treated as though he was enjoying divine favour.

Some have viewed this passage differently and taught that the "railing accusation" refers to Michael refusing to charge Satan with railing, rather than his blaspheming Satan, but the context favours the view we have taken and most agree with it.

10   Once more we are directed to the apostates by the occurrence of "these". This is the third time the men of v.4 are referred to in this way. Here their conduct is seen to be in sharp contrast to that of Michael. Thus before he was introduced in v.8, and now after he has been set forth as an example, his treatment of spiritual powers is entirely contrary to theirs. They speak evil of those unseen powers of which they know nothing. What they gain by their slander, either for themselves or for others, is difficult to imagine, but their evil hearts take pleasure in defaming someone, so the spiritual powers become the target of their unbridled tongues. They take advantage of every opportunity to defame and to display their contempt for "dignities". Not being spiritual themselves they cannot possibly understand the spiritual realm and should have been content to let the unseen and unknown powers alone, but they prefer to display their hatred toward them in the most unreasonable manner, so they are not only ignorant, but malicious. It is wisdom to be silent about that which to us is unknown and make no comments either favourable or derogatory about it.

There is a sphere with which they were fully acquainted, namely the flesh. Their natural instinct enabled them to know this realm apart from any schooling either from their fellows, or from God. Alas, even in this the natural and lower side of their being, they manifested their evil propensities by the misuse they made of their bodies. Their knowledge failed to preserve them from corruption or to enable them to rise above the brute beast which also has fleshly desires. It is expected that man, made in the image of God, will be respectful of his body and not allow it to be the instrument to fulfil unlawful lusts. These men, however, knew nothing about restraint, but were abandoned to the gratification of their beastly passions, and in so doing, brought about the inevitable result-their own destruction. They lived like beasts and had to share the same fate as they.

The principle of comparing man with the brute is quite often found in Scripture. "Be ye not as the horse, or as the mule" (Ps 32:9); "Jeshurun waxed fat, and kicked" (Deut 32:15); "we put bits in the horses' mouths, that they may obey us" (Jas 3:3); "A wild ass ... that snuffeth up the wind" (Jer 2:24) are a few samples of this. The more carnal a man is, the more like the beast he will become; the more spiritual he is, the more of the character of God he will manifest.

11   The certainty of the doom of these beastly men is clearly implied in this verse, for the three examples are selected to show that men of former times who were marked by the same features as they, fell under God's judgment. It is only here in the epistles that we have "woe" in denunciation used except when Paul uses it of himself if he failed to preach the gospel (1 Cor 9:16). It occurs often in the Gospels and also in Revelation where sometimes it is an expression of grief. Jude is so incensed at the corruption of these men and their influence that he writes as did some of the prophets of old using strong language seldom employed in this dispensation of grace. The cases he cites were all so incorrigible that none of them ever repented, but remained fixed to his chosen path. It must be stressed again that in this epistle it is not the restoration of these evil men that is attempted, for there is no hope for them, but rather the deliverance of the true saints from their evil influence.

In grouping together these three examples he again departs from chronological order, but puts them in the order suited to the development of the evils he has already denounced. Thus the way of Cain was the way of unbelief as was the sin of Israel in the wilderness mentioned in v.5; the error of Balaam corresponds to the sin of Sodom, for he managed to corrupt the Israelites in the wilderness; and the gainsaying of Core links back with the rebellion of the angels in v.6. There may be a progression in these samples, for where there is no faith as in the case of Cain, quite often corruption follows, and where corruption is present, quite often rebellion will ensue. The three men mentioned, all involved in religion, were like the apostates. Cain was a false worshipper; Balaam a false prophet; and Core (Korah) was a false priest. There is a gradation in the verse, for "gone" implies embarking on a course; "ran greedily" implies reckless abandonment to the course; and "perished" shows that the course leads to perdition.

There is much difference of opinion as to what is implied in "the way of Cain". Not a few speak of it as the "bloodless way" of approach to God and make him the first example of those who would seek to obtain favour with God by the fruit of their own hands. They have no doubt that if Cain had brought the right offering he would have found acceptance with God. However, when we turn to Gen 4, there is no mention of "blood", not even of the victim offered by Abel, but rather of its "fat", and stranger still, we read that God had respect unto Abel and to his offering, words which clearly imply that the offering was accepted because of the man who offered it, rather than the man being accepted on the grounds of his victim. The fact is that the two brothers were attempting to offer to God a "present", for that is the meaning given to the word used throughout Genesis. Even if Cain had obtained a lamb from his brother, he could not have been accepted by God, for he was offering without faith, and "without faith it is impossible to please" God (Heb 11:6). God wants no presents from the wicked, nor from those who have no confidence in Him. The "way of Cain" must extend to more than one event in his life and seems to cover his entire course including his murder of his only brother, and the life he lived afterwards, attempting to make himself happy without God by inventions which helped him feel independent of His aid. Nothing said to him could change him, but though reasoned with and shown the way to go, yet he persisted in his self-chosen course.

There is no clear statement in this epistle that these false men were guilty of persecuting the saints, but if they followed the way of Cain, this would possibly be their practice. If they did not slay them literally, they were attempting to kill them spiritually. Toward the end of the epistle those rescued from them are seen as being pulled out of the fire. As far as is known the entire race which sprang from Cain followed in his footsteps, so he not only perished himself, but was the cause of many more landing in destruction.

The evil workers not only resembled Cain in their conduct, but also showed a similarity to Balaam in their covetousness and immorality. He was a false prophet and they too speak falsely. In pursuit of his reward from Balak and his lust for honours offered, he was prepared to curse Israel. Not even the miraculous speech of the beast upon which he rode could deter him from his ambition. At length he was allowed to go, but with the restriction that he would speak only what the Lord put into his mouth. In him we have an example of goodly words being spoken by a wicked man. Had he spoken from his own heart, the message would have been different. He appeared to be close to reality with his altar, sacrifices and sublime addresses. God had taught him on the way that He could as easily have used the ass to speak instead of Balaam, so if Balaam said true things, and he did, this was no credit to him. It is obvious that all the fair speeches which left his lips, in no way changed his heart, for secretly he gave Balak the secret of how to destroy Israel, and as we all know this was by luring them into immorality and idolatry. It is not easy deciding whether the reference here is to his greed of gain, or whether his error involves also his immoral teaching, perhaps the emphasis here is upon the former. One of the worst features of these apostates denounced by Jude is that they would use their ability in religious things for their own personal gain. There were those at Crete who were "teaching things which they ought not, for filthy lucre's sake" (Titus 1:11). Satan's ministers like to be well paid for their work, and do not always believe in sacrificing their time and talents just for the sake of their cause. Balaam would never have journeyed to Moab if Balak had made no attractive offer to him. It is also interesting to note how often in Scripture covetousness and immorality are brought together, for to a great extent, the latter is a form of the former.

Jude finds in the camp of Israel in the wilderness his third example of these men who have been so variously described. Core (Korah) was a Levite and as such had his service determined for him by the Lord, but, like the angels of v.6, he was not satisfied with the position assigned to him and attempted to become a priest. In his ambition to fill the highest position in Israel, he ventured to blame Moses and Aaron for appointing themselves to their respective responsibilities. He was not afraid to speak evil of dignities, nor did he acknowledge that these men were divinely appointed. Moses even said to him, "what is Aaron, that ye murmur against him?", implying that being high-priest was not the result of his own efforts. In seeking the priesthood, he had underestimated the favour shown him as one who had charge of the tabernacle. In spite of faithful speaking by Moses, he was prepared to face the test and fill his censer to offer incense before the Lord, with the result that the earth swallowed him and those who were with him. His rebellion was short lived, and his gainsaying was quickly silenced. There may be more in "gainsaying" than mere words, for the same word used here is in Prov 17:11 LXX translated "rebellion", so acts as well as speech may be included. There can be no doubt that the saints contending for the faith would have to be prepared to face opposition and a rebellious spirit, and would have to rely on God to defend His cause, as did Moses in an earlier day.

3.   *A Threefold Description of the Evil-workers vv.12-19*

Having denounced these men by saying "woe unto them", and having shown examples of those like them in OT days who were judged for their ways, it is to be expected that Jude would be frank and disclose to the saints as clearly as possible their characteristics, for they must be known if their evil influence is to be avoided. This is exactly what he does in the verses we are about to consider. In the execution of his purpose, he searches the universe for metaphors which he skilfully uses to bring their features home to the minds of the saints in a vivid way. There are few other parts of Scripture where such a variety of figures is used in so short a space. The divisions of this section are settled by the three occurrences of "these". These divisions decrease in length, so the first is the longest and extends to v.15, the second is shorter and ends at v.18, and the third is shortest of all, being only v.19. If we examine these sections we will discover that the first reveals the character of these men and their judgment prophesied by Enoch; the second, tells of their speech and the warning of the apostles of their coming in the last days; and the third speaks of the divisions they cause, and their real deficiency-they are devoid of the Spirit.

12   There are six metaphors in vv.12-13; two of these are taken from the sea-"sunken rocks" and "surging waves"; two are from the sky-"showerless clouds" and "shooting stars"; and two are from the land-"shepherding themselves" and "stubbed-up trees". There existed in the apostolic days and for some time later what are here called "love-feasts". These social gatherings were a means to bring together in a friendly way all the saints in a locality, so that the rich could share their bounty with those less well favoured and that mutual fellowship would be fostered. Whether they were an attempt to imitate the passover of the upper room, we cannot say, but even at Corinth, there was a meal associated with the Lord's supper, and Paul had to correct their misbehaviour regarding this in his epistle. Quite early the Supper was divided from these love-feasts, lest the abuse seen at Corinth would re-appear, but still they continued into the second century, but again because of their abuse, they were abolished and nothing more is heard of them. The evil men referred to as "these" were wont to frequent such gatherings and professed to be one with the saints and to share in the feasting. Perhaps it is mainly to such gatherings they are said to have "crept in". We must note the absence of any reference to the local church in this epistle and be careful not to teach that these corrupt men were in happy fellowship in the assembly. They may have been identified with the saints and appeared to be one with them for a time, but their state as here described disqualifies them from church membership. In John's epistle the false men went out from the saints, because they were not of them, but here we have a different state for the love-feasts are sailing on dangerous seas with sunken rocks beneath them. This epistle as it were, charts the sea so that the saints would be alerted to detect the presence of these "sunken rocks". The gatherings of the saints gave great opportunities for the spread of their evil teaching and for their evil ways to be introduced to the simple in an underhand way. "Evil communications corrupt good manners" (1 Cor 15:33), so it is dangerous to associate with those who spread defilement either by what they say, or what they practise. The second metaphor is taken from pastoral life. These men "shepherded themselves" instead of shepherding the flock, so in this they displayed both their independence and their selfishness. The words of the prophet Ezekiel may have been in the writer's mind: "Woe be to the shepherds of Israel that do feed themselves! should not the shepherds feed the flocks?" (Ezek 34:2). Certainly they breathe the same sentiment. In spite of their practices being so diverse from "those of the true saints", they feel no embarrassment when they meet with them, for they feast without fear; so they are daring, because they regard no authority nor feel the need for any help from others. There may be a hint here that they not only eat, but do so to excess. The rich pasture of the well-spread table was more to them than help for their souls.

The third figure, "clouds ... without water", shows the disappointment these men caused to those who expected refreshment from them. To the man in the East, who has much need of the rain, the sight of a cloud in the sky is no small encouragement, but, as is the case in our figure, if the clouds blow away with the wind and no water falls, then all his hopes are dashed to the ground. These men put up a promising show, but empty pretence, be it ever so loud, has nothing to offer anyone, and it is folly to expect anything from it. They are very different from Moses who could say, "My doctrine shall drop as the rain, my speech shall distil as the dew, as the small rain upon the tender herb" (Deut 32:2); and from the word which goeth forth out of the mouth of the Lord which falls like rain and snow (Isa 55:10).

The fact that they are "carried about of winds" is an indication of their instability and their tendency to change. It was the desire of Paul that the Ephesian saints would not be "tossed to and fro, and carried about with every wind of doctrine" (Eph 4:14); and that the Hebrews "be not carried about with divers and strange doctrines" (Heb 13:9). Clouds laden with water move slowly; high flying and light clouds soon vanish leaving not even a trace of their appearance.

For the next metaphor he leaves the sky and returns to earth, this time to the orchard and fruit trees. These seducers are likened to autumnal fruit trees at that season of the year when, if they have borne fruit, it will be ready for gathering. The AV gives the idea that the fruit they have borne has become withered, but most agree with the RV that the thought expressed is a reference to the time of year, rather than a description of the state of the fruit. It is not that the trees are without fruit, but that they are without it at the end of autumn or at the approach of winter. Just as the clouds had no water, the trees had no fruit, so both prove disappointing. Perhaps we should make a difference between being disappointed by clouds and disappointed with fruit trees. In the former case it is widely shared, but in the latter case it is the owner alone who bears it. There is only one purpose for fruit trees and that is that they bear fruit; if they fail in this, then they are useless and must be rooted up. These men, illustrated by barren trees, are in danger of being removed by God's hand in judgment. We might compare the fig tree in Luke 13 which was threatened with the axe if it continued to be barren. When trees are said to be "twice dead", they are worse than fruitless, for a tree may be barren one year, and bear fruit the next, but dead trees could never become fruitful. Viewed in the winter, fruit trees have the appearance of being dead, but when spring time comes they are resurrected, as it were, and bud forth full of life; not so twice-dead trees, for they are not only dead for the winter, but so dead that they will never live again. In this "twice dead" some see a reference first, to their dead state as sinners like all other men, and second, to their death as apostates. Just as the true believer has life in a double sense, so these men have death in a double sense. The third fact stated about the trees is that they are "plucked up by the roots", so these men are seen as cumberers of the ground. They are completely removed from their position and from all possibility of survival. Furthermore, when trees are uprooted then the real cause of their barrenness can be discovered, for quite often it is due to disease in the roots. Again we cannot fail to notice that Jude holds out no hope for these men, he ever leaves them in hopeless doom. All that "grubbed up" trees can expect is a place in the fire.

13   Jude turns again to the sea for his next illustration, this time to its wild billows and its belching foam to which he likens the shame which arises from the activity of these corrupt men. He may be making a reference to Isaiah: "The wicked are like the troubled sea, when it cannot rest, whose waters cast up mire and dirt" (57:20). The froth and foam from such raging waves may look white and clean as they rise, but when they recede, they leave behind them the mire and dirt. These men, like them, may have appeared for a time to be upholding purity and godliness, but at length their true character became manifest as one of disgrace and shame, or shames for the word is plural. The figure of waves immediately suggests to our minds restlessness, pride, and lawlessness. These features marked the libertines here condemned, but just as the angry sea accomplishes nothing for itself, so all that results from their efforts is their own disgrace.

The sixth of these metaphors here is taken from the night-sky. Jude can see in the "wandering stars" a metaphor of these impostors, for they too appeared to shine for a time, but suddenly disappeared into the darkness. Many have put up a grand show at the start of their profession of christianity, but in a short while they gave it up. Some of these turned out to be, not only unreal, but avowed enemies of the truth. It can be staggering to young believers to discover that those they had trusted and even companied with should turn so drastically. Most of them attempt to find some excuse for the change, and even blame ill treatment of the saints for their defection. The "shooting stars", here referred to, never return to shine again, for they are enveloped in eternal darkness. They are not merely eclipsed by a cloud for a time and then shine as bright as ever when it passes, but they plunge into the dark without leaving a trace of light behind them. These false lights who were troubling the saints are seen to join the angels that sinned in the doom of eternal darkness which here is said to be preserved for them. They live in the dark and die in the dark and in it they will dwell for ever.

14   In order to vindicate the reality of the threats of judgment which he has made regarding these men, Jude cites one of the oldest prophecies extant and one which was uttered before the Deluge. The words of Enoch the seventh from Adam make clear that even in those distant days God was warning of the fate that would befall ungodly livers and the occasion when it would be executed. How the writer came into possession of this prophecy we do not know. Some will tell us that he obtained it from the apocryphal book of Enoch, but as we have already pointed out, there is great difficulty deciding the date of that composition. If it appeared about the second century AD then it could not have been Jude's source. Just as Paul was able to name the magicians who opposed Moses, though they are not included in the Exodus narrative (2 Tim 3:8), Jude can quote this prophecy without disclosing to us where or how he came to possess it. We are sure that Enoch spoke these words and that now they are included in this epistle, they are part of the inspired word of God. There may be some special reason, apart from making clear that this Enoch was not the descendant of Cain who bore that name, that he is called the "seventh from Adam". "Seven" being the complete number may have suggested to him that these words were uttered at a time when evil had become all but universal. We know that Enoch was contemporary with Adam for over three hundred years, so the corruption which resulted in the flood had developed in very early times, even during the lifetime of our first-parents. While the fulfilment of this prophecy is still future, yet it was spoken no doubt as a warning to the antediluvians, and was fulfilled in a minor way at the time of the Flood. The Lord Himself likens the days before His coming in judgment to the days of Noah, and in this way links together the two times of judgment. Just as Abraham was made aware of the destruction of the cities of the plain, so Enoch, who walked with God, was given an insight into the coming judgment, not only of that pending shortly after his day, but also in the remote future.

The prophecy divides into three parts:

1.   the Lord's coming and those who will accompany Him;

2.   the consequences of this coming-judgment and conviction of the ungodly;

3.   what He will judge-deeds and words.

The "coming" here should be compared with 2 Thess 1:7-10 where the Lord is seen coming in flaming fire to destroy those who are unbelievers. The myriads of holy ones who will accompany Him may refer to the believers of this age, or may be a reference to the holy angels, for from other Scriptures we learn that both will be in His army in that day.

15   The purpose of the Lord's coming is twofold: to execute judgment and to convict the evil-doers of their deeds and words. Quite often men are deceived into thinking that their sins are unnoticed by God, and because He does not judge sin immediately it is committed, that He has forgotten all about it. Even the saints in Jude's day may have been surprised that the deceivers were allowed to continue with their hypocrisy, but the day of reckoning is coming and then all will receive the due reward of their deeds. Not only will actions be judged, but words as well. The hard speeches may not be as injurious to the body as some of the cruel deeds, but nonetheless, they can be most hurtful, especially to the meek and tender saints of God. Some imagine that their words are not important, but they do reveal the state of the heart and quite often show the hatred in it to the Lord Himself. The apostates may not have stood forth and blasphemed the name of the Lord, but in slandering the faithful, they were belittling Him who is not ashamed to be identified with them. The threefold repetition of "ungodly" in this verse is no doubt meant to connect the judged with the "ungodly" of v.4 as well as to show why these evils have been committed and why these hard speeches have been uttered-both are because the perpetrators have no fear or reverence for God. The conviction here is not that they might repent, for when the judgment comes the time for repentance is passed; rather it is to show them why they have been judged. All who leave the bar of God will be convinced that they have had a just trial and that what has befallen them is what their sins deserved. Men in this world are slow to learn the reality of sin, and those who do will seek to have it forgiven, but in that day all the wicked will stand condemned in their own conscience as well as in the sight of God.

16   In this second description of these men, their speech, rather than their deeds, is emphasised. The words "murmurers and complainers" reveal their discontentedness in their lot, and make clear that though they have taken liberty to indulge the flesh, yet they have found no real satisfaction in so doing. They have failed to find the secret of true happiness and are strangers to what Paul could say: "I have learned, in whatsoever state I am, therewith to be content". The unbelieving Israelites in the wilderness were of the same sort, for they murmured in their tents and complained about Moses and Aaron. Many believe that if only they could be allowed to have their own way, they would be happy, but these men were not curtailed in the fulfilment of the desires of their flesh and lived only to gratify these. Still they were grumbling about their lot and possibly blaming God for His ways with them. The complaining could well be about those who would attempt to correct them, especially about the apostles and other leaders in the churches. Evil doers resent any effort to change their ways and quite often blame as thoughtless and legal those who would have a care for their souls. They have chosen the path of selfish indulgence and thought it would be smooth and pleasant, but to their disappointment, it has proved to be thorny. Tried saints have been known to sing in the midst of their afflictions, but these men have no song, but their lips breathe out their miseries.

Not only are they complainers, but they are arrogant and are puffed up with pride. This is evident in their use of "swelling words" which no doubt were intended to impress their listeners. Like Balaam before them, they were not without oratory, but in their case there was likely little substance in what they said. They used every device to curry favour with those they thought could be beneficial to them, so they showed respect to the great and important, hoping to gain some advantage from them. Even though proud and independent in spirit, yet in reality they were slaves of men. Had they shown the same regard for God as they did for their human superiors, they would not have needed to stoop to such infamy. Those who have to flatter men in order to obtain their favour pay a high price for their duplicity, for quite often, in spite of their shrewdness, they are detected by the flattered.

17   If the saints are surprised that such men as have been described are amongst them, they must have forgotten the words of the apostles who had warned of their coming. As early as Acts 20, in the record of Paul's meeting with the elders of Ephesus, we have this warning concerning "grievous wolves" entering in and men arising "speaking perverse things" (vv.29-30); and Peter writes of "false teachers among you, who privily shall bring in damnable heresies", also of "scoffers, walking after their own lusts" (2 Pet 2:1;3:3). Some have concluded from this verse that Jude is telling us that he was copying from Peter's writings and this is why there is such a close resemblance between the two epistles. We believe that both wrote independently, and that both were guided by the Lord to write what was most suited to the need of the time, and therefore, as we might expect, the result was two epistles very similar, yet distinctly different. While this reference to the apostles does not explicitly prove that Jude was not one of them, yet it goes far in that direction. We can scarcely imagine either Paul or Peter mentioning the apostles and not including themselves amongst them. In passing, we should note the way the "brother of the Lord" refers to Him. He gives Him His full title-"Lord Jesus Christ". Though Jude was reared in the same home and in the same circumstances as the Lord, yet he is conscious that the risen One stands related to him, not by the ties of nature, but by the bond of spiritual life. The carpenter of Nazareth, despised by the nation, is now the Lord of glory, and Jude, His servant, gladly owns His Lordship.

18   The apostolic warning indicated that those who would appear in the last time would be "mockers" and "walk after their own ungodly lusts", and so their prophecy was fulfilled in the men condemned in this epistle. The last time began with the first advent of Christ and will continue until His second advent. All the past led up to this wonderful time when the great promise of God was fulfilled in the manifestation of the Messiah who has appeared in the consummation of the ages. Much has yet to be fulfilled, but still, in God's reckoning, what remains of time is simply to allow for the completion of that which has already begun.

19   We come to our last reference to the apostates, and as usual they are introduced as "these". Three facts are stated about them:

1.   they cause division;

2.   they are sensual;

3.   they are devoid of the Spirit.

The AV gives the thought that they separated from the saints, but as we have earlier pointed out, they were still amongst them. The RV is correct when it makes clear that they were responsible for causing divisions amongst the saints. This can be easily understood, for wrong livers and wrong teachers cannot possibly enjoy the fellowship of the faithful, but strange as it may seem to some, there have always been those amongst the saints who have sympathy with wrong-doers, even when out of sympathy with their wrong. Perhaps these men put up a good show for a time and some, remembering this, may think they have only lapsed a little and that soon they will be restored. Alas, the men Jude writes about are beyond recovery. Still, the different judgment about them would readily lead to division amongst the saints, and thus they are the root cause of separating those who should be bound together.

In describing them as "sensual" or "natural" Jude is showing that they were in the state in which they were born, and destitute of any new nature. Moreover, they were living to gratify their animal passions and soulish desires. "The natural man receiveth not the things of the Spirit of God", so there was no possibility of these men changing their ways, nor hope of turning them into saints.

In the statement "having not the Spirit" there is revealed the root deficiency of these seducers. Whatever they may have claimed when they made a profession of Christ, their state is not the outcome of the Spirit's working, for had they been indwelt by that holy Person, then they would have developed in spiritual stature and produced the fruit of the Spirit.

As we look back over these solemn verses and ponder their sad story they disclose to us the seriousness of apostasy. There is not one bright spot in the entire passage, nor the slightest hope held out that there is any possibility of their repenting or changing their course. They are wedded to their fate, and are beyond "redemption point". Of each of them it could be said, as the Lord said of Judas, "good for that man if he had not been born".

Notes

5 Saints need to be put in "remembrance" (*hupomimnēskō*) and this is being done by the Holy Spirit (John 14:26); by the apostle (2 Pet 1: 12); by both Timothy and Titus (2 Tim 2:14; Titus 3:1); and here by Jude. "This" is changed to "all things" in the better MSS. "Afterward" (*deuteron*) literally means "second place" and refers to the second work of God which was their destruction. See 2 Cor 13:2.

6 "Kept" see "preserved" (v.1) and "kept" (v.6). Their "first estate" (*archē*) is translated "principality" in the RV here and in Eph 1:21; 3:10; Col 1:16; 2:10. It refers to the high position enjoyed by angels, while their "habitation" (*oikētērion*) has to do with their abode. "Chains" (*desmos*) are the bonds which bind prisoners etc; the word is usually plural. See Col 4:18; 2 Tim 2:9. There is a play on words in this verse. The angels "kept not" (*tēreō*) their first estate, but God "reserved" (*tēreō*) them in darkness. Thus failure to keep their dignity is matched by the confinement now enforced upon them by the Lord.

7 Here is the first of seven references in the epistle to "these" (RV). It is found again in vv.8,10,12,14,16,19. This is the only place where commentators attempt to connect it with those who immediately precede, rather than with its normal connection in the other six places where all are agreed that it refers to the men of v.4. The word "giving themselves to fornication" (*ekporneuō*) is a strengthened form of "commit fornication" (*porneuō*) and is only here in the NT, but is in Gen 38:24 LXX and there translated "played the harlot". The word "strange" (*heteros*) in "strange flesh" is here a reference to the men of Sodom and their use of their bodies contrary to nature. The word "example" (*deigma*) means a "sample" or "specimen" and is here only in the NT. "Vengeance" (*dikē*) implies the justness of the penalty. It occurs again in Acts 28:4 and 2 Thess 1:9. "Suffering" (*hupechō*) is another word found here only in the NT, Ps 89:50 LXX. "Eternal" (*aiōnios*) here is different from "everlasting" (*aidios*, v.6). The latter word is only again used in Rom 1:20. The former word lays stress on time unmeasured, the latter word denotes unchangeableness.

8 The seducers are called "dreamers" (*enupniazō*) which may refer to their vain imagination and delusions which cannot be limited to sensual dreams as in the AV, but extends here to other forms of evil such as blasphemy. They "defile" (*miainō*); the word occurs elsewhere only in John 18:28; Titus 1:15; Heb 12:15. It denotes the pollution or staining of the flesh. The ranks of angels are called "lordships" (*kuriotēs*, Eph 1:21; Col 1:16). It implies power or authority and is not limited to heavenly powers. To speak evil (*blasphēmeō*) means here to defame the "glories". In English the word blasphemy is confined to speaking against God, but this word includes all kinds of evil speaking. See vv. 8 and 10. As in 2 Pet 2:10 the term "dignities" or "glories" (*doxai*) is one of honour applied here to angels. The word "despise" (*atheteō*) means to "set aside" or "reject". It is also in Mark 7:9; 1 Cor 1: 19; Gal 2:21.

9 "Contending" (*diakrinō*) means to "separate" or "dispute" and so "contend", Acts 11:2. The word "dispute" (*dialegomai*) means to argue as in Acts 17:2; 24:12. There was a dread in Michael's heart to "dare" railing on Satan. Only here and in 2 Tim 4:27 in the epistles have we the word "rebuke" (*epitimao*), but it is often in the Gospels. It is quoted here from Zech 3:2. Both at the burial of Moses and when Joshua stood before the Lord, Satan appears to claim a legal right to resist, and on both occasions the only answer given was: "The Lord rebuke thee". " Archangel" (*archangelos*) occurs only here and in 1 Thess 4:16 in the NT. It may be based on Dan 12:1 where Michael is called "the great prince".

10 There are two different words here translated "know". The things they did not "know" (*oida*) as in v.5 signifies to "know as a fact" or to "perceive"; whereas what they "know" (*epistamai*) implies "understanding". This latter word admits of progress and is often used in Acts. "Naturally" (*phusikōs*) is a reference to the product of nature (2 Pet 2:12), and "brute" (*alogos*) implies the absence of reason. We might compare "unreasonable" (Acts 25:27). "They corrupt themselves" (*phtheirō*) means that "they are brought to destruction", so that which they did "understand" resulted in their ruin.

11 "Woe unto them" is a phrase unusual in the epistles, but often in the Gospels. It indicates the fate of these men. Neither Cain nor Core (Korah) is mentioned in 2 Peter, but Cain is referred to in 1 John 3:12. In Jude the stress is on deeds, but in Peter it is on teaching, so that may account for Balaam, the false prophet, being introduced. "Ran greedily" or "rushed" (*ekcheō*) shows that for the sake of gain these evil men plunged headlong into the same corruptions as taught by Balaam. The "error" (*planē*) includes both his evil teaching and his evil practice, and so combines his covetousness of gain and his lustful ways. Although the evil workers were still alive, yet their judgment was so sure that it is spoken of as if already it had taken place.

12 The word "spots" (*spilos*) in 2 Pet 2:13 resembles the word *spilas* found here only. It is rendered "hidden rocks" in the RV, though some, including JND, retain here the reading "spots". Perhaps the context here suits "rocks" better. "Feasting together" (*suneuōcheomai*) means to feast sumptuously or to excess. The word is only here and in 2 Pet 2:13 in the NT. They do this "without fear" (*aphobōs*), an indication of their daring. The word occurs also in Luke 1:74; 1 Cor 16:10; and Phil 1:14. The trees "whose fruit withereth " (*phthinopōrinos*) are autumnal trees or trees at the fall of the year. They are "plucked up" (*ekrizoō*). The word is found elsewhere only in Matt 13:29; 15:13; Luke 17:6.

13 The figure of angry waves "foaming out" (*epaphrizō*) is used only here in the NT. It implies that the libertines, though amongst the saints, were like the waves of the sea depositing their shameful dirt and leaving it behind them. "Shame" here is in the plural which indicates that there is a variety of shame. The "wandering stars" (*planētēs*) are mentioned only here. With them we might compare Lucifer ("day star") fallen from heaven (Isa 14:12). Both the angels (v.6) and these evil men are destined to be in the gloom of darkness and will shine no more for ever. They are in contrast to those who are "wise" who "shall shine as the brightness of the firmament ... as the stars for ever and ever" (Dan 12:3).

14 The seven from Adam are counted in this way:

1. Adam, 2. Seth, 3. Enos, 4. Cainan, 5. Mahalaleel, 6. Jared, 7. Enoch.

Only here do we learn that Enoch was a prophet. The "ten thousands" (*murias*) are "myriads" or vast numbers. The word "coming" is in the past tense, the tense of prophesy. This coming is distinct in character from the "mercy of the Lord Jesus" for which the saints look.

15 The judgment will be "executed" (*poieō*) or carried out, so the threat is no vain alarm. The Lord will not only judge but "convince" (*exelenchō*). This word is here only in the NT. *Asebes* ("ungodly") and its cognates appearing four times in the verse and repeated also in vv. 4, 18, is a key word in this epistle. Note the verbal form *asebeō* here. The "hard" (*sklēros*) speeches can be compared with John 6:60 and Jas 3:4.

16 The words "murmurers" (*gongustēs*) and "complainers" (*mempsimoiros*) are only here in the NT. The former implies that they resented how they were treated, and the latter that they were unhappy with their lot. In speaking they used "great swelling" words (*huperonkos*) which shows that they were ostentatious and boastful (Pet 2:18 is the only other occurrence). Persons in "admiration" (*thaumazo*) implies showing respect for persons. The phrase is not elsewhere in the NT but see Lev 19:15. "Advantage" here means profit, for although Jude does not stress the covetous feature of their character, yet he does mention it.

18 "The last time" or "at the end of the time" (JND) can be compared with " manifest in these last times" (1 Pet 1:20) and "in the last days" (2 Pet 3:3). "Mockers" or "scoffers" (*empaiktēs*) means those who sport or play with divine things (2 Pet 3:3 and Isa 3:4 LXX).

19 "Separate" (*apodiorizō*) means to separate by intervening boundaries or divide. There is no word in the original for "themselves", so it was the saints that they divided. The word is only here in the NT, but see Lev 20:24. The word "sensual" (*psuchikos*) means natural or soulish and is in contrast to spiritual. It occurs in 1 Cor 2:14; 15:44 and Jas 3:15. "Having not the Spirit" is in contrast to all the saints (1 Cor 7:40; Rom 8:9). These men were controlled by their natural instincts, not by the Spirit of God.

III. Exhortation (vv.20-25)

v.20 "But ye, beloved, building up yourselves on your most holy faith, praying in the Holy Ghost,
v.21 Keep yourselves in the love of God, looking for the mercy of our Lord Jesus Christ unto eternal life.
v.22 And of some have compassion, making a difference:
v.23 And others save with fear, pulling *them* out of the fire; hating even the garment spotted by the flesh.
v.24 Now unto him that is able to keep you from failing, and to present you faultless before the presence of his glory with exceeding joy,
v.25 To the only wise God our Saviour, *be* glory and majesty, dominion and power, both now and ever. Amen."

It is with no small sense of relief that we take our leave of the warnings concerning the false workers, turn to exhortations and instructions for the true saints and learn what is to characterise them in their christian living. It will be noticed as we make our way through this paragraph that it has many links, both in contrasts and in comparisons, with the former part of the epistle. Jude is anxious to show the saints that all is not lost, for in spite of the widespread apostasy which he has so strongly denounced, he is confident that there are still humble souls whose only delight is to walk with God. To such he addresses these brief exhortations and encouragements, being fully conscious that they were sorely needed in the circumstances and conditions prevailing at that time. If in the early days of the church such instructions were essential, we can safely conclude that they are even more needed in our time which is all the closer to the Lord's return.

A survey of these verses will readily reveal that they bear a threefold message. They tell us:

1.   How to be preserved in the midst of danger;

2.   How we are to treat those who have been affected by the imposters;

3.   How we are to glorify God and enjoy His preservation.

We have a duty towards ourselves, to others and to God Himself. It will be noticed that we have in them a reference to the past, "before all time", to the present, "now" and to the future, "evermore" RV. There is also a hint of the three cardinal truths of the NT: faith, though here it is what is believed rather than believing; hope, "looking for the mercy of our Lord Jesus Christ"; love, "keep yourselves in the love of God". Even more obvious is the reference to the Trinity here. We have " the only God our Saviour" (RV), "praying in the Holy Spirit" and "the mercy of our Lord Jesus Christ".

1.   *Development of Spiritual Life*
vv.20-21

20   Occupation with failure and sin, whether in apostates or in saints, can be very soul-withering, for it is both discouraging and depressing. Although Jude found it necessary to warn the saints of the seducers and to describe their features so that they might be able to identify them, yet he balances his ministry by giving here positive and encouraging instruction no less needed by the saints. They are to do more than "contend for the faith"; they are to build themselves up on it. It was the foundation on which they had rested their souls when they were converted, and the same teaching which enlightened them as sinners will also develop them as saints. Proper teaching imbibed is vital for the saints' welfare. There are those who decry so much teaching, and claim it matters little what a man believes so long as he lives right, but such fail to see that what a man believes influences his conduct. To take a broad view of the case, it was the evil teaching condemned in 2 Peter that produced the evil conduct denounced by Jude. The more the teaching of the apostles is grasped, the more will life's pattern be conformed to the mind of God. In a certain sense we accepted the "faith" the moment we trusted Christ, but it takes a lifetime for us to apprehend what that "faith" includes. Constant meditation on the word of God and conscientious application of it to our behaviour will prove its effectiveness to edify. We might compare the words of Paul, "rooted and built up in him, and stablished in the faith" (Col 2:7). Although the metaphors here are somewhat mixed, there is no confusion as to their meaning. Those who do build themselves up, are not blown about with the wind, but are steadfast and unmoveable. The "building up yourselves" is in sharp contrast to those who destroy themselves (v.10 RV).

The second participial phrase, "praying in the Holy Ghost", is a fitting companion to the first, for along with growth in our grasp of "the faith" there is ever the need for prayer. The false men could dispense with prayer and live independently of God, but the weakness of the saints ever drives them to seek His face and call upon Him for His help. Certainly those who have not the Spirit (v.19) could not possibly pray in the Spirit, but all true believers are indwelt by the Spirit and know His help especially in their prayer life. The prayer here is not the same as 1 Cor 14:15, where the thought is praying in an enraptured state in a man's own spirit, but here it is prayer engendered and energised by the Spirit and could include those unexpressed prayers mentioned in Rom 8:26. The Spirit who enables us to pray is here said to be "holy", just as the faith too was said to be "holy". Doubtless this is in contrast to the unholy living of those who had crept in amongst the saints.

It has been said that true prayer begins with God, enters into the hearts of men by the power of the Spirit, rises up to God, and is answered by Him. Those who pray by the Spirit's aid will be saved from formality, from unholy familiarity, from vain repetition, from wrath and doubting, and from being verbose. Many imposters have admitted that they find no difficulty in speaking publicly, but when it comes to praying, they find great embarrassment. There is a close link between prayer and the "most holy faith", for those who are deeply exercised in the way of truth, are ever conscious of their own helplessness and the need for strength from God to fulfil its instructions. The Word of God and prayer are said to sanctify our meat (1 Tim 4:5); the apostles gave themselves to " prayer, and to the ministry of the word" (Acts 6:4); "the word of God is quick, and powerful ... Let us therefore come boldly unto the throne of grace" (Heb 4:12,16); and "take ... the sword of the Spirit, which is the word of God: praying always with all prayer and supplication in the Spirit" (Eph 6:17,18).

21 The third statement of our text and its principal clause is "keep yourselves in the love of God". In v.1 where the word for "keep" is used it is the Lord who keeps, but here it is our own responsibility. We must be sure that we are not here being told to preserve ourselves in God's favour, for "His love floweth on fresh and full as a river", but rather to keep ourselves in the good of His love toward us, and to make sure that nothing, not even our contending for the faith, will in any way rob us of our consciousness of it. All know only too well that dealing with evil and disputing with heretics can have a hardening effect upon the heart and smother within it the warmth and joy of the love of God. The Lord taught

His disciples to abide in His love and to continue in it (John 15:9,10). It has been " bestowed upon us" (1 John 3:1), and it has been " shed abroad in our hearts by the Holy Ghost" (Rom 5:5). While here it is not our love to God, yet whatever love is present in our hearts toward Him is but the reflection of His love to us.

We come to the third participial phrase, "looking for the mercy of our Lord Jesus Christ". While His coming is not directly mentioned here, there is little doubt that it is in view. His first coming into the world was regarded as a great "mercy" (Luke 1:72,78) by those who looked for it, so too will be His second coming. The sights of the believer must be directed to the time when the apostates will no longer distress, when human failure will have ended and when eternal life will be enjoyed in its fulness. This hope will not make us ashamed, nor will it prove disappointing. Perhaps the greatest deficiency in the imposter's doctrine is that it holds out no hope, but we look for that "blessed hope, and the glorious appearing of the great God and our Saviour Jesus Christ" (Titus 2:13). Some have thought that present mercies are in view here and that there is no reference to the second advent in the phrase, but the true consummation of ,,eternal life" will be when we are raptured into His presence. Usually " mercy" is show by God, as in v.2, but here it is connected with Christ alone, for in reality He is its substance for which we look.

2.   *Treatment of Defaulters and Distinguishing between Them* vv.22-23

22   All are agreed that these two verses are the most complicated so far as textual criticism is concerned that we have in the NT. In the reading of the AV there are only two groups, but in the RV and many other translations three are mentioned. In the former case those saved from the fire are to be snatched with fear and their garments hated, but in the latter case there are those who are to be convicted, those who are to be snatched, and those who are to be pitied. Without being dogmatic and at the same time having regard to the structure of this epistle, we are inclined to the latter view, and in this we have the support of many of the most able commentators.

Perhaps before we attempt to explain the verses we ought to identify those who are to be helped, for not a few think they are the very people who have been condemned by Jude in the earlier part of the epistle. We have tried to show that for them there is no hope held out, but they are destined for the wrath of God. If this be so, then who are to be rescued? The answer is, Those who have been led astray by the impostors and who, though truly saved, yet have been caught up in the corrupt teaching and in the practices that defile. There is great need for discernment so that we can distinguish between the leaders in error and those souls who have been misled by it. Some would attempt to save all, which we know to be impossible, and others would sweep all away and never attempt to deliver the fallen.

The first group are to be convicted while they dispute. This meaning can be reached only by changing to a different text. Some think that mercy on the doubters is called for, but the word they render "doubt" has been used in v.9 and there it has the meaning of "dispute". Again the word "mercy" or "compassion" is changed to "convince" or "convict". If this be the idea, then those who differed did so in an argumentative way and needed strong handling to remove their misunderstandings. Certainly the more gentle approach is suggested in the RV, "on some have mercy, who are in doubt", but the margin gives the alternative, "while they dispute with you".

23   The second group are in more imminent danger for they are to be snatched from the fire, as the words "some save, snatching them out of the fire" (RV) imply. Not a few give these words a gospel application and suggest that we should do all we can to rescue sinners from eternal fire. However true this is in other Scriptures it is not likely to be the right interpretation here, for we judge that those to be delivered from the fire are those who have already escaped the fire of hell. Most likely the "fire" is figurative of that which destroys and refers to the solemn possibility that the lives of those who have been influenced by the apostates could be ruined and who, unless helped by the faithful, are in grave danger of being swallowed up in the morass of corrupt teaching. As most are aware the words used are taken from Zech 3:2, where we read concerning Joshua the high priest, "Is not this a brand plucked out of the fire?" The "fire" in this context refers to the furnace of Babylon, although, as in our passage, it is often used in a gospel sense. In rescuing from the fire, there is no time to lose, so the urgency of the situation demands swift action, and in most cases a certain amount of danger. All should be aware of the risk involved in seeking to help those who have gone astray, for it has to be acknowledged that some who attempted to recover those who were out of the way, became wanderers themselves, and so fell into the fire out of which they sought to rescue the perishing. Others have confessed that they were sorry to have contacted those with strange doctrine, for in attempting to restore them to the faith, they were left with thoughts and memories they wish they never had entertained; so saving from the fire is not a work to be undertaken by the novice.

The third group is not to be convicted as the first group, nor rescued as the second, but to be pitied with fear. In showing them mercy there is a consciousness of their weakness and of their simplicity. Quite often unsuspecting and gullible souls are swept away with false teaching and even learn to practise the evils of those who have deluded them. It is clear that this group has fallen into corrupt living, so they are not only misled, but have misbehaved. In spite of this they are to be treated tenderly and every effort made to bring about their recovery. Thus the pity is not to be merely passive as if that is all that can be done for them, rather it is that mercy which sees the need and is willing to risk the consequences to meet it. This is implied in the caution at the end, "in fear, hating even the garment spotted by the flesh". Those who stand aloof and express their sympathy for the plight of these defiled ones, would not have to dread any defilement from them, but those who in tenderness would attempt to turn them from their corruptions would have every cause to approach their task with carefulness lest they become defiled by contact with them. "The garment spotted by the flesh " is the inner garment which is close to the body and is here viewed as having contracted defilement from the wearer.

The thought is that in showing compassion to those who have been corrupted great care is needed lest some of the defilement is passed on to the sympathiser. Whatever mercy is dispensed by the faithful to these offenders, it is not an indication that they have any sympathy with the corruption involved, for it is still hated. The garments of those defiled by fleshly lust are viewed here as though they were leprous and dangerous to handle, loathed as detestable. Again we can trace a connection with Zech 3, for in v.3 the high priest there is said to be "clothed with filthy garments". The Lord who had chosen Jerusalem gives instruction that Joshua be provided with a change of raiment. If those here involved are truly restored to the Lord as a result of being tenderly treated, then they too will have changed garments, pure and white.

Because of the great variety of critical readings these two verses of Jude have been viewed very differently by many commentators whose understanding of Textual Criticism cannot be ignored. Nevertheless we have given what we consider to be the nearest to the original according to the evidence presently available, but should the day arrive when further light on the text becomes available then the translation may need to be adjusted accordingly.

3. *Concluding Doxology*
vv.24-25

24 This doxology, while bearing some resemblance to the one at the end of Romans, is unique and is in perfect keeping with the epistle which it closes. Almost every word of it forms an answer to the evils so strongly condemned by the body of the epistle. It divides into three parts:

1. God's power to keep;

2. His ability to set the saints spotless before Him;

3. He alone must have the glory.

The writer has said much about the fall of those in high favour and the readers may well have shuddered lest they too should fall, but he calms their fears by directing them to "him that is able to keep you from falling". Their preservation was mentioned in v.1 and there it was because of their relation with Christ; here it is divine power that will keep. A marked feature of the true saint is his sense of weakness, he is a complete contrast to the haughty independent and presumptuous impostors. His strength is in God, who can so preserve him that he will not even stumble. As the psalmist could say, "I have trusted also in the Lord; therefore I shall not slide" (26:1). This keeping is during the present life when the dangers are manifold and when the evidence of the enemy's success can be witnessed on every hand.

Distinct from present preservation is the second point in the doxology-our presentation before the Lord. His own will be set in the presence of His glory; they will be there "blameless" (JND) and this will result in scenes of exultation. The angels who sinned were once in this sphere of glory, but were cast out from it, but the preserved ones will be permanently set in it and will never be deposed from their honoured position. This presentation is in full harmony with the words of Paul regarding the church, "that he might present it to himself a glorious church ... without blemish" (Eph 5:27). There the presenter is Christ, but here it is God. In a special sense the saints will be filled with joy, and possibly this joy will be shared by other created beings, but God Himself and His Son will know it in its fulness.

The third feature of this doxology is the ascription to God of the glory due to Him. We learned in v.4 that one feature of the impostors was that they denied the only Lord God, but here the One they despised has attributed to Him all that the human mind can conceive of high qualities and virtues. The word "wise", although in Rom 16:27, is rightly omitted in the RV. This only God is our Saviour. The title is often used of Christ especially in the earlier part of the NT, but is applied to God in the later epistles, particularly in the pastorals. However, here He is Saviour " through Jesus Christ our Lord" (RV), so He saves through the instrumentality of His Son. Of the virtues here mentioned the first is "glory" which refers to His magnificence and excellence. The creature would attempt to rob Him of this unique dignity by seeking to usurp it as did Satan, but He will not give it to another, for all who have aspired to obtain it have brought about their own downfall.

The second quality ascribed here to God is His "majesty". The word here used is employed only by Greek ecclesiastical writers and indicates "greatness" and is used in Hebrews to describe the position of Christ at God's right hand (1:3; 8:1). In no other doxology does it occur. If the first virtue refers to God's state, this one has reference to His exalted position. The proud glory in their greatness, as we are sure the evil workers did who are dealt with in this epistle, but they are only mites at the best in spite of all their boasting.

The thought of God's "dominion" is often brought into doxologies as in 1 Tim 6:16; 1 Pet 4:11; 5:11 and Rev 1:6;5:13. It refers to His "might". He not only sits in majestic glory, but has unlimited strength to execute His purposes. A helpless God would be a misnomer, but the God we praise has demonstrated His might, both in creation and in resurrection.

The last of the virtues ascribed to God here is His "power" or "authority". He has unfettered sway and can do whatsoever pleases Him. His supremacy cannot be questioned, nor can any say to Him, "what doest thou?"; this right and liberty to act as He pleases distinguishes Him from all His creatures, for although some of them would like to assert their authority, yet all must render an account to Him as the supreme judge. In this word not His strength to act is before us, but rather His freedom of action.

The last words of the epistle give us one of the clearest expressions of eternity in the NT-"before all time, and now, and for evermore" (RV). These qualities are to be God's portion in a timeless way. The changes of time can sweep away much that men value and their pomp is blown away with the winds never to return again, but what God is now He has ever been and will ever be. The "amen" at the close of this and other doxologies seems to imply that while the virtues ascribed to God are initially His, yet here there is a prayer that they be His portion.

Notes

20 This is the third and last time he addresses the saints as "beloved". See vv.3,17. The exhortation "building up yourselves" (*epoikodomountes heautous*) is here only, but the verb is found in Acts 20:32; 1 Cor 3:10,12,14; Eph 2:20 and Col 2:7. The "faith" as in v.3 is the body of teaching, but here it is called "most holy" because through accepting it we have been made "holy" and it has its origin in God who is holy. The prayer is also in the power of the One who is "holy". The word used here for "praying" (*proseuchomai*) is always to God and is the most common word used for this exercise.

21 In v.1 the passive mood of "keep" is used, but here the verb is active, so human responsibility is involved. This is the basic exhortation flanked by two participles before and one after it. The idea in "looking" (*prosdechomai*) is waiting with expectancy. It occurs also in Luke 2:38; 23:5 1; Acts 24:15; and Titus 2:13.

22-23 The translation on which we have based our comments on these two verses is Alford's which reads, "And some indeed convict, when they contend with you; but others save, pulling them out of the fire; and of others have compassion with fear, hating even the garment spotted by the flesh". The chief textual critics substantially concur with this rendering, but the AV and JND have only two groups instead of three and change some of the wording considerably. The word *diakrinō* rendered "making a difference" (AV) is in the accusative case in an alternative reading and is translated "doubt" in the RV, but the same word has the meaning of "contend" in v.9, so it is well to be consistent. In the Gospels it is often translated "doubt"; essentially it embodies the idea "to separate or make a distinction" allowing it to be rendered "discern", "doubt", "judge", "stagger", "contend" and "waver". In Acts 11:2 it is used in the same sense as we have adopted here- "contend". The change from "have compassion" (*eleeō*) to "convict" (*elenchō*) has the support of the critics. The latter word has been used in v.15. For the word "pulling" (*harpazō*) or "snatching" occurs in Matt 13:19; John 10:12,28,29. The garment "spotted" (*spiloō*, see Jas 3:6) is in contrast to the "fine linen, clean and white" (Rev 19:8).

24 The word "keep" (*phulassō*, to guard or watch) is not the same as the word in v.21 which has in it more the idea of "preserve", but the difference is not great. Only here in the NT have we the word *aptaistos* ("not falling") which means "without stumbling". Those "kept" will be "presented" (*histēmi*) or "set" before the "glory" of the Lord in a "faultless" (*amōmos*) or "blameless" condition (Rev 14:5). The result of this will be "exceeding joy" (*agalliasis*) or "exultation" (Luke 1:14,44; Acts 2:46; Heb 1:9).

25   The three words "majesty" (*megalōsunē*), "dominion" (*kratos*) and "power" (*exousia*) define His "glory" as One who is high and lofty, who is mighty, and who has unlimited sway. The last word is used only here in doxologies. The boasted greatness of the imposters and their disrespect for "dignities" could never be acceptable to such a God.

Appendix A

Words in Jude

In spite of its brevity, the epistle of Jude adds a number of peculiar words to the vocabulary of the NT. The following is a list of these:

"earnestly contend" (*epagōnizomai*)	v.3
"crept in unawares" (*pareisduō*)	v.4
"giving themselves over to fornication" (*ekporneuō*)	v.7
"example" (*deigma*)	v.7
"suffering" (*hupechō*)	v.7
"naturally" (*phusikōs*)	v.10
"feasts of charity" (*agapē*)	v.12 (plural here only)
"whose fruit withereth" (*phthinopōrinos*)	v.12
"foaming out" (*epaphrizō*)	v.13
"wandering" (*planētēs*)	v.13
"murmurers" (*gongustēs*)	v.16
"complainers" (*mempsimoiros*)	v.16
"who separate themselves" (*apodiorizō*)	v.19
"falling" (*aptaistos*)	v.24

The following words occur only in Jude and 2 Peter.

"dignities" (*doxa*)	v.8; 2 Pet 2:10 (plural)
"feasting together" (*suneuōcheomai*)	v.12; 2 Pet 2:13
"ungodly deeds" (*asebeō*)	v.15; 2 Pet 2:6
"mockers" (*empaiktes*)	v.18; 2 Pet 3:3

Appendix B

Triplets in Jude

Many of the triplets in this epistle have been noted in the exposition, but a concise list of them may be of interest to some.

Threefold description of the readers:	beloved
	kept
	called
Threefold greeting:	mercy
	peace
	love
Three examples of judgment:	Israel in the wilderness
	angels
	Sodom and Gomorrah
Three examples of error:	Cain
	Balaam
	Core
Threefold description of apostates:	ungodly
	turning grace into lasciviousness
	denying the Lord
Three activities of the apostates:	defile the flesh
	despise dominion
	blaspheme dignities
Three figures of the apostates:	sunken rocks
	shepherds
	clouds
Three more figures of them:	trees
	waves
	stars
Three persons of the Godhead:	Spirit (v.20)
	God
	Christ (v.21)
Three classes to be considered:	those in dispute
	those in danger
	those in defilement
Three stages of time:	before all time
	now
	forever
Three spiritual exercises:	building
	praying
	looking

Appendix C

The Fall of Angels

There is something fascinating to the human mind in prying into the unseen and into matters about which little is revealed in Scripture. Of this we are sure there are such beings as good and bad angels, who are "spirits" and are therefore bodiless, although they may be allowed to appear at times in bodily form. Although there are myriads of them and they are in contact with earth, yet in their normal state they cannot be either seen or felt. They are of a higher order than man, and all of them left the hand of God as perfect as did Adam. Some of them appear to be higher in rank than others, for we read of Gabriel who appears to be entrusted with certain important messages and of "the archangel Michael" who is captain of the hosts. In the providence of God their Creator they had a "state" or "principality" assigned to them. This was in the light of His presence where they had the privilege of serving Him day and night. They like man were not machines, but were endowed with a will which they could exercise, and for this reason were accountable beings.

The question that has to be answered is: From where did Satan and his hosts of demons come? Certainly he was not created a deceiver, a liar nor a murderer, nor were his followers created unclean and ferocious. It is implied in 1 Tim 3:7 that the devil fell through pride and was condemned by God for it. There are a few passages in the OT which, while describing earthly kings, appear to go beyond them and give us a description of their master, Satan himself. Just as much that is said of David is descriptive of a greater than he, none less that his Son, Jesus Christ, so what is said of these evil monarchs goes beyond them and throws light on the mysterious subject of the fall of Satan. If we take this view of these passages, and most are satisfied to do so, then it follows that in the beginning he was Lucifer ("star of the morning"), and that he was full of wisdom, splendour, and pomp. Not content with the honourable position assigned to him, he aspired to set himself upon a throne and reign over all the other stars, yea he went further and sought to claim equality with God Himself (Isa 14:11-14). In writing concerning the king of Tyrus the prophet tells us that he "was lifted up, and ... said, I am a God, I sit in the seat of God" (Ezek 28:2). However true these words were of the men involved, yet they are but a reflection of the ambition which rose in the arch-enemy's heart and which brought him to ruin. It is evident that in his rebellion, he was the leader of a great host and that these are the demons so often referred to in the NT. Thus the sons of light were driven into darkness and are now known as principalities, powers, rulers of the darkness of this world, and spiritual hosts of wickedness in the heavenlies (Eph 6:12). We judge these hosts to be the fallen angels who are constantly engaged in the work of their master Satan and who work in the children of disobedience.

The judgment which followed the sin of angels involved their casting down to hell (*tartaros*) (2 Pet 2:4), their binding in darkness and their judgment in a coming day. The use of the word "chains" in the AV has given the impression that they are restricted in movement and that therefore they could never be the demons we read of in the Gospels, but the import of the passage is that they are restricted to the dens of darkness, so wherever they roam they never can escape from the darkness. The word "cast down to hell" (*tartaroō*) is a participle in the aorist tense and could be translated "tartarising" them, so it is their condition rather than their place of abode that is mentioned. Prior to their fall those angels were bright and shining lights, but since it took place they are the powers of darkness. If Satan appears as the "angel of light" he must be "transformed" to do so (2 Cor 11:14). Whatever mystery may surround their present state and operations there is no doubt about their future, for they will be judged, most likely at the great white throne, and finally cast into the lake of fire. If some of them are in deeper depths of woe now than their fellows, at the end all will be in the same abode. They are aware of the sentence passed upon them and dread its execution. The Lord's words, "I beheld Satan as lightning fall from heaven" (Luke 10: 18) would give the impression that already Satan was removed from it, whereas the casting of him out in a final sense awaits a future day (Rev 12:9), but the triumph of the seventy over the demons was, to the eye of the Lord, a token of this.

Because the LXX translates the "sons of God" as "angels" in Gen 6:2 and because of the influence of the apocryphal book of Enoch very many writers believe that the sin of the angels mentioned here and in 2 Pet 2:4 was their lust after women and their marriage to them. Indeed, some go further and claim that it was from the book of Enoch that Jude learned of their fall. If this be true, then the sin of the angels in these two passages was subsequent to the fall of Satan. One thing is sure: if Jude copied from Enoch, he definitely changed it, for in the latter the saints are to be judged, whereas in Jude it is the wicked who are to be the subject of judgment. Like most counterfeits, there is some truth in Enoch, but this is mixed with much error and is therefore the more deceitful. When it was written has never been decided, but it could well be that it was based on Jude and written by a Jew to discredit christianity. The Greek philosophy abroad at the close of the pre-christian era and the beginning of the christian had penetrated deeply into Jewish minds and produced amongst them writings which were a mixture of their own beliefs and heathen falsehoods.

There are a number of reasons for rejecting this interpretation of Gen 6. A simple reading of the first two verses shows us two facts:

1.   the increase in the earth's population and

2.   the marriages which brought this about.

The "daughters" of v.1 must be the "daughters" of v.2; likewise the "men" of v.1 must be the "sons of God" of v.2. The daughters born tell of natural generation, and sons of God tell of divine creation. That those with such a noble beginning should turn so corrupt is the surprise of the passage. There is no direct statement here that the giants were the result of a mixed marriage, nor do we ever read of women giants, so if the angels were the fathers of these giants, then all the offspring must have been males. A number who hold this theory that angels are here involved, hold also that another such fall took place before Israel entered Canaan and this too produced giants. It is clear from both Peter and Jude that only one not three occasions of angels sinning is in mind. If they are prone to lust after women, as these writers teach, is it not strange that no approach by the many angels who visited women is even hinted at in Scripture? It is strange too that God sent them on such dangerous missions if this were their weakness. As has often been said, if they assumed bodies and lusted after women, they were already fallen, and had ceased to be angels who are spirits.

It is interesting to note that Paul speaks of " elect angels" (1 Tim 5:21) and in doing so indicates that the angels above are conscious that their preservation from falling is due to God's electing grace. There will never be another sinning of angels, just as there will be no possibility of saints sinning in heaven. In heaven they neither marry, nor are given to marriage, because their spiritual bodies will never reproduce; they will be like the angels of God.